Enhancing Enterprise Intelligence

Leveraging ERP, CRM, SCM, PLM, BPM, and BI

Enhancing Enterprise Intelligence

Leveraging ERP, CRM, SCM, PLM, BPM, and BI

Vivek Kale

CRC Press
Taylor & Francis Group
Boca Raton London New York

CRC Press is an imprint of the
Taylor & Francis Group, an **informa** business
AN AUERBACH BOOK

CRC Press
Taylor & Francis Group
6000 Broken Sound Parkway NW, Suite 300
Boca Raton, FL 33487-2742

© 2016 by Vivek Kale
CRC Press is an imprint of Taylor & Francis Group, an Informa business

No claim to original U.S. Government works

Printed on acid-free paper
Version Date: 20151111

International Standard Book Number-13: 978-1-4987-0597-4 (Hardback)

Library of Congress Cataloging-in-Publication Data

Names: Kale, Vivek.
Title: Enhancing enterprise intelligence: leveraging ERP, CRM, SCM, PLM, BPM, and BI / Vivek Kale.
Description: Boca Raton : Taylor & Francis, 2016. | Includes bibliographical references and index.
Identifiers: LCCN 2015031118 | ISBN 9781498705974 (alk. paper)
Subjects: LCSH: Production planning--Data processing. | Manufacturing resource planning--Computer programs.
Classification: LCC TS176 .K319 2016 | DDC 658.5/03--dc23
LC record available at http://lccn.loc.gov/2015031118

Visit the Taylor & Francis Web site at
http://www.taylorandfrancis.com

and the CRC Press Web site at
http://www.crcpress.com

To

Tanaya and Abhishek

at the start of the new chapter in their lives

Contents

Preface xv
Acknowledgments xix
Author xxi

Chapter 1 Intelligent Enterprises 1

    Agile Enterprises 1
        Stability versus Agility 4
        Aspects of Agility 6
        Principles of Built-for-Change Systems 8
        Framework for Change Proficiency 9
        Enhancing Enterprise Agility 10
            e-Business Strategy 10
            Business Process Reengineering 11
            Mobilizing Enterprise Processes 11
        Network Enterprises 12
    Operating Strategy 14
    Enterprise-Wide Continuous Improvement Programs 15
        Lean System 15
        Theory of Constraints 19
            TOC Tools 21
        Six Sigma 23
    Time-Based Competition 28
    Enhancing Enterprise Intelligence 30
        Integrated Enterprise with ERP 30
        Customer-Centric Enterprise with CRM 31
        Customer-Responsive Enterprise with SCM 31
        Renewing Enterprise with PLM 32
        Collaborative Enterprise with BPM 32
        Informed Enterprise with BI 32
    Summary 34

Chapter 2 Enterprise Systems 35

    Evolution of ES 35
        Materials Requirement Planning 37

Closed-Loop Materials Requirement Planning.................38
Manufacturing Requirement Planning II 39
Enterprise Resource Planning...39
Extended Enterprise Systems.. 40
Extended Enterprise Systems Framework........................41
Extended Functionality.. 43
ES Packages 45
Valuing the ES-Based Enterprise 50
Enterprise Stakeholders 50
From "Built-to-Last" to "Built-to-Perform"
Enterprises 52
Aspects of Enterprise Value...53
Value to Customers.. 54
Value to Shareholders...55
Value to Managers.. 56
Value to Employees..57
Value to Vendors 58
Economic Value Add...59
Value-Based Management 60
Time Value of Customers and Shareholder Value........61
ES Metrics 63
Enterprise Performances Measurement.........................67
Balance Scorecard... 68
Financial Perspective...72
Customer Perspective..72
Internal Business Processes Perspective...........................72
Learning and Growth Perspective...................................73
Summary 73

Chapter 3   Integrated Enterprise with ERP 75

Concept of Enterprise Resources Planning 76
Enterprise Resources Planning...77
Characteristics of ERP 80
ERP Transforms the Enterprise into an Information-
Driven Enterprise... 80
ERP Fundamentally Perceives an Enterprise as a
Global Enterprise 81

ERP Reflects and Mimics the Integrated Nature of
an Enterprise 81
ERP Fundamentally Models a Process-Oriented
Enterprise..82
ERP Enables the Real-Time Enterprise..............................83
ERP Elevates IT Strategy as a Part of the Business
Strategy.. 84
ERP Represents a Major Advance on the Earlier
Manufacturing Performance Improvement Approaches ... 84
ERP Represents the Departmental Store Model of
Implementing Computerized Systems...............................85
ERP Is a Mass-User-Oriented Application
Environment... 86
Advantages of ERP 87
Enterprise Knowledge as the New Capital............................. 88
Information as the New Resource 89
ERP as the New Enterprise Architecture 91
Enterprise Business Processes...93
Enterprise Application Integration 95
Service-Oriented Architecture 97
Defining SOA 99
Services.. 100
SOA Benefits..101
Characteristics of SOA 103
SOA Applications..105
Rapid Application Integration 106
Multichannel Access..106
Business Process Management....................................107
Summary 107

Chapter 4   Customer-Centric Enterprise with CRM 109
The Concept of Customer Relationship Management 110
Customer Centricity..115
From Products to Services to Experiences.......................117
Convergence: From Marketplaces to Marketspaces 118
Customer Relationships as a Strategy..............................121
Information is Relationship... 122

Customer Capital: Customer Knowledge as the
New Capital 124
Increasing Returns and Customer Capitalism 126
Leveraging the Customer Capital 127
Compelling Customer Experiences 128
Personalization 130
Customer Loyalty 131
Customer Relationships 134
Why Cultivate Customer Relationships 135
Customer Interaction Channels 136
Internet: The Web of Relationships 137
Customer Channel Integration 137
360-Degree View of Customer 138
One-to-One Marketing 139
Permission Marketing 140
Customer Life Cycle 141
Customer Value 143
Customer Lifetime Value 144
Customer Value Management 146
Customers as Lifelong Investments 148
Customer as an Asset 148
Summary 150

Chapter 5 Customer-Responsive Enterprise with SCM 153

Concept of Supply-Chain Management 154
Supply-Chain Management Challenges 156
Supply-Chain Management 158
SCM Characteristics 159
SCM Components 160
Supply-Chain Management Framework 163
Supply-Chain Performance Framework 165
Supply-Chain Performance Measurement 169
Customer Responsiveness 170
Salient Aspects of Customer Responsiveness 174
Customer-Responsive Management 178
Networks of Resources 181
Business Webs 183
Economics of Customer Responsiveness 183

Activity-Based Customer Responsiveness........................187
Activity-Based Costing for BPR................................188
Time-Driven Activity-Based Costing 190
Responsive Activity Pricing...196
Summary 198

Chapter 6   Renewing Enterprise with PLM 201

Concept of Product Lifecycle Management........................201
Product Lifecycle Management 203
Challenges of PLM.. 204
Benefits of PLM 205
Components of PLM 207
Advantages of Using PLM.. 208
Porter's Framework of Generic Strategies..........................210
Product Life Cycle 212
Product Design Attributes..215
Product Design Approaches..218
Quality Function Deployment 218
Design for Manufacturability...................................219
Concurrent Engineering 220
Design for Sustainability... 220
Customization and Standardization....................................221
Mass Customization.. 223
Methodologies for Managing Customization................. 224
Summary 228

Chapter 7   Collaborative Enterprise with BPM 229

Process-Oriented Enterprise.. 229
Value-Add-Driven Enterprise 230
Concept of Business Process Management..........................231
Business Process... 234
Business Process Management 235
Enterprise BPM Methodology 238
Strategic Planning for Enterprise BPM........................... 238
Identifying the Business Processes in the Company.... 240
Selecting Business Processes for BPM 241
Creating Process Maps.. 242
Analyzing Processes for Breakthrough Improvements... 243

Innovative Breakthrough Improvement in Processes... 244
Implementing Designed Processes................................... 245
Measuring the Performance of Designed Processes...... 245
Business Process Reengineering.. 247
Management by Collaboration 249
Relationship-Based Enterprise..............................251
Information-Driven Enterprise 252
Process-Oriented Enterprise................................. 252
Value-Add-Driven Enterprise 253
Enterprise Change Management 254
Learning Enterprise.. 255
Virtual Enterprise.. 256
Business Processes with SOA.. 257
Process... 258
Workflow.. 260
Business Process Management 261
Business Processes via Web Services 263
Service Composition.. 264
Summary 265

Chapter 8   Informed Enterprise with BI 267
Concept of Business Intelligence (BI).................................. 267
Business Intelligence (BI) 268
Benefits of BI.. 270
Technologies of BI 272
Data Warehousing and Data Marts 272
Business Intelligence 272
Data Mining 274
Online Analytical Process....................................... 275
Applications of BI 275
Context-Aware Applications... 277
Decision Patterns as Context 279
Concept of Patterns 280
Domain-Specific Decision Patterns 284
Financial Decision Patterns.................................... 284
CRM Decision Patterns 287
CRM Decision Patterns through Data Mining 291
Summary 294

Chapter 9 Implementing Enterprise Systems 295

Mission and Objectives of the ES Project............................... 296
   Examples of Cited Reasons for Implementing ES.......... 297
Guiding Principles for ES Best Practices................................ 297
Project Initiation and Planning... 298
Critical Success Factors... 299
   Direct Involvement of Top Management......................... 299
   Clear Project Scope.. 300
   Covering as Many Functions as Possible within the
   Scope of the ES Implementation.................................... 300
   Standardizing Business Process...................................... 300
   Proper Visibility and Communication in the ES
   Project at All Stages 301
   Allocation of Appropriate Budget and Resources..........301
   Full-Time Deputation of Key Managers from All
   Departments...301
   Completing Infrastructural Activities in Time and
   with High Availability.. 302
   Instituting a Company-Wide Change Management
   Plan 302
   Training of ES Team Members 303
   Training of User Members 303
   Scheduling and Managing Interface of ES with
   Other Systems... 303
   Transition Plan for Cut Over to ES 304
Implementation Strategy 304
   Big Bang Implementation of ES Components 304
   Base Components Implemented First.............................. 305
   Implementation of ES Standard Functionality............... 305
   Pilot Site Deployment Followed by Rollouts at Other
   Sites 306
   Utilize External Consultants to Primarily Train
   In-House Functional and Technical Consultants........... 306
   Centralized or Decentralized ES Configuration............. 307
   User-Driven Functionality 307
ES Implementation Project Bill of Resources 307
   Money.. 308
   Materials.. 308

Manpower 308

Time Period 309

Information 309

Implementation Environment 309

Implementation Methodology 309

Accelerated SAP (ASAP) Methodology 311

Project Preparation 311

Business Blueprint 311

Realization 312

Final Preparation 312

Go Live and Support 312

Project Management 313

Project Organization 313

Project Control 313

Time Recording 314

Meetings 314

Project Monitoring 315

Project Reviews 315

ES Implementation 315

Preimplementation 315

Training 316

ES Installation 316

Implementation 316

Postimplementation 316

ES Support 317

ES Deployment 317

Why Some ES Implementations May Sometimes Be
Less Than Successful 318

Summary 319

Epilogue: Enterprise Performance Intelligence 321

Appendix I: SAP Business Suite 323

Bibliography 361

Index 363

Preface

As experiences with enterprise systems are being collated during the past decade or more across companies world-wide, the overall sense of elation has been missing. Despite hundreds of consultants working overtime to assuage the absence of unequivocal success of enterprise systems implementations, there is a distinct sense of puzzlement as to the real benefit of a decade-long investment into IT enablement of company operations and management.

There is no panacea for elevating or correcting the situation. One thing is clear, one cannot hope to gain much by merely migrating the traditional operations and processes to enterprise systems (ES). Traditional operations and systems are innately constrained by the limitations of manual operations and systems, consequently, migrating traditional operations and processes directly to ES pitches them at the lowest-end of the value-add spectrum. Migrating mundane operations and processes without optimization or re-design or re-engineering does not even begin to unleash the stupendous potential and power inherent in integrated enterprise-wide process-oriented information-driven real-time systems like ES–enterprise systems begin from where traditional systems reach the pinnacle of their performance! Thus, what is required is to revisit the basics of enterprise systems and rededicate ourselves to improve the application, relevance, and usage of these cross-company platforms. This book attempts to help you in that endeavor.

This book provides an overview of the characteristics and essential strengths of various categories of Enterprise Systems (ES), namely, Enterprise Resource Planning (ERP), Customer Relationship Management (CRM), Supply-Chain Management (SCM), Product LifeCycle Management (PLM), Business Process Management (BPM), and Business Intelligence (BI).

Initiating change and confronting change are the two most important issues facing today's enterprises. The ability to change business operations and processes contributes directly to the innovation bottom line. The traditional concept of change management is usually understood as a one-time event or at least a non-frequent event. But if an enterprise is looking for the capability to handle not only change management but also management of changes on a continual basis, then establishing a constellation of integrated enterprise systems such as ERP, CRM, SCM, PLM, BPM, and BI is a must!

Customary treatment of business excellence seldom highlights the change-enabling aspects of IT generally, and ES more specifically. Conventional work in this area has the now familiar refrain of the notion of business and IT alignment to assure optimal creation of business value, but it seldom discusses the very key enabler role of IT: *IT makes enterprise-wide change possible, more easily and effortlessly.*

It is phenomenally important to realize that business processes that reside or are internalized within an organization's employees are difficult to change simply because human beings naturally find it more difficult to change. However, processes that reside within computerized systems are easy to change because they are not thwarted by problems of inertia, fatigue, or lack of motivation. ES enable the essential and continual changing of processes that are so critical to the successes of an enterprise. However, the requisite rationale and supporting details are too technical to be tackled here and are beyond the scope of the objectives of this book, which is essentially focused on business management.

WHAT MAKES THIS BOOK DIFFERENT

This book presents the phenomenon of the emergence of ES such as ERP, CRM, SCM, PLM, BPM, and BI from business and technological perspectives. It attempts to demystify ES and their power and potential to transform businesses. Unlike customary work on ES, which seldom discusses the key differentiators of ES from the earlier mission-critical systems, this book brings to the fore the fact that ES collectively contribute to enhancing the intelligence quotient of the enterprise.

Enterprise intelligence can be defined as the ability to initiate change (to unsettle competitors) and confront change (initiated by competitors, regulators, and other players) in the market environment.

This book presents a case that ES enhance enterprise intelligence by enabling

1. Integrated Enterprise with ERP
   ERPs enable the integration of heterogeneous and disparate business units, functions, and processes to coordinate, cooperate, and

collaborate in aligning the business operations of the enterprise with its corporate strategy.

2. Customer-Centric Enterprise with CRM

CRMs enable the relationships with individual customers to cocreate and coinnovate solutions to the satisfaction of customers at optimal cost on an ongoing basis.

3. Customer-Responsive Enterprise with SCM

SCMs enable the flexibility to obtain the capability and capacity needed to respond quickly to individual customer requests.

4. Renewing Enterprise with PLM

PLMs enable the continuous renewal (creation and innovation) of enterprise offerings, i.e., products and services in sync with the continuous changes in customer preferences and needs and also in the changing market environment (because of the impact of competitors, regulators, activists, etc.).

5. Collaborative Enterprise with BPM

BPMs enable the reconciled, i.e., collaborative working of different cross-company stakeholders of any business process, activity, or decision in compliance with its strategy, policy, and procedures.

6. Informed Enterprise with BI

BIs enable enterprises to access current, correct, consistent, and complete information on any process or transaction to take informed decisions in compliance with its strategy, policy, and procedures.

HOW THIS BOOK IS ORGANIZED

Chapter 1 presents an overview of agile enterprises and dimensions of intelligent enterprises. Chapter 2 introduces enterprise systems and related concepts of enterprise value and enterprise performance management. Chapter 3 elaborates on the characteristics of ERP and Service-Oriented Architecture (SOA). While Chapter 4 details the CRM's focal concept of customer centricity as also a constellation of related concepts such as customer relationships, customer life cycle, and customer lifetime value, Chapter 5 presents SCM's focal concept of customer responsiveness. Product Lifecycle Management (PLM) and Product Life Cycle (PLC), which are at the heart of ongoing enterprise renewal, are discussed in Chapter 6. Chapter 7 discusses establishing a collaborative enterprise with BPM and enterprise BPM methodology. Chapter 8 deals with the realization of an informed enterprise with BI along with the novel concept of *decision patterns*. This chapter highlights the fact that any end-user application's effectiveness and performance can be enhanced by transforming it from a *bare* transaction to a transaction *clothed* by a surrounding context formed as an aggregate of all relevant decision patterns in the past. Finally, Chapter 9 presents details of various issues relating to an enterprise systems implementation project.

To give a practical context to the discussions on ES presented in the book, Appendix I provides an overview of the SAP Business Suite.

WHO SHOULD READ THIS BOOK

All who are involved with any aspect of ES projects—ERP, CRM, SCM, PLM, BPM, BI—will profit by reading this book to make a more meaningful contribution to the success of their ES implementation project(s).

The following categories of stakeholders will benefit from reading this book:

- Executives, and business and operational managers
- ES evaluation and selection team members
- ES technical and project managers, and module leaders
- ES functional and technical members
- Industry professionals interested in understanding the role of ES
- Students of engineering, management, computer, and technology courses
- General readers interested in the use of ES in organizations

Acknowledgments

I would like to thank all those who have helped me with their clarifications, criticism, and valuable information during the writing of this book.

Thanks to John Wyzalek for making this book happen and guiding it through to completion.

I thank my beloved daughters Tanaya and Atmaja for their understanding and support. And finally, thanks to my wife Girija—to whom I am grateful, beyond measure, for her continuous loving support and help.

Vivek Kale
Mumbai, India

Author

Vivek Kale has more than two decades of professional IT experience during which he has handled and consulted on various aspects of enterprise-wide information modeling, enterprise architecture, business process redesign, and e-business architecture. He has been Group CIO of Essar Group, the steel/oil and gas multi-national conglomerate of India, as well as Raymond Apparel Ltd., the textile and apparel manufacturer of India. He is a seasoned practitioner in transforming the business of IT, facilitating business agility, and enabling the Process-Oriented Enterprise. He is the author of *Implementing SAP R/3: The Guide for Business and Technology Managers*, Sams (2000), *A Guide to Implementing the Oracle Siebel CRM 8.x*, McGraw-Hill India (2009), and *Inverting the Paradox of Excellence: How Companies Use Variations for Business Excellence and How Enterprise Variations Are Enabled by SAP*, Productivity Press (2014).

1

Intelligent Enterprises

AGILE ENTERPRISES

The difficult challenges facing businesses today require enterprises to be transitioned into flexible, agile structures that can respond to new market opportunities quickly with a minimum of new investment and risk. As enterprises have experienced the need to be simultaneously efficient, flexible, responsive, and adaptive, they have transitioned themselves into agile enterprises with small, autonomous teams that work concurrently and reconfigure quickly, and adopt highly decentralized management that recognizes its knowledge base and manages it effectively.

Enterprise agility is the ability to be

1. Responsive—Adaptability is enabled by the concept of loosely coupled interacting components reconfigurable within a unified framework. This is essential for ensuring opportunity management to sustain viability.

   The ability to be responsive involves the following aspects:
   - An organizational structure that enables change is based on reusable elements that are reconfigurable in a scalable framework. Reusability and reconfigurability are generic concepts that are applicable to work procedures, manufacturing cells, production teams, or information automation systems.
   - An organizational culture that facilitates change and focuses on change proficiency.
2. The ability to be intelligence intensive or to manage and apply knowledge effectively whether it is knowledge of a customer, a market opportunity, a competitor's threat, a production process, a business practice, a product technology, or an individual's competency. This is essential for ensuring innovation management to sustain leadership.

The ability to be intelligence intensive involves the following aspects:

- Enterprise knowledge management
- Enterprise collaborative learning

 When confronted with a competitive opportunity a smaller company is able to act more quickly, whereas a larger company has access to more comprehensive knowledge (options, resources, etc.) and can decide to act sooner and more thoroughly.

Agility is the ability to respond to (and ideally benefit from) unexpected change. Agility is unplanned and unscheduled adaption to unforeseen and unexpected external circumstances. However, we must differentiate between agility and flexibility. Flexibility is scheduled or planned adaptation to unforeseen yet expected external circumstances.

One of the foremost abilities of an agile enterprise is its ability to quickly react to change and adapt to new opportunities. This ability to change works along two dimensions:

i. The number or "types of change" an enterprise is able to undergo
ii. The "degree of change" an enterprise is able to undergo

The former is termed as range, and the latter is termed as response ability. The more response-able an enterprise is, the more radical a change it can gracefully address. Range refers to how large a domain is covered by the agile response system; in other words, how far from the expected set of events one can go and still have the system respond well. However, given a specific range, how well the system responds is a measure of response or change ability.

 Enterprises primarily aim progressively for efficiency, flexibility, and innovation in that order. The Model Builder, Erector set, and LEGO kits are illustrations of enterprises targeting for efficiency, flexibility, and innovation (i.e., agility), respectively.

Construction toys offer a useful metaphor because the enterprise systems we are concerned with must be configured and reconfigured constantly, precisely the objective of most construction toys. An enterprise system architecture and structure consisting of reusable components reconfigurable in a scalable framework can be an effective base model for creating variable (or built-for-change) systems. To achieve this, the nature of the framework appears to be a critical factor. We can introduce the framework/component concept, by looking at three types of construction toys and observe how they are used in practice, namely, Erector Set Kit, LEGO Kit, and Model Builder's Kit.

You can build virtually anything over and over again with any of these toys; but fundamental differences in their architecture give each system unique dynamic characteristics. All consist of a basic set of core construction components, and also have an architectural and structural framework that enables connecting the components into an unbounded variety of configurations. Nevertheless, the Model Builder is not as reusable in practice as the Erector Set, and the Erector Set is not as reusable or reconfigurable or scalable in practice as LEGO, and LEGO is more reusable, reconfigurable, and scalable than either of them. LEGO is the dominant construction toy of choice among preteen builders—who appear to value experimentation and innovation.

The Model Builder's kit can be used to construct one object like airplane of one intended size. A highly integrated system, this construction kit offers maximum esthetic appeal for one-time construction use but the parts are not reusable, the construction cannot be reconfigured, and one intended size precludes any scalability. It will remain what it is for all time—there is zero variability here.

Erector Set kits can be purchased for constructing specific models, such as a small airplane that can be assembled in many different configurations. With the Erector Set kit, the first built model is likely to remain as originally configured in any particular play session. Erector Set, for all its modular structure, is just not as reconfigurable in practice as LEGO. The Erector Set connectivity framework employs a special-purpose intermediate subsystem used solely to attach one part to another—a nut-and-bolt pair and a 90-degree elbow. The components in the system all have holes through which the bolts may pass to connect one component with another. When a nut is lost, a bolt is useless, and vice versa; when all the nuts and bolts remaining in a set have been used, any remaining construction components are useless, and vice versa. All the parts in a LEGO set can always be used and reused, but the Erector Set, for all its modularity, is not as reusable in practice as LEGO.

LEGO offers similar kits, and both toys include a few necessary special parts, like wheels and cowlings, to augment the core construction components. Watch a child work with either and you will see the LEGO construction undergoes constant metamorphosis; the child may start with one of the pictured configurations, but then reconfigures the pieces into all manner of other imagined styles. LEGO components are plug-compatible with each other, containing the connectivity framework as an integral feature of the component. A standard grid of bumps and cavities on component surfaces allows them to snap together into a larger configuration—without limit.

The Model Builder's kit has a tight framework: A precise construction sequence, no part interchangeability, and high integration. Erector Set has a loose framework that does not encourage interaction among parts and insufficiently discriminates among compatible parts. In contrast, each component in the LEGO system carries all it needs to interact with other components (the interaction framework rejects most unintended parts), and it can grow without end.

Stability versus Agility

Most large-scale change efforts in established enterprises fail to meet the expectations because nearly all models of organization design, effectiveness, and change assume stability is not only desirable but also attainable. The theory and practice in an organization design explicitly encourages organizations to seek alignment, stability, and equilibrium. The predominant logic of organizational effectiveness has been that an organization's fit with its environment, its execution, and its predictability are the keys to its success. Organizations are encouraged to institutionalize best practices, freeze them into place, focus on execution, stick to their knitting, increase predictability, and get processes under control. These ideas establish stability as the key to performance.

Stability of a distinctive competitive advantage is a strong driver for organization design because of its expected link to excellence and effectiveness. Leveraging an advantage requires commitments that focus attention, resources, and investments to the chosen alternatives. In other words, competitive advantage results when enterprises finely hone their operations to perform in a particular way. This leads to large investments in operating technologies, structures, and ways of doing things. If such commitments are successful, they lead to a period of high performance and a considerable amount of positive reinforcement. Financial markets reward stable competitive advantages and predictable streams of earnings: A commitment to alignment reflects a commitment to stability.

Consequently, enterprises are built to support stable strategies, organizational structures, and enduring value creations, not to vary. For example, the often-used strengths, weaknesses, opportunities, and threats (SWOT) analysis encourages the firm to leverage opportunities while avoiding weaknesses and threats. This alignment among positive and negative forces is implicitly assumed to remain constant, and there is no built-in assumption of agility. When environments are stable or at least predictable, enterprises are characterized by rules, norms, and systems that limit experimentation, control variation, and reward consistent performance. There are many checks and balances in place to ensure that the organization operates in the prescribed manner. Thus, to get the high performance they want, enterprises put in place practices they see as a good fit, without considering whether they can be changed and whether they will support changes in future, that is, by aligning themselves to achieve high performance today, enterprises often make it difficult to vary, so that they can have high performance tomorrow.

When the environment is changing slowly or predictably, these models are adequate. However, as the rate of change increases with increasing globalization, technological breakthroughs, associative alliances, and regulatory changes, enterprises have to look for greater agility, flexibility, and innovation from their companies. Instead of pursuing strategies, structures, and cultures that are designed to create long-term competitive advantages, companies must seek a string of temporary competitive advantages through an approach to organization design that assumes change is normal. With the advent of the Internet and the accompanying extended "virtual" market spaces, enterprises are now competing based on intangible assets such as identity, intellectual property, ability to attract and stick to customers, and, their ability to organize, reorganize frequently or organize differently in different areas depending on the need. Thus, the need for changes in management and organization is much more frequent, and, excellence is much more a function of possessing the ability to change. Enterprises need to be built around practices that encourage change, not thwart it. Instead of having to create change efforts, disrupt the status quo, or adapt to change, enterprises should be built-for-change.

To meet the conflicting objectives of performing well against the current set of environmental demands and changing themselves to face future business environments, enterprises must engender two types of changes: The natural process of evolution, or what we will call strategic adjustments and strategic reorientations:

a. Strategic adjustments involve the day-to-day tactical changes required to bring in new customers, make incremental improvements in products and services, and comply with regulatory requirements. This type of change helps fine-tune current strategies and structures to achieve short-term results; it is steady, incremental, and natural. This basic capability to evolve is essential if an enterprise is to survive to thrive.

b. Strategic reorientation involves altering an existing strategy and, in some cases, adopting a new strategy. When the environment evolves or changes sufficiently, an enterprise must significantly adjust some elements of its strategy and the way it executes that strategy. More often than not, enterprises have to face a transformational change that involves not just a new strategy but a transformation of the business model that leads to new products, services, and customers, and requires markedly new competencies and capabilities. However, operationally all these changes can be seen as manifestations of the basic changes only differing in degrees and multiple dimensions.

Maintaining an agile enterprise is not a matter of searching for the strategy but continuously strategizing, not a matter of specifying an organization design but committing to a process of organizing, and not generating value but continuously improving the efficiency and effectiveness of the value generation process. It is a search for a series of temporary configurations that create short-term advantages. In turbulent environments, enterprises that string together a series of temporary but adequate competitive advantages will outperform enterprises that stick with one advantage for an extended period of time. The key issue for the built-for-change enterprise is orchestration, or coordinating the multiple changing subsystems to produce high levels of current enterprise performance.

Aspects of Agility

This section addresses the analytical side of agility or change proficiency of the enterprise. It highlights the fundamental principles that underlie an enterprise's ability to change, and indicate how to apply these principles in real situations. It illustrates what it is that makes a business and any of its constituting systems easy to change.

Agility or change proficiency enables both efficiency programs (e.g., lean production) and transformation programs; if the enterprise is proficient at change, it can adapt to take advantage of an unpredictable opportunity, and can also counter the unpredictable threat. Agility can embrace semantics across the whole spectrum: It can capture cycle-time reduction with everything happening faster; it can build on lean production with high resource productivity; it can encompass mass customization with customer-responsive product variation; it can embrace virtual enterprise with streamlined supplier networks and opportunistic partnerships; it can echo reengineering with a process and transformation focus; it can demand a learning organization with systemic training and education. Being agile means being proficient at change. Agility allows an enterprise to do anything it wants to do whenever it wants to—or has to—do it. Thus, an agile enterprise can employ business process reengineering as a core competency when transformation is called for; it can hasten its conversion to lean production when greater efficiencies are useful; it can continue to succeed when constant innovation becomes the dominant competitive strategy. Agility can be wielded overtly as a business strategy as well as inherently as a sustainable-existence competency.

Agility derives from both the physical ability to act (change ability) and the intellectual ability to find appropriate things to act on (knowledge management). Agility can be expressed as the ability to manage and apply knowledge effectively, so that enterprise has the potential to thrive in a continuously changing and unpredictable business environment. Agility derives from two sources: An enterprise architecture that enables change and an organizational culture that facilitates change. The enterprise architecture that enables change is based on reusable elements that are reconfigurable in a scalable framework.

Agility is a core fundamental requirement of all enterprises. It was not an area of interest when environmental change was relatively slow and predictable. Now there is virtually no choice; enterprises must develop a conscious competency. Practically, all enterprises now need some method to assess their agility and determine whether it is sufficient or needs improvement. This section introduces techniques for characterizing, measuring, and comparing variability in all aspects of business and among different businesses.

Principles of Built-for-Change Systems

Christopher Alexander introduced the concept of patterns in the late 1970s in the field of architecture. A pattern describes a commonly occurring solution that generates decidedly successful outcomes.

A list of successful patterns for agile enterprises (and systems) in terms of their constituting elements or functions or components are as follows:

a. Reusable

   Agility Pattern 1

   Self-Contained Units (Components): *The components of agile enterprises are autonomous units cooperating toward a shared goal.*

   Agility Pattern 2

   Plug Compatibility: *The components of agile enterprises are reusable and multiply replicable, that is, depending on requirements multiple instances of the same component can be invoked concurrently.*

   Agility Pattern 3

   Facilitated Reuse: *The components of agile enterprises share well-defined interaction and interface standards, and can be inserted, removed, and replaced easily and noninvasively.*

b. Reconfigurable

   Agility Pattern 4

   Flat Interaction: *The components of agile enterprises communicate, coordinate, and cooperate with other components concurrently and in real-term sharing of current, complete, and consistent information on interactions with individual customers.*

   Agility Pattern 5

   Deferred Commitment: *The components of agile enterprises establish relationships with other components in the real term to enable deferment of customer commitment to as late a stage as possible within the sales cycle, coupled with the corresponding ability to postpone the point of product differentiation as close as possible to the point of purchase by the customer.*

   Agility Pattern 6

   Distributed Control and Information: *The components of agile enterprises are defined declaratively rather than procedurally; the network of components display the defining characteristics of any "small worlds" network, namely, local robustness and global accessibility.*

Agility Pattern 7

Self-organization: *The components of agile enterprises are self-aware and they interact with other components via on-the-fly integration, adjustment, or negotiation.*

c. Scalable

Agility Pattern 8

Evolving Standards (Framework): *The components of agile enterprises operate within predefined frameworks that standardize intercomponent communication and interaction, determine component compatibility, and evolve to accommodate old, current, and new components.*

Agility Pattern 9

Redundancy and Diversity: *The components of agile enterprises replicate components to provide the desired capacity, load balancing and performance, fault tolerance as well as variations on the basic component functionality and behavior.*

Agility Pattern 10

Elastic Capacity: *The components of agile enterprises enable dynamic utilization of additional or a reduced number of resources depending on the requirements.*

Framework for Change Proficiency

How do we measure enterprise agility? This section establishes a metric framework for proficiency at change; an enterprise's change proficiency may exist in one or more dimensions of change. And, these dimensions of change can form a structural framework for understanding current capabilities and setting strategic priorities for improvement: How does the agile enterprise know when it is improving its changeability, or losing ground? How does it know if it is less changeable than its competition? How does it set improvement targets? Thus, a practical measure of change proficiency is needed before we can talk meaningfully about getting more of it, or even getting some of it.

It must be highlighted that measuring change competency is generally not unidimensional, nor likely to result in an absolute and unequivocal comparative metric. Change proficiency has both reactive and proactive modes. Reactive change is opportunistic and responds to a situation that threatens viability. Proactive change is innovative and responds to a possibility for leadership. An enterprise sufficiently proficient at reactive change, when prodded should be able to use that competency proactively and let others do the reacting.

Would it be proficient if a short-notice change was completed in the time required, but at a cost that eventually bankrupted the company? Or if the changed environment thereafter required the special wizardry and constant attention of a specific employee to keep it operational? Is it proficient if the change is virtually free and painless, but out-of-sync with market opportunity timing? Is it proficient if it can readily accommodate a broad latitude of change that is no longer needed, or too narrow for the latest challenges thrown at it by the business environment? Are we change proficient if we can accommodate any change that comes our way as long as it is within a narrow 10 percent of where we already are?

Therefore, change proficiency can be understood to be codetermined by four parameters:

- Time: A measure of elapsed time to complete a change (fairly objective)
- Cost: A measure of monetary cost incurred in a change (somewhat objective)
- Quality: A measure of prediction quality in meeting change time, cost, and specification targets robustly (somewhat subjective)
- Range: A measure of the latitude of possible change, typically defined and determined by mission or charter (fairly subjective)

Enhancing Enterprise Agility

e-Business Strategy

e-Business refers to an enterprise that has reengineered itself to conduct its business via the Internet and Web. Successful enterprises need to reconceptualize the very nature of their business.

As customers begin to buy via the Internet and enterprises rush to use the Internet to create new operational efficiencies, most enterprises seek to update their business strategies. Enterprises survey the changing environment and then modify their company strategies to accommodate these changes. This involves major changes in the way companies do business, including changes in marketing, sales, service, product delivery, and even manufacturing and inventory. Changed strategies will entail changed business processes that in turn imply changed software systems or better still, software systems that are changeable!

Business Process Reengineering (BPR)

Although, BPR has its roots in information technology (IT) management, it is basically a business initiative that has a major impact on the satisfaction of both the internal and external customer. Michael Hammer, who triggered the BPR revolution in 1990, considers BPR as a "radical change" for which IT is the key enabler. BPR can be broadly termed as *the rethinking and change of business processes to achieve dramatic improvements in the measures of performances such as cost, quality, service, and speed.*

Some of the principals advocated by Hammer are as follows:

- Organize around outputs, not tasks
- Put the decisions and control, and hence all relevant information, into the hands of the performer
- Have those who use the outputs of a process to perform the process, including the creation and processing of the relevant information
- The location of user, data, and process information should be immaterial; it should function as if all were in a centralized place

When perusing the above points it will become evident that the implementation of Enterprise Systems (ES) possess most of the characteristics mentioned.

The most important outcome of BPR has been viewing business activities as more than a collection of individual or even functional tasks; it has engendered the process-oriented view of business. However, BPR is different from quality management efforts like TQM, ISO 9000, and so on, that refer to programs and initiatives that emphasize bottom-up incremental improvements in existing work processes and outputs on a continuous basis. In contrast, BPR usually refers to dramatic top-down improvements through redesigned or completely new processes on a discrete basis. In the continuum of methodologies ranging from ISO 9000, TQM, ABM, and so on, at one end and BPR on the other, ES implementation definitely lies on the BPR side of the spectrum when it comes to corporate change management efforts.

Mobilizing Enterprise Processes

This strategy entails replacing the process or process segment under consideration by a mobile-enabled link. In the next subsection, we discuss an overview of business processes before discussing the characteristics of mobilized processes.

Mobility offers new opportunities to dramatically improve business models and processes and will ultimately provide new, streamlined business processes that never would have existed if not for this new phenomenon.

Extending Web to Wireless

The first step in the evolution of mobility is to extend the Web to wireless; this is also known as webifying. For the most part, business processes are minimally affected in this phase. The goal is to provide value-added services through mobility with minimal disruption to existing processes. An example might be creating a new company website accessible through Wireless Application Protocol (WAP) phones or Palm OS-based personal digital assistants (PDAs). Firms attain immediate value through realizing additional exposure and market presence, and customers realize value through additional services.

Extending Business Processes with Mobility

The next step in the evolution of mobility is to extend existing business processes. New opportunities to streamline company business processes emerge and evolve to produce new revenue opportunities. One example is the way that mobility extends business processes through a supply-chain optimization model. New business processes emerge through these new mechanisms that ultimately shorten the supply-chain cycle, thus minimizing error and maximizing efficiency and realizing the utmost customer satisfaction. Real-time tracking and alert mechanisms provide supply-chain monitors with the capability to monitor shipments and product line quality in ways that traditional business models were not capable of doing.

Enabling a Dynamic Business Model

The final phase in the evolution of mobility is the one that has only been touched upon in today's world. The unique attributes of mobility will provide new and exciting ways of managing processes and allow for efficiencies never before attainable. The convergence of wireless technologies with existing business models will result in fully dynamic business processes.

Network Enterprises

Agile companies produce the right product, at the right place, at the right time, at the right price for the right customer. As pointed out by Jagdish Sheth in these times of market change and turbulence, the half-life (i.e., the time within which it loses currency by 50%) of customer knowledge is getting shorter and shorter. The difficult challenges facing businesses today require organizations to transition into flexible, agile structures that can respond to new market opportunities quickly with a minimum of new investment and risk.

As enterprises have experienced the need to be simultaneously efficient, flexible, responsive, and adaptive, they have turned increasingly to the network form of organization with the following characteristics:

- Networks rely more on market mechanisms rather than on administrative processes to manage resource flows. These mechanisms are not simple arms-length relationships usually associated with independently owned economic entities. Instead, to maintain the position within the network, members recognize their interdependence and are willing to share information, cooperate with each other, and customize their product or service.
- While a network of subcontractors has been common for many years, recently formed networks expect members to play a much more proactive role in improving the final product or service.
- Instead of holding all assets required to produce a given product or service in-house, networks use the collective assets of several firms located along the value chain.

The agile enterprise is composed of small, autonomous teams or subcontractors who work concurrently and reconfigure quickly to thrive in an unpredictable and rapidly changing customer environment. Each constituent has the full resources of the company or the value chain at its disposal and has a seamless information exchange between the lead enterprise and the virtual partners.

Thus, a network enterprise is a coalition of enterprises that work collectively and collaboratively to create value for the customers of a focal enterprise. Sometimes, the coalition is loosely connected, at other times, it is tightly defined, as in the relationship between Dell and its component suppliers. An enterprise network consists of a wide range of companies—suppliers, joint venture (JV) partners, contractors, distributors, franchisees, licensees, and so on—that contribute to the focal enterprise's creation and delivery of value to its customers. Each of these enterprises in turn will have their own enterprise networks focused around themselves. Thus, relationships between enterprises in the network both enable and constrain focal companies in the achievement of their goals. Therefore, liberating the potential value in customer relationships hinges on enterprises effectively managing their non–customer–network relationships.

> Though they appear similar, there are fundamental differences between the agile and lean approaches for running a business. Lean production is, at heart, simply an enhancement of mass production methods, whereas agility implies breaking out of the mass production mold and into mass customization. Agility focuses on economies of scope rather than economies of scale, ideally serving ever-smaller niche markets—even quantities of one—without the high cost traditionally associated with customization. A key element of agility is an enterprise-wide view, whereas lean production is usually associated with the efficient use of resources on the operations floor.

OPERATING STRATEGY

Operating strategy can be expressed in terms of the degree of responsiveness expected for an customer order. It can be defined as

$$\text{Degree of Responsiveness (DOR)} = \frac{\text{Customer Fulfillment Cycle}}{(\text{Manufacturing Time} + \text{Distribution Time})}$$

As an illustration, in the order of magnitude, DOR can range from 0.01 to about 5 corresponding to

- Purchase from a Retail Outlet
- One-of-a-kind Product or Project

As an illustration, Figures 1.1 and 1.2 present, for different operating philosophies, a snapshot schematic of DOR versus product flow and planning techniques, respectively.

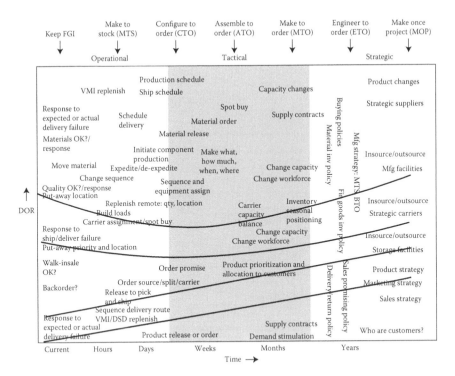

FIGURE 1.1
DOR, product flow decisions, and operating philosophies.

ENTERPRISE-WIDE CONTINUOUS IMPROVEMENT PROGRAMS

Lean is a proven approach for becoming an excellent operational system, Six Sigma is a program for attaining world-class quality improvement, Theory of Constraint is an unsurpassed tool for identifying and removing bottlenecks, and SCOR is an industry-wide analytical methodology.

Lean System

Lean System is based on the Toyota Production System, which Toyota has been perfecting for more than five decades. Toyota Production System (TPS) was inspired by the Ford production system. In 1950, when Toyota Motor Company was in trouble, Eiji Toyoda went to Detroit to learn from the legendary Ford Motor Company how to improve his family's business.

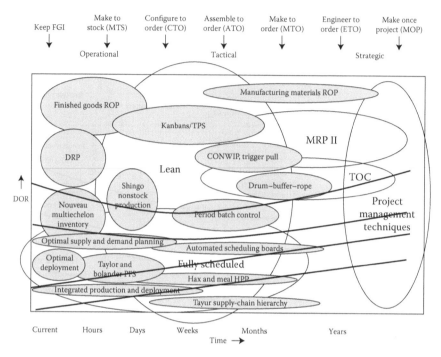

FIGURE 1.2

DOR, product planning techniques, and operating philosophies.

He spent three months in Detroit, studying Ford's manufacturing techniques in detail and looking for ways to transport them to Toyota. His conclusion was that while Henry Ford's concept of mass production was probably right for 1913, it was not responsive to the demands of the 1950s. The result was the design of a fundamentally different system, the TPS, which enabled the Japanese automobile industry to overtake Detroit.

Toyota is now recognized as a benchmark of superior performance among the world's best-run, most successful manufacturing companies. The central organizing concept of Toyota can be described as multiproduct flow. The major difference with Ford, and it is a major one, is that Toyota was not constrained to one product. Toyota applied the principle of flow to a range of products: Different models go down the same line without preventing the goals of minimal throughput time and of low inventory targets. Toyota still achieved an inventory turn (ratio of sales divided by WIP) approaching 300 (compared to Ford's inventory turns of about 200 and GM's inventory turns of about 8). Toyota took Ford's challenge of synchronization two steps beyond Ford: The first step was to introduce multiproduct flow, and the second was equalization of the cycle times for every part.

Lean applies a unique process mapping approach called Value Stream Mapping. The current-state Value Stream Map documents the materials and information flow. Value stream mapping always starts with the customer and includes both material and information flow. In addition, key information is gathered about each value stream operation. The second step is the creation of a future-state Value Stream Map, which is done by assuming that lean practices have been applied to the value stream. Projects are identified based on the changes needed to transform current-state processes into future-state processes. Lean tools are then applied to the improvement projects. When projects are completed, the process is repeated to create a new set of projects. This iterative process continues forever in the pursuit of perfection.

Lean identifies five key concepts:

- Value is defined by the customer.
- Value stream is the information and material flow from suppliers' suppliers to customers' customers.
- Flow is the synchronized continuous movement of material through the value stream.
- Pull is a product usage signal from the customer to other participants in the supply chain.
- Perfection is the never-ending pursuit of zero waste.

The Lean System is predicated on four clear values and seven principles, and has as its goal eliminating waste and increasing customer value forever by optimizing people, materials, space, and equipment resources. It specifies seven forms of waste to be eliminated:

1. Overproduction—making more than is needed
2. Transport—excessive movement of materials
3. Motion—inefficient movement of people
4. Waiting—underutilization of people
5. Inventory—material lying around unused
6. Overprocessing—manufacturing to a higher quality standard than expected by the customer
7. Defect correction—time spent fixing defects, including the part that gets thrown away and the time it takes to make the product correctly (Figure 1.3)

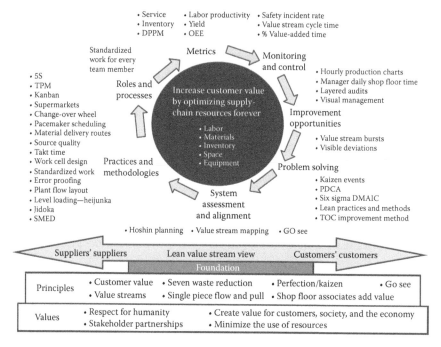

FIGURE 1.3

Lean system improvement cycle.

Lean is a holistic supply-chain operational system best practice with imbedded continuous improvement capability linked to customer value. The repetitive cycle of "standardize, level load, stabilize, and create flow" ensures continuous regeneration of improvement opportunities as perfection is pursued. Problem solving in lean is a combination of prescriptive standard practices and scientific problem solving; when none of the existing Lean prescriptive solutions is directly applicable, this allows for development of new solutions. Lean engages the entire enterprise in the improvement effort centering around the shop floor operators, so that continuous improvement is part of everyone's job. Finally, Lean imparts the continuous improvement system and culture with a common language, tools, goals, and objectives.

 Understanding Lean philosophy fully is a challenge. Lean has been explained by a set of principles and concepts that tie its practices together into a system comparatively recently. Lean is not easily scalable: The fastest complete systems implementations take two to three years, as an enterprise absorbs an immense amount of specific knowledge and applies it to its value streams. Building a team of internal Lean experts also takes two to three years before members have implemented all Lean system practices. Lean implies a committed shop floor management team for sustained gains and to lead the next level of improvement—which is very difficult to retain. Often the early results from Lean are difficult to map to bottom-line benefits. So it necessitates enlightened financial leadership to either change some of the financial operational measurements or educate their organizations on how to look at financial benefits created by Lean. In fact, inventory reduction that results improvement in working capital will likely cause a short-term reduction in output, which will reflect negatively on factory costs or cost of goods as a percentage of sales metrics.

Theory of Constraints

The Theory of Constraints (TOC) was developed by Eli Goldratt and collaborators. It became broadly known in 1984 when Goldratt's book *Goal* was published. TOC views an enterprise as a system with resources linked together to meet the enterprise's goals. TOC views enterprises as systems with resources linked together to meet an organization's goal. All systems have a constraint that limits the system's capacity to improve and better meet or exceed its goal. Enterprises have limited resources, so it is critical that resources be applied to reduce or eliminate constraints to maximize success. TOC methodology includes improvement tools that use rigorous root-cause analysis to define the solution. The methodology also identifies all the assumptions and conditions needed to ensure the success of a proposed solution. These very conditions and assumptions become the basis for action items for implementation plans. TOC improvement tools are effective both for continuous improvement or breakthrough problem solving.

Over the course of the 1980s, Eli Goldratt introduced a powerful set of concepts called TOC. The theory represents a philosophy of operations management, a management system, and a set of tools/principles to improve operations. Initially, TOC promotion focused around the fact that most manufacturing operations have a few bottleneck steps that limit the throughput of the plant under typical product mixes. The goal of planning, then, should be to schedule these bottleneck steps efficiently so as to achieve maximum throughput, to schedule steps before and after the bottlenecks in order to best support the bottlenecks, and to elevate the constraints by adding capacity there, thus shifting the binding constraints to elsewhere in the system. The drum–buffer–rope scheduling methodology was invented to support plant operations to exploit constraints to the maximum possible (get maximum throughput through them) and subordinate other manufacturing steps to the constrained ones. As TOC evolved, greater emphasis was placed on the fact that the principles apply not just to manufacturing but to supply-chain operations as a whole and even to non–supply-chain activities like project management.

These principles led to a universal five-step methodology for business improvement:

1. Identify the system's constraints
2. Decide how to exploit the system's constraints
3. Subordinate everything else to the earlier decision
4. Elevate the system's constraints
5. If in the previous steps a constraint has been broken, go back to step 1

The Theory of Constraints takes a holistic systems view of all operations of a plant or supply chain. Applied to a business, the TOC purpose is to increase profit. It focuses system improvement on increasing throughput as the best way to add more value. Improvement or elimination of a current constraint results in more throughput, at which point a new system constraint is identified. This continuous cycle drives performance improvement forever.

TOC includes concepts used to schedule operations. The constrained operation is scheduled in a specific product sequence, aligning resource use to meet customer demand. This system termed as Drum–Rope–Buffer scheduling sets the pace for all other operations:

i. Upstream, raw materials are subordinated to the constrained operation to make sure materials are available when needed to support the constrained operations schedule.
ii. Downstream operations must flow, and are therefore planned and run with sufficient capacity so that all products made by the constrained operation can be processed.
iii. Time buffers are used upstream from the constraint so promised shipment dates are met, protecting promised dates from inevitable process variability. Work is released into production at a rate dictated by the drum and started based on a predetermined total process buffer length.

When sales is the constraint, TOC has an approach for solving these problems, which includes use of its problem-solving tools combined with TOC accounting, market segmentation, and pricing strategies to identify what needs to change in order to increase sales. This is a unique feature of TOC compared with other problem-solving methodologies.

The metrics used in TOC measure the value add produced. Key TOC metrics are

- T: Throughput value of sales less materials cost
- I: System's raw material inventory
- OE: Operating expenses
- Conversion Ratio: Dividing T by OE gives a productivity measurement, that is, the rate at which operating expenses are converting raw materials into T
- Inventory Turnover: Dividing T by I, the money generated from sales divided by raw material inventory cost measures inventory turnover

TOC Tools

TOC employs five tools as follows:

1. What to Change
   Current Reality Tree: The current reality tree is a tool used to identify the root cause of a core problem that has no known solution, in order to eliminate initial undesirable effects. The current reality tree is a type of flowchart that depicts the cause-and-effect relationships that exist for the object of interest. The tree is normally built using a storyboard-type approach, starting with a listing of the effects to be remedied. The contributing factors that perpetuate these effects are associated with them and listed accordingly. This type of analysis is performed again on the perpetuating factors and is continued until what in essence would be the root cause of the problem can be identified. This simplistic explanation can become quite convoluted in practice when the situation under study has multiple effects to remedy and many associated contributing factors.

   One of the expected outputs of creating a current reality tree is to identify the root causes that are perpetuating the effects to be remedied. Once these causes are identified, then they provide a focus for subsequent efforts.

2. Objective for Change

Evaporating Cloud: The evaporating cloud identifies requirements that the solution must satisfy. The first step is to state the core problem and define what should replace it. The current core problem exists because it satisfies an organizational need or requirement. This means defined solutions must satisfy needs currently satisfied by whatever caused the core problem and by whatever will replace it.

Future Reality Tree: The future reality tree defines the desirable effects of the solution, which will become the improvement project objectives. Future reality trees create a complete picture of positive and negative consequences of the proposed solution defined in the evaporating cloud process. Each undesirable effect discovered in making the current reality tree is reviewed to define its opposite, i.e., desirable effect. These desirable effects become implementation plan objectives. They are also inputs examined using the prerequisite tree.

3. How to Change

Prerequisite tree: The prerequisite tree defines conditions that need to be in place to achieve future reality tree defined objectives. Prerequisite trees ensure all necessary conditions are identified and objectives are set to ensure implementation plans meet them. Projects are implemented efficiently by defining the best sequence to meet these conditions and they are included as input to the transition tree.

Transition tree: The transition tree creates detailed plans to implement the objectives defined in the prerequisite tree. Intermediate objectives and action plans supporting them are delegated to teams or individuals. Teams use transition trees to break down the actions needed to achieve the assigned objectives. These transition tree objectives and actions are used in implementation reviews to ensure that overall project objectives are met.

Systems always have constraints to be eliminated, so TOC will always regenerate opportunities for improvement. The heart of the TOC methodology is the focus on the system constraint, which ensures that all resources are applied to maximize the system improvement benefit. The TOC thinking process is based on the scientific method, that is, it identifies the root cause(s) of a problem and develops effective solutions. The thinking process is useful for making both incremental and breakthrough improvements.

Understanding TOC thinking fully is a challenge. Becoming proficient in applying TOC takes time because the language and rigorous improvement methodology are not easily understood. TOC thinking provides no prescriptive solutions but rather a very rigorous scientific method problem-solving process. It ensures focus on the most important defect, the real problem is well understood, root causes are defined, and implementation will treat all the root causes and mitigate any unintended consequences. The entire company leadership team must be on board in leading the use of TOC across the company because at some point in the journey the constraint will move to all the operating functions in the organization. If TOC is applied only in manufacturing and the supply chain without total organizational involvement, the maximum potential benefit will not be achieved. As in Lean, TOC also needs an enlightened financial leadership to change some of the financial operational measurements or educate the organization on how to look at the financial benefits created by TOC.

Six Sigma

Six Sigma is a business improvement approach that seeks to find and eliminate causes of mistakes or defects in business processes by focusing on outputs that are of critical importance to customers. Six Sigma projects should be customer focused. The key element of any customer–supplier relationship is a clear understanding of what customer expectations are. The message received from gaining a clear understanding of customer expectations is sometimes referred to as the voice of the customer.

Six Sigma can be applied to any process that needs improvement. Potential projects are defined to fill gaps between current performance and the level required to achieve the success as envisaged in the annual business plan of the company. By targeting the areas of the business plan with the greatest critical gaps, organizational effort is focused and prioritized; projects are also identified by examining the defects affecting the achievement of business objectives or obvious variability in processes. Brainstorming and analysis of current processes are then often used for bottom–up generation of potential projects. Process performance may be compared to an entitlement level, a level of performance that may represent the best short-term performance ever achieved for such a process. Once the projects are defined, the five-step Six Sigma DMAIC (define, measure, analyze, improve, control) process is used.

DMAIC is the primary Six Sigma tool for reducing variability in existing processes. DMAIC, without doubt, has proven itself a very powerful tool for improvement at 3M and a number of other well-known companies. It is a rigorous process that relies heavily on statistical methodologies and techniques. Projects which follow a prescribed five-step process are completed within a specified time frame resulting in quick impact on the business. During the early stages of Six Sigma implementation, projects are completed in four to six months; however, once the Master Black Belts and Black Belts gain experience and become more proficient, projects can get completed faster.

> Six Sigma requires an investment in infrastructure. The training of Master Black Belts and Black Belts. Most leading Six Sigma practicing companies have their own certification process, which requires successful completion of projects. A Master Black Belt has the same technical skills as a Black Belt but is normally also trained in leadership and program management. They are usually responsible for a number of Black Belts. Black Belts are intensively trained in all Six Sigma DMAIC skills and tools, they are expected to complete projects and coach Green Belts who are leading their own projects.

For Six Sigma, it is imperative that strong management support exists. The efforts expended must have buy-in from management because various resources will be utilized and personnel will be called upon throughout the project to invest time and energy. The commitment needs to be there or you are doomed to failure. In addition to management support, the personnel involved in the project need to be adequately trained in the methodology of Six Sigma in order to properly apply the tools. The level of training is commensurate with the role an employee plays in the Six Sigma scheme of things. The typical roles that exist in the world of Six Sigma are black belts, master black belts, green belts, executive sponsors, champions, and process owners.

The objective or focus of the project team needs to be related to the organizational goals and results in a financial benefit to the company. In order to verify that the team's efforts have resulted in a financial benefit, it is imperative that effective metrics are evaluated. Once the project team screens through the maze of potential metrics and selects those most appropriate to the organizational goals, then the team is poised to initiate the project. A Six Sigma effort is a project that has a predetermined objective, a planned life cycle, and requires the allocation of resources for completion. Therefore, many of the basic tenets of "project management" apply to the execution of a Six Sigma project, and its successful execution and monitoring of status are accomplished in the same fashion as any other project, using Gantt charts, PERT charts, etc.

 The execution of a Six Sigma project uses a structured method of approaching problem solving, termed DMAIC, primarily used for improving existing processes, stands for Define, Measure, Analyze, Improve, Control. DMADV, which is used for improving designs, stands for Define, Measure, Analyze, Design, Verify.

The purpose of DMAIC is to improve growth, cost, or working capital performance of a business. It is a five-step improvement methodology based on the vigorous use of statistical methods. Potential improvement projects receive high priority when their elimination or improvement is necessary to achieve the annual business plan, for example, defects that result in customer dissatisfaction, high cost, high inventories, or other negative financial measures. Once the "hopper" of potential projects is identified, the projects are prioritized to align with the business's priorities and started through the five-step process. Six Sigma DMAIC is a methodology for reducing variation, decreasing defects, and improving quality when the root cause is unknown and not easily identifiable.

The process turns input X's into output Y; Six Sigma DMAIC identifies defects (Y's) in the output of processes that need improvement through better control of key input and process variables (X's). The five phases are as follows:

1. Define. This phase clearly defines the goal of the project:
   - What is the undesirable process variability or defect that must be eliminated?
   - What is the benefit if there is zero waste and a well-defined project charter which
     - is driven by a business strategy and a business plan improvement goal

    – reflects the voice of the customer in project metrics
    – clearly defines project objectives
    – defines the scope of the project appropriately to ensure it can be accomplished in four to six months or less

2. Measure. This phase clearly defines the current process, establishes metrics, and validates the measurement quality:
   - What is the measurement of the output defects (Y)?

   Many statistical tools are available to the Six Sigma professional, including probability analysis, box plots, scatter diagrams, and trend analysis. All these measures will provide some understanding of how the data are distributed, but a deeper grasp can be obtained with the probability density function and cumulative distribution function. Measurement system analysis is an evaluation of the amount of variability that is being introduced into your data values as a result of the measuring equipment you are using.

   Process flowchart, process mapping, or value stream mapping gives a road map of potential opportunities to focus on.

3. Analyze. This phase clearly defines the root causes of variation:
   - Selecting enough input variables (X's) to make analysis feasible
   - Using multivariables studies to determine which X's have the most impact on the output defects (Y)
   - Planning initial improvement activities

   There are numerous statistical tools to analyze data: Simple linear regression, correlation coefficient, multivariable analysis, coefficient of determination, goodness of fit test, analysis of variance, nonparametric tests, the Spearman rank correlation coefficient, Kruskal–Wallis one-way analysis of variance by ranks, Mann–Whitney U-test, Levene's test, Mood's median test, etc. The challenge is to use the most appropriate tool for the situation in order to make the best decisions.

4. Improve. This phase clearly identifies relationships between critical X's and the output defects (Y) are quantified and selected to verify the proposed solutions by
   - determining the effect critical X's have on the output defects (Y) using designed experiments
   - developing the sequence of experiments
   - identifying the critical inputs that need to be controlled
   - defining and piloting solutions to resolve problem root causes

   There are three primary methods that the Six Sigma professional may want to consider when beginning to attempt to improve a process: Design of experiments, response surface methodology, and evolutionary operations. Experimentation performed without utilizing design of experiments effectively only looks at one factor at a time, and ends up drawing erroneous conclusions because an interaction effect that may exist between factors goes unobserved; another is that without comparing various levels of all factors simultaneously, there may be no insight as to what is the optimal combination of factor levels. That is where design of experiments comes in. With design of experiments, you can look at multiple levels of multiple factors simultaneously and make decisions as to what levels of the factors will optimize your output.

There are various types of experimental designs you can draw upon depending on what you are trying to evaluate, namely, randomized and randomized block designs, full factorial designs, fractional factorial designs, mixture experiments, and Taguchi designs.

5. Control. This phase ensures that the process maintains the gains achieved, is neutral or positive for customers, and controls the critical X's through

- a well-executed control plan
- the identification of the control plan process owner
- tracking financial results for a year

There is a need to build an appropriate level of control into the process to assure that it does not backslide into an undesirable state. This can be achieved by tools like statistical process control (SPC) and some of the Lean tools. SPC is to provide the operator with real-time feedback as to whether or not a process is functioning in control. There are a host of different types of charts that can be utilized depending on the type of data collection desired including X-bar/R, X/MR, EWMA, etc., and attribute charts include c, p, u, np, etc. Lean tools include the 5Ss, the kaizen blitz, kanban, poka-yoke, total productive maintenance, and standard work.

Six Sigma's major strength is that its project focus, measurable defect elimination, and direct financial benefits are easily understood by the business's leadership and aligned with their need to meet the annual business objectives. Rigorous control plans are established as a part of finalizing Six Sigma projects to ensure improvements become permanent and result in a good bottom-line profit for the business. Six Sigma should measure only hard savings, cost, or cash benefits that are actually tracked to an operating budget, inventory, accounts payable, or accounts receivable balance.

This would ensure that some true net financial benefit will show up in the profit and loss statement. Six Sigma creates a company-wide improvement methodology allowing employee team members to engage in problem solving and maximizing their improvement capacity. Six Sigma's fact-based problem-solving rigor gives a good level of confidence that true root causes are being addressed and creates data-based thinking throughout the enterprise. Six Sigma necessitates maintaining a team of experts for implementation and ongoing support; since the training is focused on deployment of the tool set, it is relatively easy to scale up quickly.

> Six Sigma identifies projects that resolve known process defects and variations or gaps between current performance and the requirements of the operating plan. What Six Sigma does not have is assessment tools that look at overall enterprise or plant processes to continuously generate opportunities and connect improvements to the entire system. Consequently, a few years of eliminating low-hanging fruit results in a declining number of Black Belt projects, making return on Six Sigma infrastructure investment more difficult to justify and sustain. Six Sigma has no process or tools for ensuring complete alignment of metrics and projects across the entire enterprise. Goal trees, also called Y-trees, are used to align projects with business goals. This is not effective in assuring alignment of metrics across enterprises nor in prioritizing projects to meet the metrics. This can lead to less than optimum results at minimum, and potentially to projects that serve one function without contributing to overall business improvement. Six Sigma solutions are not prescriptive: Solutions have to be identified, developed, tested, and then implemented. Even using shared project databases and encouraging replication of solutions are ineffective in creating prescriptive solutions.

TIME-BASED COMPETITION

Time-Based Competition (TBC) was invented by George Stalk and his colleagues from the Boston Consulting Group. Time-Based Competition is defined as "the extension of JIT principles into every facet of value delivery cycle, from research and development through marketing and distribution." Both concepts, TBC and JIT, have the same goals: *eliminate waste in the production or service delivery process.* Waste is anything that does not add value to a product or a service. In many instances, waste involves activities which do not contribute to the value of the company. Through the elimination of waste time, more time can be spent on value-added activities. While JIT looks more at the operations function, TBC considers the whole value chain and focuses on the total time required to produce and deliver products and services.

Time-Based Competition gains significance because of the enormous opportunities for time reductions that can be achieved across processes: On average, 95-per cent of the process time has been evaluated as non-value-adding.

The basic principle of Time-Based Competition is to react faster on changes in the environment and to be more flexible than competitors in order to grow faster. One of the key issues in Time-Based Competition is to reduce the development time of new products and services. Shorter lead times generate many secondary effects, such as higher efficiency, higher supplier reliability, and flexibility. Besides the primary effect of being faster, Time-Based Competition also generates secondary effects in costs and quality. A flexible operations process, a fast reaction, and innovation are the key elements in order to attract profitable customers. The new company strategy is "the highest value for the lowest cost in the shortest time."

Time reduction essential for achieving Time-Based Competition can be achieved through measures such as

- simplification, removing process complexity that has accumulated over time
- integration, improving information flows and linkages to create enhanced operability and visibility
- standardization, using generic best-practice processes, standardized components and modules, and information protocols
- concurrent working, moving from sequential to parallel working by using, for example, teams and other forms of process integration
- variance control, monitoring processes, and detecting problems at an early stage so that corrective action can be taken to avoid problems with quality and waste

- automation, applied to improve the effectiveness and efficiency of entities and activities within the supply-chain process
- resource planning, allocating resources in line with operational best practice. For example, plan by investigating bottleneck activities and consider use of multiskilled workforces to provide resource flexibility

Becoming a time-based competition is a strategy that goes hand-in-hand with Total Quality Management. Eliminating non–value-adding activities or preventing rework in order to work faster are strategies totally in line with quality management; there is a bilateral relationship between speed and quality. While quality is a necessary condition in order to produce or deliver goods or services quickly, speed can be considered as a component of quality because it contributes to the satisfaction of customers.

ENHANCING ENTERPRISE INTELLIGENCE

Enterprise intelligence can be defined as the ability to initiate change (to unsettle competitors) and confront change (initiated by competitors, regulators, and other players) in the market environment.

Enterprises are not only expected to be effective and efficient, but they should also be able to adapt to the frequent changes driven by globalization, in other words, be agile. Enterprise agility has become even more important in these times of globalization, particularly in times of continuous organizational change, which is often caused by an increasing pace of innovation, collaboration with other enterprises, new challenges in the market, societal changes, or technology advancements. The enterprises that can best respond to fast and frequently changing markets, will have better competitive advantages than those that fail to sustain the pace dictated by the process of globalization. And, this can be realized through enterprises acquiring better control and efficiency in their ability to manage the changes in their enterprise processes.

Integrated Enterprise with ERP

ERPs enable the integration of heterogeneous and disparate business units, functions, and processes to coordinate, cooperate, and collaborate in aligning the business operations of the enterprise with its corporate strategy. An integrated enterprise is a prerequisite for all subsequent evolutionary stages of the enterprise, namely, the customer centric, customer responsive, renewing, collaborative and, finally, informed enterprise. It is the bedrock for not only realizing time-based competition (see section "Enterprise-Wide Continuous Improvement Programs") but also the essence of BPM, BPR, etc. (see Chapter 7, section "Enterprise BPM Methodology").

Customer-Centric Enterprise with CRM

CRMs enable the relationships with individual customers to cocreate and coinnovate solutions to the satisfaction of customer at optimal cost on an ongoing basis. This importance of customer relationships is based on a simple fact: It can cost four to seven times more to replace a customer than it does to retain one. A major step in retaining a customer is to realize that whereas customer relationships are not all about information, all customer-related information is certainly about customer relationships. Chapter 4 provides a reference framework for business operations based on customer relationships rather than the traditional four Ps (product, positioning, price, and promotion).

Customer-Responsive Enterprise with SCM

SCMs enable the flexibility to obtain the capability and capacity needed to respond quickly to individual customer requests. SCM is important because companies have come to recognize that their capacity to continuously reinvent competitive advantage depends less on internal capabilities and more on their ability to look outward to the networks of business partners in search of the resources to assemble the right blend of competencies that will resonate with their own enterprises and with core product and process strategies. The ultimate core competency an enterprise may possess is in the ability to continuously assemble and implement market-winning capabilities arising from collaborative alliances with their supply-chain partners.

SCM provides companies with the ability to be both flexible (i.e., able to manipulate productive assets, outsource, deploy dynamic pricing, promotions, etc.) and responsive (i.e., able to meet changes in customer needs for alternate delivery quantities, transport modes, returns, etc.). SCM enables whole channel ecosystems to proactively reconfigure themselves in response to market events, such as introduction of a disruptive product or service, regulatory and environmental policies, financial uncertainty, and massive market restructuring, without compromising on operational efficiencies and customer service.

Renewing Enterprise with PLM

PLMs enable the continuous renewal (creation and innovation) of enterprise offerings, i.e., products and services in sync with the continuous changes in customer preferences and needs as also the changing market environment (because of impact of competitors, regulators, activists, and so on). PLM allows the management of product design processes (PDPs) (functional analysis, configuration management, change management, etc.) associated with the product, along its entire life cycle. PLM plays an essential role by managing product data in all phases of its life cycle (design, industrialization, manufacturing, delivery, recycling, etc.) and especially during the product design phase.

Collaborative Enterprise with BPM

BPMs enable the reconciled, i.e., collaborative working of different cross-company stakeholders of any business process, activity, or decision in compliance with its strategy, policy, and procedures. The significance of a process to the success of the enterprise's business is dependent on the value, with reference to the customer, of the collaboration that it addresses and represents. In other words, the nature and extent of the value addition by a process to a product or service delivered to a customer is the best index of the contribution of that process to the company's overall customer satisfaction or customer collaboration. Customer knowledge by itself is not adequate; it is only when the enterprise has effective processes for sharing this information and integrating the activities and actions of frontline workers, and has the ability to coordinate the assignment and tracking of work that enterprises can become effective.

Informed Enterprise with BI

BIs enable enterprises to access current, correct, consistent, and complete information on any process or transaction to take informed decisions in compliance with its strategy, policy, and procedures. BI is the process of

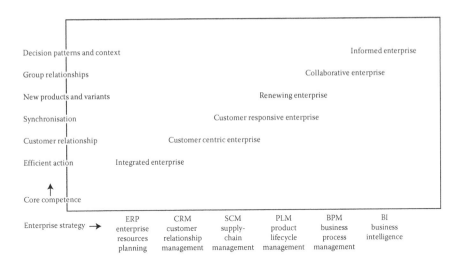

FIGURE 1.4
Types of enterprises enabled by Enterprise Systems (ES).

using advanced applications and technologies to gather, store, analyze, and transform the overload of business information into actionable knowledge that provides significant business value. The concept of BI has been introduced into the marketplace in order to enhance its ability to make better and more efficient business decisions.

To realize a long-lasting competitive advantage, an organization needs to have rapid and continuous innovation and dynamic coupling of processes so that they cannot be easily duplicated. Moreover, firms also need to leverage on resources such as structural capital, human capital, and relationship capital to achieve sustainable competitive advantage. With BI systems connected to customer relationship management, enterprise resource planning, human resource and finance systems, information can be produced in a more accurate and timely manner. BI systems thus make up a complex solution that allows decision makers to create, aggregate, and share knowledge in an organization easily, along with greatly improved service quality for efficient decision making (Figure 1.4).

Companies can define and track Enterprise Intelligence Quotient (EQ) on lines of the IQ defined for human intelligence (see "Epilogue: Enterprise Performance Intelligence").

SUMMARY

This chapter discusses the needs and characteristics of agile enterprises. It presents various strategies adopted for enabling enterprise agility ranging from e-Business transformations to mobilizing business processes. The chapter then describes sequentially manufacturing strategy, enterprise-wide continuous improvement programs (Lean System, Theory of Constraints and Six Sigma) and time based competition. The later part of the chapter describes the dimensions of enterprise intelligence, namely, integrated enterprise, customer-centric enterprise, customer-responsive enterprise, renewing enterprise, collaborative enterprise, and informed enterprise.

2

Enterprise Systems

The Enterprise System (ES) is an information system that integrates business processes with the aim of creating value and reducing costs by making the right information available to the right people at the right time to help them make good decisions in managing resources proactively and productively. An ERP is comprised of multi module application software packages that serve and support multiple business functions. These large automated cross-functional systems were designed to bring about improved operational efficiency and effectiveness through integrating, streamlining, and improving fundamental back-office business processes.

Traditional ES (like ERP systems) were called back-office systems because they involved activities and processes in which the customer and general public were not typically involved, at least not directly. Functions supported by ES typically included accounting, manufacturing, human resource management, purchasing, inventory management, inbound and outbound logistics, marketing, finance, and to some extent engineering. The objective of traditional ES in general was greater efficiency, and to a lesser extent effectiveness. Contemporary ES have been designed to streamline and integrate operation processes and information flows within a company to promote synergy and greater organizational effectiveness, and innovation. These newer ES have moved beyond the back office to support front-office processes and activities like those fundamental to customer relationship management.

EVOLUTION OF ES

ES have evolved from simple Materials Requirement Planning (MRP) to ERP, Extended Enterprise Systems (EES) and beyond. Table 2.1 gives a snapshot of the various stages of Enterprise Systems (ES).

TABLE 2.1

Evolution of Enterprise Systems

System	Primary Business Need(s)	Scope	Enabling Technology
MRP	Efficiency	Inventory management and production planning and control	Mainframe computers, batch processing, traditional file systems
MRP II	Efficiency, effectiveness, and integration of manufacturing systems	Extending to the entire manufacturing firm (becoming cross functional)	Mainframes and minicomputers, real-time (time-sharing) processing, database management systems (relational)
ERP	Efficiency (primarily back office), effectiveness, and integration of all organizational systems	Entire organization (increasingly cross functional), both manufacturing and nonmanufacturing operations	Mainframes, mini- and microcomputers, client/server networks with distributed processing and distributed databases, data warehousing, mining, knowledge management
ERP II	Efficiency, effectiveness, and integration within and among enterprises	Entire organization extending to other organizations (cross functional and cross enterprise partners, suppliers, customers, etc.)	Mainframes, client/server systems, distributed computing, knowledge management, Internet technology (includes intranets, extranets, portals)
Interenterprise Resource Planning, Enterprise Systems, Supply-Chain Management, or whatever label gains common acceptance	Efficiency, effectiveness, coordination, and integration within and among all relevant supply-chain members as well as other partners or stakeholders on a global scale	Entire organization and its constituents (increasingly global and cross cultural) comprising global supply chain from beginning to end as well as other industry and government constituents	Internet, Service Oriented Architecture, Application Service Providers, wireless networking, mobile wireless, knowledge management, grid computing, artificial intelligence

Materials Requirement Planning (MRP)

The first practical efforts in the ES field occurred at the beginning of the 1970s, when computerized applications based on MRP methods were developed to support purchasing and production scheduling activities. MRP is a heuristic based on three main inputs: The Master Production Schedule, which specifies how many products are going to be produced during a period of time; the Bill of Materials, which describes how those products are going to be built and what materials are going to be required; and the Inventory Record File, which reports how many products, components, and materials are held in-house. The method can easily be programmed in any basic computerized application, as it follows deterministic assumptions and a well-defined algorithm.

MRP employed a type of backward scheduling wherein lead times were used to work backwards from a due date to an order release date. While the primary objective of MRP was to compute material requirements, the MRP system proved also to be a useful scheduling tool. Order placement and order delivery were planned by the MRP system. Not only were orders for materials and components generated by an MRP system, but also production orders for manufacturing operations that used those materials and components to make higher level items such as subassemblies and finished products.

As MRP systems became popular and more and more companies started using them, practitioners, vendors, and researchers started to realize that the data and information produced by the MRP system in the course of material requirements planning and production scheduling could be augmented with additional data and used for other purposes. One of the earliest add-ons was the Capacity Requirements Planning module which could be used in developing capacity plans to produce the master production schedule. Manpower planning and support for human resources management were incorporated into MRP. Distribution management capabilities were added. The enhanced MRP and its many modules provided data useful in the financial planning of manufacturing operations, thus financial planning capabilities were added. Business needs, primarily for operational efficiency, and to a lesser extent for greater effectiveness, and advancements in computer processing and storage technology brought about MRP and influenced its evolution. What started as an efficiency oriented tool for production and inventory management was becoming increasingly a cross-functional system.

Closed-Loop Materials Requirement Planning (Closed-Loop MRP)

A very important capability to evolve in MRP systems was the ability to close the loop (control loop). This was largely because of the development of real-time (closed-loop) MRP systems to replace regenerative MRP systems in response to changing business needs and improved computer technology—time-sharing was replacing batch processing as the dominant computer processing mode. With time-sharing mainframe systems the MRP system could run 24x7 and update continuously. Use of the corporate mainframe that performed other important computing task for the enterprise was not practical for some companies, because MRP consumed too many system resources; subsequently, some companies opted to use mainframes (now growing smaller and cheaper, but increasing in processing speed and storage capability) or minicomputers (could do more, faster than old mainframes) that could be dedicated to MRP. MRP could now respond (update relevant records) to timely data fed into the system and produced by the system. This closed the control loop with timely feedback for decision making by incorporating current data from the factory floor, warehouse, vendors, transportation companies, and other internal and external sources, thus giving the MRP system the capability to provide current (almost real time) information for better planning and control. These closed-loop systems better reflected the realities of the production floor, logistics, inventory, and more. It was this transformation of MRP into a planning and control tool for manufacturing by closing the loop, along with all the additional modules that did more than plan materials—they planned and controlled various manufacturer resources—that led to MRP II. Here too, improved computer technology and the evolving business needs for more accurate and timely information to support decision making and greater organizational effectiveness contributed to the evolution from MRP to MRP II.

Manufacturing Requirement Planning II (MRP II)

The MRP in MRP II stands for Manufacturing Resource Planning rather than materials requirements planning. The MRP system had evolved from a material requirements planning system into a planning and control system for resources in manufacturing operations—an enterprise information system for manufacturing. As time passed, MRP II systems became more widespread, and more sophisticated, particularly when used in manufacturing to support and complement computer-integrated manufacturing (CIM). Databases started replacing traditional file systems allowing for better systems integration and greater query capabilities to support decision makers, and the telecommunications network became an integral part of these systems in order to support communications between and coordination among system components that were sometimes geographically distributed, but still within the company.

Enterprise Resource Planning (ERP)

During the late 1970s and early 1980s, new advances in IT, such as local area networks, personal computers, and object-oriented programming, and more accurate operations management heuristics, allowed some of MRPs deterministic assumptions to be relaxed, particularly the assumption of infinite capacity. MRP II was developed based on MRP principles, but incorporated some important operational restrictions, such as available capacity, maintenance turnaround time, and financial considerations. MRP II also introduced simulation options to enable the exploration and evaluation of different scenarios. MRP II is defined as business planning, sales and operations planning, production scheduling, MRP, capacity requirements planning, and the execution support systems for capacity and material. Output from these systems is integrated with financial reports such as the business plan, purchase commitment report, shipping budget, and inventory projections in dollars. An important contribution of the MRP II approach was the integration of financial considerations, improving management control and performance of operations, and making different manufacturing approaches comparable. However, while MRP II allowed the integration of sales, engineering, manufacturing, storage, and finance, these areas continued to be managed as isolated systems. In other words, there was no real online integration and the system did not provide integration with other critical support areas, such as accounting, human resource management, quality control, and distribution.

The need for greater efficiency and effectiveness in back-office operations was not unique to manufacturing, but was also common to nonmanufacturing operations. Companies in nonmanufacturing sectors such as healthcare, financial services, air transportation, and the consumer goods sector started to use MRP II-like systems to manage critical resources. Early ERP systems typically ran on mainframes like their predecessors, MRP and MRP II, but many migrated to client/server systems where networks were central and distributed databases more common. The growth of ERP and the migration to client/server systems really got a boost from the Y2K scare. Many companies were convinced of the need to replace older mainframe-based systems, some ERP and some not, with the newer client/server architecture.

An analysis of performance of ES shows that a key indicator is the level of enterprise integration. First-generation MRP systems only provided limited integration for sales, engineering, operations, and storage. Second-generation MRP II solutions enhanced that integration and included financial capabilities. ERP systems enabled the jump to full enterprise integration. Finally, CRM and SCM systems are expanding that integration to include customers and suppliers. In this history, there is a clear positive trend of performance improvement, coinciding with the diffusion of ES functional innovations. If we assume that ERP, CRM, and SCM systems achieve real integration, the next stage is likely to be ES that allow for the integration of a group of businesses.

EXTENDED ENTERPRISE SYSTEMS (EES)

The most salient trend in the continuing evolution of ES is the focus on front-office applications and interorganizational business processes, particularly in support of supply-chain management. At present greater organizational effectiveness in managing the entire supply chain all the way to the end customer is a priority in business. The greater emphasis on front-office functions and cross-enterprise communications and collaboration via the Internet simply reflects changing business needs and priorities. The demand for specific modules/capabilities in particular shows that businesses are looking beyond the enterprise. This external focus is encouraging vendors to seize the moment by responding with the modules/systems that meet evolving business needs. In this renewed context, ES enable enterprises to integrate and coordinate their business processes. They provide a single system that is central to the enterprise and ensure that information can be shared across all functional levels and management hierarchies.

ES are creeping out of the back office into the front and beyond the enterprise to customers, suppliers, and more, in order to meet changing business needs. Key players such as Baan, Oracle, PeopleSoft, and SAP have incorporated Advanced Planning and Scheduling (APS), Sales Force Automation (SFA), Customer Relationship Management (CRM), Supply-Chain Management (SCM), Business Intelligence, and E-commerce modules/capabilities into their systems, or repositioned their ES as part of broader Enterprise Systems suites incorporating these and other modules/capabilities. ES products reflect the evolving business needs of clients and the capabilities of IT, perhaps most notably those related to the Web. Traditional ES (i.e., ERP) have not lost its significance because back-office efficiency, effectiveness, and flexibility will continue to be important. However, the current focus seems more to be external as enterprises look for ways to support and improve relationships and interactions with customers, suppliers, partners, and other stakeholders. While integration of internal functions is still important, and in many enterprises still has not been achieved to a great extent, external integration is now receiving much attention.

Extended Enterprise Systems (EES) Framework

The conceptual framework of EES consists of four distinct layers:

- Foundation layer
- Process layer
- Analytical layer
- E-business layer

Each layer consists of collaborative components described in Table 2.2

  a. Foundation layer
     The foundation layer consists of the core components of EES which shape the underlying architecture and also provide a platform for the EES.

TABLE 2.2

Four Layers of EES

Layer		Components
Foundation	Core	Integrated Database (DB)
		Application Framework (AF)
Process	Central	Enterprise Resource Planning (ERP)
		Business Process Management (BPM)
Analytical	Corporate	Supply-Chain Management (SCM)
		Customer Relationship Management (CRM)
		Supplier Relationship Management (SRM)
		Product Life cycle Management (PLM)
		Employee Life cycle Management (ELM)
		Corporate Performance Management (CPM)
Portal	Collaborative	Business-to-consumer (B2C)
		Business-to-business (B2B)
		Business-to-employee (B2E)
		Enterprise Application Integration (EAI)

EES do not need to be centralized or monolithic. One of the core components is the integrated database, which may be a distributed database. Another core component is the application framework, which also can be distributed. The integrated database and the application framework provide an open and distributed platform for EES.

b. Process layer

The process layer of the concept is the central component of EES which is Web-based, open, and componentized (this is different from being Web-enabled) and may be implemented as a set of distributed Web services. This layer corresponds to the traditional transaction-based systems. ERP still makes up the backbone of EES along with the additional integrated modules aimed at new business sectors outside the manufacturing industries. The backbone of ERP is traditional ERP modules such as financials, sales and distribution, logistics, manufacturing, or HR.

The EES concept is based on Business Process Management (BPM). ERP has been based on "best-practice" process reference models but EES primarily build on the notion of the process as the central entity. EES include tools to manage processes: Design (or orchestrate) processes, to execute and to evaluate processes (Business Activity Monitoring), and redesigning processes get effect in real time. The BPM component allows for EES to be accommodated to suit different business practices for specific business segments that otherwise would require effort-intensive customization. EES further include vertical solutions for specific segments such as apparel and footwear or the public sector. Vertical solutions are sets of standardized preconfigured systems and processes with "add-ons" to match the specific requirements of a specific sector.

c. Analytical layer

The analytical layer consists of the corporate components that extend and enhance the central ERP functions by providing decision support to manage relations and corporate issues. Corporate components are not necessarily synchronized with the integrated database and the components may easily be "add-ons" instituted by acquiring third-party products/vendors. In the future, the list of components for this layer can get augmented by newer additions such as Product Life cycle Management (ERP for R&D function) and Employee Life cycle Management (ERP for human resources).

d. E-Business layer

The e-business layer is the portal of EES and this layer consists of a set of collaborative components. The collaborative components deal with the communication and integration between the corporate ERP II system and actors such as customers, business partners, employees, and even external systems.

Extended Functionality

E-Commerce is arguably one of the most important developments in business in the last 50 years, and M-Commerce is poised to take its place alongside or within the rapidly growing area of E-Commerce. Internet technology has made E-Commerce in its many forms (B2B, B2C, C2C, etc.) possible. Mobile and wireless technology are expected to make "always on" Internet and "anytime/anywhere" location-based services (also requiring global positioning systems), as well as a host of other capabilities characteristic of M-Business, a reality. One can expect to see ES geared more to the support of both E-Commerce and M-Commerce. Internet, mobile, and wireless technology should figure prominently in new and improved system modules and capabilities.

The current business emphasis on intra- and interorganizational process integration and external collaboration should remain a driving force in the evolution of ES in the foreseeable future. Some businesses are attempting to transform themselves from traditional, vertically integrated enterprises into multi enterprise, "recombinant entities" reliant on core-competency-based strategies. Integrated SCM and business networks will receive great emphasis, reinforcing the importance of IT support for cross-enterprise collaboration and interenterprise processes. ES will have to support the required interactions and processes among and within business entities, and work with other systems/modules that do the same. There will be great need for business processes to span organizational boundaries (some do at present), possibly requiring a single shared interenterprise system that will do it, or at least communicate with and coprocess (share/divide processing tasks) with other ES.

Middleware, ASPs, and enterprise portal technologies may play an important role in the integration of such modules and systems. Widespread adoption of a single ASP solution among supply-chain partners may facilitate interoperability as all supply-chain partners essentially use the same system. Alternatively, a supply-chain portal (vertical portal), jointly owned by supply-chain partners or a value-added service provider that coordinates the entire supply chain, and powered by a single system serving all participants, could be the model for the future. ASP solutions are moving the ES within the reach of SMEs, as it costs much less to "rent" than to "buy."

The capability of Web Services to allow businesses to share data, applications, and processes across the Internet may result in ES of the future relying heavily on the Service Oriented Architecture (SOA), within which Web Services are created and stored, providing the building blocks for programs and systems. The use of "best-in-breed" Web Service-based solutions might be more palatable to businesses, since it might be easier and less risky to plug-in a new Web Service-based solution than replace or add-on a new product module. While the "one source" alternative seems most popular at present, the "best-in-breed" approach will be good if greater interoperability/integration among vendor products is achieved. There is a need for greater "out of the box" interoperability, thus a need for standards.

Data warehouses and Knowledge Management System (KMS) should enable future ERP systems to support more automated business decision making and they should be helpful in the complex decision making needed in the context of fully integrated supply-chain management. More automated decision making in both front-office and back-office systems should eliminate/minimize human variability and error, greatly increase decision speed, and hopefully improve decision quality. Business

Intelligence (BI) tools which are experiencing a significant growth in popularity, take internal and external data and transform it into information used in building knowledge that helps decision makers to make more *informed* decisions.

> Greater interoperability of diverse systems and more thorough integration within and between enterprise systems is likely to remain the highest priority for all enterprises. An environment for business applications much like the "plug and play" environment for hardware would make it easier for enterprises to integrate their own systems and have their systems integrated with other organizations' systems. Such an environment necessitates greater standardization. This ideal "plug and play" environment would make it easier for firms to opt for a "best-in-breed" strategy for application/module acquisition as opposed to reliance on a single vendor for a complete package of front-office, back-office, and strategic systems.

ES PACKAGES

In the past few decades, all of us have witnessed a procession of different methodologies, tools, and techniques emanating from the software industry that have had tremendous impact on the very nature and operations of business enterprises. But in the midst of all this turmoil, one fact has remained constant and that has been the lack of productivity improvements, irrespective of the extent and nature of computerization.

But right from the start, there was an even more basic problem in terms of the number of software applications that were actually completed and implemented successfully. Much has been written on the software crisis that engulfed information service groups in the 1980s. The reasons were multifold:

- With the advent of PC-like functionalities, users were becoming more aware and demanding.
- Consequently, applications were becoming bigger and more complex.
- Correspondingly, productivity was reducing rather than increasing.

- Software development times were increasing and cost and time over-runs were fairly routine.
- Quality trained professionals were always in short supply, resulting in increased costs for programmers; hence, systems development costs were ever increasing.
- Mortality of systems was very high.

On average, out of the total number of IT systems under development, more than half used to be canceled; of the remaining half, only about two-thirds were delivered. Half the delivered systems never got implemented, while another quarter were abandoned midway through the implementation. Of the residual quarter of the delivered systems, half failed to deliver the functionality required by the management and were therefore scrapped. Only the remaining half of the systems was used after great modifications, which entailed further delays and costs in an almost never-ending process.

One of the root causes identified for these problems was the inherent weakness of the phase in which requirements were captured and analyzed. This phase never seemed to get the correct and complete requirements. As a result, completed projects never seemed to deliver on the promised functionality and had to be recycled for more analysis and development. Maintenance and enhancements were called for indefinitely and became harder to undertake as time went by. Because individuals often changed midway, both on the development and user sides, system requirements changed frequently and the whole process continued indefinitely. This is primarily because there is a fundamental disconnect between the business and the IT/IS people. Notwithstanding how much both parties try to bridge the gap, there is a fundamental chasm between the perception of a business user and what is understood by the systems staff; both classes of people speak different languages. Even if systems personnel tried to increase precision by using methodologies and specification tools, they were never able to ratify the documented requirements completely because users were unfamiliar with these tools.

Typically, surveys found that 50%–80% of IT/IS resources were dedicated to application maintenance. The ROI in IT was abysmally low by any standard of measurement and expectation. With IT/IS budgets stretching beyond the capabilities of most organizations, there was a compelling need for a radically new approach that could result in actual usable functionality that was professionally developed, under control, and on time.

The traditional software implementation involving the development of applications was characterized by the following:

- Requirement-driven functional decomposition
- Late risk resolution
- Late error detection
- Use of different languages or artifacts at different phases of the project
- Large proportion of scrap and rework
- Adversarial stakeholder relationship with non-IT users
- Priority of techniques over tools
- Priority of quality of developed software rather than functionality, per se
- Greater emphasis on current, correct, complete, and consistent documentation
- Greater emphasis on testing and reviews
- Major effort on change control and management
- Large and diverse resource requirements
- Schedules always under pressure
- Greater effort on projected or estimated target performance
- Inherent limitations on scalability
- Protracted integration between systems

Many alternate strategies were devised like CASE (Computer-Aided Software Engineering) and prototyping; however, none were able to cross this basic hurdle. CASE provided a more rigorous environment for requirement analysis and design, and automated to a large extent the subsequent development of code, testing, and documentation efforts. The increased time spent on requirement definition with the users was envisaged to lead to systems that were closer to the user's actual requirements. On the other hand, prototyping was designed to address the requirement capture issue by making the users directly participate in the process of defining the requirements. This was mainly focused on the screen and reports design because these were the elements that could be visualized directly by the user. However, none of these strategies really resolved the problem. Packages like ERP and CRM adopted a totally different approach by providing the most comprehensive functionality within the package. Company personnel were only expected to pick and choose whatever was required by the company actually using the package. Thus, ES packages effectively short-circuited the whole issue

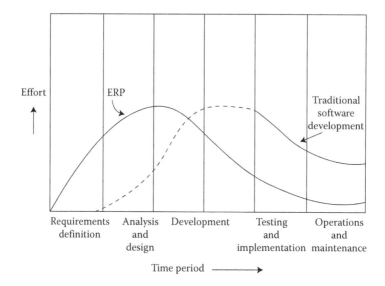

FIGURE 2.1

Comparison of effort expended during ERP and traditional software development life cycle.

of capturing requirements. The traditional project life cycle consisting of analysis, design, development, testing, and implementation was transformed to the ES implementation life cycle consisting merely of requirement mapping, gap analysis, configuring and customizing, testing, and implementation.

Figure 2.1 shows a comparison of effort expended during ES and the traditional software development life cycle.

This ultimately led to the ERP and ES revolution that we are witnessing today.

Unlike traditional systems, the ES software implementations involving the implementations of pre-engineered ready-to-implement application modules are characterized by the following:

- Primacy of the architecture, process-oriented configurability
- Primacy and direct participation of the business user
- Early risk resolution
- Early error and gap detection
- Iterative life cycle process, negligible proportion of scrap and rework
- Changeable and configurable functionality

- Participatory and cohesive stakeholder relationship with non-IT users
- Priority of functionality over tools followed by techniques
- Quality of the functional variability and flexibility of the available functionality
- Greater emphasis on current, correct, complete, and consistent documentation of customizations
- Greater emphasis on integration testing
- Actual demonstration of functionality at all phases of the project
- Twin categories of resource requirements—functional and technical
- Schedules devoid of long-term cascading impact
- Demonstrated performance
- Larger span of scalability
- Efficient integration between systems

Off-the-shelf packages, and especially enterprise-wide solutions such as ES, were considered as the best approach for confronting the software crisis of the 1980s. This was because of the following:

- ES ensure better validation of user requirements directly by the user.
- ES ensure consistent quality of delivered functionality.
- ES provide a cohesive and integrated information system architecture.
- ES ensure a fair degree of standardization.
- ES provide a consistent and accurate documentation of the system.
- ES provide outstanding quality and productivity in the development and maintenance of the system.

As companies are reporting their couple of decades of experience in implementing and operating on ES, a base of experience seems to support the fact that companies that plan and manage the use of ES are usually successful. It is no longer a matter of learning only new technology, it is now about applying the new technology effectively and addressing the problems of inertia and resistance to change across the enterprise. Today, the recognized management decision is not whether to use ES but rather when to use ES and which ES package to use.

VALUING THE ES-BASED ENTERPRISE

ES enable an enterprise to operate as an integrated, enterprise-wide, process-oriented, information-driven, and real-time enterprise. As organizational and environmental conditions have become more complex, globalized, and therefore competitive, processes provide a framework for dealing effectively with the issues of performance improvement, capability development, and adaptation to the changing environment.

In turn, continued value addition along every business process has become an essential prerequisite for viability of not only a particular process, but also for that of the enterprise as a whole. Here is the fundamental rationale for measuring and valuing an enterprise in terms of the value determinants that are relevant to all stakeholders of an enterprise. These include not only the traditionally known stakeholders of a company, like the company's investors and customers, but also the suppliers, managers, and employees of the company as well.

An enterprise-wide solution like SAP or Siebel, which embodies the process-oriented view of the enterprise, must provide the means for evaluating and maximizing the value delivered by the enterprise to all its stakeholders. The first half of this chapter provides a fairly detailed introduction to such a perspective on the value created by an enterprise. It also discusses the now-popular Balance Scorecard (BSC) approach for valuation of an enterprise or the enterprise of a company. It suggests an interpretation of the scorecard in terms of the value to the five primary stakeholders of an enterprise: Customers, vendors, investors, managers, and employees.

Enterprise Stakeholders

An enterprise is defined by a constellation of collaborations. All collaborative relationships are truly stakeholder relationships; thus, a company is truly a continuum of collaborative stakeholder relationships. A corporation is embedded in a network of interdependent stakeholder relationships that are defined mutually and dynamically. The competitive response of an enterprise is the result of all such stakeholder relationships or collaborations. One of the earliest proponents of what is known as stakeholder theory is R. E. Freeman, who wrote "Strategic Management: A Stakeholder Approach." The stakeholders are investors, owners, management, political groups, customers, community, employees, trade associations, suppliers, alliance partners, government, competitors, and so forth.

Two kinds of stakeholders exist: Primary and secondary. Primary stakeholders are those entities that are effected directly by the success or decline of a company such as investors, financial institutions, customers, suppliers/vendors, employees, and so on. Secondary stakeholders such as the media, government, and regulatory agencies are affected only indirectly by the varying fortunes of the company, but they definitely exercise influence on the functioning of the company. Sometimes this influence may not only exceed the influence of the primary stakeholders, but may also prove to be decisive for the enterprise.

For the value created by an enterprise, the five stakeholders of primary importance are

- Customer
- Investors
- Vendors
- Managers
- Employees

Collaborations are characterized by contracts that can range from explicit to the implicit. These contracts specify or allude to what the company can expect from each stakeholder in achieving its objectives and what each stakeholder can expect in return from the enterprise. For instance, explicit contracts are contracts whereby a customer pays a predetermined amount of money for availing of the company's products or services. Similarly, implicit contracts are contracts whereby an employee gets a promotion, depending upon the performance with reference to the expectations set at the beginning of the concerned period.

It is with reference to these contracts, whether implicit or explicit, that every stakeholder invests capital in the continued and envisaged future success of the company; this capital could be financial, managerial, intellectual, environmental, social, and so forth. The continued involvement, interest, and commitment of the stakeholders are dependent on the stakeholders getting a reasonable return on investment (ROI). This ROI could be different for different stakeholders. For the customers, it could be in terms of assured competitive products, services, support, and upgrades in the future. For the vendors, it could be in terms of assured supply contracts on favorable terms. For the investors, it could be in terms of an assured dividend in the future.

For the managers, it could be in terms of an assured rise up the corporate ladder and for the employees of the company, it could be in terms of assured security, professional development, and career growth.

From "Built-to-Last" to "Built-to-Perform" Enterprises

In the early 1980s, Peters and Waterman published a study of forty-three major American corporations. The sample included such household names such as Disney, Boeing, IBM, Mars, McDonalds, Dupont, Levi–Strauss, Procter and Gamble, 3M, Caterpillar, Hewlett Packard, Kodak, Wang, and Atari. All forty-three companies were selected because they had been innovative and adaptable over reasonably long periods, i.e., "built to last" enterprises. The study reached the conclusion that the cause of the excellence displayed by these companies lay in eight prominent attributes that they shared in common.

The eight attributes were

- Stick to the knitting
- Close to the customer
- Productivity through people
- Autonomy and entrepreneurship
- Hands on and value driven
- Bias for action
- Simple form and lean staff
- Simultaneous loose–tight properties

Each of them had a characteristics pattern of actions, position, posture, and process associated with them. The conclusion drawn was that, if others imitate these eight attributes, they too would become excellent.

The eight-attribute plan proved to be a disappointment because, within five years, two-thirds of the companies in the sample had slipped from the pinnacle. A number of other studies followed since then, but none can be judged to have found the best way for all companies to excel in business. For instance, except for General Electric, of the top 12 companies that made up the Dow Jones index in 1900, none survive today. Almost 40% of the names which made up the Fortune 500 ten years ago have disappeared, whilst of the 1970 list, 60% have been acquired or folded up. Clearly, the best run and most widely admired companies are unable to sustain their market-beating levels of performance for an extended period of time. The very processes that enable them to survive over the long term, thwart them from renewal and reinvention, and, finally, fossilize them.

This seems to suggest that one of the fundamental tenets of business that a company should be "built to last" is seriously flawed. Rather than aiming for continuity, enterprises should aim for changes or variations to ensure "built-to-perform" enterprises (see section "The Performance Prism"). Analogous to Michael Porter's concept of the value chain that essentially reflects costs at various stages, one can conceive of a causal "performance chain" running from activities to costs to revenues to the valuation of the enterprise in the capital markets. Enterprises should innovate, renew, and reinvent themselves and their businesses to survival in the turbulent market environment. Please also refer to Inverting the Paradox of Excellence (Kale 2014) for an alternate view on the success and survival of companies that is inspired by the principle of "Evolution by Natural Selection" in biosciences.

Aspects of Enterprise Value

From the perspective of the collaborative enterprise, it is evident that a single stakeholder cannot sustain an appreciable ROI for itself at the cost of the other stakeholders. For instance, shareholder value cannot be maximized indefinitely by reducing product quality or customer service, negotiating arbitrarily lower rates from suppliers/vendors, or by cutting down remuneration of the employees. An ROI for different stakeholders is not in opposition to each other, it is not a "zero-sum game." We have already seen concrete proof of this in the last century when manufacturing quality and cost were mistakenly believed to be in opposition to each other. As it has been shown in the 1990s, an enterprise can achieve excellent quality at reduced costs.

Although all companies focus on creating value for all constituencies, these efforts do not or are not able to address all the constituencies simultaneously. An enterprise does not usually have the capabilities to track the information that is essential for maintaining a cross-functional view of the impact of efforts for

- Improving value addition activities at local activity centers
- Minimizing the nonvalue addition activities at local activity centers

The apparent improvement in value addition or nonaddition activities needs to be tracked enterprise wide across all functions and constituencies.

This is because value addition or nonvalue addition at a local level may not be so for the company as whole. It has been well accepted by now that output of the organization as a whole cannot be maximized only by maximizing the output of each constituting organizational unit or activity. For overall efficiency and effectiveness, a unit may often have to undertake activities that are essentially non–value-added at the operational level of the unit. ES like SAP or Siebel provide such a system that generates, retains, analyzes, and reports on parameters that can track activity-level measures of performance, revenues, and expenditures. More importantly, Siebel highlights cross-functional dependencies of activities across the enterprise.

Value to Customers

Value to customers is one of the most important values that is created by the company. Customers value the product/service not only in terms of its innate use, but also in terms of its price relative to the competition. This in turn leads to other satellite criteria that ultimately lead to customers' continued patronage of the company's products. Customers look for

- Responsiveness
- Price
- Quality
- Flexibility
- Utility
- Variability, or the range of options
- Reliability
- Standardized interfaces and auxiliary systems
- Durability
- Maintainability
- Upgradability
- Support
- Service
- Innovation

Some of these properties characterizing a product/service may be in opposition to each other; the constellation of values that become applicable may vary from one product to another. Moreover, over the course of time, even the values for one particular product or closely related products may undergo changes. As we have seen in Chapter 7, section "Value-Added View of Business Processes," the value shifts may happen because of competitive products, changes in technology, or changes in regulatory conditions. In fact, in the absence of other causes, value shifts may also occur merely because of the customer's illusive urge for innovation and the need for more than ordinary experiences. Added to this is the complication arising from the fact that the customer base itself is not static and keeps on changing dynamically, depending on the shift in critical value determinants (CVDs).

The customary way to determine the relative importance of value determinants is through customer satisfaction surveys and subsequent customer value analysis to generate normalized customer satisfaction indices. These indices may differ, depending on the objectives of the customer value analysis.

Value to Shareholders

Shareholders expect a reasonable ROI in the long term. It must be mentioned that whereas none can deny that higher returns are the basic motives for any investment, shareholders also value their contribution in the creation of wealth and job opportunities for their community. They derive immense satisfaction by sharing the created wealth with the community through the employees of the company. If a company demonstrates that it is utilizing its capital competitively and has a viable strategy that will sustain this rate of return or better it in the future, they will continue to maintain their financial interests in the company.

From the traditional earnings point of view, for industrial enterprises geared to mass production strategies, the investors look for Return-on-Capital-Employed (ROCE), Earnings per Share (E/S), Return on Assets (ROA), etc., in terms of integrity and quality of accounting information like

- Relevance
- Reliability
- Neutrality
- Fidelity
- Verifiability
- Comparability
- Consistency

However, the earnings point of view has not proven to be a reliable indicator of the value of a company. It is primarily oriented toward existing and past values and is not geared to address its arc in the future. Earnings is a static concept that uses linear projections based on the figures of the last accounting year. The underlying assumption in the traditional approach is that a company's value can be forecast based on its reported earnings. That this is erroneous has been established beyond doubt by the fact that market values of successful companies have always been greater than twice its book value.

On the other hand, the cash flow perspective sees value as a function of the expected future cash flows, which reflects the company's value in the long term and makes due allowance for the attendant risks. Unlike the accounting approach, in the cash flow approach, a strong correlation has been found to exist between the market price per share and predicted value per share based on cash flow forecasts.

According to the cash flow perspective, the investors look for

- Increased future surplus cash flows
- Assured future cash dividends
- Share price appreciation

For a company with relatively small capital, the earnings and cash flow perspective may not produce appreciably different results, but, even in such cases when we factor in accounts payable and inventories, the two approaches may provide highly divergent views.

Value to Managers

By convention, in the discussions on stakeholders, senior managers are usually grouped with owner/investors, which is incorrect. Managers with their responsibilities for driving the growth and profitability of the company have a different perspective of the values that are important to them vis-à-vis the owner/investors.

Senior managers look for the following:

- The freedom to articulate the vision of the enterprise and translate the same into objectives for the enterprise
- The latitude to focus on a select set of strategies and tactics

- The latitude to form the management team that believes in this vision and gels with this approach
- The facility to define the measures of performance for the enterprise as a whole as well as for individual business and operational managers
- The authority to allocate and deploy systems and resources for executing plans
- The authority to institute and implement systems for measuring and reporting on the measures of performance for different functions and levels of the enterprise at predefined time periods or on an ad hoc basis
- The latitude to mold the policies and procedures in line with the company's vision
- The latitude to commit research and development (R&D) efforts on technological and managerial issues that they perceive to be of importance for the future
- Remuneration that is commensurate with risks and targeted tasks

With the increase in the pace and pulse of businesses, the leeway available for CEOs and other senior executives has been diminishing continuously. The window of tolerance for failing revenues or periods of executing corrective strategies is progressively becoming smaller. In such circumstances, hard-driving managers become conscious of the value that is catalyzed by them for the enterprise and the returns that they accrue to themselves. It is a supreme irony of our times that, with their increasing power and prestige, the CEOs and members of a management team are also most vulnerable to being summarily replaced due to perceived nonperformance.

Value to Employees

As described in the section "Management by Collaboration" in Chapter 7, the dynamic changes in the market and global competition being confronted by companies have resulted in more flexible enterprises. These organizations are populated with empowered workers who are multi skilled with enhanced responsibilities. No organization can sustain the generation of value at high levels for extended periods without a corresponding value add to the employees of the company.

Employees value factors such as the following:

- Opportunities for participating and contributing significantly to the activities of the enterprise
- Reasonable compensation
- Opportunities to learn, develop skills, and handle challenging roles
- Access to all relevant information and resources for making decisions and discharging their responsibilities creditably
- Opportunities for recognition and rewards
- Opportunities for advancement
- Opportunities for training

The integrated, real-time, and transparent access to relevant data provided by ES empower traditionally deprived members of the enterprise to make timely decisions and derive the satisfaction of being involved meaningfully in ensuring the well-being of the company.

In many ways, the value for employees is analogous to the value for external customers. Like the customers of the company, the effectiveness of employee value is gauged through employee satisfaction surveys that are administered on a periodic basis.

Value to Vendors

In recent times, vendors are getting increased recognition for the value that they add not only to the final output of an enterprise, but also to its profitability. Vendors play a major role in enhancing the overall performance of the enterprise be it in terms of quality, input costs, overheads, responsiveness to changes in the market, and so forth. Increasingly, they are perceived more as enterprise partners, rather than as the traditional adversaries to be browbeaten to lower prices.

Vendors in turn look for the following values in the value-creating enterprise of a company:

- Steady order commitments
- Optimal lead times
- Immediate information on deliveries, rejects, returns, and so on in terms of the quantity and control information (such as delivery note numbers and batch numbers)
- Systematic invoice verification
- Prompt payments for verified and accepted invoices

- Interfaces with an enterprise-wide, implemented system like Siebel
- Sharing changes in production schedules
- Sharing changes in the positions of inventories vis-à-vis production orders and so on
- Sharing results and analysis of quality tests on supplied materials
- Participation in plans of new products, models, technologies, and production processes

As mentioned in the section "Management by Collaboration" subsection "The Virtual Enterprise" in Chapter 7, only mature Customer Relationship Management (CRM) like Siebel can provide the backbone for holding together the virtual value chain across such collaborative relationships with vendors.

Economic Value Add (EVA)

Economic Value Add (EVA) is a new type of managerial accounting criterion that recognizes that capital, whether equity or borrowed, is simply another resource used in the enterprise.

Traditional accounting methods, that are transaction based, take into account sales (i.e., revenue) and expenses (i.e., purchase and interest payments) for computing profitability that is determined by the measure of the Return on Investment (ROI) defined by

$$\text{Return} = (\text{Revenue} - \text{Expense})$$

EVA treats both stockholder capital (i.e., equity capital with zero dividends and its average return of about 6% higher than long-term governmental bonds, as its cost) and borrowed capital (with its interest payment as its cost) as expense items. Consequently, if the enterprise uses a combination of borrowed and shareholder capital, the cost of capital is a weighted average of the two costs. As EVA is computed as revenue less expenses (including all expenses such as purchases, capital, and taxes), EVA is a genuine measure of the value created from the enterprise operations at various levels.

Once capital is seen as a resource, the focus shifts from a simplified Return on Investment (ROI) to the Yield on Investment (YOI) that primarily measures revenue generated for the capacity scheduled. The emphasis shifts to minimizing the amount of resources used for generating revenue, that is, to increase the efficiency with which the stockholder equity is used. Accordingly the managers are prompted to aim for the following at the operational level:

- Use less capital
- Earn more profit without using more capital
- Invest capital in as high-return projects as possible

Because of the critical role played by employees in the operations of the enterprise, most EVAs incorporate a method for distributing bonuses and dividends to employees. EVA effectively expands the definition of owner-ship beyond that of shareholders (who share the risk of the venture) to also include employees whose participation and commitment also contributes to the success of the enterprise.

Value-Based Management

For delivering superior stakeholder value, especially shareholder value, a company's management must not only be able to formulate strategies, but should also be able to execute them. Value-based management (VBM) ensures the implementation of a corporate strategy by directly linking the strategy, finance, and operations within a company. By linking strategic objectives to resource allocation and performance management, the opera-tional decision making is focused fully on delivering the strategic objectives.

To be effective, VBM entails combining the internal, external, historic, and predicted views with the financial and nonfinancial drivers of the business. Leveraging VBM essentially involves the following four steps:

1. Understanding what factors drive value
2. Finding out where value is created or destroyed
3. Establishing value as the criterion for decision making
4. Embedding value into the corporate culture

The financial-oriented VBMs currently in vogue are primarily aimed at operationalizing VBM so that individual members of a company can perceive and identify with the shareholder value that is contributed by the various functions and activities within the enterprise. But, it must be noted that there is already recognition that the financial-oriented view needs to be supplemented with a value-add view of manufacturing directly. ERP systems basically perpetuate the philosophy of top-down, build-to-stock, and supply-driven mass-producing manufacturing strategy. The value-add view of manufacturing is in line with the increasing emphasis on

- Demand pull reflected in order changes
- Flow manufacturing entailing fast changeovers

Like the Corporate Performance Monitor (CPM) discussed later, it is possible to envisage a Manufacturing Performance Monitor (MPM) that monitors real-time manufacturing processes in terms of various technical and economic value drivers.

Time Value of Customers and Shareholder Value

A company's market valuation or shareholder value is the sum total of the envisaged lifetime values (LTVs) of its current and future customers, that is, its customer capital. Customer capital is like a miner's canary—the bird whose death signals dangerous conditions in mines. It is the most accurate (if grisly) leading indicator of the enterprise's competitive advantage as well as that of its partners and competitors.

In this framework, the total value of the company, its market capitalization, is equal to the present value of the total predictable lifetime value (LTV) of its current and future customers, discounted for risk. Figure 2.2

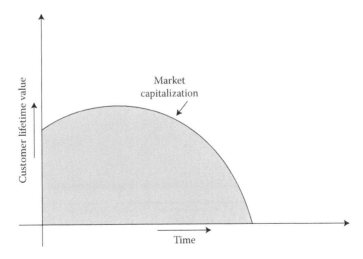

FIGURE 2.2
Market capitalization in terms of Customer Life Time Value (CLTV).

shows the CLTV curve: A graph of Customers-Projected Lifetime Value against Time. The earlier quarters are more accurate as they are based on information on the sales pipelines, work-in-process, and backlog orders that contribute in making these earlier numbers more reliable. But further out on the curve, the envisaged numbers are based more on extrapolations of investments and trends. With the increasing risks associated with progressive forecasts into the future, the present value placed on them progressively decreases to zero. The area under the curve represents the customer's market capitalization. The objective of any management team to increase the shareholder value then translates into increasing the area under this curve.

As evident from looking at the CLTV Curve in Figure 2.3, this is achievable in the following two ways:

1. Increasing the customer-differential gap (CUG) that corresponds to the gap between the enterprise customer's lifetime value (CLTV) and those of the closest competitors.
   The CUG can be enhanced by
   • Migrating the customers to higher value alternatives of the current offerings.
   • Increasing the range/type of offerings.

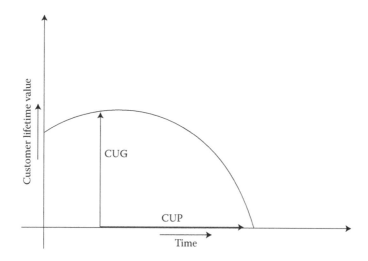

FIGURE 2.3
Higher market capitalization in terms of higher CUGs and longer CUPs.

- Increasing the total quantum of consumption of current offerings.
- Reducing dramatically the cost of serving the existing customers.
- Acquiring new customers!

The increase in CUG effects the height of the curve because, assuming the cost structure is unaltered, CUG directly impacts both sales and gross margins positively to show up as increased earnings.

2. Increasing the length of the customer-differential period (CUP) for which the enterprise can sustain the CUG once the superior returns generated by the enterprise start attracting additional competition.

A long CUP is typically a function of high barriers to entry for competitors' intent on a portion of the same market or high switching costs for customers and partners contemplating defecting to the enterprise's competitors. Long CUPs contribute to higher stock price by increasing the duration of the period of such customer differential. Long CUPs effectively represent a reduction in the long-term risks, resulting in much lower discount rates applied to such risks, which in turn results in extending the curve even further toward the right side.

Thus, the management of shareholder value effectively transforms into sustaining increasingly higher customer lifetime values (CLTVs) for a longer duration of time, that is, higher CUGs and longer CUPs. Although CUGs and CUPs are interdependent, CUPs primarily represent the sustainability of CUGs, and the enterprise must focus first on CUPs and then on CUGs. This is because while effects on CUGs are short lived and can be corrected easily, the effects on CUPs are more far reaching and have a bigger impact on stock price than CUGs. Generally, traditional enterprises with a P&L focus already have the tool for managing the CUGs, but they do not have a tool to manage the CUPs.

All line functions need to reevaluate their old metrics to ensure that they are current with the customer-centric and customer-responsive stances of twenty-first-century enterprises. We discuss these issues next.

ES Metrics

Metrics help companies track and assess their performance and, more importantly, evaluate the returns on their CRM initiatives. In the process of implementing CRM, managers have to deal with a huge amount of data with the ultimate goal of evaluating managerial performances based on the value that each individual customer brings to the firm. In order to record and quantify those evaluations, managers need a set of indicators that measure customer values. Metrics perform this role.

The benefits of developing and using metrics are significant to companies. Some of the key benefits that accrue to the firm are

- Tighter control over business processes and CRM activities
- Means to measure changes in revenues, costs, and profits
- Benchmarks and targets to attain certain levels of performance
- Measures on return on investment (ROI)
- Aid in the acquisition and retention, preventing churn, and assisting win back of profitable customers
- Realigning marketing resources to maximize customer value

There are two broad categories of metrics, brand level and customer level. Brand-level metrics are metrics that measure the brand's competitiveness in the market, such as market share, customer equity, sales growth, and so on. Customer-level metrics break down those brand-level metrics to the individual customer, such as acquisition cost per customer, size of wallet, and so on. A combination of brand-level and customer-level metrics gives managers a complete picture of how the firm or the brand fares in the market, as well as how its customer needs differ on an individual level, and how to leverage these differences to enhance the overall competitiveness of the firm. Determining which metric(s) to measure and manage should depend on how each metric relates to the desired short-term or long-term outcome. If the metric(s) chosen cannot be quantifiably related to desired outcome measures such as profitability and shareholder value, the metric(s) generally may not be worth measuring and managing.

Table 2.3 presents some commonly used metrics at both brand level and customer level. Given the multiplicity of dependencies and influencing factors, the selection of the right measures is a complex task. There is a need for a framework under which multiple measures are integrated and related to each other so that a set of measurements should not be perceived to be in opposition to others. Moreover, there is also a need to have the right balance between financial and nonfinancial measures, which is the focus of the section "Balance Scorecard."

TABLE 2.3

Brand- and Customer-Level Matrices

Metric	Definition	Use of Metric
Market share	The percentage of a firm's sales to the sales of all firms in a given market	Brand level
Sales growth	The increase or decrease in sales volume or sale value in a given period compared to that in the previous period	Brand level
Acquisition rate	The proportion of prospects converted to customers	Brand level
Acquisition cost	The acquisition spending of a focal firm per prospect acquired	Brand level and customer level
Retention rate	The average likelihood that a customer *makes a repurchase* from the focal firm in period t, given that this customer has purchased in the last period $t - 1$	Brand level and customer level
Defection rate	The average likelihood that a customer *defects* from the focal firm in period t, given that this customer has purchased in the last period $t - 1$	Brand level and customer level
Survival rate	The ratio of customers who continue to remain as customers (survive) until a period t from the beginning; of observing these customers	Brand level
Average lifetime duration	The average duration customers continue to remain as customers	Brand level
P-active	The probability of a customer making a repurchase (being active) in a given period	Customer level
Win-back rate	The ratio of acquisition of customers who had been lost in an earlier period	Brand level
Share-of-wallet	The ratio of total sales of all customers of the focal firm in a product category to the total spending of those customers in the product category across all different firms	Brand level and customer level
Size of wallet	The total spending of a customer on a product category across all different firms	Customer level

(Continued)

TABLE 2.3 (*Continued*)

Brand- and Customer-Level Matrices

Metric	Definition	Use of Metric
Share of category requirement	The ratio of the sales volumes of a particular product category of the focal firm or brand to the total sales volumes of the product category in the market Also considered the market share of a firm or a brand with respect to a particular product category	Brand level and customer level
Past customer value	The gross contribution of a customer when adjusted for the time value of money	Customer level
RFM value	RFM stands for Recency, Frequency, and Monetary value: • Recency indicates the most recent purchase date of a customer • Frequency measures how often a customer purchases from the firm • Monetary value measures the average per transaction spending of a customer	Customer level
Customer lifetime value	The total discounted contribution margins of a customer (excess of recurring revenues over recurring costs) to the focal firm over a specific time period	Customer level
Customer equity	The total lifetime value of all customers of the focal firm	Brand level

Enterprise Performances Measurement

It is important to define the right measures for assessing a company's performance and its progress toward its declared goals and objectives. ES assist in monitoring and managing the measures of performances (MOPs) to enhance the company's operational performance. With its integrated and real-time availability of operational data, ES have the enabling environment to create, monitor, and manage enterprise value. ES provide the empowered platform for SMEs to address the competitive demands of the rapidly changing marketplace and be successful in terms of

1. Improved customer relations and management
2. Reduced cycle time
3. Improved quality
4. Increased sales volumes
5. Improved margins
6. Reduced product development time
7. Reduced manpower for routine operations
8. Improved market share

The process of monitoring the MOPs can be guided by the value determinants that have been identified for the company. The value determinants can then be prioritized as well as customized suitable for the different activities within the company. Additions and deletions to the selected measures will be likely, depending on the market situations or alterations in the emphasis and focus of the measures already implemented.

The following lists show some of the performance factors that could be considered for measuring the excellence of the processes in ES.

The sales and distribution measures of performance factors are as follows:

- The number of new customers
- The number of one-time customers
- The number of customers retained
- The number of repeat orders and type
- The customer order-to-delivery time
- The number of nonstandard or customized orders
- The number of errors per order shipped
- The percentage of back orders as a percentage of total orders
- The percentage of on-time first delivery to customers
- The percentage of on-time complete deliveries to customers

BALANCE SCORECARD (BSC)

A company's emphasis is not on the capability to ingest the latest technology per se, because that would continue to change in future too. The emphasis is related more to the capability to confront any changes in the market with a strategy that will not only make customers continue to value the company's products and services, but also differentiate them effectively from those provided by the competitors. This is the subtle reason why a few years back General Motor's much known foray into highly automated manufacturing facilities to beat the Japanese on productivity and quality was not very successful. Thus, a company needs a management system to assess and evaluate its strategy in terms of competitiveness and performance in the future. There is also the important need for the company to be able to dynamically monitor the progress and performance of the execution of these strategies, which will then enable the company to administer any corrections or adjustments based on the real-time operational feedback received from such a system. The BSC is precisely such a strategic management system that enables an enterprise to monitor and manage the execution of its value-adding and value-creating strategies effectively. Enterprises also need an information system that would empower them to implement the BSC.

The BSC aims to provide a balance between the external and internal measures of performance, between short- and long-term objectives, between financial and nonfinancial measures, and between lagging and leading indicators. It is not limited to being merely a measurement and control system, but has actually developed over the course of time into a full-featured management system for the successful implementation of a company's strategy.

The BSC provides companies with a framework for translating the company's vision and strategy into a coherent set of performance measures. The BSC derives the objectives and measures of the value determinants or the corresponding performance drivers based on the vision and strategy of the company. As shown in Figure 2.4, the BSC framework is constituted of the following four perspectives:

- Financial
- Customer
- Internal business processes
- Learning and growth

Financial	Customer
Operating income growth Same store sales growth Inventory turns Expense/sales growth ratio	Frequency of purchases Units per transection Transection size Customer feedback
Internal	**Learning and growth**
Category market shape Category margin Sales psf Quality/returns Out of stock	Employee climate survey Turnover Strategic skill coverage Systems versus plan

FIGURE 2.4
The Balance Scorecard (BSC) framework.

The BSC retains the financial perspective of the company's performance that is essentially based on past performance and is valid for short-term performance in the immediate future. However, it supplements this traditional perspective with those of the customer and the internal system, process, and people that determine the company's value-generating potential and hence long-term future financial performance i. The customer's perspective ensures the continual relevance of the products and services provided by the company. The internal perspective of business processes and people ensures that the company surpasses customers' expectations on critical value determinants such as quality, timeliness, innovation, and service. It is in this sense that the BSC represents a balance between the external value determinants of the customers and shareholders, and the corresponding internal value drivers of the critical systems, business processes, and people.

Two kinds of value drivers exist: Outcome and performance. Outcome drivers are lagging indicators such as financial measures that are objective, quantifiable, and are past-facing. On the other hand, performance measures are leading indicators that link with the company's strategy and provide the rationale for achievements of the outcome drivers. Although performance drivers are future-facing, the impact and effectiveness of performance drivers on outcome measures is highly subjective. This is compensated by the dynamic nature of the BSC system that treats evaluation and feedback as an important element of the framework. The value drivers are constantly under test for continued relevance in the market and any deviations observed in the customer's value determinants are immediately cascaded in terms of changes in the value drivers' measures or the value drivers themselves. This corresponds to the learning and growth perspective of the BSC framework. It represents the capability of institutional learning, which is the powerful concept of "double-loop" learning referred to in Chapter 7, section "Management by Collaboration," subsection "The Learning Enterprise" that gives tremendous advantages to companies in these times of rapidly changing markets.

In fact, the whole BSC framework is based on a perceived cause-and-effect relationship between the various strategies, organizational elements, and processes of the enterprise. It is in the context of these assumptions that the BSC also incorporates the cause-and-effect relationships in terms of the relationships between the various outcome and performance drivers. For instance, the ROCE driver (in the financial perspective) is dependent on customer loyalty (in the customer perspective). Customer loyalty is dependent on the enterprise's product quality and responsiveness (in the internal business processes perspective), which in turn is dependent on the minimization of product defects, knowledge of the customer's prior transaction history, recorded preferences, and so on (learning and growth perspective). It is because of this that the multiple objectives and measures of the BSC do not entail complex trade offs but can easily be integrated into a consistent framework of 20–25 value drivers that can help navigate the strategy of the company successfully through the turbulent marketplace.

The strategic management of enterprises using the BSC involves the following stages:

1. Mapping the company strategy into the BSC framework in terms of the strategic objectives and drivers for the BSC. This might also involve reconciling or prioritizing among various objectives or defining differing objectives and drivers for different divisions. This stage identifies all processes that are critical to the strategic performance of the enterprise. It must be noted that the BSC is a methodology for implementing a company strategy and not for formulating one. This is another reason why it is highly suitable for incorporation into the SAP SEM solution.

2. Communicating the link between the strategic objectives and measures throughout the enterprise at all levels. This might also involve operationalizing the defined set of measures to the specifics of the local circumstances for the various departmental and functional units of the company. BSCs are usually defined at the level of strategic

business units (SBUs), but for a multidivisional company, the defined BSC might incline more toward the financial perspective.

3. Setting targets, devising aligned strategic initiatives, and planning/ scheduling initiatives to achieve a breakthrough performance. This might also include financial planning and budgeting as an integrated part of the BSC. From the customer's perspective, this step should include requirements of both existing and potential customers.

4. Enhancing performance through feedback and learning, based on operational data and reviews. This might entail reprioritizing or changing the performance thresholds or even the value drivers themselves. The latter might become necessary either because of the changes in the marketplace or because the selected set of value drivers might be ineffectual.

Figure 2.5 shows the BSC approach to create a strategy-focused organization.

In the BSC framework, the financial perspective enables a reality check of the strategic management activity of the enterprise. This is because

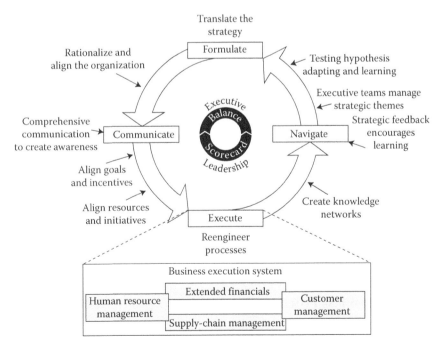

FIGURE 2.5
BSC approach to create a strategy-focused company.

all strategic initiatives meant for improving quality, flexibility, and customer satisfaction might not necessarily translate into improved financial results. If the improved operational outcome as seen from the other three perspectives defined by the company does not end in improved financial results, it might be a powerful indicator of the need for reformulation of the strategy itself. All cause-and-effect relationships that knit a BSC program must eventually link to financial objectives. Therefore, the financial perspective is preeminent among all perspectives of the BSC framework.

Financial Perspective

As mentioned above, financial performance measures indicate whether a company's strategy, implementation, and execution are translating into bottom-line financial results. Depending on the business strategy, the financial objectives could be in terms of

- ROCE, economic value add (EVA) or operating income, and maintaining the market share
- Rapid sales growth and increased market share
- Maximize the generation of cash flow

Customer Perspective

The customer perspective mainly addresses customer- and market-oriented strategies that would deliver improved financial results. This involves the identification of market segments of interest, value propositions for each of these segments, and measures that would help in ascertaining the performance of the company in the selected segments.

The basic outcome measures for this perspective could be

- Customer acquisition
- Customer satisfaction
- Customer retention
- Customer profitability

Internal Business Processes Perspective

The internal business processes perspective provides focus on the business processes that are critical to the success of the enterprise. These processes selected for improvement could be existing processes (as discussed in Chapter 6, section "Selecting Business Processes for BPR") or they could also be entirely new processes conceived as a consequence of the strategy of the company. For instance, an excellent example of such a process could be a provision for a Web-based procurement of a company's goods and services.

Learning and Growth Perspective

The learning and growth perspective addresses the need to build and maintain an appropriate infrastructure for the long-term growth and success of the company. Contributions from the other perspectives, especially regarding envisaged shifts in customer value, might identify the technologies and products essential to the continued relevance of the company's offerings in the marketplace. These contributions might encompass the following:

- People's skills
- Information and support systems
- Organizational processes and procedures

This perspective comprehensively covers employee-related issues such as employee satisfaction, employee training, advancement and promotion policies, employee-friendly policies and procedures, productivity-multiplying application environments, and so forth.

The standard BSC framework talks of only four perspectives, but, if required, the framework can be supplemented with additional perspectives of stakeholders discussed in the section "Enterprise Stakeholders." In view of the increased importance of supply-chain management (SCM) for the extended collaborative enterprises of today, a prime candidate for addition would be the suppliers/vendors of the company.

SUMMARY

This chapter began with a look at the evolution of Enterprise Systems (ES) followed by the description of the extended enterprise systems.

It then presented the characteristics of ES packages which are examples of commercial off-the-shelf packaged systems (COTS). The chapter then addressed issues related to valuing the ES-enabled enterprise. The last part of the chapter presented an overview of the Balance Scorecard (BSC) as an example of the performance management system.

3

Integrated Enterprise with ERP

In the early days, the most important systems in manufacturing companies were known as MRP-based systems. After two decades, MRP systems evolved into MRP II, but it was many years before ERP systems were first implemented, and these systems continue to evolve.

In the 1960s, MRP emerged with the rapid evolution of computers. The main emphasis of these systems was to manage inventory, and the use of MRP helped companies control their inventory based on actual demand rather than reorder points. To do this, MRP used a set of techniques that took into account bills of material data, inventory data, and the master production schedule to predict future requirements for materials. A finished product was subdivided into its components, and for every component, a time schedule was developed. Based on this list, using computers, all necessary information required for the production of this specific product could be obtained in a very short time. The critical subcomponents could be tracked easily and, if necessary, could be obtained quickly to support on-time production. The critical path (time, resources, etc.) could be defined, and orders could be organized in order to prevent time delays in receipt of materials. However, even this simple procedure became tedious once the number of parts increased. Thus, a computer was essential to carry out these features of MRP. To sum up the benefits of MRP, it reduced the level of inventory a company needed to maintain, reduced production times by improving coordination and avoiding delays, and increased the company's overall efficiency.

In the 1980s, companies transitioned to MRP II. This system allowed manufacturers to optimize materials, procurement, manufacturing processes, and so forth, while at the same time providing financial and planning reports. The underlying idea behind the MRP II concept was to integrate MRP with further manufacturing functions and other business functions. MRP II was designed to assist in the effective planning of all resources available to a manufacturing company. Ideally, it addressed operational planning in units and financial planning in dollars and included a simulation capability with which to answer what-if questions. It included business planning, sales and operations planning, production scheduling, MRP, and capacity requirements planning, along with executive support systems that could be used to balance capacities and materials.

Toward the end of the 1980s, many business processes such as logistics, procurement, and financial accounting needed to be integrated to allow companies to operate at their maximum efficiency. Actually, software systems to automate each of these internal business processes already existed, and these were very efficient in their own areas. However, their relative autonomy and limited real-time interaction was a major problem that had to be solved. The divisions did not exchange data with each other, or even if they did exchange data, it was poorly coordinated, which caused substantial problems that decreased the efficiency of the systems. For example, it was impossible for accounting systems to exchange data with manufacturing systems, and the time lag for exchanging data was so large that it brought no benefits to either division.

CONCEPT OF ENTERPRISE RESOURCES PLANNING

The main focus of ERP has been to integrate and synchronize the isolated functions into streamlined business processes. ERP evolved considerably over the next 30 years as a result of continuous improvements in business management and the development of new information technologies. The ERP concept was first implemented at the end of the 1980s with the development of better client/server technology that enabled the implementation of an ERP system. ERP is a cross-functional enterprise backbone that integrates and automates many internal business processes and information systems within the sales and distribution, production, logistics, accounting, and HR functions of a company.

ERP not only coordinates several divisions but also enables companies to enter data only once for the information to be distributed to all the integrated business processes. ERP systems consist of several integrated suites of software modules, which share common data and provide connectivity. Once the data have been recorded, they are available for all the company's divisions. The information about the processes in the company is represented consistently and is up to date in all business divisions at all times.

 There is a substantial difference between the concept of Enterprise Resources Planning (ERP) and Enterprise Resources Planning Systems (ERP Systems). ERP is a concept of much broader scope than the ERP Systems that implement a subset of the tenets of ERP. In this chapter, after introducing the concept of ERP, the chapter focuses on leveraging the ERP-oriented capabilities of the enterprises, while Appendix I presents an overview of the ERP functionality provided by SAP Business Suite (see Appendix I "SAP Business Suite").

ENTERPRISE RESOURCES PLANNING

There is no generally accepted definition of ERP in the offerings in the market. Not only is there little agreement on what it really stands for, there is even less agreement on what constitutes an ERP package, how it should be used, the potential of productivity gain, the impact on the enterprise, the costs involved, the personnel needed, or the training needed for the ERP personnel. Its characteristics are not limited to the ERP products and tools that are currently available in the market, and it is certainly not a technique or methodology. It is preferable not to contain ERP within a single set of current ideas but to look at ERP as a developing area of enterprise computerization with expanding boundaries. There is every reason to believe that the boundaries described for ERPs in this book will be constantly enlarging in the coming years. Notwithstanding all this caveats, ERP could be defined reasonably as follows:

Enterprise Resources Planning (ERP) software applications package is a suite of preengineered ready-to-implement integrated application modules catering to all the business functions of an enterprise and which possesses the flexibility for configuring and customizing dynamically the delivered functionality of the package to suit the specific requirements of the enterprise. ERP enables an enterprise to operate as an integrated enterprise-wide process-oriented information-driven real-time enterprise.

ERPs can provide this comprehensiveness and flexibility because at the heart of the system resides a computer-aided software engineering (CASE)-like repository that stores all details of these predeveloped applications. These details include every single data item, data table, and software program that is used by the complete system. For instance, SAP has more than 800 application process definitions stored in about 8000 tables within its repository. It also has additional support subsystems that help it to manage, secure, and maintain the operations of this package on a day-to-day basis. ERPs are a major development based on the initial ideas about information engineering put forward by Clive Finkelstein in Australia around 1980. He crystallized the basic idea that systems analysis could be engineered. Information engineering approaches essentially treat the application development environment as an application in itself. The development can be designed and managed with an expectation that the users will request many changes; the systems are designed to accommodate such changes. The integrated application repository holds a full set of correlated information regarding the application, which also greatly facilitates documentation, testing, and maintenance. The major development of ERPs over the information engineering approaches was in terms of providing a predefined already-built-in comprehensive functionality of the application systems.

The success of ERP packages is based on the principle of reusability. It is not a very new concept in the computer industry. The origin of reusability goes back almost to the beginning of the computer era in the middle of the last century when it was recognized early that far too much program code was being written and rewritten repeatedly and uneconomically. Very soon, most of the programming languages provided for routines or packets of logic that could be reused multiple times within individual programs or even by a group of programs. Databases enabled the reuse of data, resulting in a tremendous surge in programmer productivity. Similarly, networks permitted reuse of the same programs on different terminals or workstations at different locations. ERP basically extended the concept of reusability to the functionality provided by the package. For instance, any ERP is based on the essential commonality that was observed in the functioning of companies within an industry. ERPs built a reusable library of normally required processes in a particular industry; and all that implementing ERP customers had to do was to select from this library all those processes that were required by their company. From a project effort and cost that was essential for the development and implementation using the traditional software development life cycle (SDLC), ERP reduced the project effort and cost only to that associated with the implementation phase of the SDLC. A comparison of the traditional SDLC and postmodern ERP implementations is shown in Figure 2.1. Even though the cost of implementing ERP may seem higher than that for the traditional systems, ERPs get implemented sooner and, therefore, start delivering all the benefits much earlier than traditional systems. The fabled library of 800 best-of-class processes made available right from SAP R/3 is like building blocks or components that can be reused by any customer to build their system quickly and at a considerably reduced cost.

In the early 1990s, all software crisis situations underwent a dramatic change with the arrival of ERP systems. ERPs changed the basic developmental model of implementing computerized systems within enterprises to that of implementing off-the-shelf ready-made packages that covered every aspect of the function and operations of an enterprise. It provided an integrated set of functional modules corresponding to all major functions within the enterprise. It engendered the concept of implementing all these modules as an integrated whole rather than in piecemeal fashion. Although there have not been any published results as yet, it became an accepted fact that enterprises that implemented ERPs only for a part of their enterprises or only for a few select functions within their enterprises did not benefit greatly. And, for the first time in the history of IT, ERPs gave indication of the recognition of the fact that the business processes of an enterprise were much more fundamental than time-invariant data characterizing various aspects of the enterprise. And, most importantly, ERPs elevated information systems (IS) from a mere enabler of business strategy of an organization to a significant part of the business strategy itself. Thus, ERPs brought to an end the subsidiary and support role that IT had played throughout the last few decades. But in turn, the very nature of IS has also undergone a complete transformation (see section "ERP Elevates IT Strategy as a Part of the Business Strategy"). Implementation of an ERP within an enterprise was no longer a problem of technology; it was a business problem. ERPs have been the harbingers of a paradigm shift in the role of the IS/IT function within an enterprise. The writing of this book was also motivated by the need to address these fundamental changes in the very nature of IS/IT activity within an enterprise.

CHARACTERISTICS OF ERP

The distinguishing characteristics of ERP are as follows:

1. ERP transforms an enterprise into an information-driven enterprise.
2. ERP fundamentally perceives an enterprise as a global enterprise.
3. ERP reflects and mimics the integrated nature of an enterprise.
4. ERP fundamentally models a process-oriented enterprise.
5. ERP enables the real-time enterprise.
6. ERP elevates IT strategy as a part of the business strategy.
7. ERP represents a major advance on the earlier manufacturing performance improvement approaches.
8. ERP represents the new departmental store model of implementing computerized systems.
9. ERP is a mass-user-oriented application environment.

In the remaining part of this section, we introduce the concept of ERP and deal with each of these characteristics of ERP systems. There is also a need of a unifying framework that would bring together the various aspects of an ERP implementation. These include aspects of business competitiveness, information-based organizations, integrative and collaborative strategies, process-oriented real-time operations, employee empowerment, information capital and knowledge assets, organizational learning, business engineering, change management, virtual value chains, and strategic alliances.

ERP Transforms the Enterprise into an Information-Driven Enterprise

All computerized systems and solutions in the past were using past-facing information merely for the purpose of referring and reporting only. ERP, for the first time in the history of computerized systems, began treating information as a resource for the operational requirements of the enterprise. But, unlike traditional resources, the information resource as made available by ERPs can be reused and shared multiple times without dissipation or degradation. The impressive productivity gains resulting from ERPs truthfully arise out of this unique characteristic of ERPs to use information as an inexhaustible resource.

ERP Fundamentally Perceives an Enterprise as a Global Enterprise

In these times of divestitures, mergers, and acquisitions, this is an important requirement. Unlike some of the earlier enterprise-wide solutions available on mainframes, ERPs cater to corporate-wide requirements even if an enterprise is involved in disparate businesses like discrete industries (manufacturing, engineering, etc.), process industries (chemicals, paints, etc.), and services industries (banking, media, etc.). ERP enables the management to plan, operate, and manage such conglomerates without any impediments of mismatch of systems for different divisions.

Although it may seem a minor point, ERP also permits the important functionality of enabling seamless integration of distributed or multilocation operations; we consider this aspect in the next section.

ERP Reflects and Mimics the Integrated Nature of an Enterprise

Notwithstanding the different ways in which the enterprises are structured and organized, enterprises function essentially in an integrated fashion. Across the years, the turf-preservation mentality has been rigidified even in computerized systems deployed for various functions. Under the garb of the fundamentally different nature of activities and functions, many information systems mushroomed within an organization reenforcing rather than lessening the heterogeneity of systems. This led to problems of incompatibility, differing standards, interfacing issues, limited functional and technological upgrade paths, costly maintenance, high operating costs, costly training and support activities, inconsistent documentation, and so on. Instead of providing the strategic leverage necessary for the business operations of the enterprise, IS/IT systems were a constant drain on the enterprise and, truthfully, increased their reaction times to the changes observed in the market space.

ERP with its holistic approach and its demand for integration dissolve all such efficiency dissipating spurious processes not only in their IS/IT aspects but also in their actual functions. With a single centralized transparent, current, consistent, and complete database of all enterprise-related data, ERP in a masterstroke eliminated all wait times associated with all intracompany interactions. Integration as embodied in ERP eliminates many a non–value-added (NVA) processes. With its laser-like focus on best-of-business practices, ERP demonstrates glaringly the essential futility of routine bureaucratic mechanization within enterprises; it brings in consistency, discipline, and fast reaction times in the operations of a company. Thus, whereas finance may aim for minimizing stock, the purchasing function may want to maintain a buffer stock to avoid out-of-stock situations. Similarly, marketing may want production of more varied product models to cater to the requirements in the market, whereas the production function may want to lessen the number of different kinds of products for reducing setup times and related costs. By promoting cross-functional processes and work teams, ERP like SAP provides a powerful medium for supporting, reconciling, and optimizing the conflicting goals of different functions of the enterprises.

ERP Fundamentally Models a Process-Oriented Enterprise

As organizational and environmental conditions become more complex, globalized, and, therefore, competitive processes provide a framework for dealing effectively with the issues of performance improvement, capability development, and adaptation to the changing environment. Process modeling permits the true comprehension of the characteristic structure and dynamics of the business. Business processes are the most important portions of the reality that had been ignored by traditional information systems. The traditional IT process modeling techniques, methodologies, and environments are a misnomer, for they truly model only the procedures for operating on the data associated at various points of the business subprocesses, while themselves are never mirrored within the system.

Conventional systems primarily store only snapshots of discrete groups of data at predefined or configured instants of time along a business process within an enterprise. This predominating data-oriented view of the enterprise as implemented by traditional IT systems is the most unnatural and alien way of looking at any area of human activity. The stability of the data models, as canonized in the conventional IT paradigm, may have been advantageous for the systems personnel, but for the same reason, they would have been unusable (and unacceptable) to the business stakeholders within the enterprises. Traditional systems could never really resolve this simple dichotomy of the fact that systems based on leveraging on the unchanging data models, although easy to maintain, can never describe the essentially dynamic nature of businesses. The lack of facilities for modeling business processes and business rules was the root cause of the resulting productivity paradox mentioned in the beginning of this section.

ERPs for the first time recognized the fundamental error that was being perpetuated all these past decades. Although many of the ERP packages still carry the legacy of the data-oriented view, the parallel view of business process and business rules is gaining prominence rapidly. This can also be seen to be the reason for the rapidly maturing groupware and workflow subsystems within the core architecture of current ERP systems.

ERP Enables the Real-Time Enterprise

ERP has engendered the earlier only imagined possibility of a real-time enterprise. Even before the arrival of ERPs, companies had witnessed the power and perils of operating an online system which provided on-the-system direct registration of business transactions as well as immediate updates or posting to the relevant master and transaction data files. ERP has made this possible on enterprise-wide scale and has realized tremendous gains in efficiencies and productivity by extending, as it were, the concept of JIT to the whole of the enterprise. Every system is a collection of many subsystems and processes with lifecycle times of varying durations. A system that can respond effectively within the lifecycle time of some of the smaller life cycles can be considered to be functioning essentially in a real-time mode. As per this definition, for example, as far as the solar system is concerned, with reference to a life cycle of earth's rotation period of 365 days, forecasting the climatic conditions anytime within a period of 365 days could be termed as functioning in a real-time mode! In analogy with this, for better appreciation of real-time responsiveness, enterprises could define enterprise standard time (EST). This could be defined based on the following:

1. A central reference location within the enterprise
2. An optimal cycle time in days or weeks suitable for all functions within the enterprise

All responses within the enterprise could be measured with reference to this EST. Enterprises that can cut down their EST relentlessly would be able to sustain their competitiveness in the market. And this would become achievable to a large extent because of the instant availability of relevant information to all concerned members of the company provided by ERP. Information is only relevant when it is available within a cycle of EST; information furnished after this period ceases to act as a resource and rapidly ends up being of value only for recording and reporting purposes (see last paragraph in section "Information as the New Resource"). A continuous effort for reducing EST would result in kind of customer responsiveness that would be unimaginable in earlier times.

Furthermore, the real-time responsiveness of the enterprise coupled with the earlier mentioned enterprise-wide integration also enable enterprises the powerful capability of concurrent processing that would be impossible without ERPs like SAP. Enterprises can obtain tremendous efficiencies and throughputs because of this ability to administer in parallel many related processes that are not fully or partially interdependent. In non-ERP enterprises, such closely related processes are typically done sequentially because they are usually handled by the same set of personnel, who may be obviously constrained to address them only in a sequence. An illustration of this could be ad hoc analysis that may have to be done simultaneously on a set of POs and corresponding vendors/suppliers, deliveries, invoices, and so on. ERPs like SAP can perform all these concurrently because of ready availability of all relevant, complete, and consistent information at the same time.

ERP Elevates IT Strategy as a Part of the Business Strategy

The coming of ES heralded an enhanced role for IT systems. They are no longer the support functions of the earlier years. If someone is under that illusion, they will pay a very high price, maybe even in terms of the corporeal death of the enterprise itself. Now the real focus of IS/IT systems is no longer its alignment with the business strategy of the enterprise but on how to give it a competitive edge; it is part of the business necessities and priorities. Because of the complexity of increasing business change and uncertainty, IS/IT is business strategy incarnate!

And this arises primarily from the fact that information itself has become a vital resource for an enterprise in the same league as traditional resources such as manpower, materials, money, and time.

ERP Represents a Major Advance on the Earlier Manufacturing Performance Improvement Approaches

ERP is the latest in the succession of approaches that have been adopted throughout the history of enterprises for the improvement of enterprise-level performances. ERPs have realized the failed dream of improvements that were expected from the MRP II-based manufacturing resources

TABLE 3.1

Timeline of Performance Improvement Movements in the Century

1690	Division of Labor	Adam Smith
1890	Scientific Measurement	Frederick Taylor
1900	Mass Production	Henry Ford
1920	Industrial Engineering	F. Gilberth and Frederick Taylor
1930	Human Relations Movement	Elton Mayo
1950	Japanese Quality Revolution	J. M. Juran and W. E. Deming
1960	Material Requirement Planning (MRP)	William Orlicky
1970	Manufacturing Resource Planning (MRP II)	Oliver Wright
1970	Focused Factory	Wickham Skinner
1980	Total Quality Movement (TQM)	Philip Crosby
1980	Supplier Chain Management (SCM)	
1980	Just-in-Time (JIT)	Taiichi Ohno
1980	Computer Integrated Manufacturing (CIM)	
1980	Optimized Production Technology (OPT)	Eliyahu Goldratt
1980	ISO 9000	NASI
1980	World Class Manufacturing (WCM)	Richard Schonberger
1990	Mass Customization	Stan Davis and Joseph Pines II
1990	Lean Manufacturing	J. Womack, D. Jones and D. Roos
1990	Business Process Reengineering (BPR)	Michael Hammer
1990	Enterprise Resource Planning (ERP)	
1990	Customer Relationship Management (CRM)	Frederick Riechheld
1990	Product Lifecycle Management (PLM)	
1990	Business Intelligence (BI)	

planning systems of the 1970s. ERPs have enabled combining the hard approach of MRP II with the much more broadly scoped soft approaches of World Class Manufacturing (WCM) that were widely adopted during the 1980s. The WCM included such powerful approaches such as JIT, TQM, benchmarking, lean manufacturing, HR development movement, and, later in the 1990s, BPR. Table 3.1 gives a list of major enterprise performance improvement movements during the last century. ERPs provide the basic platform for devising techniques and tools for better implementations of the earlier approaches.

ERP Represents the Departmental Store Model of Implementing Computerized Systems

The coming of ERP has been the death knell of the development model of IS systems and, along with it, has gone the concept of requirements capture, modeling languages, development of software programs, testing, and so on that have usually been associated with the conventional developmental model. In its place, for the first time, is the end-user-friendly model of what one could call the departmental store model of computerized systems. The reference here is to the fact that rather than going through the complexities of specifying and getting a job done for you, you walk into a departmental store and from the array of functional goodies on display, pick and choose the functionality required by you. An ERP is the analog of the great departmental store of functionalities or processes required within an enterprise. ERP makes the transition from the world of carefully engineered and running systems to, as it were, the world of consumers where the value of the delivered functionality is based not on its pedigree but only on what, how, where, and when it can be used gainfully.

This then is the final commoditization of the IS/IT products and services!

ERP Is a Mass-User-Oriented Application Environment

Compared to the degree of involvement of functional managers and end users into traditional software project implementations, their participation in ES implementations may definitely seem unusual. ERP brings computerization to desktops and in this sense is an end-user-oriented environment in the true sense of the word (see Table 3.2). Unlike traditional systems, where users accessed the system directly only in well-defined pockets within the

TABLE 3.2

Back-Office Automation Technology versus Relationship Building Technology

	Traditional Back-Office Automation Technology	**Relationship Building Technology**
1. Strategic focus	Internal: Operational efficiency	External: Customer relationship
2. Key business benefit	Control cost	Drive corporate performance
3. Expertise required to develop applications	Algorithmic optimization	Business knowledge (e.g., sales, marketing, customer service)
4. Industry focus	Manufacturing	Services
5. Nature of process flows	Structured, deterministic	Unstructured, spontaneous
6. Process focus	Transactional	Relationship Building
7. Number of internal users	10s–100s	1000s to millions
8. Number of external users	10s–100s	Millions

enterprise, in ERP end users are truly the personnel actually involved with the operations of the business. Because of the intense involvement of a sizable portion of the workforce of the company with the ERP implementation right from the beginning, the probability of them embracing the system and not struggling against the system is much higher. They also act as the advocates and facilitators during and after the implementation phase.

ADVANTAGES OF ERP

The implementation of ERP engenders the following business and technical advantages:

- Reconciling and optimizing the conflicting goals of different divisions or departments; the transparent sharing of information with all concerned departments also enables cross-functional collaboration that is essential for the success of the millennium enterprise standardization of business processes across all the constituent companies and sites, thus increasing their efficiencies.
- Ability to know and implement global best practices.
- Altering the function-oriented organization toward a more team-based cross-functional process-oriented enterprise, thus leading to a more flexible, flatter, and tightly integrated enterprise.
- ERP provides a responsive medium for undertaking all variants on process improvement programs and methodologies including process innovation, process improvement, and business process redesign.
- ERP also provides a responsive medium for quality improvement and standardization efforts including QC, QA, and TQM.
- ERP being process-oriented is a fertile ground for implementing activity-based management (ABM) efforts, be it for budgeting, costing, efficiency, or quality.
- ERP provides the best conduit for measuring the benefits accruing to enterprises by their implementation by monitoring the ROI of not only money but also manpower, materials, time, and information. This could be in terms of various parameters such as cost, quality, responsiveness, and cycle time. Thus, ERP could assist in the implementation of, for instance, the balanced scorecard within the enterprise.

- ERPs, because they customarily implement best-of-class practices, provide the best means for benchmarking the organization's competitiveness.
- An ERP enables an enterprise to scale up its level of operations drastically or even enter into different businesses altogether without any disruption or performance degradation.
- Real-time creation of data directly during the actual physical transaction or processes by the persons who are actually responsible for it.
- Pushing the latest data and status to the actual operational-level persons for better and faster decisions at least on routine issues; empowering and giving ownership to the operational personnel at the level of actual work (this automatically does away with problems associated with collection of voluminous data, preparation, entry, corrections of inaccuracies, backup, etc.).
- Integration of the data of the enterprise into a single comprehensive database.
- Online availability of correct and up-to-date data.

ERP provides the most current, correct, consistent, complete operational data that can be populated into the enterprise data warehouse for analysis and reporting.

ERP greatly reduces the cost of maintaining systems. The vendor shoulders the responsibility of enhancing functionalities, providing technical upgrades as well as incorporating the latest country-specific regulations and statutory requirements.

ENTERPRISE KNOWLEDGE AS THE NEW CAPITAL

Adam Smith started the industrial revolution by identifying labor and capital as the economic determinants of the wealth of a nation. In this century, however, the size of the land, mass of labor, and materials that you may possess might be worthless if you do not control the related know-how. In the twenty-first century, know-how will reside and flourish in people's minds; what might matter more are how many enterprising and innovative people you have and the freedom that they have in realizing their dreams. It will be the century of information economics.

ERP like SAP also acts as transformers of the knowledge which resides in the heads of the operational and subject experts into a more explicit and accessible form. This corresponds exactly to the tacit knowledge talked about by I. Nonaka and H. Takeuchi in their book titled "The Knowledge Creating Company." These could be learning experiences, ideas, insights, innovations, thumb rules, business cases, concepts or conceptual models, analogies, and so on. They exhort companies to convert the illusive, unsystematized, uncodified, and can-be-lost knowledge of the corporation into explicit knowledge that can be codified, collated, and managed like any other capital investment; this could be in the form of documents, case studies, analysis reports, evaluations, concept papers, internal proposals, and so on. Most importantly, it is available for scrutiny and can be improved on an ongoing basis. ERP performs the invaluable service of transforming implicit knowledge into explicit form.

Information as the New Resource

Having covered the context of ERP in this chapter, it is time now to state that the importance of ERP packages like SAP is not because of the total integration of various modules, single-point data entry, data integrity, ad hoc reporting, instant access to information, end-user computing, etc., provided by them. The importance arises primarily from the fact that information is by now the fifth resource (the first four being manpower, materials, money, and time). And, unlike other resources, this resource is inexhaustible—it can be shared infinitely without any reduction. Thus, if we can use information as substitute for other resources (which we can see below), we can use it many times over without any appreciable further cost. Among all resources, this is one resource that in practical terms almost defies the universal law of increase of entropy as understood in the physical sciences.

Traditionally, competitive advantage came from strategies based on the following value determinants:

1. Cost (ownership, use, training support, maintenance, etc.)
2. Time (cycle time, lead time, etc.)
3. Response time (lead time, number of handoffs, number of queues, etc.)
4. Flexibility (customization, options, composition, etc.)

5. Quality (rework, rejects, yield, etc.)
6. Innovation (new needs, interfaces, add-ons, etc.)

But because everyone has squeezed (and continue to do so) as much as one can from the preceding value determinants in the last few decades, now the only source for competitive strategy of substantial value, which remains to be exploited in a major way, is from the latest new-found resource:

Information (correctness, currency, consistency, completeness, clarity, compliance, availability, security, etc.)

Traditionally, the basic resources have been manpower (before the agricultural revolution), materials (before industrial revolution), capital (before the information revolution till the mid-twentieth century), and time (since the mid-1950s). In certain sense of the term, these basic resources are considered interchangeable. Likewise, since the mid-twentieth century, information has become the fifth resource, and it is almost a substitute for manpower, materials, capital, and even time.

For instance, JIT permits us to order for just the right kind of material at the right time at the right place, therefore reducing inputs of manpower in ordering, handling, storing, etc. It also results in reduced materials inventory and, hence, cost of storage mechanisms, cost of locked capital, etc.

The availability of detailed and up-to-the-minute information on production runs can result in up-to-the-minute information on

- Production plan for the next run
- Hence, material requirements for the next run
- Hence, issue of materials from the main stores for the next run
- Hence, stock at hand in the stores for the next run
- Hence, material to be ordered for the next run

It is not difficult to see that this ultimately results in drastically increased throughputs and reduced business cycle times, which is equivalent to improved production or technological processes through the use of improved resources. Traditionally, appreciably higher throughputs and lower production/business cycles could only be possible through innovation in technology and/or production methods or process. How information as provided by ERPs is a resource of an organization can be seen from the analogy with fuel that drives automobiles: Information as made available by ES greatly increases the speed of business processes within the enterprise. Evidently, this is a class apart from what is achievable with the manual or even fragmented legacy computerized systems. Enterprise-wide JIT, and not just the one confined primarily to the production department only, is impossible without integrated postmodern computerized systems such as ERPs for correct, current, consistent, and complete information.

Thus, information is a practical and tangible substitute for manpower, materials, money, and time in real commercial terms. And though manual JIT systems are possible, only computerized ERP systems can give you JIT even in industries such as airlines, credit cards, electronic banking, and courier services, which do not work in a batch mode of production but are essentially functioning in a real-time mode.

We can take this analogy even further. In any industry, like that for any other traditional raw materials, companies need the information resource preprocessed in massive amounts that has to be correct, current, consistent, and so on. And only complete and integrated ERP packages like SAP can provide this operational raw material required in massive amounts. It should be specially noted that only an ERP implemented within an enterprise enables the optimal utilization and efficient conversion of such a seemingly intangible resource like information into tangible resource, which is also a highly perishable resource!

ERP AS THE NEW ENTERPRISE ARCHITECTURE

ERP provides the architecture for the realization of the dimensions of variations discussed in Inverting the Paradox of Excellence (Kale 2014).

Shared values: ERP truly makes it possible to operate as a collaborative value-add-driven enterprise. It is difficult to imagine such a company operating on manual or even nonintegrated systems, which, because of the inherent delays of information transfer between them, would not function in the real-time mode. ES permit learning happening in any part of the enterprise to be incorporated into the system even on a daily basis.

Strategy: ERP enables the realization of an organization that has a vision to be competitive by raising the level of skills and competencies of its personnel so that they can respond better, faster, and at optimal cost to the changing business situations every day.

Structure: For the millennium enterprise, the ERP system provides visibility to the responsibility-oriented organization structure rather than the designation-oriented structure of the earlier times. It provides instant communication and interaction with all members who are involved in a particular activity or process irrespective of their reporting department or designation.

Stuff: ERP enables the definition, management, planning, production, and delivery of products or services. They empower the enterprise to compose or develop new products or services and add them seamlessly to traditional processes established for defining, manufacture, and delivery of products to the end customers.

Style: ERP enables access to data to all concerned personnel to keep track of the enterprise's overall performance with reference to the company's goals as well as their own contribution to the same on a daily basis. This engenders a sense of involvement and transparency that had not been achievable earlier.

Staff: ERP enables access to data to all concerned personnel to keep track of the enterprise's overall performance with reference to the company's goals as well as their own contribution to the same on a daily basis. This engenders a sense of involvement and transparency that had not been achievable earlier.

Skills: ERP is equipped to fully maintain a repository of skills (and skill sets) across the whole base of employees. It can query for a specific skill, or shortlist for upgrade of skills, or register acquisition of new skills at an individual or group level. ERP can also help plan and schedule skills that need periodic refreshing on a systematic basis.

Systems: ERP implements all essential systems and procedures to their bare-minimum necessity level. It provides for adequate control without encumbering the work that directly contributes in the value add delivered to the external or internal customers. ERP enables the process-oriented enterprise that may not always be feasible to realize physically, for instance, by locating all concerned members of a team in one place. It also makes it possible for members to participate efficiently and effectively in more than one business-critical process.

Sequence: ERP can enable the handling of the discrete or continuous process requirements of any enterprise. ERP also enables the handling of any or a mix and match of both modes of production depending on the enterprise's requirement. Any changes planned in the production flow by reason of changes of products, materials, production process, quality, and so on can be accommodated readily.

ENTERPRISE BUSINESS PROCESSES

Businesses take inputs (resources) in the form of material, people, and equipment and transform these inputs into goods and services for customers. Managing these inputs and the business processes effectively requires accurate and up-to-date information. For example, the sales function takes a customer's order, and the production function schedules the manufacturing of the product. Logistics employees schedule and carry out the delivery of the product. If raw materials are needed to make the product, production prompts purchasing to arrange for their purchase and delivery. In that case, logistics will receive the material, verify its condition to accounting so that the vendor can be paid, and deliver the goods to production. Throughout, accounting keeps appropriate transaction records.

Most companies had unintegrated information systems that supported only the activities of individual business functional areas. Thus, a company would have a marketing information system, a production information system, and so on, each with its own hardware, software, and methods of processing data and information. This configuration of information systems is known as silos because each department has its own stack, or silo, of information that is unconnected to the next silo; silos are also known as stovepipes. Such unintegrated systems might work well within individual functional areas, but to achieve its goals, a company must share data among all the functional areas. When a company's information systems are not integrated, costly inefficiencies can result. For example, suppose two functional areas have separate, unintegrated information systems. To share data, a clerk in one functional area needs to print out data from another functional area and then type the information into his/her area's information system. Not only does this data input take twice the time, it also significantly increases the chance for data-entry errors. Alternatively, the process might be automated by having one information system write data to a file to be read by another information system. This would reduce the probability of errors, but it could only be done periodically (usually overnight or on a weekend) to minimize the disruption to normal business transactions. Because of the time lag in updating the system, the transferred data would rarely be up-to-date. In addition, data can be defined differently in different data systems, such as calling products by different part numbers in different systems. This variance can create further problems in timely and accurate information sharing between functional areas.

The functional business model illustrates the concept of silos of information, which limit the exchange of information between the lower operating levels. Instead, the exchange of information between operating groups is handled by top management, which might not be knowledgeable about the functional area (see Figure 3.1a). In the quickly changing markets of

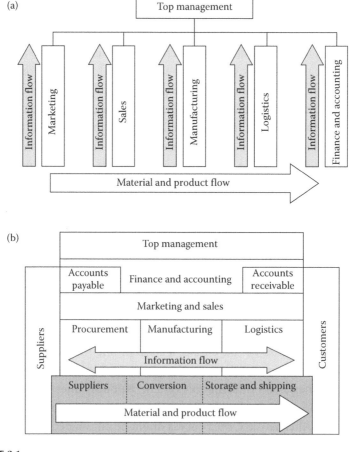

FIGURE 3.1
Information and material flows in (a) functional business model and (b) a business process model.

the 1990s, the functional model led to top-heavy and overstaffed enterprises incapable of reacting quickly to change. This led to view a business as a set of cross-functional processes, as illustrated in Figure 3.1b. In the process-oriented model, the flow of information and management activity is horizontal across functions, in line with the flow of materials and products. This horizontal flow promotes flexibility and rapid decision making and stimulates managers to see the importance of managing business processes. Now information flows between the operating levels without top management's involvement.

ENTERPRISE APPLICATION INTEGRATION

In these times of market change and turbulence, enterprises are confronted with the increasing need to interconnect disparate systems to satisfy the needs of the business. It is estimated that 35%–60% of an enterprise's IT resources are spent on integration. Enterprise application integration is the creation, maintenance, and enhancement of leading-edge competitive functionality of the enterprise's business solutions by combining the functionality of the existing legacy applications, commercial off-the-shelf (COTS) software packages, and newly developed custom applications via a common middleware.

Enterprise applications are software applications developed to manage the business operations, assets, and resources of an enterprise. Their development process integrates the work of at least four groups, namely, GUI developers responsible for the design and development of widgets to ease human–computer interaction; application programmers focusing on coding the business logic for the solution of a particular business problem; database managers building data models to structure and manage data storage, access, security, and consistency; and finally, application integrators for integrating existing applications and available technologies with the new applications.

In principle, there is no difference between enterprise applications and regular software applications other than the specific business purpose they are developed for. As the nature of business goals and processes vary, software solutions delivered for specific business problems vary as well. As a consequence, the number and variety of applications delivered for each solution increase the complexity of managing the overall IT system.

While having an automated solution to business problems increases effectiveness and efficiency and reduces cost, managing the complexity of the automated solution is a new business problem that companies have to deal with separately.

A high-level blueprint of a standard application template for a company can reduce that complexity. In response to this need, the design characteristics, limitations, interfaces, and rules of developing enterprise applications have been documented. This high-level description, the blueprint, of how an application should be developed to satisfy the business goals is known as Enterprise Application Architecture. This architecture defines an organizing structure for software application elements and the resources, their relationships, and roles in an organization. Enterprise applications are usually developed independent of each other, and each of these applications manage their own data in their specific database system. This leads to data heterogeneity and inefficiency because the same data elements are stored multiple times in different databases. This creates the problem of managing the same logical data object stored in multiple data stores. Differences in data structures as well as in semantics are also possible. One of the challenges facing enterprises today is the task of integrating all these applications within the enterprise, even though they may use different operating systems and employ a variety of database solutions. Simplistic approaches soon become unmanageable as the number of applications to be integrated increases. Enterprise Application Integration (EAI) has the task of making independently developed applications that may also be geographically dispersed and may run on multiple platforms to work together in unison with the goal of enabling unrestricted sharing of data and business processes.

In order to accomplish this goal, middleware vendors provide solutions to transform, transport, and route the data among various enterprise applications. EAI faces significantly more management challenges than technical challenges, and its implementation is time consuming and needs substantial resources, particularly in upfront design. Among the software applications for managing company assets and resources, the most commonly used are Enterprise Resource Planning (ERP), Customer Relationship Management (CRM), Supply-Chain Management (SCM), Business Intelligence Applications, and Human Resource (HR) Applications. ERP is probably, the most general class of enterprise software that attempts to integrate all departments and functions across a company. ERP incorporates many different families of more specific enterprise applications. CRM solutions focus on strategies, processes, people, and technologies used by companies to successfully attract and retain customers for maximizing profitability, revenue, and customer satisfaction. Enterprise Content Management solutions provide technologies, tools, and methods used to capture, manage, store, preserve, and deliver content (document, voice and video recordings, etc.) related to organizational processes across an enterprise. SCM solutions focus on the process of planning, implementing, and controlling the operations of the supply chain, which includes the flow of materials, information, and finances as they move in a process from supplier to manufacturer, to wholesaler, to retailer, and to consumer. HR Management solutions provide a coherent approach to the recruitment and management of people working in enterprises.

SERVICE-ORIENTED ARCHITECTURE

Integration seems to be one of the most important strategic priorities mainly because new innovative business solutions demand integration of different business units, business systems, enterprise data, and applications. Integrated information systems improve the competitive advantage with unified and efficient access to information. Integrated applications make it much easier to access relevant, coordinated information from a variety of sources. It is clear that replacing existing systems with new solutions will often not be a viable proposition. Companies soon realize that the replacement is more complicated, more complex, more time consuming, and more costly than even their worst-case scenarios could have predicted: Too much time and money have been invested in them, and there is too much knowledge incorporated in these systems. Therefore, standard ways to reuse existing systems and integrate them into the global, enterprise-wide information system must be defined.

The modern answer to application integration is a SOA with Web Services; SOA is a style of organizing (services), and Web Services are its realization. An SOA with Web Services is a combination of architecture and technology for consistently delivering robust, reusable services that support today's business needs and that can be easily adapted to satisfy changing business requirements. An SOA enables easy integration of IT systems, provides multichannel access to systems, and automates business processes. When an SOA with its corresponding services is in place, developers can easily reuse existing services in developing new applications and business processes.

A service differs from an object or a procedure because it is defined by the messages that it exchanges with other services. A service's loose coupling to the applications that host it gives it the ability to more easily share data across the department, enterprise, or Internet. An SOA defines the way in which services are deployed and managed. Companies need IT systems with the flexibility to implement specialized operations, to change quickly with the changes in business operations, to respond quickly to internal as well as external changes in conditions, and consequently gain a competitive edge. Using an SOA increases reuse, lowers overall costs, and improves the ability to rapidly change and evolve IT systems, whether old or new.

An SOA also maps IT systems easily and directly to a business's operational processes and supports a better division of labor between the business and technical staff. One of the great potential advantages of solutions created using an SOA with SOAP or REST Web Services is that they can help resolve this perennial problem by providing better separation of concerns between business analysts and service developers. Analysts can take responsibility for defining how services fit together to implement business processes, while the service developers can take responsibility for implementing services that meet business requirements. This will ensure that the business issues are well enough understood to be implemented in technology and the technology issues are well enough understood to meet business requirements.

Integrating existing and new applications using an SOA involves defining the basic Web Service interoperability layer to bridge features and functions used in current applications such as security, reliability, transactions, metadata management, and orchestration; it also involves the ability to define automated business process execution flows across the Web Services after an SOA is in place. An SOA with Web Services enables the development of services that encapsulate business functions and that are easily accessible from any other service; composite services allow a wide range of options for combining Web Services and creating new application functionality.

As a prerequisite, one will have to deal with a plethora of legacy technologies in order to service-enable them. But the beauty of services and SOA is that the services are developed to achieve interoperability and to hide the details of the execution environments behind them. In particular, for Web Services, this means the ability to emit and consume data represented as XML, regardless of development platform, middleware, operating system, or hardware type. Thus, an SOA is a way to define and provision an IT infrastructure to allow different applications to exchange data and participate in business processes, regardless of the operating systems or programming languages underlying these applications.

Defining SOA

SOA provides an agile technical architecture that can be quickly and easily reconfigured as business requirements change. The promise of SOA is that it will break down the barriers in IT to implement business process flows in a cost-effective and agile manner that would combine the best of custom solutions as well as packaged applications while simultaneously reducing lock-in to any single IT vendor.

A Service-oriented architecture (SOA) is a style of organization that guides all aspects of creating and using business services throughout their life cycle (from conception to retirement), as well as defining and provisioning the IT infrastructure that allows different applications to exchange data and participate in business processes regardless of the operating systems or programming languages underlying these applications. The key organizing concept of an SOA itself is a service. The processes, principles, and methods defined by SOA are oriented toward services; the development tools selected by an SOA are oriented toward creating and deploying services; and the runtime infrastructure provided by an SOA is oriented to executing and managing services.

A service is a sum of constituting parts including a description, the implementation, and the mapping layer (termed as transformation layer) between the two. The service implementation, termed as the executable agent, can be any environment for which Web Service support is available. The description is separated from its executable agent; one description might have multiple different executable agents associated with it and vice versa. The executable agent is responsible for implementing the Web Service processing model as per the various Web Service specifications and runs within the execution environment, which is typically a software system or programming language environment. The description is separated from the execution environment using a mapping or transformation layer often implemented using proxies and stubs. The mapping layer is responsible for accepting the message, transforming the XML data to be native format, and dispatching the data to the executable agent.

Web Service roles include requester and provider; a requester can be a provider and vice versa. The service requester initiates the execution of a service by sending a message to a service provider, which executes the service and returns the results, if any specified, to the requester.

Services

Services are coarse-grained, reusable IT assets that have well-defined interfaces (or service contracts) that clearly separate the service accessible interface from the service technical implementation. This separation of interface and implementation serves to decouple the service requesters from the service providers so that both can evolve independently as long as the service contract remains unchanged.

A service is a location on the network that has a machine-readable description of the messages it receives and optionally returns. A service is therefore defined in terms of the message exchange patterns it supports. A schema for the data contained in the message is used as the main part of the contract between a service requester and a service provider; other items of metadata describe the network address for the service, the operations it supports, and its requirements for reliability, security, and transactional integrity. However, developing a service is quite different from developing an object because a service is defined by the message it exchanges with other services, rather than a method signature. A service usually defines a coarse-grained interface that accepts more data in a single invocation than an object because of the need to map to an execution environment, process the XML, and often access it remotely. Services are executed by exchanging messages according to one or more supported message exchange patterns (MEPs), such as request/response, one-way asynchronous, or publish/subscribe. Services are meant to solve interoperability problems between applications and for use in composing new applications or application systems, but not meant like objects to create the detailed business logic for the applications.

From a business perspective, services are IT assets that correspond to real-world business activities or identifiable business functions that can be accessed according to the service policies related to

- Who is authorized to access the service
- When the service can be accessed
- What is the cost of using the service
- What are the reliability levels of using the service
- What are the performance levels for the service

A service is normally defined at a higher level of abstraction than an object because it is possible to map a service definition to a procedure-oriented language, such as COBOL or PL/1, or to a message queuing system such as JMS or MSMQ, as well as to an object-oriented system such as J2EE or the .NET Framework. Whether the service's execution environment is a stored procedure, message queue, or object does not matter; the data are seen through the filter of a Web Service, which includes a layer that maps the Web Service to whatever execution environment is implementing the service. The use of XML in Web Services provides a clear separation between the definition of a service and its execution so that Web Services can work with any software system. The XML representation of the data types and structures of a service via the XML schema allows the developer to think solely in terms of the data being passed between the services without having to consider the details of the service's implementation. This is quite in contrast to the traditional nature of the integration problem that involves figuring out the implementation of the service in order to be able to talk to it.

One of the greatest benefits of service abstraction is its ability to easily access a variety of service types, including newly developed services, wrapped legacy applications, and applications composed of other newer and legacy services.

SOA Benefits

SOA delivers the following business benefits:

a. Increased business agility: SOA improves throughput by dramatically reducing the amount of time required to assemble new business applications, from existing services and IT assets. SOA also makes

IT significantly easier and less expensive to reconfigure and adapt services and IT assets to meet new and unanticipated requirements. Thus, the business adapts quickly to new opportunities and competitive threats, while IT quickly changes existing systems.

b. Better business alignment: As SOA services directly support the services that the enterprise provides to customers.

c. Improved customer satisfaction: As SOA services are independent of specific technology, they can readily work with an array of customer-facing systems across all customer touch points that effectively reduce development time, increase customer engagement time, and, hence, increase customer solutioning, enabling enhanced customer satisfaction.

d. Improved ROI of existing assets: SOA dramatically improves the ROI of existing IT assets by reusing them as services in the SOA by identifying the key business capabilities of existing systems and using them as the basis for new services as part of the SOA.

e. Reduced vendor lock-in and switching costs: As SOA is based on loosely coupled services with well-defined, platform-neutral service contracts, it avoids vendor and technology lock-in at all levels, namely, application platform and middleware platform.

f. Reduced integration costs: SOA projects can focus on composing, publishing, and developing Web Services independently of their execution environments, thus obviating the need to deal with avoidable complexity. Web Services and XML simplify integration because they focus on the data being exchanged instead of the underlying programs and execution environments.

Technical benefits of SOA include the following:

a. More reuse: Service reuse lowers development costs and speed.

b. Efficient development: As services are loosely coupled, SOA promotes modularity that enables easier and faster development of composite applications. Once service contracts have been defined, developers can separately and independently design and implement each of the various services. Similarly, service requesters too can be designed and implemented based solely with reference to the published service contracts without any need to contact the concerned developers or without any access to the developers of the service providers.

c. Simplified maintenance: As services are modular and loosely coupled, they simplify maintenance and reduce maintenance costs.

d. Incremental adoption: As services are modular and loosely coupled, they can be developed and deployed in incremental steps.

Characteristics of SOA

a. Dynamic, Discoverable, Metadata Driven
Services should be published in a manner by which they can be discovered and consumed without intervention of the provider. Service contracts should use metadata to define service capabilities and constraints, and should be machine readable so that they can be registered and discovered dynamically to lower the cost of locating and using services, reduce corresponding errors, and improve management of services.

b. Designed for Multiple Invocation Styles
Design and implement service operations that implement business logic that supports multiple invocation styles, including asynchronous queuing, request/response, request/callback, request/polling, batch processing, and event-driven publish/subscribe.

c. Loosely Coupled
This implies loose coupling of interface and technology; interface coupling implies that the interface should encapsulate all implementation details and make them nontransparent to service requesters, while technology coupling measures the extent to which a service depends on a particular technology, product, or development platform (operating systems, application servers, packaged applications, and middleware).

d. Well-Defined Service Contracts
Service contracts are more important than service implementations because they define the service capabilities and how to invoke the service in an interoperable manner. A service contract clearly separates the service's externally accessible interface from the service's technical implementation; consequently, the service contract is independent of any single service implementation. The service contract is defined based on the knowledge of the business domain and not so much on the service implementation. The service contract is defined and managed as a separate artifact, is the basis for

sharing and reuse, and is the primary mechanism for reducing interface coupling.

Changing a service contract is generally more expensive than modifying the implementation of a service because while changing a service implementation is relatively a localized effort, changing a service contract may entail changing hundreds or thousands of service requesters.

e. Standard Based

Services should be based on open standards as much as possible leading to the following benefits:

- Minimizing vendor lock-in by isolating from proprietary, vendor-specific technologies and interfaces
- Increasing the choice of service requesters for alternate service providers and vice versa

It is important to base the service-level data and process models on mature business domain standards as and when they become available. This is in addition to complying with technology standards such as SOAP, WSDL, UDDI, and the WS* specification.

f. Granularity of Services and Service Contracts

Services and service contracts must be defined at a level of abstraction that makes sense to service requesters as also service providers. To achieve this, services should perform discrete tasks and provide simple interfaces to encourage reuse and loose coupling.

An abstract interface at the appropriate level of granularity promotes ready substitutability, which enables any of the existing service providers to be replaced by a new service provider without affecting any of the service requesters.

g. Stateless

Services should be stateless because they scale more efficiently as any service request can be routed to any service instance. In contrast, stateful interactions do not scale efficiently because the server needs to track which service is serving which client and cannot reuse a service until the conversation is finished or a time-out has occurred.

Thus, services should be implemented so that each invocation is independent and does not depend on the service maintaining client-specific conversations in memory or in persistent state between the invocations.

h. Predictable Service-Level Agreements (SLAs)

The service delivery platform must provide service-level management capabilities for defining, monitoring, incident logging, and metering of SLAs for service usage. SLAs should be established early because they affect service design, implementation, and management. There should also be provision for fine-tuning of SLAs based on the feedback of ongoing operations.

Typically, SLAs define metrics for services such as response time, throughput, availability, and meantime between failures. Above all, SLAs are usually tied up to a business model whereby service requesters pay more for higher or more stringent SLAs but charge a penalty when service providers default on their SLA commitments.

i. Design Services with Performance in Mind

Service invocation should not be modeled on local function calls since local transparency may result in a service that is on another machine on the same LAN or another LAN or WAN.

SOA Applications

An SOA can be thought of as an approach to building IT systems in which business services are the key organizing principle to align IT systems with the needs of the business. Any business that can implement an IT infrastructure that allows it to change more rapidly than its competitors has an advantage over them. The use of an SOA for integration, business process management, and multichannel access allows any enterprise to create a more strategic environment, one that more closely aligns with the operational characteristics of the business. Earlier approaches to building IT systems resulted in systems that were tied to the features and functions of a particular environment technology (such as CORBA, J2EE, and COM/DCOM) since they employed environment-specific characteristics such as procedure, or object, or message orientation to provide solutions to business problems. The way in which services are developed aligns them better with the needs of the business than was the case with previous generations of technology. What is new in the concept of SOA is the clear separation of the service interface from execution technology, enabling choice of the best execution environment for any job and tying all these executional agents together using a consistent architectural approach.

Rapid Application Integration

The combination of Web Services and SOA provides a rapid integration solution that readily aligns IT investments and corporate strategies by focusing on shared data and reusable services rather than proprietary integration products. These enterprise application integration (EAI) products proved to be expensive, consumed considerable time and effort, and were prone to higher rates of failure. Applications can more easily exchange data by using a Web Service defined at the business logic layer than by using a different integration technology because Web Services represent a common standard across all types of software. XML can be used to independently define the data types and structures. Creating a common Web Service layer or overlay of services into the business logic tiers of application also allows you to use a common service repository in which to store and retrieve service descriptions. If a new application seeks to use an existing service into one of these applications, it can query the repository to obtain the service description to quickly generate (say) SOAP messages to interact with it. Finally, the development of service-oriented entry points at the business logic tier allows a business process management engine to drive an automatic flow of execution across the multiple services.

Multichannel Access

Enterprises often use many channels to ensure good service and maintain customer loyalty; therefore, they benefit from being able to deliver customer services over a mixture of access channels. In the past, enterprises often developed monolithic applications that were tied to a single access channel, such as a 3270 terminal, a PC interface, or a Web browser. The proliferation of access channels represented a significant challenge to IT departments to convert monolithic applications to allow multichannel access. The basic solution is to service-enable these using an SOA with Web Services that are good for enabling multichannel access because they are accessible from a broad range of clients, including Web, Java, C#, and mobile devices. In general, business services change much less frequently than the delivery channels through which they are accessed. Business services refer to operational functions such as vendor management, purchase order management, and billing, which do not vary very often, whereas client devices and access channels are based on new technologies, which tend to change.

Business Process Management

A business process is a real-world activity that consists of a set of logically related tasks that, when performed in an appropriate sequence and in conformity with applicable rules, produce a business outcome. Business process management (BPM) is the name for a set of software systems, tools, and methodologies that enable enterprises to identify, model, develop, deploy, and manage such business processes. BPM systems are designed to help align business processes with desirable business outcomes and ensure that the IT systems support those business processes. BPM systems let business users model their business processes graphically in a way that the IT department can implement; the graphical depiction of a business process can be used to generate an executable specification of the process. Unlike traditional forms of system development where the process logic is deeply embedded in the application code, BPM explicitly separates the business process logic from other application code. Separating business process logic from other application code renders increased productivity, reduced operational costs, and improved agility. When implemented correctly, enterprises can quickly respond to changing market conditions and seize opportunities for gaining competitive advantage.

SOA with Web Services can better automate business processes because Web Services help achieve the goals of BPM more quickly and easily.

SUMMARY

ERPs enable the integration of heterogeneous and disparate business units, functions, and processes to coordinate, cooperate, and collaborate in aligning the business operations of the enterprise with its corporate strategy. After introducing the concept of ERP, the chapter describes the characteristics of ERPs and their advantages. It introduces the powerful new concept of information as a resource which is a substitute for tangible resources such as materials, money, manpower, etc. In the context of the essential requirements for integration and the challenges of the traditional approaches to enterprise application integration (EAI), the chapter introduced the concept of service-oriented architecture (SOA) that enables realizing business process as Web Services (see Chapter 7, section "Business Processes with SOA"). It highlights the benefits and characteristics of SOA for modern enterprises.

4

Customer-Centric Enterprise with CRM

Customer Relationship Management (CRM) is a holistic approach to identifying, attracting, and retaining customers. CRM deals with creating a customer-centric enterprise. This involves two major aspects: Customer centricity and customer responsiveness. All activities must eventually add value to the customer reflected in their willingness to pay for the products and/or services; nonvalue adding elements should be excised swiftly in Internet-time because customers have numerous other choices. This entails focusing all strategies, plans, and actions on the customer rather than the traditional focus on the products and/or services. As originally proposed by Fred Reichheld: It is a question of transitioning from zero defects to zero defections.

Additionally, enterprises must ensure seamless and real-time integration between

- Customer-facing demand generating processes
- Back-end demand fulfilling intra- or interenterprise supply-chain processes

An effective CRM strategy aims at achieving the following:

- Continuously attract new customers
- Gain customer insight and manage intimacy
- Retain profitable customers and phase-out nonprofitable customers
- Establish long-term relationships with current customers
- Increase the customer spend and profits by cross-selling and upselling

This book takes a stance that customers are not the exclusive preserve of the marketing function, but are the key to an enterprise's enduring and compounding competitiveness and success.

 There is a substantial difference between the concept of Customer Relationship Management (CRM) and Customer Relationship Management Systems (CRM Systems). CRM is a concept of much broader scope than the CRM Systems that implement a subset of the tenets of CRM. In this chapter, after introducing the concept of CRM, the chapter focuses on leveraging the CRM-oriented capabilities of the enterprises, while Appendix I includes an overview of the CRM functionality provided by SAP Business Suite (see Appendix I "SAP Business Suite").

THE CONCEPT OF CUSTOMER RELATIONSHIP MANAGEMENT (CRM)

Customer Relationship Management (CRM) can be defined as the customer-centric business strategy that encompasses all business models, processes, methodologies, and techniques for closing the gap between an organization's current and potential performance in acquisition, growth, and retention of valuable customers for mutual benefit.

In an era where the advantages based only on product features and add-on services are shortened to a "click of a customer" (see section "The Customer Triggered Company"), the key to success is to forge long-term, profitable relationships with valuable customers. This involves two major aspects: Customer centricity and customer responsiveness. CRM aims to identify the customers that are most profitable to the company, and optimizes relationships with those customers.

Figure 4.1 presents the underlying Customer Relationship Framework for the whole book.

Whereas this view may lead to increased services and incentives for customers that provide the greatest returns to the company, it may also result on the other hand, in reduced services or even strong disincentives for nonprofitable customers. If a company or enterprise were to put

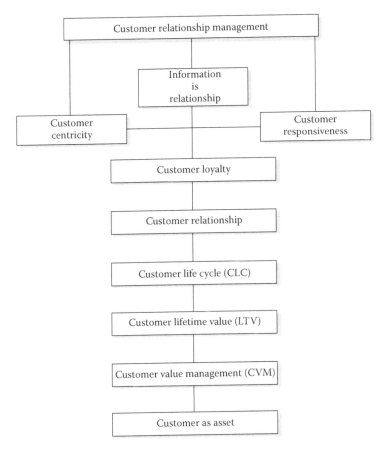

FIGURE 4.1
The customer relationship framework.

more of its efforts into its existing customers, it would make sense that it did this with customers that had the greatest potential. This means that at some point, it has to start to lose those customers that are not ones that offer long-term future value—this might be because of transaction spend, the value of a customer, or the cost of transacting or dealing with that customer or customer group. All customers are not created equal! Consequently, the traditional customer-centric slogan should be transformed to: Valuable (i.e., Profitable) customers are always right.

Thus, even customers compete for bestowing their custom! Customer retention is extremely important for companies because it is more efficient and effective to retain a current customer than gain a new one. Companies can generate additional revenue and profits without incurring the costs for acquiring new customers. In light of this, management is really concerned

FIGURE 4.2
Marketing techniques for different types of customers.

with having the right product in the right place, at the right price, at the right time, in the right condition for the right customer.

Don Peppers and Martha Rogers pioneered the concept of one-to-one marketing made possible by the advent of computer-assisted database marketing. Figure 4.2 represents the entire spectrum of customers and the corresponding marketing techniques. The horizontal axis measures the diversity of customer needs and the vertical axis measures the differentiation in "customer valuations." The representative businesses for each of the quadrants are as follows: Gas Station, bookstore, airline, and computer systems company.

According to Don Peppers and Martha Rogers:

- Businesses with relatively undiversified customer needs and relatively uniform customer valuations will do best with mass marketing techniques (refer to section "Customer Value").
- Businesses with diversified customer needs but uniform valuations can benefit from target marketing.
- Businesses with relatively undiversified customer needs but with highly differentiated customer valuations will benefit immensely with a key accounts management approach.
- Businesses with highly diversified customer needs and highly differentiated customer valuations will benefit from one-to-one customized marketing.

How does one handle a set of highly differentiated customers having a large diversity of needs?—through customer responsiveness that is discussed in Chapter 5. In the remaining part of this section, we deal with the various facets of CRM.

The enterprise' business model governs both its business strategy and its use of IT. Figure 4.3 shows the product-process change matrix that illustrates the four distinct business models based on

- The dimensions of change (product or process change)
- The fundamental nature of change (dynamic or stable)

On the vertical axis, product change reflects changes in the demand for goods or services because of competitor moves, shifting customer preferences, or entering new geographical or national markets. On the horizontal axis, process change means altering the procedures or technologies used to generate, produce, or deliver the corresponding products or services. Taken together these factors result in four distinct business models, as listed below:

- Mass Production: In these enterprises the primary use of technology is to automate tasks.
- Invention: In these enterprises, technology must support collaborative efforts amongst teams or a set of individuals.

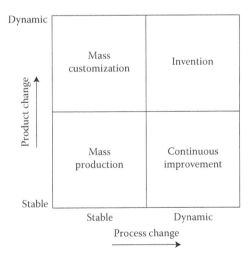

FIGURE 4.3
Business models.

- Continuous Improvement: In these enterprises, technology must augment tasks by enhancing people's deep process knowledge and skills. It can also link people and processes across functions to provide customer-focused, horizontal, informational flows enabling them to continuously improve the processes they execute.
- Mass Customization: In these enterprises, technology must not only automate tasks, augment knowledge and skills, but most significantly must also automate relationships between processes and people.

The advent of the Total Quality Management (TQM) movement in the USA led to the emergence of customer satisfaction measures; and efforts aimed at improving and sustaining them led to greater emphasis on customer centricity. The total quality management turned attention to customer needs and forced a rethinking of traditional management methods.

One of the keys to mass customization is the use of dynamic business networks within and amongst enterprises. These are formed out of a set of loosely coupled autonomous business process capabilities with a linkage system that allows them to be reconfigured instantly for any particular customer order. By engineering the flexibility of the processing units and coordinating the flow of resources (materials or services) between these units, the mass customizer can produce an almost infinite variety of base products or service, at a cost that is competitive when compared even with a mass producer. Whereas labor in the mass production design is organized to perform repetitive tasks according to a singular command and control system, the mass customizer organizes labor to routinely respond to an ever-changing set of rules and commands. The mass customizer organizes labor to work effectively in a dynamic network of relationships and to respond to work requirements defined by dynamically changing customer needs. Although there is apparently a great degree of centralization in both of these models, there is a fundamental difference in the nature of centralization: In case of mass production, all decision making is centralized, whereas in the case of mass customizer it is only the coordination and control that is centralized. The mass customizing enterprises centralizes the allocation of work to different processing units to produce the customer's product or service order. (See Chapter 1, section "Agile Enterprises," Chapter 5, section "Business Webs (B-webs)," and Chapter 6, section "Mass Customization.")

CUSTOMER CENTRICITY

CRM is a different approach to business that involves relationship marketing, customer retention, and cross selling leading to customer extension (see section "Customer Life Cycle (CLC)"). CRM represents a culmination of a long-evolutionary shift in the traditional thinking of business. Until the last few decades, the business of the global economy was, essentially, manufacturing. The focus on goods rather than services led to a product-focused, mass-market marketing strategy resulting in a high cost of acquiring new customers, and a low cost for customers switching to other brands.

Table 4.1 compares the traditional mass marketing approach with that of the relationship-oriented customized marketing.

There has always been a focus on customer needs, but with the advent of computers, there has been a shift away from producing goods or providing services, toward discovering and meeting the needs of the individual customer. The challenge to the company's future is not necessarily from the competitors, but from its own complacency toward its customers. Product differentiation is eroding. The change is driven by intensified compensation, deregulation, globalization, and saturation of market segments.

TABLE 4.1

Traditional Mass Marketing versus Customized Relationship Marketing

	Traditional Mass Marketing	**Customized Relationship Marketing**
Objective	Mass Marketing	Customer as an Individual
Focus	Customer Acquisition	Throughout Customer Life
Timetable	Transaction Term	Medium to Long Term
Performance Indicators	Market Share, Product Profitability	Wallet Share of the Valuable (i.e., Profitable) Customers
Customer Knowledge	Segment-Based Habits, Behavior Modeling, Occasional Market Research	Individual-Based Habits, Behavior Modeling, Prediction
Product	Stand-Alone Product	Product and Service
Price	General Price Reductions	Customer Loyalty-Based Differential Pricing
Channels	Traditional Channels	New Technology Channels
Sales	Salesman as the *lone hunter*	Team Sales Sales Automation
Communication	One Way Brand Oriented	Two Way Interactive Personalized

Internal business processes are being reengineered as never before, but process changes are initiated, designed, implemented, and evaluated in terms of meeting the needs of the customer (see Chapter 7, section "An Enterprise BPM Methodology"). These businesses are organized for customer centricity and responsiveness, not for the routine performance of standardized predefined tasks.

Customer needs and values can be defined in terms of the following:

- The need for relationship: Customers with a high "need for relationship" place a high value on the supplier's ability to understand their needs, their organization, strategy, and challenges; and their future plans.
- The need for information: Customers with a high "need for information" place a high value on the supplier's ability to provide all relevant information on the company, its products, and services enabling them to make an informed decision regarding using the company's products and services.

Accordingly, Figure 4.4 presents a map that classifies customers depending on what customers value most:

- Transaction oriented
- Relationship oriented

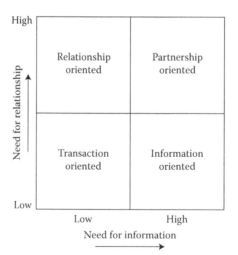

FIGURE 4.4
Types of customer relationships.

- Information oriented
- Partnership oriented

For a successful CRM program that can produce bottom-line financial results, customer centricity needs to pervade the whole of the demand and supply chain. A process view, as embodied in CRM, assists in achieving this by integrating the downstream customer-facing processes with upstream supply-chain processes. As emphasized throughout this book, the process view cuts through the impeding organizational boundaries to focus on business results for the satisfaction of the end customer.

From Products to Services to Experiences

By the middle of the last century, products, goods, and property came to increasingly mean an individual's exclusive right to possess, use, and, most importantly, dispose of as he/she wished to in the market. By 1980s, the production of goods had been eclipsed by the performance of services. These are economic activities that are not products or construction, but are transitory, are consumed at the time they are produced (and, thus, cannot be inventoried), and primarily provide intangible value. In a service economy, it is time that is being commoditized, not prices or places or things—this also leads to a transition from P&L to market cap as the base metric of success; what the customer is really purchasing is the access for use rather than the ownership of a material good. Since the 1990s, goods are becoming more information intensive, interactive, and are continually upgraded, and, are essentially evolving into services. Products are rapidly being equated as cost of doing business rather than as sales items; they are becoming more in the nature of "containers" or "platforms" for all sorts of upgrades and value-added services. Giving away products is increasingly being used as a marketing strategy to capture the attention of the potential customers. But with the advent of electronic commerce, feedback, and workflow mechanisms, services are being further transformed into multifaceted relationships between service providers and customers; and technology is becoming more of a medium of relationships. In the servicized economy, defined by shortened product life cycles and an ever-expanding flow of competitive goods and services, it is customer attention rather than resources that is becoming scarce.

The true significance of a customer's attention can be understood the moment one realizes that time is often used as a proxy for attention. Like time, attention is limited and cannot be inventoried or reused. In the current economy, attention is the real currency of business and, to be successful, enterprises must be adept in getting significant and sustained mind share or attention of their prospects or customers. As with any other scarce and valuable resource, markets for attention exist both within and outside the enterprise. For extracting optimum value, real time and intelligent enterprises must impart optimal attention to the wealth of operational and management information available within the enterprise. This fact alone should automatically put a bar on overzealous reengineering and downsizing efforts (although reengineering and other cost-cutting tactics are necessary, it is essential to ascertain if undertaking such tactics will contribute to the delivery of superior or at least "on par" value to the customers) (see Chapter 1, section "Time-Based Competition").

One major result of this trend toward the importance of experience has been the blurring of lines between the content (the message) and container (the medium) in the market, which we describe in the next section (see Figure 4.5).

Convergence: From Marketplaces to Marketspaces

Traditional capitalism considered market share as the prime determinant of profits. Market share was a classic example of the zero sum game, where increase of market share by one company was typically at the expense of corresponding loss by other(s). Market share, which is a lagging indicator, does not distinguish in favor of valuable, satisfied, or repeat customers. On the other hand, market spaces are defined with reference to a customer's perception of the delivered value and the resulting market size may be essentially limitless. Market spaces typically emerge because of the convergence across disparate or differing industries. For instance, the convergence of computers, data communication, telecommunications, and media industries have resulted in the emergence of one of the biggest market spaces with possibly the largest growth opportunities in recent times.

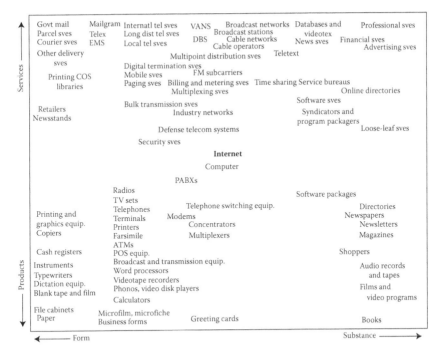

Govt mail	Mailgram	Internatl tel sves	VANS	Broadcast networks	Databases and	Professional sves
Parcel sves	Telex	Long dist tel sves		Broadcast stations	videotex	
Courier sves	EMS	Local tel sves	DBS	Cable networks	News sves	Financial sves
				Cable operators		Advertising sves
Other delivery			Multipoint distribution sves	Teletext		
sves		Digital termination sves				
Printing COS		Mobile sves	FM subcarriers			
libraries		Paging sves	Billing and metering sves	Time sharing Service bureaus		
			Multiplexing sves			Online directories
		Bulk transmission sves		Software sves		
Retailers			Industry networks	Syndicators and		
Newsstands				program packagers		Loose-leaf sves
		Defense telecom systems				
		Security sves				

Internet

Computer

PABXs

	Radios		Software packages	
	TV sets			Directories
Printing and	Telephones	Telephone switching equip.		Newspapers
graphics equip.	Terminals	Modems		Newsletters
Copiers	Printers	Concentrators		Magazines
	Farsimile	Multiplexers		
	ATMs			
Cash registers	POS equip.			Shoppers
Instruments	Broadcast and transmission equip.			Audio records
Typewriters	Word processors			and tapes
Dictation equip.	Videotape recorders			Films and
Blank tape and film	Phonos, video disk players			video programs
	Calculators			
File cabinets	Microfilm, microfiche			
Paper	Business forms	Greeting cards		Books

◄────── Form   Substance ──────►

FIGURE 4.5

Spectrum of offering (product/service) versus medium (or form or container)/message (or substance or content).

Convergence describes the phenomenon in which two or more existing technologies, markets, producers, boundaries, or value chains combine to create a new force that is more powerful and more efficient than the sum of its constituting technologies. The value chain migration alludes to the development of real-term systems that integrate supply-chain systems and customer-facing systems, resulting in a single and unified integrated process.

This convergence is primarily because of three factors:

- The digitization of information to enable the preparation, processing, storage, and transmission of information regardless of its form (data, graphics, sound and video, or any combination of these)
- The rapidly declining cost of computing that has enabled computing to become ubiquitous and available with sufficient power (see Chapter 7, note "Moore's Law")
- The availability of broadband communications is critical to convergence because multimedia is both storage intensive and time sensitive

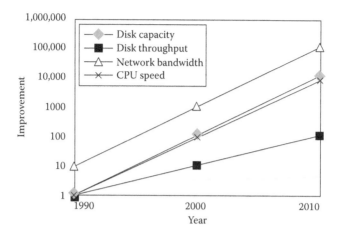

FIGURE 4.6
Hardware trends in the 1990s and the last decade.

Figure 4.6 presents hardware trends in the 1990s and the current decade.

Table 4.2 gives a comparison of communications technologies in terms of the approximate time required to send a file with a size of 1 MB.

The merging of previously disparate technologies, products, and information to give rise to compelling new products and services also underscores the concept of the merging of the container and content that we referred to earlier. Convergence increasingly means that products in the experience economy (see section, "From Products to Services to

TABLE 4.2

Comparison of Communication Technologies

Communications Technology	Bandwidth	Time for Sending 1 MB File
Modern using analog signal over phone line	28.8 kB/s	5 min
ISDN using digital signal over phone line	128 kB/s	1 min
T1 using digital signal over private phone line	1.5 MB/s	16 s
Cable using Modern digital signal over Ethernet	10 MB/s	0.80 s
T3 using digital signal over private phone line	45 MB/s	0.53 s
ATM using digital signal over ATM-switched network	155 MB/s	0.05 s
ATM using digital signal over ATM-switched network	1 GB/s	0.008 s

Experiences") combine the attributes of both content and container in novel ways to create new value chains.

Customer Relationships as a Strategy

Customer relationship strategy is emerging as one of the most important components of corporate strategy. A well-executed customer relationship strategy can result in a number of quantitative benefits including greater ability to upsell and cross-sell, improved customer retention, and reduced cost of service and support.

Customer relationship management has emerged as a corporate strategy driven by the following factors:

- Implosion of product life cycles: This has robbed companies from enjoying the sustained financial benefits of being product innovators for sustained periods. Competitors introduce alternative, substitute, and even improved products much more rapidly.
- Explosion of new technologies: They are enabling even nascent players to compete effectively with established players not only in terms of superior technology but in terms of flexibility, reliability, maintainability, costs, and so on.
- Explosion of new distribution channels: Companies need to effectively integrate interactions through newer technology-driven channels such as the Internet, wireless, telephone, mobile sales, kiosks, ATMs, etc.
- Explosion of competitors: The convergence of industries such as computers, networking and data communications, TV and print media, publishing, and so on, have radically redefined the traditional boundaries between industries resulting in an explosion of the number and kinds of competitors (see section "Convergence: Creation and Growth of Market Spaces").

Ongoing changes rule the marketplace. The only permanent factor is the customer and abiding relationships with the customer alone can buffer the impact of change. Thus, only those enterprises that nurture customer relationships can survive product obsolescence, and overcome the onslaught of superior competitors and still manage to maintain profitability.

Traditionally, competitive advantage came from strategies based on the following value determinants:

Cost	Ownership, use, training support, maintenance, and so on
Time	Cycle time, lead time, and so on
Response time	Lead time, number of handoffs, number of queues, and so on
Flexibility	Customization, options, composition, and so on
Quality	Rework, rejects, yield, and so on
Innovation	New needs, interfaces, add-ons, and so on

Most enterprises have squeezed (and continue to do so) as much as they can from the above value determinants in the last few decades. Now, one of the sources for competitive strategy of substantial value that remains to be exploited in a major way is from enterprise relationships, especially customer relationships, which are truly the real source of revenue.

For instance, in a B2B environment, a leading supplier of aggregates and industrial materials harnessed its CRM systems to help build loyalty and retain customers. However, the company faced the challenge of rapid growth through acquisition of synergetic businesses. The company grew from $140 million in revenues and seven locations in 1997 to $360 million in revenues and 21 locations in 2000. Now it was distributing throughout the United States. With the addition of many new products to its product portfolio (through the acquisitions) the company wanted to be sure that it was maximizing its cross-selling opportunities and that the salesmen had as much information about the different products and each of the customers as possible. This was because the company could no longer depend on the sales representatives "knowing it all" at any instance of time.

Information is Relationship

Companies cannot have relationships with the customers unless they "know" them, i.e., unless they have detailed information on them. Companies have a wealth of knowledge in the files and records that customer-facing employees have on customer interactions. The best way to leverage this knowledge is to free it from the shackles of experience, institutionalize it, and transfer it in real time to all employees, so that they are empowered to build relationships with customers.

As stated earlier, companies are finding it harder and harder to differentiate on factors that prevailed in the 1980s—product quality, operations, logistics, and business processes. Across the last decade, the quality of products has improved, many companies have undertaken business process reengineering (BPR) with reference to enterprise processes, and many businesses have also streamlined their supply and distribution channels. In this environment it has become essential for companies to identify new ways to attract new customers, to maximize the value from each existing customer, and to retain the most profitable ones. Studies show that maintaining loyalty can increase customer profitability between 25% and 85%. Knowing who your customers are and what they are buying is a major step toward ensuring their loyalty without necessarily increasing the costs.

The approximate value of a customer can also be estimated easily based on the information on the defection rate and the profitability of customers by year. Since,

$$\text{Average life of customer} = \frac{1}{\text{Attrition rate}}$$

It is evident that profits are determined not by sales but by the retention rate.

A major step in this direction would be to realize that whereas customer relationships are not all about information, all customer-related information is certainly about customer relationships. And everything else being the same, there is a huge potential in leveraging on the totality of information that is gathered from all the interactions that the company has with each customer. This is achievable by

a. Knowing the customer better than the competition does
b. Employing that knowledge to create better and more personalized interactions in future
c. Incorporating or embedding the costs of switching to competing solutions into current customer relationships

It is interesting to realize that as much as 80% of the sales process maybe controlled by specific knowledge of a customer's business. Information as relationships can help in enhancing the effectiveness of the various functions within the company:

- In sales, it helps companies to make the offers that are most likely to be accepted, and to focus sales efforts on the highest lifetime-value customers

- In after-market service, it reduces customer hassles, lowers costs, and streamlines repair and return processes
- In marketing, it is key to planning, executing, and evaluating campaigns
- In manufacturing and distribution, it helps to forecast optimally delivered solutions
- In design, it guides in the development of product features and style
- In finance, it helps in managing credit risks and opportunities

Customer information-bases within CRMs like SAP CRM, consist mainly of two components, viz., a customer database and an enterprise-level statistical database. A customer database typically contains

- Descriptive data such as the customers' name, address, and phone number
- The customer's status data, such as outstanding balance, line of credit, and preexisting conditions
- The customer's life-style preference data, such as meals, clothes, cars, housing, and allergies
- The customer's history such as search history, purchase history, returns, failed deliveries, complaints, recommendations, and any other data that could affect the customer's relationship with the firm

Customer Capital: Customer Knowledge as the New Capital

Adam Smith helped start the industrial revolution by identifying labor and capital as the economic determinants of the wealth of a nation. In this century, however, the size of the land, mass of labor, and materials that you may possess might be worthless if you do not control the related know-how including customer know-how.

 The information about an asset is more important than the asset itself. This stance also opens up possibilities ranging from coownership, options on ownership, etc., to owner-ship for access/use or even ownership-by-consumption.

In the twenty-first century, know-how will reside and flourish in people's minds; what might matter more are how many enterprising and innovative people you have and the freedom that they have in realizing their dreams. It will be the century of information economics, and, in particular, customer economics. Traditional capitalism made companies more efficient by the classical means of cutting costs of producing and distributing volumes of offerings, rather than giving customers the value they were after. This is why more than two thirds of the companies identified in The Search of Excellence in 1982 fell from grace within five years. Similarly, this is also why so many companies in the Fortune 1000 improved their margins between the mid-1980s and 1990s, but fewer than 40 companies actually grew their total shareholder value by more than 25 percent (see also Chapter 2, section "From 'Built-to-Last' to 'Built-to-Perform' Enterprises"). In contrast to traditional capitalism where it was scarce offerings (and, thus, resources) that produced wealth, in customer capitalism, it is intangible customer relationships that are driving growth and prosperity in the networked economy (see Chapter 5, section "Networks of Resources").

CRM systems like SAP CRM also act as transformers of the knowledge that resides in the heads of the operational and subject experts into a more explicit and accessible form. This corresponds exactly to the tacit knowledge talked about by I. Nonaka and H. Takeuchi in their book titled "The Knowledge Creating Company." These could be learning experiences, ideas, insights, rules of thumb, business cases, and so on. They exhort companies to convert the illusive, unsystematized, uncodified and "can-be-lost" knowledge of the corporation and its customers into explicit knowledge that can be codified, collated, and managed like any other capital investment. This could be in the form of documents, case studies, analysis reports, evaluations, concept papers, internal proposals, and so on. Most importantly, it is available for scrutiny and can be improved on an ongoing basis. CRM performs the invaluable service of transforming the implicit customer-related knowledge into the explicit form (see Chapter 5, section "Best Practice Guidelines").

Customer capital has gained importance because of the following trends:

- Information-based targeted marketing is becoming more efficient and effective than unfocused mass marketing because of factors such as affordable information technology, sophisticated statistical modeling, low-cost communications, and flexible fulfillment.

- Enterprises are no longer dependent solely on the vertical channel systems to control customers' buying behaviors.
- Enterprises utilizing all the data on customer purchase behavior are not only acquiring new customers, retaining existing ones, and cross selling more effectively, they are also linking this data with the corresponding cost data much more efficiently as well.
- Customers have access to comprehensive comparative data on competing solutions resulting in barriers to switch to competing solutions dropping dramatically.
- Competitors' targeted acquisition efforts to wean away more attractive customers are undermining enterprise's mass marketing strategies entailing more-profitable customers subsidizing less-profitable ones to achieve targeted profits.

Increasing Returns and Customer Capitalism

Traditional capitalism encourages managers to focus on short-term rewards that eventually lead to diminishing returns. In contrast, customer capitalism focuses on becoming the customer's preferred choice to ensure an enduring and compounding competitive advantage and sustainable growth, eventually leading to increasing returns, i.e., positive, disproportionate gains over time. With customer capitalism, customers "lock on" to a corporation; and such customers become the most effective barrier to competitive entry. However, this "lock in" is very different from the product "lock in" envisaged in the traditional offering-based mass marketing approach. The latter is primarily based more on product architecture and standards which once established give the customer little or no option and give the corporation quasi-monopolistic powers for as long as that particular technology wave lasts.

Increasing returns are the consequence of a combination of network effects and minimal marginal costs. This situation typically occurs when enterprises have very large start-up costs but very low marginal costs; this effect becomes pronounced with incidence of network effects. Network effects is manifested as a change in the benefit, or surplus, that a customer derives from goods when the number of other customers using similar kind of goods changes. The classic example of this case is the use of fax machines, whose value rises rapidly dependent on the number of other people using similar machines.

Please note that while the positive loops of increasing returns reinforce successes, in reverse, they will also aggravate losses. If an enterprise falters in delivering value to its customers, the "value gap" will get amplified rapidly to pull the enterprise down a descending spiral of ever-decreasing customer values and number of customers.

Leveraging the Customer Capital

Each piece of information in the enterprise, including that residing in the company's information systems, has a value. This value is primarily associated with the manner in which this piece of information is utilized by the enterprise for remaining competitive, providing good customer service, and optimizing e-business operations. If CRM is not to be used as a past-facing system merely for recording and reporting purposes but more as a future-facing handler of strategic information and relationships, implementation of all the basic components corresponding to the businesses of the enterprise is essential. The enterprise should consider a "big bang" implementation of ES, wherein all the base components of the ES (relevant to the enterprise's area of business) are implemented and put in production together. By implementing only certain components of the system, the company cannot hope to reap more significant benefits than those accruing from traditional systems. A piecemeal approach of progressive implementation should be abandoned because delaying the implementations of all basic components together only delays the benefits of a fully functional CRM and, therefore, incurs opportunity costs.

In analogy with the Metcalfe's Law for networks (see note on "*Metcalfe's Law and Network Effects*" below), the value of customer information can be assessed to be proportional to

$$n^m \times d$$

where,

n is the average number of active users

m is the average number of employees involved in any business process from different departments

d is the number of interacting departments involved in the primary business processes of the enterprise

One of the major users of CRM are database marketers whose objective is to automate the process of interacting with the customers to

Identify the customers or prospects with high-profit potential using mountains of data about prospective customers and their buying behavior

Build and execute campaigns that impact this behavior favorably to the benefit of the enterprise's business

Data mining applications automate the process of searching the mountains of data to find patterns that are good predictors of purchasing behaviors based on analyses of past activity. Data mining uses well-established statistical and machine-learning techniques to build models that predict customer behavior.

Table 4.3 lists the various mechanisms that an enterprise can employ to retain, leverage, and enhance its customer capital.

COMPELLING CUSTOMER EXPERIENCES

For an enterprise to get the positive reinforcing loops that produce the increasing returns of customer capitalism depends on its ability to link benefits and deliver a totally integrated experience to its customers over time. The pervasiveness and convergence of information technology are transforming traditional feature-benefit-oriented marketing to experiential marketing. As recognized by B. Joseph Pine II and James Gilmore, experiences have emerged as the latest step in the progression of economic value. However, the experience economy envisaged by them is only another manifestation of the overarching customer economy whereby customers are now demanding not only the quality of the enterprise solutions and services, but also the quality of the experience of using these solutions and services. While solutions and services are external to the customer, experiences are inherently individualistic, involving and engaging the customer's attention directly. The competitive edge in future would lie in staging engaging, compelling, and memorable experiences. Thus, the same product delivered with the same portfolio of surround services may still be perceived to generate varying

TABLE 4.3

Loyalty Models

Name	Description
Personal profile/ data	Customers are averse to furnish or confirm the same information again. This model involves maintaining and sharing existing customer databases to obviate the need to demand the same information again across related functions or corresponding Call Centers, Service Centers, Web sites, etc.
Lethargy	Customers are averse to negotiate the interaction or dialog mechanisms with the enterprise again and prefer to stick to the familiar experiences including searching, assessing, evaluating, configuring, ordering, and paying. Loyalty through lethargy is a very powerful loyalty mechanism.
Customized service	Customers vote for identified and customized service that creates a personalized experience of excellence attributable to the enterprise. The customized service can get configured over time through either user-selected options or a customer profile maintained current.
Making it easier to do business with the enterprise	Customers appreciate informed and nonintrusive assistance while doing business with the enterprise. The information and assistance gets calibrated dynamically suitable to the available customer profile and the current flow of the interaction or dialog.
Personal involvement	In later stages of customer bonding, customers have a great desire to be involved and identify with the specific product design, development, and production support activities or with the brand or even the enterprise as a whole. User groups, vendor-sponsored development communities, sponsored case studies, etc., are manifestations of customers wanting to share a sense of ownership with the enterprise.
Free services, discounts, and promotional incentives	All customers get reassured with occasional rewards for continued relationship with the enterprise—even if, in real terms, these only have a notional value.
Payments	Customers are gratified if they are rewarded, even with small monies or points, for specific actions or activities, be that satisfaction surveys, suggestions on promotional slogans, etc.
Sole supplier	This is akin to attaining the Everest of loyalty whereby customers return again and again despite numerous other hardships.

levels of value depending on the final rendering or performance for individual customers.

Customer-responsive enterprises recognize that customers may not be aware of what they really need unless they experience it and, hence, realize the importance of anticipating rather than reacting to express need after it is too late.

Personalization

Relationships evolve and grow through trust, responses, and the mutually beneficial exchange of value. Personalization is a combination of technology and prior information to tailor customer interactions with the enterprise. Using information previously obtained or provided in real time about these and other customers, the conversation between the parties is altered dynamically to fit the customers' interests, preferences, and needs, so that the interaction/transaction locates the best-suited product or service with minimal expenditure of time and cost. Deliveries are personalized to suit the evolving, unique, and multiple needs of individuals, as opposed to only providing the standard offering in that range that the company makes or has in stock at that moment of time. This strengthens the bonding that enables the corporation to be proactive, and the deliveries to be more customized—this is what gets customers to "lock in" (see "Increasing Returns and Customer Capitalism" earlier).

Delivering content, products, services, and pricing specific to a unique customer's interests and needs is based on collection of information about individual customer preferences, interests, and buying behavior by employing the following techniques:

Customer profiling aggregates data from allied Web sites based on the identification (ID) made available when the customer arrives on an event venue or a Web site.

Collective filtering involves utilizing the prior experiences of a customer or similar customers to devise responses to individual customers.

Advantages of personalization are as follows:

- Higher degrees of customer service to the customer by anticipating their needs delivering content, products, services, or pricing information that meets their needs
- Improving the efficiency of the interaction thus enhancing the likelihood of a purchase being made during the current visit
- Increasing the level of knowledge about customers and understanding why and how they prefer to do business with the organization
- Establishing a relationship that encourages customer relationship and enhanced customer bonding

- Improving the performance with customer site by using tracking to provide insight into factors that have a salutary effect on the performance of the application

CUSTOMER LOYALTY

Traditionally, companies have focused on winning customers, rather than retaining them. The conventional wisdom was that a dominating market share typically translated into production economies of scale and the ability to become a low-cost producer. The goal was to continually add customers to replace those customers that defected to the competitors and also to grow the market share.

However, lately, financial analysis of the cost of customer acquisition versus the cost of retention has shown that, for most enterprises where the cost of acquisition is high, keeping customers can be a more profitable strategy. It is estimated that it can cost four to seven times more to replace a current customer than it does to retain one. On the average, US companies lose half their customers every five years. It is easier to get existing customers to try new capabilities than to engage and acquire new ones. The cost of contacting existing customers, researching their needs, and getting them to begin using new services is minimal compared with acquiring new customers. It is easy to see how effective this approach of "customer loyalty" can be if we recognize that the revenue accruing from customers follows the Pareto's Law: 20% of the customer base accounts for 80% of the revenues and more than 110% of the profits generated by a company. A study published in Harvard Business Review by Reichheld and Sasser concluded that some companies could boost profits by almost 100% by retaining just 5% more of their customers. Mass unfocused marketing is a thing of the past. As stated earlier, as much as 80% of the sales process may be controlled by specific knowledge of a customer's business. As the marketing spend needs to show a higher return on investment, a longer-term relationship becomes essential.

The relative costs for acquiring, retaining, and winning back a lost customer is as follows:

Cost of retaining a current customer	1×
Cost of acquiring a new customer	5× to 10×
Cost of winning back a lost customer	50× to 100×

Customized Relationship Marketing recommends that companies identify their most valuable customers (MVC), and then have a close relationship with them. Many companies may use ABC analysis (for example, identify top 20% customers who account for 80 percent of sales) to identify their MVCs. However, this maybe a misguided effort because, being a lag measure, this would lead to concentration of efforts on customers who although are currently contributing to the profitability of the company may not necessarily have long-term profit potential. The best way of assessing the long-term profit potential of customers is through their Life Time Value (LTV), which we discuss in section "Customer Value Management (CVM)" below.

While most companies measure some form of customer satisfaction, that measure does not determine customer loyalty: Reasonably satisfied customers often defect to the competition. Customer loyalty is different from customer satisfaction per se. For instance, higher-levels of customer satisfaction do not necessarily translate into repeat purchases and, therefore, increased sales and profits. A related problem is that even in enterprises such as departmental stores, that are critically dependent on access to data on loyalty schemes, may possibly be using only about 2 percent of the data to which they have access to. One of the primary reasons for this is the sheer volume of data that is being captured inside these enterprises. For instance, a regular shopper may buy 50 to 100 items during a monthly visit. Many of these stores have 10 to 20 check-out points operating at any moment in time. These can process on an average about 12 customers an hour for 10 hours a day. So, each and every day they are open, they are gathering between 60,000 and 240,000 data points per store. Even for an midsized supermarket chain with about 200 stores, working 7 days a week, this would result in something like 65 million to 340 million data points per working week!

Table 4.4 compares the traditional customer satisfaction-oriented approach with that of the value orientation of relationship marketing.

Customer loyalty is characterized by repeat purchases and a willingness to continue the relationship. Loyal customers

- Stay longer
- Cost less to service
- Buy more
- Provide higher margins
- Purchase across product lines
- Demonstrate immunity to the lure of competition
- Demonstrate less price sensitivity

TABLE 4.4

Customer Satisfaction Orientation of Traditional Mass Marketing versus Value Orientation of Customized Relationship Marketing

Traditional Mass Marketing's Customer Satisfaction Orientation	**Customized Relationship Marketing's Customer Value Orientation**
Focuses on the product—emphasizes the firm's offering or tactical solution	Focuses on the customer/product interaction—emphasizes fundamental needs of customer
Emphasizes product attributes and features	Considers all aspects of the customer/product interaction, viz., attributes, values, and consequences
This is inherently more short term and unstable, leads to incremental or marginal product/service change and improvement, and results in historical orientation	Is inherently more long term and stable, leads to innovation and radical improvements, and has a future orientation
Typically fails to measure trade-offs that determine customer value	Measures the trade-offs that determine customer value
Often difficult to assess in the absence of consequence-level information	Helpful to assess because of available interaction-level information and actionability

There are various ways to represent progress up the ladder of customer loyalty. The Customer Pyramid is one such approach that assists in planning for enhanced relationships with the company's prospects and customers; and is also helpful in visualizing the progress toward higher-value relationships. Figure 4.7 presents the Customer Pyramid consisting of the following:

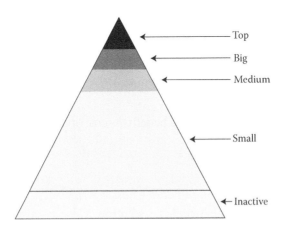

FIGURE 4.7
Customer pyramid.

a. "Top" that are the top 1% revenue customers
b. "Big" that are the next 4% revenue customers
c. "Medium" that are the next 15% revenue customers
d. "Small" that are the next 70% revenue customers
e. "Inactive" that are the remaining 10% revenue customers

The objective of enhanced customer loyalty then translates into the movement of customers in, up, and out of this pyramid. It helps in getting new customers into the pyramid, getting a larger share of the business of the existing customers, and prevents losing those who are most profitable. A 2% upward migration in the customer pyramid can mean 10% more revenues and 50% more profit. Hence, CRM initiatives that are targeted at getting, growing, and keeping valuable customers result in revenue and profit increases that represent very high returns on the company's CRM investments.

CUSTOMER RELATIONSHIPS

In today's world of decreasing margins, increasing competition, and an ever-changing business environment, corporate success depends on an enterprise's ability to build and maintain loyal and valued customer relationships.

In a market where loyalty has plummeted and the cost of acquiring new customers is prohibitive, companies have turned to their current customers in an attempt to retain and maximize the business potential from them.

The value of relationship can be expressed as follows:

Value of Relationship

$$= \text{future value} \sum_{l=1}^{M} (\text{expected benefits}_l - \text{cost of obtaining the benefits}_l)$$

where
expected benefits = *economic cost + hassle + risk*
cost of obtaining the benefits = solution value = (customer value × customer *fit*)
economic cost is typically the cost of delivered solution

hassle includes all noneconomic costs, such as effort required to place orders and locate potential providers

risk includes all the uncertainties about the delivered solution and the cost of protecting against risk such as insurance, inspections, and contracting

fit is delivered solution effectiveness of the customized individual deliveries

The customer-responsive enterprise adds value for the customer even by eliminating the hassle required to research the product and learn how to use it. When relationships exist uninterruptedly for extended periods of time, they improve need diagnosis and deliver solution effectiveness as well as establish procedures that minimize the hassle of communicating needs and responses.

Why Cultivate Customer Relationships

The relationship-oriented enterprise sees the customer not as a single sale but as a long-term relationship in which the value of future solutions will always be greater than the value of any existing transactions. Relationships not only define and determine expectations, but also minimize transaction costs. Good relationships obtain substantial outcomes with a minimum of effort (i.e., cost and hassle). When relationships are positive, solutions are more effective, and the effort expended for making these solutions also get reduced (e.g., the hassles, risks, or transactions).

Such a relationship results in several benefits because

- The parties understand and trust each other
  - Parties have shared values
  - Have confidence in each other
  - Rely on each other
  - Communicate clearly
  - Work more easily together
- The parties are more committed and responsive
  - The parties are willing to pay a premium for the mutual commitment
  - The parties are mutually persuasive rather than coercive
  - The parties resolve delivered solution errors or other differences amicably

- The parties are predictable to each other
- It not only reduces the time to diagnose needs of the customer, but also reduces diagnosis errors
- The parties develop the solutions jointly
- The parties integrate schedules mutually

Relationships based purely on contracts may not be long lasting because no contract can be comprehensive enough to cover all possible future eventualities. The purpose of a contract is primarily to eliminate uncertainties regarding delivered solution commitments in terms of scope, functionality, schedule, costs, etc. Consequently, especially in these times of market change and turbulence, contracts tend to restrict responsiveness of the relationships and, hence, eventually the responsiveness of the respective enterprises.

Customer relationships are important because they establish customer expectations. When expectations are realistically high, customers call to seek solutions for their needs. Once the customer does call, the provider needs to respond and reassure the customer. Customers empower people and organizations they trust. Each time their needs are met, the customer's trust is increased. Even if the delivered solution is below expectations, trust levels get restored if the provider accepts responsibility for the problems and makes a good recovery. Few managers realize that more than 80% of customers return if their complaints are resolved quickly.

Customer Interaction Channels

To strengthen customer relationships, companies draw on and integrate information from a wide range of resources to develop insights into customer wants, needs, and values. These sources may include direct contacts, customer information systems, sales reports, call center data, market surveys, focus groups, billing data, demographic studies, and so forth. This may also include prior records and analysis of interactions of the customer with the enterprise. The customer may interact with different units of the business through different channels, but the enterprise must have a coordinated, consistent, and complete picture of the customer available throughout the enterprise. All these impart a greater degree of stability, continuity, and predictability to the customer base, which eases the planning and operations all along the supply chain.

Customers are demanding more access and interaction points with their suppliers. In addition to getting more information from the companies with which they do business, customers are demanding more ways of interacting with those companies—including phone, fax, e-mail, Web, mail, on-site, and so on. Most companies practicing CRM set up call centers, which are able to provide customized services to individual customers. This further enhances the enterprise's organizational memory about the customers' interactions with the company. While these interactions are momentary and could be across many interaction channels, the organizational memory about these interactions (and, therefore, the customer) can be made persistent by incorporating them within the growing customer knowledge base.

Accessibility creates responsiveness. In terms of sales, responsiveness depends upon how easy it is for the prospect or the customer to reach the company through multiple modes of communication and how fast the enterprise can respond. On the other hand, responsiveness in service also depends upon the speed of reply and action (which in turn is dependent upon the speed of executing the corresponding business processes). More than the product itself, it is often the degree of responsive support and service received by a customer that decides between a loyal customer and a lost customer.

Internet: The Web of Relationships

The Web is a key factor in the emergence of CRM as an important technology. The emergence of the Web, like printing and telegraph earlier, has caused a fundamental change in the ease with which people communicate with each other. The Web has enhanced by a quantum measure the ability of many more people to produce information, disseminate it to a much larger audience and that too at much lower cost, much more easily. In some cases, the Web simply offers a new and better way to perform existing services, such as checking an account balance. But other Web applications offer novel products and services that are possible only through Web technology. Customer self-service is the best example of the Web's enablement of customer relationships. It is estimated that a typical banking transaction at a local branch costs about 50% by telephone, 30% at an ATM, and, only 1% on the Web!

Customer Channel Integration

Once we have a proliferation of channels, the objective is to make the sales and marketing as efficient and effective as possible whilst also delivering rapid growth, reduced sales expenses, and seamless services. Figure 4.8

	Engage	Transaction	Fulfill	Service	
Face to face			●	●	$400
Partners				●	$250
Call center		●		●	$40
Electronic	●	●		●	$1

	Transaction costs ($)
In-branch teller	3.00
ATM	0.80
Telephone	0.60
PC banking	0.50
Internet banking	0.05

FIGURE 4.8
Channel costs and channel integration.

illustrates how the strategy of channel integration can be effective in reducing costs whilst also providing the complete functional coverage demanded by customers.

360-Degree View of Customer

In the customer-centric approach, the goal is to provide personal service—recreating the individual attention, flexibility, and understanding that the best neighborhood stores have always provided to their most valued customers—on a mass scale. Meeting this goal involves solving the "many-to-many" problem, i.e., many people within different departments of the enterprise interacting with many different customers. None of the information on interactions is shared across these different departments, leaving all employees involved with only partial information. Each employee has at the most only a fragmentary view of the customer resulting in possibly below-par service, inappropriate product offering and pricing, and ineffective branding. To address this effectively and inefficiently, each of the company's representatives who interacts with the customer needs to have a clear and complete picture of that customer's activity. This holistic picture is what is termed as the "360-degree view."

Achieving a 360-degree view of the customer is critical to

- Interact with a customer in a fully informed way
- Assess the customer's potential value correctly
- Determine the programs that could realize this potential value from each customer

The key is to integrate in a single environment the related data that comes from all points of interaction with the customer. This can be achieved effectively by a CRM system like SAP CRM which will give each employee at each customer touch point a 360-degree view of the Customer. SAP NetWeaver, that is a critical enabler of enterprise-wide integration of diverse applications across various products and divisions, affords the enterprise a 360-degree view of its customer relationships across multiple channels of interaction. It enables every customer to perceive the enterprise as a whole, and also expect to be recognized and valued by the enterprise as a whole. By tracking and managing interactions with individual customers, and making the customer history available across the enterprise, such a system provides companies with the data they need to improve relationships across the board.

One-to-One Marketing

In the traditional mass marketing approach, companies use demographic segments—segments based on standard demographic measures, such as age, income, geography, gender, and marital status—to divide up their customer base and define the marketing program. Whilst this is a step in the direction of recognizing the fact that not all customers are same, this does not address the problem adequately. The problem is that demographic segments tend to be very large or coarsely grained because of which major differences among individual members of such segments, and the corresponding marketing opportunities, are overlooked. This is also the primary reason that standard response rates for direct marketing, such as direct mail, are only about 2 percent.

Don Peppers and Martha Rogers introduced the notion of one-to-one marketing in their hit book, The One to One Future. This advocates the move toward more fine-grained segments, with the ultimate goal of reaching the segment of one. 1-to-1 Marketing treats each customer as an individual, based on a holistic view, with consistent actions across all touch points, and to think in terms of wallet share of each customer rather than that of market share.

Permission Marketing

It is estimated that, by 2004, e-business marketers took advantage of the e-mail channel by sending more than 200 billion e-mails to reach customers, increase their brand visibility, and jump-start sales. This is primarily because e-mail marketing has been assessed to achieve purchase rates as high as four times those achievable using traditional direct mail methods. But with the increasing use of the Internet and other digital channels as vehicles for marketing or selling, the need to manage customer data more effectively in line with government rulings has become very important.

The Distance Selling Directive implemented from June 4, 2000 requires

- The consumer to be provided with information in a clear and comprehensible manner and in good time before concluding any distance contract
- The consumer has the right to the cancel a distance contract within a specified "cooling-off" period
- The consumer cannot be targeted for unsolicited e-mails, faxes, and automatic calling systems for distance selling purposes, unless the consumer has consented to be contacted by the vendor enterprise in that way

Permission marketing is an approach to selling goods and services in which a prospect explicitly agrees in advance to receive marketing information. Conceived by Seth Godin, Yahoo!'s Internet marketing pioneer, permission-based marketing seeks to build trust and involve customers by putting them in control of asking the enterprise to keep them up to date on information and offers that are of specific interest to them. The objective is to gain permission from customers to keep them informed by e-mail, SMS, WAP, or through official channels, on a regular basis of things that are of interest to them.

CUSTOMER LIFE CYCLE (CLC)

Customer relationships evolve over time along with their needs and expectations from companies at various stages. The concept of a customer life cycle provides a framework for understanding and managing these differences at various stages of relationship with the company. Support for the existence of CLC comes from the various studies and research undertaken on new product acceptance, and, Recency, Frequency and Monetary (RFM) analyses.

The different types of customers are as follows:

- Prospects: This is the precustomer stage, where the prospects are not customers yet, but they represent potential value for the enterprise. In fact, managing prospects is much more difficult than managing even disgruntled customers at a later stage. This is because all customers have predefined thresholds of cost, quality, and price for making the "buy" decision. If the company's offerings are not perceived to exceed such thresholds, it may not result in a purchase. But, on the other hand, exceeding them overly also may prove to be counterproductive as such very high expectations are likely to be unmet resulting in difficulty in retaining such customers later.
- First-Time Buyers: A company's customer capital is heavily dependent upon the potential value of first-time buyers. Customers achieve this stage upon making their first purchase. At this stage, the customer is highly vulnerable to defection due to even minor disappointments or the lure of a competitor's offerings.
- Core Customers: Customers advance to this stage when they begin to make repeat purchases regularly. At this stage, the relationship has stabilized, the expectations have stabilized as well and, finally, there are no major changes in the customer's needs or product specifications. An occasional product failure does not trigger defection or even a reevaluation of the firm's offerings. Core customers have the highest and most stable retention rates, they also account for the highest sales per customer.
- Defectors: Customers may reach this stage either because of a massive, though rarely occurring, failure on part of the company or a compelling alternative offering from a competitor or, in a few cases,

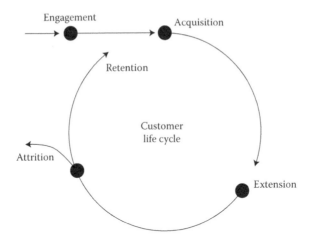

FIGURE 4.9
Various stages during the Customer Life Cycle (CLC).

frequently recurring failure that goes unaddressed by the company for an extended period of time despite repeated reporting by the customer.

Figure 4.9 shows the various stages during the Customer Life Cycle (CLC). The focus of the activities during the various phases are as follows:

a. Customer Engagement: To contact a new customer through marketing, advertisement, telemarketing, personal selling, direct mail, promotions, and publicity.
b. Customer Acquisition: To increase customer involvement through collection of as much information about the customer as possible, understand the buying context, purchase conditions and associated costs, offer postpurchase reassurance, promote the price–value relationship, and, finally, develop the foundation for a long-term relationship.
c. Customer Retention: To create long-term, committed, and loyal customers, develop a service philosophy, identify and close service gaps, manage retention-related costs, increase responsiveness to customers, measure customer satisfaction, and reward positive customer behavior.
d. Customer Extension: To extend the customer's loyalty through first defining loyalty parameters and discover customer lifetime, determine customer lifetime value (see below), learn customer needs and extended needs (e.g., upsell), search and communicate solutions

(e.g., cross-sell), counter defection rates and patterns, bond closely with customers, manage loyalty costs, and reward loyal behavior. Initially, Amazon only sold books, then it added CDs, and now it also sells DVDs, toys, electronics, computer peripherals, and much more. The customer capital model leads to greater customer value once the firm understands how to apply it as a business model.

e. Customer Attrition: To reduce defection rates and patterns through identification of defection parameters (both controllable and uncontrollable), focus on "at risk" customers, arrange loyalty schemes, programs and events, felicitate and reward loyal customers, improve customer satisfaction ratings, extend customer lifetime, discover customer "wish lists" to propose effective customized solutions, and improve customer spend. Despite questionable on-time reliability and poor customer service, the airline industry has been able to foster high loyalty by instituting barriers to the customer's exit including increasing the customer's cost of switching to competitors. For instance, frequent-flyer programs pitch the customer's status in the next year dependent upon the mileage clocked in the current year.

To grow, an enterprise needs to acquire customers at a rate greater than its defection or attrition rate. Unlike customer satisfaction, the attrition rate being unambiguous is an excellent predictor of long-term (non)profitability. To increase its profits, an enterprise must place as much emphasis on reducing customer defections as it does on new customer acquisitions.

Customer Value

Customer Value (CV) is the long-term financial value that a customer delivers to a business and, therefore, is a result of the following factors:

- All income streams, right from the initial purchase through all the subsequent purchases
- All direct variable costs associated with managing the customer
- The envisaged length of the customer's relationship with the enterprise
- The customer's propensity to recommend the company to other prospective customers
- The resulting final value discounted, at an appropriate rate, to calculate the net present value

Customer value could be of different kinds:

a. Historic Value: What has been the total CV till date
b. Current Value: Assuming the current customer behavior to remain the same, what will be the CV in the future
c. Potential Value: What could the customer be worth if we cost-effectively cross-sell, increase their useful life with the company, and encourage them to recommend us
d. Influence Value: What is the value of the sales that the customer indirectly influences through reference, referrals, and the like

 Cocreation or coproduction of customer value occurs when the enterprise delivers the value desired by the customer with the active participation of the customer. This is such a significant concept that it would need another book in itself to explore it to its full potential and depth. In the cocreation of value, the customer contributes time, effort, or resources essential for the selection, production, packaging, and delivery of the offering or services. Because of the coparticipation of the customer in the production and delivery of the offering and services, inherently, there is an assured minimum level of customer satisfaction. ATM systems, Self-Service Restaurants, etc., are typical examples of value cocreating systems, but the best exemplars of value cocreating systems are Internet-based applications.

Customer Lifetime Value

As mentioned above, the Customer Lifetime Value (LTV) is measured typically on an individual customer basis by tracking all transaction and expense details. This information is used to project the Net Present Value of future revenue streams from this customer throughout the envisaged lifetime of this customer.

The kinds of data that are essential for calculating LTV include

a. Customer Transaction History
   - What was the revenue generated from the purchase
   - What was purchased
   - How much was purchased
   - When it was purchased

- Where it was purchased
- What were the special offers/promotions
- What was returned/canceled

b. Revenue History
  - Initial Revenue
  - Incremental Revenue
  - Service and Support Revenue

c. Promotion History

d. Costs
  - Acquisition costs
  - Product costs
  - Incremental sales costs
  - Incremental product costs
  - Ongoing service and support costs

A general formula for LTV can be defined as follows:

Customer LTV = Value (Initial Revenue – Costs)

$\qquad$ + Net Present Value (Loyalty * (Future Revenue – Costs)

$\qquad$ + Net Present Value (Loyalty * Influence Value)

The LTV for various customers may also be helpful in identifying several groups of customers who have similar patterns of behavior, which in turn could be helpful in tailoring value propositions to such identified groups of customers.

The Customer Lifetime Value (LTV) is easier to predict if it incorporates a recurring number of the corresponding product's use cycle(s). For instance, if the average use cycle of a vehicle costing $20,000 is five years, the CV for a single vehicle owning customer with the relevant "customer lifetime" of about 40 years, may range between $140,000 and $200,000. The LTV of this customer will be much larger because of additional values representing warranty, maintenance, repair, and other services during the use cycle of a vehicle.

 This is based on the powerful idea of business cycles or the constituent product use cycles. A database of the ownership and use history of product(s) can be used to perform sales projections, at any moment of time, for a specific period for a named prospective customer. It is possible to predict the requirements of a company with a reasonable accuracy based on

- The average use life cycle of a product
- The average innovation cycle of the underlying technology
- The business cycle of the particular company as well as the concerned industry
- The purchase history of the company for the relevant product

This kind of information on enterprises used strategically for sales and marketing could help in improving

- Efficiency of the sales by reducing the time to sell
- Effectiveness of the sales by entering the natural procurement cycle at an appropriate time as predicted by this analysis

CUSTOMER VALUE MANAGEMENT (CVM)

In the process of reorienting the business around the customer, companies are increasingly realizing that not all customers are equal. Different customers provide different revenues to the companies, they choose its products and services for different reasons and, finally, they also defect for different reasons. This range of customer behavior results in widely differing values across the customer base, in terms of customers' future revenue to the business. To maximize profitability, it is important for companies to determine the future value of prospects and customers, so that they can differentiate their marketing activity and business processes to optimize future revenues and return on investment.

Customer Value Management (CVM) is the management of processes and communications designed to maximize Customer Lifetime Value (CLTV) by closing the gap between the current and potential Customer Value (CV). CVM provides a way of measuring and improving the value delivered by the customer to the business and using this as the basis for decision making. It identifies those customers that really count; identifying what it is that they want as individuals (or as groups) and determining how to deliver it profitably.

CVM improves profitability and delivers greater Return On Investments (ROI) by assisting in the following:

- Targeting acquisition efforts and activities at those prospects with the greatest CV
- Developing stronger and more profitable relationships with existing customers
- Observing shifts in CV that reflect changes in customer behavior
- Identifying the gap between current value and potential value, i.e., the value gap to drive targeted cross-sell/upsell campaigns as well as measure improvements in CV
- Ensuring that scarce financial and staff resources are allocated to interactions with those customers with the largest proven CV or potential CV

Any business initiative can be assessed in terms of the how much it contributes in increasing the CV versus the costs involved. But CVM is more than just a new method for calculating the value of a customer relationship or a new way that a business allocates marketing resources and efforts. It is a total marketing system that entails the need to build enterprises, processes, and performance measures that work together to maximize the value of customer capital. In contrast with the traditional brand management approaches that focus primarily on brand equity, CVM treats customer capital as the primary marketing asset. Table 4.5

TABLE 4.5

Comparative Features of Customer Capital and Brand Equity Approaches

	Customer Capital Approach	**Brand Equity Approach**
Product and service quality	Create strong customer preference	Create high customer retention
Advertising	Create brand image and position	Create customer affinity
Promotions	Deplete brand equity	Generate repeat buying and enhance customer lifetime value
Product development	Use brand extensions to sell related products	Use relationships to sell other products
Segmentation	Based on customer characteristics and benefits	Based on observed customer buying behavior
Channels of distribution	Multistage distribution system	Direct distribution to customer
Customer service	Enhance brand image	Enhance customer affinity

compares the features of these two approaches. Whereas, traditional mass marketing and tactics revolve around segmentation, targeting, and positioning CVM is driven by the acquisition, retention, and add-on selling model. In the case of CVM, the marketing mix is determined by the stage of the customer life cycle.

Mass customization of products and services enables companies to market "off–the-shelf" products and services as tailored to individual customers. This reduces the need for standard offerings and their associated carrying costs. However, this is possible only if the vendor has an accurate profile of the individual customer; a good CRM program will generate and maintain this kind of information. Building such a profile also facilitates cross selling of products and services through the different delivery channels available, adding incremental revenues. It can also reduce time to market new products as potential latent demand can be quickly identified and addressed.

Customers as Lifelong Investments

Relationship-based enterprises view customers as lifelong investments and, therefore, their primary objective is to maximize the sum total of the time value of current and envisaged future customers. Relationship-based enterprises focus on accomplishing the intricate and long-term goal of "owning" the customer.

Traditional offering-based enterprises are focused on maximizing the ROI on customers as early on in the relationship as possible because once the competition sets in, the margins and payoff would invariably go down leading to the regime of rapidly diminishing returns. Figure 4.10a shows the classic product life cycle or the "S" curve for offering-based enterprises. On the other hand, customer-responsive enterprises are more focused on maximizing the sum of the area under the curve, i.e., the sum total of the time value of current and envisaged future customers. Figure 4.10b shows the characteristic exponential curve for the relationship-based enterprise. Initially the returns are minimal or even reducing; thereafter with increasing inputs of resources, the returns increase exponentially.

Customer as an Asset

In the framework being proposed here, the customer is akin to a financial asset that enterprises can measure, manage, and maximize like any other

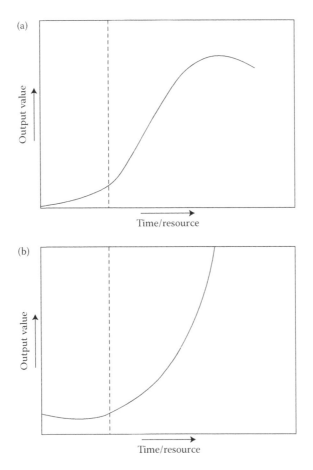

FIGURE 4.10
Value curve. (a) Value curve for Offering-based Enterprises, (b) value curve for Relationship-based Enterprises.

asset. Enterprises can use financial valuation techniques and information about customers to optimize the acquisition, retention, cross-selling and upselling of additional products to an enterprise's customers, and that maximizes the value of the customer relationship throughout its life cycle.

Enterprises that take a customer asset approach differ significantly from those that treat brand equity as the primary marketing asset. The brand approach focuses on activities that maximize a brand's total revenues and the greatest possible returns on the brand investment. Rather than confining attention to singular brands, the customer asset approach focuses on the sum total of net income stream across all brands and

TABLE 4.6

Comparison of Marketing Mix for Customer Equity and Brand Equity Approaches

Element of the Marketing Mix	Customer Equity Approach	Brand Equity Approach
Segmentation	Behavioral segmentation based on the customer base	Customer characteristics and benefit segmentation
Product and service quality	Creates high customer retention rate	Create strong customer preference
Product development	Acquire products to sell to the installed customer base	Use brand name to create line extensions into new areas
Advertising	Create customer bonding and affinity	Create brand image and position
Promotions	Create repeat buying and enhance customer lifetime value	Momentarily enhance perceived value for money; but this depletes brand equity
Customer service	Enhance customer bonding and affinity	Enhance brand image
Channels of distribution	Direct distribution to customer	Multistage distribution system

services. Table 4.6 compares the characteristic features of the marketing mix for the customer equity and brand equity approaches.

Chapter 2, section "Time Value of Customers and Shareholder Value" elaborates on the concept that a company's market valuation/capitalization is truly dependent on the sum total of the envisaged life time value of its current and future customers. The market valuation in turn determines the company's share price on the stock markets. Patricia Seybold was the first one to point out that the success in the customer economy will depend on companies managing their enterprises by and for customer value—they will have to use customer lifetime value (CLTV) as a strategic management tool. The company's source of investor value will increasingly be based on the value of their customer franchise, the lifetime customer value of their present and future customers.

SUMMARY

Customer relationship strategy is emerging as one of the most important components of corporate strategy for competitive differentiation and shareholder value. The concept of CRM aims at identifying the customers that are more profitable to the company, and helps in optimizing relationships with those customers. In today's world of decreasing margins, increasing competition, and an ever-changing business environment, corporate success depends on an enterprise's ability to build and maintain loyal and valued customer relationships. The key to forge long-term, profitable relationships with valuable customers is customer centricity. A major step in this direction is to realize that whereas customer relationships are not all about information, all customer-related information is certainly about customer relationships.

5

Customer-Responsive Enterprise with SCM

Companies have always known that leveraging the strengths of business partners could compensate for their own operational deficiencies, thereby enabling them to expand their marketplace footprint without expanding their costs. Still, there were limits to how robust these alliances could be due to their resistance to share market and product data, limitations in communication mechanisms, and inability to network the many independent channel nodes that constituted their business channels. In addition, companies were often reluctant to form closer dependences for fear of losing leverage when it came to working and negotiating with channel players. SCM is important because companies have come to recognize that their capacity to continuously reinvent competitive advantage depends less on internal capabilities and more on their ability to look outward to the networks of business partners in search of the resources to assemble the right blend of competencies that will resonate with their own organizations and core product and process strategies.

In today's business environment, no enterprise can expect to build competitive advantage without integrating their strategies with those of the supply-chain systems in which they are entwined. In the past, what occurred outside the four walls of the business was of secondary importance in comparison to the effective management of internal engineering, marketing, sales, manufacturing, distribution, and finance activities. Today, a company's ability to look outward to its channel alliances to gain access to sources of unique competencies, physical resources, and marketplace value is considered a critical requirement; creating "chains" of business partners has become one of today's most powerful competitive strategies. No company can survive and prosper isolated from its channels of suppliers and customers. The ultimate core competency an enterprise may possess is in the ability to continuously assemble and implement market-winning capabilities arising from collaborative alliances with their supply-chain partners.

CONCEPT OF SUPPLY-CHAIN MANAGEMENT (SCM)

The supply-chain focus of today's enterprise has arisen in response to several critical business requirements that have arisen over the past two decades. To begin with, companies have begun to look to their supplier and customer channels as sources of cost reduction and process improvement. Computerized techniques and management methods, such as enterprise resource planning (ERP), business process management (BPM), Six-Sigma, and Lean process management, have been extended to the management of the supply chain in an effort to optimize and activate highly agile, scalable manufacturing and distribution functions across a network of supply and delivery partners. The goal is to relentlessly eradicate all forms of waste where supply-chain entities touch while enabling the creation of a linked, customer-centric, "virtual" supply channel capable of superlative quality and service.

In the twenty-first century, companies have all but abandoned strategies based on the vertical integration of resources. On the one side, businesses have continued to divest themselves of functions that were either not profitable or for which they had weak competencies. On the other side, companies have found that by closely collaborating with their supply-chain partners, new avenues for competitive advantage can be uncovered. Achieving these advantages can only occur when entire supply chains work seamlessly to leverage complementary competencies. Collaboration can take the form of outsourcing noncore operations to channel specialists or leveraging complimentary partner capabilities to facilitate the creation of new products or speedy delivery to the marketplace.

As the world becomes increasingly "flat" and the philosophies of lean and continuous improvement seek to reduce costs and optimize channel connections, the element of risk has grown proportionally. Companies have become acutely aware that they need agile, yet robust connections with their supply-chain partners to withstand any disruption, whether a terrorist attack, a catastrophe at a key port, a financial recession, or a devastating natural event like Hurricane Katrina. Enterprises such as

Dell Computers, Microsoft, Siemens, and Amazon.com have been able to tap into the tremendous enabling power of SCM to tear down internal functional boundaries, leverage channel-wide human and technological capacities, and engineer "virtual" enterprises capable of responding to new marketplace opportunities. With the application of integrative information technologies to SCM, these and other visionary companies are now generating the agile, scalable enterprises capable of delivering to their customers revolutionary levels of convenience, delivery reliability, speed to market, and product/service customization.

SCM provides companies with the ability to be both flexible (i.e., able to manipulate productive assets, outsource, deploy dynamic pricing, promotions, etc.) and responsive (i.e., able to meet changes in customer needs for alternate delivery quantities, transport modes, returns, etc.). SCM enables whole channel ecosystems to proactively reconfigure themselves in response to market events, such as introduction of a disruptive product or service, regulatory and environmental policies, financial uncertainty, and massive market restructuring, without compromising on operational efficiencies and customer service. Today's marketplace requirement that companies be agile as well as efficient has spawned the engineering of virtual enterprises and interoperable processes impossible without supply-chain collaboration. The conventional business paradigms assumed that each company was an island and that collaboration with other organizations, even direct customers and suppliers, was undesirable. In contrast, market-leading enterprises depend on the creation of pan-channel integrated processes that require the generation of organizational structures capable of merging similar capabilities, designing teams for the joint development of new products, productive processes, and information technologies, and structuring radically new forms of vertical integration.

Globalization has opened up new markets and new forms of competition virtually inaccessible just a decade ago. Globalization is transforming businesses and, therefore, supply chains, strategically, tactically, and operationally. As they expand worldwide in the search of new markets, profit from location economies and efficiencies, establish a presence in emerging markets, and leverage global communications and media, companies have had to develop channel structures that provide them with the ability to sell and source beyond their own national boundaries. Integrating these supply channels has been facilitated by leveraging the power of today's communications technologies, the ubiquitous presence of the Internet, and breakthroughs in international logistics.

The merger of the SCM management concept and the enabling power of integrated information technologies are providing the basis for a profound transformation of the marketplace and the way business will be conducted in the twenty-first century. The application of breakthrough information technologies has enabled companies to look at their supply chains as a revolutionary source of competitive advantage. Before the advent of integrative technologies, businesses used their supply-chain partners to realize tactical advantages, such as linking logistics functions or leveraging a special competency. With the advent of integrative technologies, these tactical advantages have been dramatically enhanced with the addition of strategic capabilities that enable whole supply chains to create radically new regions of marketplace value virtually impossible in the past. As companies implement increasingly integrative technologies that connect all channel information, transactions, and decisions, whole channel systems will be able to continuously generate new sources of competitive advantage through electronic collaboration, enabling joint product innovation, online buying markets, networked planning and operations management, and customer fulfillment.

Supply-Chain Management Challenges

The major business challenges for companies developing supply-chain strategies include developing capabilities to manage:

1. Value: The value challenge is for suppliers to anticipate and identify what customers value in order to supply a bundle of goods and services that equate with value in order to exchange money for products.
2. Volume: The volume challenge is for suppliers to supply in volumes of their choice, at a time determined by the supplier, preferably in a standardized form. This was a characteristic of the mass-production era.
3. Volatility: The volatility challenge is for suppliers to meet the demands of customers when required by ensuring that capacity can be increased when demand is high and lowered when demand is lowered without incurring excessive or unnecessary cost.
4. Velocity: The velocity challenge is for suppliers to enhance or degrade the speed of response.
5. Variety: The variety challenge is for suppliers to customize products and services per the customer requirements.

6. Variability: The variability challenge is for suppliers to exercise management control in ensuring that goods and services satisfy the quality and deliver criteria per the customer requirements.

7. Visibility: The visibility challenge is for supplier's core capability for managing the total supply chain from source to consumer. Visibility or transparency ensures that parties within the total supply chain know what the current pipeline looks like.

 The integration of systems, policies, and procedures across organizational boundaries between enterprises working together within a supply chain to satisfy the customer has been the catalyst for visibility whilst technology provided the means for achieving the same. Information and communication technology has allowed enterprises to frequently view status reports on sourcing, procurement, production, logistics, and customer demand ensuring that there are no blockages, unnecessary inventories, or unplanned cost build up.

8. Virtuality: The virtuality challenge is for suppliers to replace inventory with information through the creation of digital supply chains supported by ICT. Companies need to focus their attention on customers by creating capabilities that deliver market-driven supply-chain strategies.

Companies need to look at the ways in which they interact with customers at every level, and view each of the above challenges from a customer perspective to devise corresponding supply-chain strategies:.

• Sustainability—Must offer customers' consistent value. For example, based on preferences. Value not simply in their preferences for time, place, cost, flexibility, dependability, and quality. Must identify order qualifiers and order winners and compete managing complexity.

• Service—The ability to deliver different quantities of goods through managing capacity not simply operationally but strategically (no longer sufficient to rely on economies of scale). Developing capabilities to manage capacity flexibly to deliver products and services to customers when they are required in the quantities demanded, e.g., from mass production to mass customization (from n to 1).

- Speedy response—Developing responsive capabilities to deliver goods and services when they are required, e.g., efficient consumer response, quick response.
- Suited to customer requirements—Developing flexibility capabilities—e.g., agile, lean supply chains, innovations, and new product developments.
- Standards—Developing supply-chain strategies to assure customer quality standards are met effectively and cooperating within supply chains to compete across supply chains.
- Systems focused on customer satisfaction—Redesigning business processes and developing enabling strategies for all relevant parties including customers to view supply-chain information relevant to them (e.g., collaborative, cooperative rather than competitive strategies).
- Structures and relationships—For example, developing digital supply-chain strategies to replace unnecessary inventory movements by moving and exchanging information instead of goods.

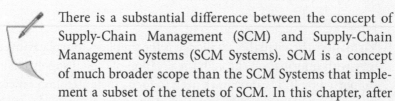 There is a substantial difference between the concept of Supply-Chain Management (SCM) and Supply-Chain Management Systems (SCM Systems). SCM is a concept of much broader scope than the SCM Systems that implement a subset of the tenets of SCM. In this chapter, after introducing the concept of SCM, the chapter focuses on leveraging the SCM-oriented capabilities of the enterprises, while Appendix I includes an overview of the SCM functionality provided by SAP Business Suite (see Appendix I "SAP Business Suite").

Supply-Chain Management (SCM)

Supply-Chain management (SCM) can be defined as the management of intra- and interorganizational processes and activities with the objective of fulfilling customer requirements by delivering goods and services from the point of origin to the point of consumption to the overall lowest costs at the right time and at the highest level of quality.

In order to realize a supply chain, apart from the focal company, numerous different companies are involved from the point of origin of raw materials to the point of consumption by end users; they include raw material/component suppliers, manufacturers, wholesalers/distributors, retailers, and customers. Different customers may need different products and different services, and a different set of companies may be involved for delivering to different customers. Even for the same portfolio of products, different customers may require a different set of value-added services. The last key element in the definition of SCM is the simultaneous focus on cost minimization, time reduction, and quality optimization.

SCM Characteristics

Supply chains can be structured in different forms to improve business performance in areas such as operational efficiency, agility, lean management, customer satisfaction, inventory levels, and response time to market. Once a supply chain is completed and integrated, the supply-chain partners need to evaluate how they are performing in terms of its major functions: The physical, financial, and informational flows.

a. Physical Flow: Physical flow is the actual movement of goods or the delivery of services across the supply chain. All supply-chain partners attempt to optimize the physical flow to ensure that customers receive goods on time and at a reasonable price. information and funds flow play supporting roles to ensure the core supply-chain functions smoothly and efficiently from one business partner to another. At the same time, business partners must closely collaborate with each other and streamline the physical flow to reduce waste. Success at moving physical flow can lower costs and increase revenues. Retailers promote goods to customers in an effective manner so that revenues increase and the quality of customer service improves. If customers are satisfied with the goods purchased, retailers will continue to order from manufacturers. Moving physical goods from upstream to downstream supply chain seamlessly is indispensable to the sustainability of a supply chain.

b. Information Flow: When goods move from one location to another, information requires updation and dissemination to supply-chain partners. The absence of information synchronicity can result in overstocking, backorders, poor decision-making processes, distrust between supply-chain partners, and slow responses to market changes. The real significance of information emerges when information substitutes for traditional physical and funds flow as far as possible till such time when physical goods or funds actually have to move.

c. Funds Flow: When goods move or services are provided, business partners expect monetary compensation from their customers. Funds need to flow in order to support the movement of goods and services from their origins to their final delivery to the end user and vice versa.

Funds flow is essential to sustain the operation of a supply chain because

- A total of 80% of revenue dollars is spent on supply-chain activities.
- Services account for 18% of the total revenue.
- An internal physical supply chain typically contains more than 70% of organizational assets.
- An average of 55% of total revenue in a company is spent on purchased materials.
- Maintenance, repair, and operations (MRO) activities account for 7% of the total revenue in a company.

SCM Components

a. Demand management is the SCM process that balances the customers' requirements with the capabilities of the supply chain. With the right process in place, management can match supply with demand proactively and execute the plan with minimal disruptions. In particular, if managers are proactively managing the demand management process, they need to manage their company's activities that influence customer demand patterns, such as end-of-quarter promotions or financial terms of sale that cause customers to react in totally unexpected ways. Thus, the demand process not only includes forecasting, but also strategies for synchronizing supply and demand, increasing flexibility and reducing variability. A good demand management system uses point-of-sale and key customer data to reduce uncertainty and provide efficient flows throughout the supply chain. In advanced applications, customer demand and production rates are synchronized to manage inventories globally.

The output from demand management is important for several reasons. It can help the company with decisions regarding inventory levels, production planning, transportation requirements, etc. It also provides information required to organize labor, equipment, raw material, and semimanufactured goods. It may also be useful in predicting cost levels for assessing future procurement challenges.

b. Order fulfillment is the SCM process that includes all activities necessary to define customer requirements, design a logistics network, and enable an enterprise to meet customer orders while minimizing the total cost of delivery. More than the functional requirements of logistics, order fulfillment needs to be executed cross functionally and also with the coordination of key suppliers and customers. For example, in complex global enterprises, the finance function provides requisite information regarding tax rates, tariffs, and exchange rates that determines the selection of the appropriate network configuration, thus, affecting the overall profitability. The objective is to develop a seamless process from the suppliers through the focal enterprise onto its various customer segments.

c. Customer relationship management is the SCM process that includes all activities related to identifying customers, building, and continuously enhancing customer relationships, increasing awareness of the company's products and services that address the needs of the customer, enable company's sales, marketing, services, and support to the final satisfaction of the customer.

d. Product development and commercialization is the SCM process that includes all activities for developing and bringing products to market jointly with customers and suppliers. The product development and commercialization process team coordinates with the CRM process teams to identify customers' articulated and unarticulated needs; develop production technology with the manufacturing flow management process team keeping in mind the manufacturability aspects of the product; and select materials and their suppliers in conjunction with the SRM process teams to manufacture and provide the best overall supply-chain process for a particular market/product combination.

e. Manufacturing flow management is the SCM process that includes all activities necessary to move products through its own plants and facilities as also to obtain, implement, and manage manufacturing flexibility in the supply chain via the network of the manufacturing facilities of their suppliers and subsuppliers. Manufacturing flexibility reflects the ability to make a wide variety of products in a timely manner at the lowest possible cost. To achieve the desired level of manufacturing flexibility, planning, and execution must extend beyond the four walls of the manufacturer to other concerned members of the supply chain.

f. Sourcing Management is the SCM process that includes activities for matching the manufacturing plan to corresponding requirements of raw materials and components. Sourcing decisions are especially important when product costs become a significant portion of its price. This involves sales forecasts being broken down to actual needs for items necessary for manufacturing the products. Some components might be manufactured internally and only the corresponding raw materials need to be procured for producing them. For others, semimanufactured or even finished goods can be procured from other company-operated locations or from external suppliers.

g. Supplier relationship management (SRM) is the SCM process that includes all activities related to interactions with suppliers. It is the counterpart of customer relationship management in that just as a company needs to develop relationships with its customers, it also needs to foster relationships with its suppliers. A company forges close relationships with a small subset of its key suppliers and manages an arm's-length relationships with others. The objective of SRM is to build and maintain relationships with key suppliers to enhance value creating capability and advantage. SRM processes are focused on data that provides information regarding suppliers of raw materials, components, semimanufactured goods and services, and so on.

h. Returns management is the SCM process by which activities associated with returns, reverse logistics, gatekeeping, and avoidance are managed within the enterprise and across key members of the supply chain. The correct implementation of this process enables management not only to manage the reverse product flow efficiently but also to identify opportunities to reduce unwanted returns and to control reusable assets, such as containers. The concept of returns avoidance is a key aspect of this process that differentiates it from reverse logistics. The largest type of returns is consumer returns since it is a result of the perception that a flexible returns policy increases total revenue; marketing returns consist of product returns from downstream inventory positions; products get returned by reason of slow sales turnover, quality problems, or changes in the product mix; asset returns comprise of recapture and repositioning of assets like in the case of reusable containers; product recall corresponds to recalling a product due to quality or safety issues; and environmental returns are typically triggered by government regulations. Avoidance has to be with activities that minimize the number of return requests; this dictates that quality standards must be met before the product leaves the company. Gatekeeping refers to the process of minimizing the number of items that are allowed to flow from the reverse channels. This must be achieved without any adverse effect on customer service.

SUPPLY-CHAIN MANAGEMENT FRAMEWORK

Figure 5.1 shows the Supply-Chain Operating model consisting of three principal flows, namely, materials, information, and cash. The squares represent different companies and the lines of connection represent the flows between different companies. The company under consideration is termed as the focal company and is shown in the middle of the figure. Activities and processes related to the conversion of goods from the suppliers (and supplier's suppliers and so forth) up to the focal company are called upstream. Activities and processes from the same focal company to its customers (and customer's customers and so forth) are called downstream. A network structure appears in the figure containing different layers of suppliers as well as customers. Up to and from the focal company, there are first-tier customers and first-tier suppliers. Upstream, the supplier's supplier is the second-tier supplier and the same tier structure occurs downstream (see Figure 5.2).

Figure 5.3 shows supply-chain structures for different industries.

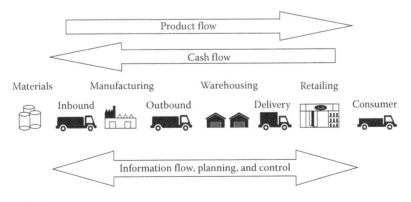

FIGURE 5.1
Classic supply-chain operating model.

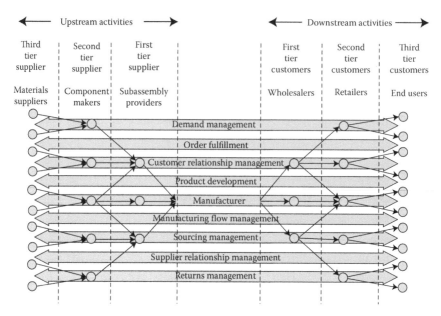

FIGURE 5.2
Network structure in supply chain.

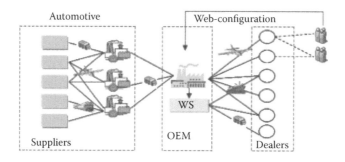

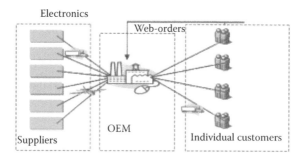

FIGURE 5.3
Supply-chain structures examples.

Four SCM patterns can be highlighted:

a. Internal pattern: This corresponds to the activities and process flow of material, information, and cash within the company under focus. Elements in the internal supply chain may be the function and process related to demand management, order handling, planning, sourcing and purchasing, inventory management, warehousing, manufacturing, transportation, and quality inspection.

b. Bilateral pattern: This corresponds to the activities and process flow of material, information, and cash between two companies or two companies within the same group. The bilateral pattern spans the whole spectrum of business relationships from transaction-based arm's-length relationships to close business relationships based on trust and shared information. This pattern can be applied in projects like Vendor Managed Inventory (VMI) that seek to make optimization between the focal company and one of its suppliers.

c. Chain pattern: This corresponds to a linear chain of companies engaging in goods and services. The chain is as vulnerable as its weakest link in the "chain."

d. Network pattern: This corresponds to the richest interaction in global and complex business networks with the exchange of material and information occurring both horizontally and vertically. Moving beyond the traditional linear chain, the network pattern highlights optimization between the focal company and several of its competing suppliers.

Supply-Chain Performance Framework

The growing importance of the management of supply chains has motivated researchers and practitioners to develop and implement measures that can be used to establish supply-chain performance. The measurement of supply-chain performance requires the creation of an interorganizational assessment system. Such systems can feasibly be used to identify high-performance entities and best practices.

a. Volume
   Customers now prefer customized products that are aligned with their specifications and preferences.

Key concepts associated with volume are
1. Product functionality and features are cocreated with customers
2. Products are engineered on platforms incorporating all the prerequisite systems and support
3. Production processes that use postponement to configure the final product as close as possible to the point of delivery

b. Volatility

Enterprises need the prompt ability to scale up or scale down operations, or engage or disengage outsourced capacities depending on the surge or slack in customer demand. This would enable avoiding lost sales or preventing lost operational capacities matching the volatility in customer demands.

Key concepts associated with volatility are
1. Lead time essential for initiating scaling up or down internal capacities, or engaging or disengaging external outsourced capacities
2. Resources essential for initiating scaling up or down internal capacities, or engaging or disengaging external outsourced capacities

c. Velocity

The result of increasing operational velocity will translate into an increase in asset velocity-inventory and cash flow. Far too often, enterprises try to increase asset velocity by reducing inventory without appropriate changes in policies and processes to reduce time and/or increase frequency. This customarily results in poorer customer service. Without the underlying changes (in reducing time and increasing frequency), inventory reduction will only result in lost sales and poorer customer service.

Inventory turns or the number of days of inventory are the two most popular ways to measure inventory velocity. Inventory turns measures the number of times the inventory turns over during a year. It is calculated as the annual Cost of Goods Sold (COGS)/Average Inventory during the year. The number of days of inventory is the Average Inventory/Average Daily Cost of Goods Sold. Correspondingly, the Cash Flow Velocity is the sum of Account Receivable days minus the Accounts Payable days.

While reducing time, one distinguishes between four characteristic times:

- Need time: The time between when a customer requests a product or service and when they need to get that product or service fulfilled
- Lead time: The time it takes to fulfill a customer request
- Cycle time: The time taken for each of the process elements
- Wait time: The time between process elements, spent waiting for people, resources, assets, materials, cash, and so forth, to start a process element

The gap between the need time and lead time is what creates the need for inventory.

Unlike the time element of velocity, the frequency aspect of velocity has largely been neglected. Frequency of sourcing, manufacturing, replenishment, and customer service have a critical role in improving velocity. Improving frequency directly improves the velocity of operations and reduces cycle stock requirements dramatically. Since forecasts have to be made over a shorter duration, the safety stock requirements also decline. Just like manufacturing frequency needs to be traded off with setup time and costs, replenishment frequency will have to be traded off with truckload considerations. If truckload considerations come in the way of increasing frequency, multistop routes that together make a truckload can be another strategy to increase the replenishment frequency.

Thus, key concepts associated with velocity are

1. Asset velocity is the result of improving operational velocity
2. The gap between need time and lead time determines the amount of inventory needed
3. Frequency is a largely untapped way of increasing velocity

d. Variety

Customers demand more and more differentiated offerings. If there is a way you can deal with variety without its associated costs of complexity, you have got the best of both worlds—the variety that customers love, with the simplicity that employees and shareholders love. The 80/20 rule is one of the best ways to measure variety; what this rule states is that 20% of causes contribute to 80% of the results. The 20% of the businesses, customers, employees, processes, facilities, and products that contribute to 80% of the revenues, economic surplus, and cash flow represent good variety.

Thus, key concepts associated with variety are
1. Variety or complexity tends to slow down systems
2. Distinguish between good and bad variety in the context of businesses
3. Costs of differentiation and increased variety are more than compensated for by increased revenues
4. Complexities and costs associated with increased variety outweigh the increased revenues

e. Variability

Processes will always have variability in the inputs (e.g., supplier lead time variability, yield, etc.) they receive, the outputs they produce (e.g., customer demand variability, product quality, etc.) and the products and services they deliver (e.g., fill rate, plan compliance, etc.).

Key concepts associated with variability are
1. All processes have variability: There is variability in the inputs they receive, the outputs they produce, and in the resources, costs, and time they consume to produce those outputs.
2. Controlling variability: Minimizing it wherever possible; if not, minimizing its impact by buffering against the variability where it matters most.
3. Differentiating between common causes that do not need intervention and special causes that can be improved.

f. Visibility

Visibility problems exist not only between enterprises, but is also equally prevalent within enterprises. Enterprises create teams to ensure specialized competencies are created and nurtured. Over time, each of the teams starts to work within its silos, and the walls that get created distort visibility across the enterprise. Each team begins to create its own set of numbers (forecasts, inventory buffers) that result in a lot of local optimization, but at the cost of global optimization. This distorts "demand" and creates "bullwhip" effects within the enterprise.

The beer game illustrates the distortions caused by poor visibility. The three participants in the game—the retailer, the wholesaler, and the marketer or manufacturer—share little data among themselves other than the orders placed. Each participant also tries to maximize his or her "patch." As a result, when there is a small change in demand at the retailer's end, it causes a "bullwhip" effect that results in bigger changes in "demand" for the wholesaler, and even bigger changes in "demand" for the marketer/manufacturer. First there is growing demand that cannot be met. Orders build throughout the system; inventories get depleted and backlogs grow. Then the beer arrives en masse while incoming orders suddenly decline, and everyone ends up with large inventories they cannot unload.

Key concepts associated with visibility:

1. Improve visibility within the organization by designing policies, processes, performance measures, and systems that breakdown the visibility barriers between marketing, sales, planning, manufacturing, distribution, and transportation
2. Gain visibility to customers' sales at the stores, the events, and promotions they are planning and their impact on forecasts, and the inventories they have at the stores and DCs
3. Provide visibility to suppliers

g. Virtuality

Enterprise need the ability to instanciate internal real or outsourced virtual business electronic-processes essential for any part of the operations.

Key concepts associated with virtuality are

1. Interoperable business electronic-processes
2. Characteristic metrics and measures for monitoring the virtual processes which can be looped back to the virtual process for sfine-tuning the performance of the concerned operations

Supply-Chain Performance Measurement

The growing importance of the management of supply chains has motivated researchers and practitioners to develop and implement measures that can be used to establish supply-chain performance. The measurement of supply-chain performance requires the creation of an interorganizational assessment system. Such systems can feasibly be used to identify opportunities for improved supply-chain efficiency and competitiveness, to help understand how companies operating in supply chains affect each other's performance, to support the supply chain in satisfying consumer requirements and to assess the result of an implemented initiative.

Any business may be able to identify a multitude of measures to provide some perspective on supply-chain performance. These can be categorized into

a. Strategic
   - Total cash flow time
   - Rate of return on investment
   - Flexibility to meet particular customer needs
   - Delivery lead time
   - Total cycle time
   - Level and degree of buyer–supplier partnership, and
   - Customer query time
b. Tactical
   - Extent of cooperation to improve quality
   - Total transportation cost
   - Truthfulness of demand predictability/forecasting methods
c. Operational
   - Manufacturing cost
   - Capacity utilization
   - Information-carrying cost
   - Inventory-carrying cost

CUSTOMER RESPONSIVENESS

It comes as a revelation that customers are neither necessarily looking for more products and services, nor are they looking for a wider range of choices. Customers simply want solutions to their individual needs—when, where, and how they want it. The goal of a responsive enterprise is the cost-effective delivery of an interactively defined need of a customer.

In traditional mass marketing, the primary focus is on the offering and the goal is the sales transaction (see Table 4.4, "Customer Satisfaction Orientation of Traditional Mass Marketing versus Value Orientation of Customized Relationship Marketing"). It is the offering (whether tangible or intangible) that must be defined, produced, and distributed. All measures of activity, viz., cost, revenue, and profits, are based on the offering. Mass marketing enterprises emphasize deterministic planning, e.g., the best offering, the best way to produce and deliver the offering, and the best way to inform potential customers about the offering, and so on. The "best" method is typically based on the anticipated need of a prototypical customer who represents the needs of the target market. Success depends on how many customers buy the offering. In customized marketing, the focus is on flexibility—the flexibility to obtain the capability and capacity needed to respond quickly to a wide variety of individual customer requests. Customer-responsive activities are used to find the best way to solve individual customer needs. In customized relationship marketing (or, in short, customized marketing), the emphasis is on delivered solution effectiveness (i.e., how well the individual problems are communicated, diagnosed, and solved) and delivered solution efficiency (how few resources are required to solve the problems).

While mass marketing enterprises try to sell a single product to as many customers as possible, customized marketing enterprises try to sell to a single customer as many products across as many different product lines over as long a period of time as possible. CRM Systems like SAP CRM gives enterprises the ability to interact "One-to-One" with individual customers and the ability to produce in response to individual customer requests.

The mass marketing and customized marketing approaches are organized very differently. The mass marketing approach anticipates customer needs and defines solutions before interacting with the customers, while the customized marketing approach involves developing a process that allows interaction with each individual customer One-to-One to define his or her need and then to customize the delivered solution in response to that need. Each type of marketing requires a different type of enterprise.

When the inflexibilities are because of natural causes beyond control of the enterprise, competitors will not be able to gain a responsive edge and, hence, competitive advantage. However, to the degree that inflexibilities are institutionally caused by organizational structure, processes, or strategies, the inflexibility is self-inflicted, and the enterprise should definitely be liberated from such inflexibilities to make it customer responsive. True customer centricity is reflected in the enterprise transitioning from providing customers a range of choice offerings to providing solutions to the specific needs of the customers; until the enterprise becomes customer centric, the emphasis will be on the offering, not on the responsiveness. In the offering-based approach, when the range of offerings is small and demand is relatively stable, enterprises can focus on producing and mass marketing more new offerings, and, rely on the customer attending to the best of these offerings. As against this, in the customer-responsiveness-based or customized marketing approach, rather than merely proliferating the number of offerings, enterprises focus on meeting the individual needs of customers.

 It must be emphasized that contrary to common perception, responsiveness as an alternative approach to management has applications not only for services but also for production activities.

Whereas, offering-based enterprises are characterized by "top-down management," customer-responsive enterprises are "bottom-up management" oriented. As the response is guided by prior organizational experience that is embodied in the best-practice guidelines that are readily available to all frontline workers, the delivery is necessarily effective and efficient. Customer-responsive enterprises are knowledge based rather than plan based. This knowledge base consists of knowing how to divide the envisaged work into tasks, identify individual delivery units capable of performing it, assigning the work/tasks, and monitoring activities to ensure that the tasks are completed as per agreed requirements. Unless the knowledge is captured, it will only be available to those who have experienced it or learned about it. Because it is modifiable, rather than a plan, the captured knowledge becomes a list of "best practices" to guide responses to requests in future. Conditional best-practice guidelines specify the processes required for diagnosing needs and developing customized delivery plans. We discuss development of best practices in the section "Best-Practice Guidelines Management."

a. Advantages of Customer Responsiveness
   The various advantages of customer responsiveness are
   - Improve the fit between the customer's need and what the enterprise delivers
   - Increase profits through customer retention
   - Increase profits by reducing costs
   - Makes the enterprise more change-capable
   Responsiveness reduces costs for the providers by reducing capital costs, making planning activities more efficient and effective, and increasing capacity utilization. The section "Economics of Customer

Responsiveness" looks at several aspects of costs associated with customer responsiveness.

b. Responsiveness Reduces Costs

But can an enterprise be more responsive at reduced cost? Yes! In a career spanning about four decades, Taiichi Ohno spent years fine tuning the principles for controlling costs that became the foundations of the world famous Toyota Production System. He surprisingly discovered that not only the best way for increasing revenue but also the best way to reduce cost of automobile production was to make the system more flexible and responsive! This is akin to the situation in the 1960s and 1970s when manufacturing quality and costs were mistakenly believed to be in the opposition to each other; however, by early 1990s it was clearly established that not only can an enterprise achieve excellent quality at reduced costs but it was also imperative for its success.

Ohno discovered that the best way to reduce cost was also the best way to make the enterprise more responsive: Customer-responsive management was the most cost-effective way to solve customer needs. Toyota found that to control costs, they had to separate capacity scheduling (capacity management) from the work dispatching (task assignments): The responsiveness was not necessarily limited because of the constraints, or inflexibilities, or limitations of the infrastructure but primarily because of the inflexible way the deliveries are scheduled and assigned (i.e., coordinated, monitored and, if delayed, expedited).

c. Customer Responsiveness is Activity Based

Customer responsiveness is activity based, where every activity is constituted of four parts:

- The first is an event (whether internal, external, regular, or dramatic) that triggers the response
- The second defines the actions or tasks (guided by existing or customized best-practice guidelines) that need to be taken in response to the event
- The third, is the assignment (i.e., JIT coordination) of the identified actions to resources with appropriate capability and capacity, in response to the event. Assignment minimizes lead time and thus contributes in enhancing flexibility
- Finally, the desired benefits are delivered to the customer

Salient Aspects of Customer Responsiveness

A major part of the following sections has been inspired by the insightful book entitled "Customer-Responsive Management: The Flexible Advantage" authored by Frank W. Davis and Karl B. Manrodt. The literature on enterprise responsiveness is rather limited, but this book is an exception and had a lasting impression on the author in that it ignited an abiding interest into the nature of responsiveness and the characteristics of responsive enterprises.

Salient aspects involved with Customer Relationship Management are as follows:

a. Needs Diagnosis Management

This involves activities related to identifying, discovering, or understanding the needs of prospects or newer needs of existing customers. Traditional offering-based or mass marketing enterprises typically achieve this through product catalogs, demonstrations, or even product data sheets. However, responsive enterprises achieve this through dialog with the customer regarding their operational or design issues problems, inefficiencies, and so on.

b. Best-Practice Guidelines Management

Best-practice guidelines management is to response-based enterprises what strategic and tactical planning is to offering-based or mass marketing enterprises. It is the management of the enterprise's knowledge base by collecting newer needs encountered, solutions proposed and delivered by frontline workers, and its dissemination to the frontline workforce on a continual basis. It involves activities like development of new guidelines when new resources become available; dynamic modification of existing guidelines when new situations are encountered; and, the periodic review of existing guidelines for continuous improvement.

There are two major categories of best-practice guidelines:

- Needs diagnosis
- Defining work, identifying resources/capacity, assigning work, and coordinating deliveries

The guideline should identify each task required, the skill needed to perform that task, the timing of the task, the conditions under which the task needs to be performed, and the capacity required to perform the task.

Processes are under continual review to verify the result and assess the delivered solution effectiveness and efficiency of adopting best-practice guidelines.

c. Responsive Task Management

Responsive task management is not unlike project management except that

- Customer requirements are often more similar than different, but never completely identical
- Instead of a single big project, it is a series of smaller projects or tasks
- Lead time is typically shorter

It deals with the prioritized assignment list that is used to determine, plan, assign, and coordinate the work steps composing the deliveries to the individual customers. It also deals with the best-practice guidelines that must be developed to oversee the assigning, tracking, and delivery process.

d. Responsive Capacity Management

Responsive capacity management is the process of maximizing capacity utilization to deliver benefits to their customers. It is the process of minimizing unutilized capacity because whereas delivered capacity generates revenue, unutilized capacity creates only additional cost as this wasted capacity cannot be inventoried. As discussed in the following, capacity is scheduled in the short term but sold only in the real term.

The various methods utilized to maintain high utilization are as follows:

- Forecasting needs so that access capacity is not scheduled in the short term—the ideal situation being the matching of capacity scheduling to capacity utilization.
- Cross training of employees so that the same capacity can be used for a wider variety of tasks; this is counter to the tendency of specialization in mass production or offering-based enterprises.
- Developing cooperative networks for real-term flexibility; the main driver for this method is the fact that the cost of transactions coupled with the cost of interfacing, collaboration, coordination, and communication between enterprises maybe be lower than the cost of those transactions being undertaken by a vertically integrated enterprise. Mass production or offering-based enterprises are more

amenable to "cooperative partnerships" that are oriented toward long-term, steady-state, and continuous relationships. Typically, a customer will have a limited number of cooperative partnerships because while it ensures the customer a consistent and reliable supply of know-how and offerings, it also ensures steady business for the provider. However, customer-responsive enterprises, rather than limiting the number of partners, lay more emphasis on developing a large network of providers (each having their own special core competency) to increase the range of capabilities that they can access to meet their customer's needs. Instead of emphasizing steady-state relationships, customer-responsive enterprises focus more on obtaining a greater diversity of capabilities by enabling ready access to a broader network of solution-delivering units (i.e., resources) that are available for assigning on an as-needed basis at any instant, at a lower cost, seamlessly, and with minimal friction.

Please also see the section "Economics of Customer Responsiveness" below.

e. Resource Interface Management

Interface management is not unlike channel management whose prime objective is to minimize the number of interfaces and to continuously optimize the performance of the existing interfaces in line with the business objectives and strategies of the enterprise. The more diverse the final customer needs, the broader the network necessary to provide access to more core competencies (i.e., capabilities); the greater the variation in capacity needs, the greater the depth of the network required to ensure the capacity required for each core competency. For enterprises to be flexible, they need access and the ability to integrate, assign, and coordinate the delivered solution at a very low cost. Whereas efficient network interface management enables network members to actually become additional solution-delivering units for the response-based enterprise just as in-house delivery units do, inefficient interface management forces the enterprises to integrate vertically, thus, limiting its options for access solely to the capabilities (i.e., core competencies) of its in-house delivery units.

With successful interface management, an enterprise has advantages like

- Virtually all enterprises can become part of the delivery network
- Thus, the enterprise has virtually unlimited capability and capacity at its disposal to serve the needs of its customers

- Thus, the enterprise can focus on meeting the needs of the customer unfettered by the need to find a revenue-generating use for existing unused in-house capacity

f. Customer Service Management

As discussed in Chapter 4, section "From Products to Services to Experiences," products are rapidly being equated as the cost of doing business rather than as sales items; they are becoming more in the nature of "containers" or "platforms" for all sorts of upgrades and value-added services. This allows the enterprise to initiate and maintain a long-term relationship with the customer. By this reason platforms are often sold at cost, or even being given away free, in the expectation of selling even more lucrative services to the customer over the lifetime of the product, or rather, more correctly, the lifetime of the customer!

In these times of rapid product obsolescence and continual onslaught of superior competitors a sustainable competitive advantage can only be obtained through services, such as

- Tailor-made designs
- Just-in-time logistics
- Installation of equipment
- Customer training
- Documentation of goods
- Maintenance and spare part service
- Service recovery and complaints management
- Handling of enquiries
- Customer-oriented invoicing
- Pricing below market standard

In the servicized economy, defined by shortening product life cycles and the ever expanding flow of competitive goods and services, it is customer attention rather than resources that is becoming scarce. Giving away products is increasingly being used as a marketing strategy to capture the attention of potential customers. A growing number of enterprises are giving away their products for free to attract customers, and then charging them for managing, upgrading, and servicing for uninterrupted availability and usage of the products. Microsoft, after initially missing the Internet-wave, invested massively to come up with a reasonably competitive Internet

Explorer (IE) Web browser, but decided to give away this Web browser for free to its customers.

Especially in the case of software companies, the cost of producing and delivering individual product orders is almost zero, hence, if enough number of customers "hook" on to the company's product and if the enterprise can set its product as an industry standard, it can sell upgrades and services at significant margins. The more the number of customers linked together through an enterprise's program (see note "Metcalfe's Law and Network Effects" below), the more the benefits to each of the participating customers and, consequently, the following are more valuable:

- Services provided by the enterprise (at much lower cost, because the costs are spread across a much larger installed base of customers)
- The attendant long-term relationships with the customer

Customer-Responsive Management

The traditional philosophy of management focused on mass production was developed during the twentieth century. The foundation of mass production is based on

- Eli Whitney's concept of interchangeable parts
- Ford's development of the production line
- Frederick W. Taylor's scientific management
- GM and Dupont's cost accounting methods

Mass-production management focused on large-scale production and mass marketing of standardized, low-cost products produced for homogenous markets. Customers' are researched so that the right product is offered to the market place. This approach results in centralized product planning, process planning, production scheduling, and market planning that is separated from the daily operations. When the change is gradual and incremental, the traditional make-and-sell enterprises focus on optimizing the efficiency of execution in terms of the following:

- Predicting or forecasting or projecting market demand
- Minimizing the cost of making and selling the corresponding offering

In contrast, when the customer-driven change becomes rapid and essentially unpredictable, adaptiveness takes precedence over efficiency: Enterprises need to sense the needs of the customer early and respond in the real term, individual customer by individual customer. The sense-and-respond enterprise becomes a pool of modular capabilities that can be dynamically configured and reconfigured to respond to the customer's latest requirements. Therefore, in make-and-sell enterprises the plan comes first, while in the sense-and-respond enterprises the customer comes first; make-and-sell enterprises primarily focus on what is common among many customers rather than what is different about individual ones (see Chapter 4, section "One-to-One Marketing"). The customer commitment rather than the command-and-control structure defines the dynamic interactions between the modular capabilities.

Customer-Responsive Management (*crm*) enables enterprises to be more adaptable to changing conditions and responsive to smaller markets. The responsiveness could be in terms of

a. Timeliness (e.g., a schedule)
b. Time window (i.e., by a specified time range)
c. Priority (e.g., a dynamic dispatch list)

It recognizes that forecasting and planning become more difficult as the marketplace and environment become more turbulent. The detailed planning of work is done at the front line. The purpose of flexible planning is not to plan all the details of the work but to plan the infrastructure that is necessary to enable and facilitate individual-level changes. *crm* emphasizes taking steps that minimize the time and cost required to recognize and respond to changes. Whereas mass production was based on defining a product and designing the most efficient means of producing large quantities of a product, *crm* designs flexible processes that could make it easier to respond to changing conditions.

Thus, *crm* consists of two major relationships: One relationship is with the customers to identify and diagnose needs, and the second relationship is with the network of suppliers who make the deliveries. For offering-based enterprises, the former corresponds to the marketing function (e.g., market research, product planning, advertising, sales, and customer service) and the later corresponds to the operations function (e.g., purchasing, production, supply-chain logistics, and human resources). For traditional offering-based enterprises, logistics is generally understood as the process of managing the efficient flow and storage of raw materials, in-process inventory, finished goods, and information for conformance with customer requirements. But within the *crm* framework, this logistics concept transforms to the coordination of deliveries that are responsive to individual customer requests using a network of resources, and integrated by flexible processes and communications.

 As emphasized brilliantly by Frank Davis (see Frank W. Davis and Karl B. Manrodt), for achieving responsiveness, the separation of assignment and delivery is critical. It is the frontline worker who interacts with the individual customer to determine individual needs. These individual needs are then used in conjunction with the conditional best-practice guidelines to develop the individual delivery plan. The individual delivery plan, which itemizes each task, schedule, and the responsible person, becomes the prioritized assignment list or Kanban. This list is used to assign each task dynamically to the resource network and also to record the results.

The offering-based deterministic enterprise uses highly structured systems or channels to develop a plan that not only includes the product design but also the channels that will be used to deliver the product to the customer. When enterprises do not have the flexibility to respond to a wide variety of needs, a different system must be established to meet each type of need. This makes it very expensive to respond to new markets. In contrast, the customer-responsive enterprise tends to build and uses networks of resources that it can call upon to respond to a wide range of needs. The customer-responsive enterprise is able to put together a large combination of resources to respond according to initial-conditions-determined best-practice guidelines to a wide range of needs.

The role of the responsive enterprise is to develop an infrastructure that facilitates the integration of the provider network into the solution process and, the assigning and monitoring of each delivery. When the infrastructure works, the relationship is effective and hassle free; otherwise it is frustrating and unresponsive. Similarly, when the infrastructure works, the delivery is efficient and coordination cost is low; otherwise the delivery is late and ineffective, and special recovery mechanisms such as expediting, inspection, signoffs, and approvals must be implemented to work around these shortcomings of the infrastructure. These recovery mechanisms unduly increase expense, slow delivery, and make the enterprise inflexible and unresponsive.

Thus, to be able to respond, the enterprise must create an enterprise infrastructure that includes

- Best-practice guideline development to maintain a repertoire of delivery practices
- Resource network development that identifies resources, interfaces, and builds relationships to ensure that the resources are available when needed
- Information infrastructure development that integrates and coordinates individual deliveries

 The Internet is the classic illustration of a "neural network" on a large scale that displays a "top-down" oversight combined with a "bottom-up" cooperative delivery of digital content.

It displays characteristic features of

- Network Effects
- Small Worlds Networks (SWN)
- Cooperative Patterns
  etc.

We touch upon these topics briefly in the sections below.

Networks of Resources

The customer-responsive enterprise is not aware of the exact needs of the customer until the customer calls them. Therefore, the enterprise cannot ever be more responsive to its customers than its delivery units are to it. The enterprise's ability to respond is determined by the capability and capacity available for assignment. Consequently, customer-responsive enterprises constantly seek to expand core competencies, i.e., capabilities, and the capacity for assignment to serve customers. The more capability and capacity that is available, the more customers can be served.

Because responsive enterprises typically deliver benefits to customers in the form of products, information, or even money, an enterprise utilizes a wide range of resources. Resources typically provide functions (or services) such as transport, storage, security, or processing. The range of resources includes

- Transportation networks resources like satellites (for communication movement), datacom (for data movement), truck lines (for products movement), airlines (for people movement)
- Storage resources such as computer hard disk storage-banks (for e-data or e-content), voice mails (for messages), e-mails (for information messages), warehouses (for products), hotels (for people)
- Security resources like PINs and e-passports (for computer authentication), vaults or refrigeration units (for products), escort services or smart cards or identity cards (for people)
- Processing resources like data processing centers (for data and information), fulfillment centers (for products), janitorial services (for facilities), healthcare providers (for people)

Each of these resources would have a core competency. An enterprise cannot be more responsive than their resources enable them to be. To make responsive deliveries, the enterprise must be able to build a network of resources, develop guidelines that allow the integration of the resources into the delivery task, and information systems that allow the coordination and assigning of work to these resources. The resource units may either be owned by the responsive enterprise or may have a relationship with the responsive enterprise. Not withstanding the legal nature of these collaborative relationships, which could either be a collaborative exclusive partnership or intermittently used network, these resources have to be "always-on," i.e., available when needed, and have the capability and capacity needed to respond to the responsive enterprise's dynamic assigning and monitoring requirements.

Infrastructure development is not a one-time effort, but must evolve continually to allow the enterprise to stay ahead of competition and keep pace with technology and environmental changes. For instance,

- As new customer needs evolve, the infrastructure must enable these needs to be satisfied
- As new resources become available, the infrastructure must readily integrate the new resource into the delivery process

- As new technology becomes available, the infrastructure must allow newer options for communicating, coordinating deliveries, and relating with customers
- As new measurement techniques become available, the infrastructure must incorporate them to enhance delivery coordination and monitoring

The network of resources achieves two apparently contradictory goals: A greater ability to respond to customer needs and a reduction in the cost of the response.

 In fact, analogous to Sun's vision of "Network is Computer," one can say that "Network is Resource Provider!" (see Kale 2014).

Business Webs (B-Webs)

Don Tapscott introduced the concept of a Business Web (B-Web) as a cluster of businesses coming together particularly over the Internet. B-Webs are the mechanisms for accumulation of digital capital consisting of three parts:

1. Human capital: Is the sum of the capabilities of individuals in the enterprise including skills, knowledge, intellect, creativity, and know-how
2. Customer capital: Is the wealth contained in an enterprise's relationships with its customers
3. Structural capital: Is the knowledge embodied in enterprise procedures and processes

The rise in affiliate marketing and the existence of Internet-based Extranets or Exchanges are examples of the rise of B-Webs.

Economics of Customer Responsiveness

Unlike the case of mass production enterprises that define average cost per unit in terms of the constituent fixed and variable costs, customer-responsive enterprise classifies costs into three components, viz.

- Fixed capacity costs: Are incurred to acquire or develop facilities, tools, and skills
- Scheduled capacity costs: Are incurred when the acquired facilities, tools, and skills are scheduled so that they become available to serve customers
- Service delivery costs: Are the costs incurred when the benefits are actually delivered to the individual customer

Consequently,

i. The total capacity costs are the combination of both fixed capacity and scheduled capacity costs
ii. Total service delivery costs are the sum of total capacity costs and service delivery costs

While fixed capacity costs remain unchanged even in the long term; scheduled capacity costs are variable costs in the short term; and service delivery costs are variable costs even in the real term.

For responsive enterprises, revenues are determined in real time when the enterprise interacts with the customer. Therefore, for responsive activities capacity acquisitions, modifications, or abdications are decided on a long-term basis, capacity is scheduled on a short-term basis, and, capacity is committed on a real term (or real time or immediate term) basis. While the capacity acquisition costs are based on the long-term trends analysis, the capacity is usually scheduled on a periodic basis such as accounting periods because of the availability of the relevant information on sales, production, costs, revenue, and inventory on which the schedule is based. As against this, the capacity is committed on the basis of a real-term operational data available in CRM systems like SAP CRM.

Moreover, the role of inventory changes radically in the process of the enterprise becoming more customer responsive. In the mass production (i.e., mass marketing) approach, inventory greatly simplifies the task of managing an offering-based enterprise because it allows the enterprise to manufacture products and ship finished goods to the marketplace in anticipation of market demand. It is the key for enabling various functions like purchasing, production, distribution, and sales to function independently and also seek optimal performance independently. There is no major emphasis on extensive coordination, planning, and scheduling, as inventory is used to buffer purchasing, planning, and scheduling. In times of market uncertainty and turbulence, inventory

- Desensitizes decision making
- Enables longer lead times
- Reduces flexibility
- Reduces complexity of coordination

Thus, in offering-based enterprise the local functional efficiencies and strategies are truly at the cost of increased inventory and inventory-carrying costs at the enterprise level. However, in the mass customization (i.e., customized marketing) approach, enterprises seek minimization of inventory because this not only reduces the costs but also enhances the enterprise's flexibility, i.e., ability to respond to changing conditions. But increase in flexibility also increases the complexity of coordination; the enterprise has to shift from the deterministic planning and scheduling management approach to the protocol and assignment method of coordination.

 However, inventory could change from a large user of capital (because inventory turns slower than payment terms) to a source of capital for financing retail outlets by dramatically increasing the normal inventory turns to much more rapid inventory churns. An inventory churning 24 times per year generates cash flow fast enough to provide its value in working capital to help finance the building of a new store.

As pointed out by Frank Davis, a customer-responsive enterprise does not have the luxury of inventory to buffer real-term variations and reduce management complexity. Although capacity has to be scheduled in anticipation of customer requests, the use of capacity can only be scheduled after receiving such a customer request. If the provider scheduled too much capacity, the excess capacity gets wasted because capacity cannot be preserved in an inventory. But, on the other hand, if inadequate capacity is scheduled, some users are likely to go unserved. As the service delivery costs are typically less than 10 percent of the total delivery costs explained earlier, the profitability of the enterprise depends on reducing the fixed and scheduled capacity costs and maximizing the percent utilization.

For minimizing wasted capacity, responsive enterprises have to enable more flexible scheduling in the short term and higher utilization in the real term. This can be achieved through

- Economies of scope: Approach that allows the provider to increase capacity utilization (e.g., percentage billable hours, load factors, occupancy rates, etc.) through cross training of the workforce.
- Economies of use: Approach that seeks to utilize every unit of scheduled capacity to generate revenue to minimize the amount of non-revenue generating and wasted capacity.
- Economies of modularity: Approach that seeks greater flexibility to schedule capacity by developing modules so that less capacity can be scheduled when the demand is expected to be low. The more modular the organizational structure, the more efficiently the enterprise can respond to variation in expected capacity utilization. One way of increasing modularity is through networking.
- Economies of networking: Approach that seeks to allow enterprises the flexibility to focus on changing customer needs rather than to be burdened with finding a revenue-generating use for inflexible resources. Resources can either be acquired or networked: Responsive enterprises will typically acquire resources where expected demand is continual and stable, whereas, if there is a greater variation in the expected capability and capacity needs, the enterprise will network with resources on an as-needed basis. Acquired resources become fixed capacity costs, whereas networked resources become variable service delivery costs because they are paid on a per-use basis. It may be more efficient to have the resource in-house on a per-hour basis, but on a per-use basis it is more efficient to network for the resources. Thus, the network approach not only enhances the flexibility to respond to the customer needs, but it also makes this possible at a much lower cost!

 The purpose of a network is to provide the enterprise with the range of capabilities and capacities it needs to serve its customers' diverse needs while at the same time maintaining the cost of the resource as a service delivery cost (which is a variable cost in the real term) rather than as a capacity cost (which is a fixed cost in the real term).

Activity-Based Customer Responsiveness

The customer responsiveness of an enterprise is really dependent on the corresponding business processes or activities. As explained in Chapter 1, in CRM the focus is on flexibility—the flexibility to obtain the capability and capacity needed to respond to a wide variety of individual customer requests. Customer-responsive activities are used to find the best way to solve individual customer needs. In customer-responsive activities, the emphasis is on delivered solution effectiveness (i.e., how well are the individual problems communicated, diagnosed, and solved problems) and delivered solution efficiency (how few resources are required to solve the problems).

Enterprises that deploy customer-responsive activities have the following objectives:

- Building relationships so that customers become "conditioned" to contact the enterprise first whenever they have a need
- Establishing the enterprise to provide effective diagnoses and response whenever customers make such contact with the enterprise
- Creating the capability and processes to enable customer-facing members to cultivate deep and long-term relationships with customers; and cost effectively coordinate each individual delivery of benefits

The traditional mass marketing or mass production approach considered a process to be a way to produce a product; it focuses on limitations (e.g., setup time, resource availability, capability of the existing workforce) and develops the most efficient process that can function within the constraints. The focus is on coping with internal limitations (often self-inflicted) instead of on becoming more responsive to customers and the changing business climate. The emphasis is on control rather than performance. As against this, mass customization obtains its flexibility by viewing the process as a way of converting resources into products so that a single process can be used to produce many different products. The balance of control and power has shifted from producers to the customers. Mass customization develops processes to minimize or eliminate limitations (e.g., reduce setup time, locate alternative resources, expand capabilities of current workforce, and develop a network of resources). Customer-responsiveness management develops numerous best-practice guidelines to guide frontline workers as they interact with customers to plan deliveries and enable them to modify them, if necessary, to improve the customer fit.

Therefore, for an enterprise to be totally flexible in responding to individual customers, the enterprise must develop three things:

1. Process(es) for interacting with individual customers and defining their individual needs
2. Conditional best-practice guidelines for defining how the enterprise will respond to various type of customer requests
3. A dynamic assigning system that allows Just-in-Time (JIT) assignment of work for delivery to resources with appropriate capability and capacity

Activity-Based Costing (ABC) for BPR

ABC is a way of linking an enterprise's market positioning to its internal cost structure, i.e., capability. The basic premise is that activities that are realized via the processes, consume resources and convert them into products and services that are usable by customers. Thus, costs are the consequence of resource decisions, and income the consequence of the business processes that deliver value to customers. In other words, the requirement is to improve resourcing decisions as a means of managing costs, and to improve processes as the means of improving business effectiveness leading to improved customer loyalty and, therefore, revenue.

The ABC data is useful as a source to support:

• Profitability management, such as costing and profitability analysis, customer and product mix decisions, and support for marketing decisions
• Revenue and performance management, such as resource to volume and service level changes, activity budgeting, and cost driver analysis

The principle of ABC is based on knowledge of activities, the reason of their existence and the factors that drive them. The BPM effort helps in identifying a list of cost drivers that are allocated to the various activities. These could include

• Volume of materials used, labor hours consumed, parts produced
• Number of new parts, new suppliers, new prototypes

- Number of customers, orders raised, invoices sent
- Number of design modifications, customer warranty claims

and so on. The database of activities can then be aggregated into "pools" of activities that have common cost drivers. By assigning such pools of activities to "objects" (such as products, distribution channels, customer groups), a proper allocation of product and customer costs is then derived.

To build up activity-based product costs, the total for any one product (or a group) would be the sum of

$$\sum_{l=1}^{M} \{\text{Activity-based product costs}\}_l$$

$$= \sum_{l=1}^{M} \left\{ \begin{array}{l} \text{Direct material and labor} \\ + \text{volume-dependent overheads} \\ + \text{variable cost driver-dependent overheads} \end{array} \right\}_l$$

Similarly, to build up activity-based customer costs, the total for a customer (or a group) would be the sum of

$$\sum_{l=1}^{M} \{\text{Activity-based customer costs}\}_l$$

$$= \sum_{l=1}^{M} \left\{ \begin{array}{l} \text{Activity-based product costs} \\ + \text{volume-dependent customer costs (e.g.,} \\ \text{packaging materials or cost of delivery)} \\ + \text{variable cost driver-dependent overheads} \end{array} \right\}_l$$

ABC provides the basis to understand product and customer profitability and allows the management to make decisions both on positioning and capability—the twin pillars of BPM. The understanding of product and customer costs that comes from using ABC provides its real value when the revenue resulting from the total activity within a business area is related to the costs of achieving that revenue.

It is usually possible to trace revenue to customers only if the enterprise operates a billing system requiring customer details or if a membership scheme like a store card or loyalty program is in place. Costs vary from customer to customer on account of

- Customer acquisition costs—sales calls and visits, free samples, engineering advice, and so on
- Terms of trade or transaction—price discounts, advertising and promotion support, extended invoice due-dates, and so on
- Customer service costs—handling queries, claims and complaints, demands on sales person and contact center, and so on
- Working capital costs—cost of carrying inventory for the customer, cost of credit, and so on

If an enterprise wants to assess which of its customers are profitable, it has to be able to trace costs as well as revenues to the customers (see note "Customer-centric Activity-Based Revenue Accounting (ABRA)"). In Chapter 2, section "Economic Value Add (EVA)," we look at the EVA concept for assessing performance of responsive enterprises.

Time-Driven Activity-Based Costing (TDABC)

Conventional ABC systems had many drawbacks in that they were expensive to build, complex to sustain, and difficult to modify. Their reliability was highly suspect as the cost assignments were based on individuals' subjective estimates of the percentage of time spent on various activities. It also made unrealistic assumptions like

- Identified activities (e.g., processing customers orders or enquiries) take about the same amount of time without any variations for particular circumstances
- Resources work at full capacity without discounting for idle or unused time

Moreover, implementing an ABC system for realistic enterprise scenarios (a few hundred activities, few hundred thousand cost objects, and time duration of a couple of years) quickly ended up confronting computational challenges of gargantuan proportions requiring huge computational resources that were beyond the capabilities of normal enterprises. Because of the subjectivity, time-consuming surveying and data-processing costs of ABC systems, many enterprises either abandoned ABC entirely or localized it in isolated units or ceased updating their systems, which left them with out of date and highly inaccurate estimates of the business process, product, and customer costs.

Time-driven activity-based costing (TDABC) gives enterprises an elegant and practical option for determining the cost and capacity utilization of their processes and the profitability of orders, products, and customers. Based on this accurate and timely information, enterprises can prioritize for business process improvements, rationalize their offering variety and mix, price customer orders, and manage customer relationships.

TDABC avoids the costly, time-consuming, error-prone, and subjective activity surveying task of conventional ABC by skipping the activity definition stage and therefore, the very need to estimate allocations of the departments' costs to the multiple activities performed by the department (Robert Kaplan and Steven Anderson).

TDABC defines activity costs with only two parameters:

a. Capacity cost rate for the department executing the activity or transaction
b. Capacity usage time by each activity or transaction processed in the department

Thus,

$$\text{Activity-based cost} = \text{Capacity cost rate} * \text{Capacity usage time}$$

where,

$$\text{Capacity cost rate} = \frac{\text{Cost of capacity supplied}}{\text{Practical capacity of resources supplied}}$$

And, the cost of capacity supplied is the total cost of the department executing the activity or transaction.

Practical capacity of resources supplied is the actual time employees, machines, and equipment perform productive work.

Capacity usage time is observed or estimated time for performing the activity or transaction.

Both these parameters can be estimated and validated easily and objectively. These estimates are not required to be precise; a rough accuracy is adequate. Cost of capacity includes cost of all the resources such as personnel, supervision, equipment, maintenance and technology, and so on, that are supplied to this department or business process. However, the practical capacity of resources supplied is usually lower as compared to the rated capacity because it excludes the cost of unused resources on account of scheduled breaks, training, meetings, setting time, maintenance, and so on.

Table 5.1 compares the conventional activity-based costing (ABC) and time-driven activity-based costing (TDABC).

TDABC does not require the simplifying assumption, unlike that for conventional ABC, that all customer orders or transactions are the same and require the same amount of time for processing. TDABC is not only more accurate but also granular enough to capture the variety and complexity of actual operations. For example, it allows time estimates to vary on the basis of particular requirements of individual customers, or orders such as manual or automated orders, orders for fragile or hazardous goods, expedited orders, international orders or orders from a new customer without an existing credit record. It achieves this through the simple mechanism of altering the unit time estimates or adding extra terms to the departmental time equation on the basis of the order's activity characteristics. Thus, TDABC can readily incorporate many more variations and complexities (in business process efficiencies, product volume and mix, customer order patterns, and channel mix), which adds accuracy at little additional cost and effort, and with fewer number of equations compared (i.e., without creating an exploding demand for estimates data, storage, or processing capabilities), than conventional ABC. TDABC models expand only linearly with variation and complexity by merely adding terms in the time equation; but a department is still modeled as one process with one-time equation.

Consequently, the expressions for the total costs presented in the previous section get modified to

$$\sum_{l=1}^{M} \{\text{Activity-based product costs}\}_l$$

$$= \left\{ (\text{capacity cost rate}) * \left(\sum_{l=1}^{M} \text{capacity usage time} \right)_l \right\}$$

TABLE 5.1

Conventional ABC versus Time-Driven ABC

Conventional Activity-Based Costing	Time-Driven Activity-Based Costing
Tedious, costly, and time consuming to build a model that is error prone, difficult to validate, and localized model	Easier, inexpensive, and faster to build an accurate and enterprise-wide model
Drives cost first to the activities performed by a department and then assigns the activity costs down to orders, products, and customers on the basis of subjective estimates (based on interviewing and surveying process) of the quantity of departmental resources consumed by various activities	Drives costs directly to the transactions or orders using specific characteristics of particular business processes, products, and customers
Complexity and variations are incorporated by adding more activities to the model increasing its complexity and subjectivity, resulting in lower accuracy, and creates an exploding demand for estimates data, storage, and processing capabilities	Incorporates complexity and variations that add accuracy at little additional cost and effort without creating and exploding demand for estimates data, storage, and processing capabilities
Calculates cost driver rates by taking into account the full-rated capacity of resources without discounting for idle or unused resources	Calculates cost driver rates by taking into account only the practical capacity of resources supplied by discounting for idle or unused resources, rather than the full-rated capacity of the resources
As most of the data are estimates furnished by employees in respective areas, it has to be fed separately into systems for further processing; data being localized, this model cannot provide integrated view of enterprise-wide profitability opportunities	Integrates well with order and transaction-specific data already available from ERP/CRMs like SAP CRM, thus providing integrated view of enterprise-wide profitability opportunities
Cannot be easily updated to accommodate charging or anticipated circumstances	Can be easily updated by simply estimating the unit times required or by adding additional terms in the time equation for each changed or anticipated activity
Being based primarily on users' insights and conjectures, cannot provide visibility into process efficiencies; since it ignores idle or unused capacity, capacity utilization is at 100% by definition	Provides transparent visibility to process efficiencies and capacity utilization
Being already based primarily on users' insight and conjectures, cannot guide user with identifying the root cause of problems	Furnishes granular information to assist users with identifying the root cause of problems

(Continued)

TABLE 5.1 (*Continued*)

Conventional ABC versus Time-Driven ABC

Conventional Activity-Based Costing	Time-Driven Activity-Based Costing
Not a universal model; cannot be applied to other companies even within the same industries	Can easily be applied to other companies in the same or even industries with similar business processes; hence, useful in M&A
Being based primarily on users' insights and conjectures cannot act as a correct or consistent basis for initiatives like business process reengineering, benchmarking, lean management, and enterprise performance management	Potentially unable in initiatives like business process reengineering, benchmarking, lean management, enterprise performance management, balance scorecard, and supply chain management

and

$$\sum_{l=1}^{M} \{\text{Activity-based customer costs}\}_l$$

$$= \left\{ (\text{capacity cost rate}) * \left(\sum_{l=1}^{M} \text{capacity usage time} \right)_l \right\}$$

 Significance of Time-Driven Activity-Based Costing (TDABC). TDABC plays an increasingly significant role in strategy and operations of an enterprise because of reasons like the following:

1. Time is a decisive factor in all efforts for process improvements, business process re-engineering (BPR), enterprise performance management (EPM), balanced scorecard (BSC), and so on, because of the criticality of wait times, lead times, cycle times, handover processes across department boundaries, etc. By contributing through increased accuracy at dramatically reduced complexity, efforts, resources, costs, etc. TDABC plays a determining role in enabling all such exercises.

2. Along the critical path of departmental business processes, any drastic imbalances in the capacity usage times of the various processes or subprocesses will highlight the potential for dramatic improvements in terms of complexity, efforts, resources, materials, technology, costs, and so on and will become obvious candidates for detailed scrutiny. This will usually result either in a BPR initiative or even in restructuring or reconfiguration of the department(s).

3. Based on the analysis of capacity cost rate, TDABC plays a crucial role in deciding the boundaries of an enterprise, that is, in bifurcation of core activities (that get executed in-house) from noncore activities (that can get outsourced). TDABC is critical for addressing the issues of dramatically reduced response times, turnaround times, high throughputs, increased accuracy, etc. Hence, the reason that all customer-facing processes like call centers or contact centers, customer service or customer response desks, and help desks is usually outsourced.

TDABC plays an increasingly significant role in the strategy and operations of an enterprise because of reasons like

i. Time is a decisive factor in all efforts for process improvements, business process reengineering (BPR), enterprise performance management (EPM), balance scorecard (BSC), and so on because of the criticality of wait times, lead times, cycle times, handover processes across department boundaries, etc. By contributing through increased accuracy at dramatically reduced complexity, efforts, resources, costs, etc., TDABC plays a determining role in enabling all such exercises.

ii. Along the critical path of departmental business processes, any drastic imbalances in the capacity usage times of the various process or subprocesses will highlight the potential for dramatic improvements in terms of complexity, efforts, resources, materials, technology, costs, and so on, and will become obvious candidates for detailed scrutiny. This will usually result either in a BPR initiative or even in restructuring or reconfiguration of the department(s).

iii. Based on the analysis of capacity cost rate, TDABC plays a crucial role in deciding the boundaries of an enterprise, i.e., in bifurcation of core activities (that get executed in-house) from noncore activities (that can get outsourced). TDABC is critical for addressing the issues of dramatically reduced response times, turnaround times, high throughputs, increased accuracy, etc. Hence, the reason that all customer-facing processes like call centers or contact centers, customer service or customer response desks, help desks, etc., are usually outsourced.

The TDABC model simulates the actual business processes deployed across the enterprise. In addition to addressing the improvement of inefficient processes and transforming nonprofitable products and customers, an enterprise can also use TDABC to tackle the issue of excess capacity revealed by the application of this model. An enterprise can use the TDABC model as the core of its budgeting process to link its strategic plan, and sales and production forecasts to the specific demands for capacity required to implement the plan and realize the forecast. Thus, TDABC can assist in deciding on the capacity the company needs to supply in the future.

Responsive Activity Pricing

For the sake of completeness, we will touch briefly on the issues related to the pricing of responsive activities for BPM.

Some of the relevant characteristics of customer-responsive activities are as follows:

- There is no standardized product for which there is a market price. As the delivered solution is customized to each individual customer's need, the value of the delivered solution is determined by how well the solution solves the customer's need and must be priced separately.
- There are no products that are tradable; delivery services are not tradable. Therefore, there is no market price for the delivery service.
- There are no products to inventory, only capacity that continuously perishes if it is not utilized to deliver benefits.
- Commitments to the customers are made on a real-time basis.

Thus, the emphasis must be on pricing in the immediate run to maximize the yield that can be obtained from the capacity scheduled in the short run, i.e., minimizing wasted capacity (or maximizing capacity utilization) and maximizing the customer value of capacity. The objective must be to not only collectively cover the fixed capacity costs but also to profit through contributions from customers; or in other words, the objective is to maximize contribution to fixed capacity and to profit from each sale. The price will range between the customer value at the upper limit and the larger of the cost of delivery or the competitor's price at the lower limit.

However, the final price is determined by the customer's perception of a reasonable price in light of the corresponding hassles (to identify the right solution) and the risks (see Chapter 4, section "Customer Relationships"). Evidently, the customer will pay a premium for response commitments such as guaranteed-response, time-of-day, lead time, response-level, and so on.

The frontline worker can make the pricing decision based on information such as customer value, cost of delivery, competitor's charges, and alternative use of capacity.

 A singular drive to minimize costs to the exclusion of all other factors underlies many disastrous managerial decisions. In analogy with ABC, one can conceive of ABRA that involves assigning revenues and costs explicitly to both individual customers, and processes or activities. Like ABC, ABRA also envisages the enterprise as a collective whole of activities. ABRA would engender the firm to be designed around customer-facing units where activities, costs, and revenues converge on the customer. ABRA would enable the fundamental shift from the enterprise to the customer by shifting the focus from the performance of the enterprise as a whole to the activities performed by the enterprise (along with their associated costs and revenues).

ABRA is based on the following:

- Activities of the enterprise
- Activity costs
- Revenues resulting from activities
- Measure of performances as the revenues resulting from activities less the cost of performing them

Like ABC, ABRA also identifies activities, activity revenues, revenue drivers, and revenue objects. Because value added for the customer cannot be observed directly, the contribution of activities to customer revenues is estimated by analyzing the relevant data. After assessing the activity costs by using ABC, the profitability of each activity is assessed by comparing activity revenues with activity costs. Ultimately, ABRA separates the offerings contributing to customer profitability from those incurring costs.

Some other relevant characteristics of ABRA are

- By allocating costs to customers and revenue to activities and, hence, by enabling comparison of revenues to costs customer by customer and activity by activity, ABRA also provides the rationale for evaluating and compensating individual performance
- An ABRA-like approach can also be used for focusing on transactions driving customer loyalty or retention; the costs and revenues will change suitably to aspects that are relevant to the changed context

ABC is useful wherever the enterprise offerings are clearly separable from the underlying specifications and can also be made to particular specifications (known to add value for the customer); the corresponding activities and costs can be identified and optimized (including elimination), and performance can be improved without varying these specifications. In contrast, ABRA may be useful in improving performance in cases like delivery of services (which are innately time dependent and perishable) where the specifications that are adding value are not known comprehensively and, moreover, are inseparable from the corresponding activity or activities.

SUMMARY

This chapter showed how SCMs enable the flexibility to obtain the capability and capacity needed to respond quickly to individual customer requests. After introducing the concept of SCM, the chapter described the characteristics and components of SCM. After looking at the supply-chain performance framework, we looked at issues of measurement. The last part of the chapter presented aspects of customer-responsive management with special emphasis on activity-based customer responsiveness including Time Driven Activity Based Costing (TDABC) and responsive activity pricing.

6

Renewing Enterprise with PLM

Fierce competition in global markets drives companies to perform better. Product Lifecycle Management is an essential tool for coping with the challenges of increasingly demanding global competition and ever-shortening product and component lifecycles. New and better products must be introduced to markets more quickly, with more profit and less labor, and from financial and environmental perspectives, the lifecycle of each product must be better controlled. In order to perform well financially, companies must be able to make informed decisions concerning the lifecycle of each product in their portfolio. Winner products must be introduced to market quickly and poorly performing products must be removed from the market. To do this effectively, companies must have a very good command of the lifecycle of each product. A good command of product and process definitions over a large product portfolio requires that ways of operation and IT-systems must support each other flawlessly.

CONCEPT OF PRODUCT LIFECYCLE MANAGEMENT (PLM)

The traditional paradigm for the management of a company's products was departmental-oriented: Marketing decided which products were needed by the market; engineering designed them; manufacturing produced them; and sales supported them. Each new product was developed from scratch, its functionality was paramount; its structure, relationship with other products, and degree of reuse of existing parts were seen as minor issues. With time, the departmental approach led to an environment of incompatibilities at departmental borders, waste, gaps, contradictory versions of the same data, information silos, islands of automation, over-lapping networks, duplicate activities, serial work, ineffective fixes, and product recalls. The end result was long product development and support cycles, customers having problems with products, reduced revenues, and higher costs.

Product Lifecycle Management (PLM) system supports the management of product information by storing and managing it according to many business tools (for example, project management tools, CAD, CAM, etc.). It also allows the management of product design processes (PDPs) (functional analysis, configuration management, change management, etc.) associated with the product, along its entire lifecycle. These PDPs organize the creation, exchange, use, and evolution of product information. In a constantly changing environment industrial companies face an increasingly challenging customer and competitor base. To remain competitive, a company must develop the business agility to enable it to meet customer demands that are increasingly immediate, as well as broader changes in its market environment and its own functioning. To do so, it must adopt diverse approaches to facilitate collaborations and improve product development. Among these approaches, PLM plays an essential role by managing product data in all phases of its lifecycle (design, industrialization, manufacturing, delivery, recycling, etc.) and especially during the product design phase.

 PLMs enable the continuous renewal (creation and inno-vation) of enterprise offerings, i.e., products and services in sync with the continuous changes in customer prefer-ences and needs as also the changing market environment (because of impact of competitors, regulators, activists, and so on).

There is a substantial difference between the concept of Product Lifecycle Management (PLM) and Product Lifecycle Management Systems (PLM Systems). PLM is a concept of much broader scope than the PLM Systems that implement a subset of the tenets of PLM. In this chapter, after introducing the concept of PLM, the chapter focuses on leveraging the PLM-oriented capabilities of the enterprises, while Appendix I includes an overview of the PLM functionality provided by SAP Business Suite (see Appendix I "SAP Business Suite").

PRODUCT LIFECYCLE MANAGEMENT (PLM)

Product lifecycle management (PLM) can be defined as the business process that the company's products go through all the way across their lifecycles; from the very first idea for a product all the way through until it is retired and disposed of. With PLM, product architecture, the portfolio of products, platform products, product families, and the relationship of a product to other products are all important.

Whatever the product made by a company, an enormous volume and a variety of product data are needed to develop, produce, and support the product throughout its lifecycle. The scope of information being stored, refined, searched, and shared with PLM has expanded. PLM is a holistic business concept including not only items, documents, and BOMs, but also analysis results, test specifications, environmental component information, quality standards, engineering requirements, change orders, manufacturing procedures, product performance information, component suppliers, and so forth. Modern PLM system capabilities include workflow, program management, and project control features that standardize, automate, and speed up operations. Web-based systems enable companies easily to connect their globally dispersed facilities with each other and with outside enterprises such as suppliers, partners, and even customers. PLM is a collaborative backbone allowing people throughout extended enterprises to work together more effectively.

Most PLM systems adopt workflow management approaches and propose basic workflow design and workflow engines to cope with PDPs. These approaches do not usually handle dynamic behaviors, such as dynamic changes on running workflow instances. However, PDPs are emergent and nondeterministic because of the creativity aspect in manufacturing product design projects. Furthermore, various unpredictable situations may occur during PDPs due to external constraints (e.g., evolving customer requirements, changing standards, subcontractor or supplier constraints, etc.) and/or internal constraints (e.g., changes in business priorities and opportunities, delays, technical feasibility problems, staff/resource availability, etc.). PDPs are thus constantly changing. Reflecting these changes on time is critical and represents an ongoing challenge. The automated support of business operations is necessary to reflect such changes and is provided by PLM.

Today's complex products require the collaboration of large specialist networks. In this kind of supplier and partner network, product data must be transferred between companies in electronic form, with a high level of information security. Overall, PLM can also be considered as a tool for collaboration in the supply network and for managing product creation and lifecycle processes in today's networked world, bringing new products to market with less expenditure of time and effort.

PLM is useful not only in discrete operations (component assembly) but also in process (blending) industries such as foods, pharmaceuticals, and chemicals. Process industries are often highly regulated, with strict formula/ recipe management, process standards and documentation, safety, version control, laboratory testing, health, environmental, and other regulatory compliance requirements where PLM adds value. PLM is also useful when the product is a structured service, such as banking, financial services, or insurance. Although the product is less tangible than manufacturing, the essential requirements of product data and life cycle management are very similar. Thus, PLM may be useful for a manufacturing company that delivers services in combination with, or in addition to, their manufactured products.

Challenges of PLM

Manufacturing enterprises have historically developed separate systems for managing the product design process and manufacturing operations. These systems evolved to optimally address the differing needs of engineering and manufacturing. Design engineering, manufacturing engineering, production planning, and technical sales all have a rightful claim to ownership of product data. In a fluid environment they must each concurrently review, edit, and approve the product data, without violating the integrity of the information or disrupting the smooth and rapid flow of the development and production processes.

PLM must manage a substantial volume of unstructured knowledge and intellectual property in the form of communications, spreadsheets, drawings, diagrams, still photos, video and audio clips, and other document types that are not stored in a transactional database. In a concurrent development environment, the information flow between customers, suppliers, outsourcers, marketing, sales, service, design engineering, and manufacturing engineering can be fast and furious. Engineering documents may be in a constant flux, routing through multiple creation and approval pathways, with individuals editing multiple versions during the document's life cycle. Concerns abound of security, ownership, version control, approvals, search, retrieval, reporting, and cross referencing of information.

PLM is a strategy supported by a collection of tools and techniques, rather than a single, integrated system. Effective PLM implementation strategy also requires a change in organizational culture, extending the boundaries of confidential collaboration, workflow, and communication to customers and partners. If done skillfully, concurrent engineering practices supported by a collaborative PLM technology infrastructure may nurture strategic partnerships that add value far beyond the traditional supplier–customer relationship.

Benefits of PLM

Successfully managing PLM offers several business benefits including the following:

- Shortens the time to market
- Reduces research and development (R&D) costs
- Optimizes product designs
- Improves product quality
- Reduces waste
- Increases the success rate of new products

PLM improves operational efficiencies because groups all across the value chain can work faster through advanced information retrieval, electronic information sharing, data reuse, and numerous automated capabilities, with greater information traceability and data security. This allows companies to process engineering change orders and respond to product support calls more quickly and with less labor. They can also work more effectively with suppliers in handling bids and quotes, exchange critical product information more smoothly with manufacturing facilities, and allow service technicians and spare part sales reps to quickly access required engineering data in the field.

With PLM, people are trained to think about the product across its lifecycle. For example, engineers designing a product take account of how it will be manufactured and how it will be disassembled and recycled. The recycling specialists keep up to date with environmental laws and keep development engineers informed. Together, they work out how to design products that can be disassembled quickly, and how to reuse parts in new products. People look to add value and create revenues across the lifecycle. Opportunities include developing new environment friendly products, providing customized products, providing services to support product use, refurbishing existing products, and taking financial and environmental responsibility for products produced in low-cost countries. Experience from product operations is used in development of future products. Feedback about the use of one generation of a product helps improve future generations. Products that have reached the end of their life are disassembled, and some parts are reused in the start of life of new products.

The benefits of operational PLM go far beyond incremental savings, yielding greater bottom line savings and top-line revenue growth not only by implementing tools and technologies, but also by making necessary changes in processes, practices, and methods and gaining control over product lifecycles and lifecycle processes. The return on investment for PLM is based on a broader corporate business value, specifically the greater market share and increased profitability achieved by streamlining the business processes that help deliver innovative, winning products with high brand image quickly to market, while being able to make informed lifecycle decisions over the complete product portfolio during the lifecycle of each individual product.

 PLM can result in impressive cost savings, with many companies reporting pay-off periods of one to two years or less based solely on reduced development costs. PLM also enables better control over the product lifecycle. This gives opportunities for companies to boost revenue streams by accelerating the pace at which innovative products are brought to market. Excellent lifecycle control over products also gives new opportunities to control product margins more carefully and remove poorly performing products from the market. This set of benefits, driving top-line revenue growth and bottom-line profitability, makes ROI extremely compelling, leading to PLM being treated as a competitive necessity for manufacturers.

COMPONENTS OF PLM

PLM is appropriately described as a strategy supported by a collection of tools and techniques, rather than a single integrated application. Many of the information technology components of PLM have existed independently for years and have been gathered as integrated suites of PLM tools:

    a. Authoring Tools—Computer-aided design (CAD), computer-aided manufacturing (CAM), computer-aided engineering (CAE), and 3D visualization tools.

    b. Requirements Management—Provides input to design and engineering processes and may be used in conjunction with techniques such as Quality Function Deployment (QFD) throughout the conceptualization, creation, manufacturing, and distribution of products. These tools keep track of marketing and customer issues, functional and technical requirements, quality, safety, usability, serviceability, manufacturability, and cost factors while helping to manage the flow of information, and evaluate constraints and trade-offs caused by design decisions.

    c. Product Data Management (PDM)—Creates a unified record of the design, specifications, characteristics, production, and distribution of products. This includes structured data stored in various relational databases and unstructured data contained in a wide variety of electronic document formats. Product data include detailed specifications on the items, Bills of Materials, routings, delayed change effectivity information, work instructions, sourcing, and compliance information.

    d. Engineering Change Management/Control (ECM/ECC)—Routes change order, notification, and approval information through various pathways, managing multiple document versions, revision audit control, new part signoffs, compliance validation, and quality management.

    e. Configuration Management—Provides change control and tracking for as-designed, as-manufactured, and as-serviced product information. For example, if a part has to be replaced in a product years later, the system can locate the original version, configuration, design, and specific materials that are required for service.

    f. Sourcing Management—Provides supplier management tools including specifications management and history, supplier performance management, certification, and testing.

g. Collaboration and Knowledge Management—Includes such diverse software tools such as scheduling, communications, collaboration, groupware, visualization, documentation, version control, exceptions management, storage, search, retrieval, reporting, data analysis and mining, security, and administrative tools to enable a geographically distributed product development team over the duration of a lengthy product life cycle. Such a process-oriented, cross-boundary system exposes vital and confidential company knowledge to outside parties, requiring a strong system of security and document control.

h. Quality Assurance, Regulatory Compliance, Environmental Health and Safety Management—Offers capabilities that vary widely by environment: Food, pharmaceuticals, chemicals, hazardous materials, consumer goods, automotive and transportation, aerospace, defense, government, contracting, etc.

i. Program and Project Management—Provides control over scope, time, cost, risk, schedules, and resource requirements during the design and engineering process. When program and project management are integrated within PLM, they provide the capability to link and communicate changes in design to the overall project change management process, controlling overall scope, quality, cost, and risk.

ADVANTAGES OF USING PLM

i. Manufacturability: Most production costs are designed into the product and process long before the job is sent to the shop floor. When manufacturing engineering cooperates with design engineering in the early stages of product design, they can influence decisions on manufacturability, cost, and quality for which they will later be held accountable. PLM facilitates effective collaboration among these and other participants.

ii. Standardization: In addition to the central management of product information, the establishment of design, development, and manufacturing standards leads to greater standardization and reusability of designs, tools, components, and processes. This in turn may enable group technology, cellular production, reduction of inventory, reduced purchasing and manufacturing lead time, improved quality, and serviceability. PLM becomes the system of record for product definition data, eliminating redundant and potentially conflicting versions of information that often proliferate within an organization.

iii. Aid to Continuous Improvement: PLM tools add value to continuous improvement efforts by codifying design and development, production, and customer service practices to ensure standardization of work.

iv. Marketing and Sales Support: By publishing product information through a public Internet or secure extranet Portal, customers may be able to help themselves, leading to better decisions and a faster sales cycle. In fact, good Web-based product information may be an essential sales and customer service tool for a manufacturer that delivers high knowledge content within its products. However, in some environments there are legitimate reasons to restrict the amount of technical content that is offered freely without qualified interaction with a human being, because there may be a risk that the information may be misunderstood or misused. In that case, a PLM system may provide the appropriate information to a sales team, who then skillfully manage the customer relationship, through the combination of CRM and PLM.

v. Communication and Collaboration: By making vital product design standards and information available to the team, all stakeholders may be united in a streamlined process. Development projects often involve colocation, where project personnel representing the various stakeholder companies are located together, enabling more rapid and frequent decision making and exchange of ideas. On the other hand, collaboration, knowledge management, and security tools can help development teams electronically colocate anywhere in the world. When a team works around the world they also work around the clock, further accelerating the pace of development. PLM offers a variety of tools for enabling such communication and collaboration. Regardless of the physical arrangement of the team, when a company uses PLM and concurrent engineering effectively, it creates a framework for a strong working relationship among the parties, which may nurture a lasting competitive advantage.

vi. Lead Time Reduction: There is a natural tendency to squander time on the front end of any project because issues, tasks, and priorities are not yet clearly defined. In fact, the time on the front end of the project is more valuable (compared with that at the back end) because the opportunities for differentiation and the creation of competitive advantage are highest in the early stages of market opportunity.

Through the development of standard processes and information flows, aided by knowledge management and collaboration tools, PLM reduces lead time during the early design stage, accelerating time to market.

vii. Intellectual Property Management: Vital intellectual property is often stored in people's heads; this poses a significant risk to companies that have significant intellectual property valuation bound to their aging workforce. In addition to retirement, there are many causes for knowledge to be irretrievably lost: Hiring by a competitor, disability, death, relocation, or role change. If a manufacturing enterprise does not capture and institutionalize its knowledge and processes, it may be guilty of not protecting vital company assets. The positive side of this argument is that by documenting this knowledge it may be preserved and extended throughout the enterprise. PLM can institutionalize this knowledge to mitigate this risk appreciably albeit at additional cost.

viii. Reduction of Administrative Waste: As physical documents propagate across an enterprise, more time and effort are required to complete any task or process. When vital product and process data are not available electronically, and made accessible through intuitive search tools, then a higher-skilled individual must invest valuable time to retrieve and interpret the information to address low-value questions. When multiple versions of key documents are circulating, the risk of serious errors, omissions, oversight, and miscommunication is great. And the use of manual documentation creates a security risk, while naturally limiting an enterprise's ability to extend its collaborative development efforts across suppliers, customers, locations, languages, and time zones. PLM tools can conserve much of this energy and efforts expended in manual document management.

PORTER'S FRAMEWORK OF GENERIC STRATEGIES

The most widely known strategy framework is the three generic strategies introduced by M. Porter. Subsequently, Porter added a further aspect to his model, whether the strategic target is industrywide or focused on a particular segment.

The three generic competitive strategies are as follows:

a. Differentiation strategy dictates that the firm creates a product offering that is perceived industrywide as being unique. The differentiation can take many forms: Design, brand, technology, features, customer service, dealer network, and many more. The firm differentiates itself along several dimensions. While costs are not allowed to be ignored, they are not the primary strategic target. If differentiation is achieved, above-average returns can be yielded due to the defensible position it creates. Differentiation has proven to be a viable strategy resulting in brand loyalty and lower sensitivity to price.
   - Margins that avoid the urge for a low-cost position
   - Decreased buyer power due to a lack of comparable alternatives
   - Entry barriers for competitors
b. Overall Cost Leadership strategy dictates that the firm constructs efficient and appropriately scaled facilities, pursue cost reduction based on the experience curve, and tightly control direct costs and overhead. Even though lower cost relative to competitors is the major strategic target, a watchful eye must be placed on quality, service, and customer satisfaction. Achieving overall cost leadership yields above-average returns due to the lower costs, while competitors have competed away their profits.
c. Focus strategy dictates that the firm caters to a particular segment only (e.g., one particular buyer group, geographic market, etc.). It bases its above-average returns on serving a particular target very well, i.e., more efficiently than competitors competing more broadly. A focus strategy either achieves differentiation by better meeting the needs and wants of the particular target it focuses on, or manages to maintain lower costs in serving this target, or both. The differentiation or lower cost position is not achieved for the entire market, but only for the narrow market target.

Although, initially cost leadership and differentiation were regarded as being incompatible, subsequently hybrid competitive strategies combining the above strategies were explored. While the generic hybrid strategies (high relative differentiation/high relative cost position and low relative differentiation/low relative cost position) were only ascribed an average competitive position, the combination of high relative differentiation position and a low relative cost position was considered powerful. The strategy resulting from such a hybrid combination of differentiation (customization) and cost leadership (standardization) is called *mass customization*

PRODUCT LIFE CYCLE (PLC)

If you put a pair of rabbits in a meadow, you can watch their population go through an exponential growth pattern at first. As with every multiplication process, one unit brings forth another. But the population growth slows down later as it approaches a ceiling—the capacity of a species' ecological niche. Over time, the rabbit traces an S-shaped niche. Over time, the rabbit population traces an S-shaped trajectory. The rate of growth traces a bell-shaped curve that peaks when half the niche is filled. The bell-shaped curve for its rate of growth and the S-shaped curve for the total population constitute a pictorial representation of the natural growth process, that is, how a species population grows into a limited space by obeying the laws of survival.

A product's sales follow the same pattern as the product fills its market niche, because competition in the marketplace is intrinsically the same as in the jungle. The cumulative number of units sold is shown in Figure 6.1. Table 6.1 lists characteristic product cycle times by industry.

The PLC is used to map the life span of a product. There are generally four stages in the life of a product. These four stages are the introduction stage, the growth stage, the maturity stage, and the decline stage. There is

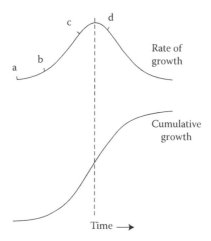

FIGURE 6.1
S-curve and the PLC.

TABLE 6.1

Characteristic Product Cycle Times by Industry

Description	Life Cycle (Years)	Development Cycle (Years)
Financial services	0.2	0.2
Silicon foundries	0.5	0.5
Retailing, entertainment	1.0	1.0
Fashion and textiles	1.5	1.5
Software	2.0	2.0
Electronics	2.5	2.5
Computers	3.0	3.0
Medical and dental	3.5	3.5
Automobiles	4.0	4.0
Metal products	4.5	4.5
Photographic	5.0	5.0
Chemicals, paper	6.0	6.0
Publishing	7.0	2.0
Aircraft	7.0	7.0
Biotechnology	8.0	3.0
Pharmaceuticals	10.0	10.0
Mining	11.0	6.0
Lodging, hotels	11.0	3.0
Foods	11.0	2.0
Tobacco	11.0	1.0
Forestry, oil, and gas reservoirs	12.0	12.0
Military weapons	12.0	2.0
Communication systems	20.0	20.0
Transportation systems	20.5	20.5

no set time period for the PLC and the length of each stage may vary. One product's entire life cycle could be over in a few months; another product could last for years. Also, the introduction stage may last much longer than the growth stage and vice versa. Figure 6.1 also illustrates the four stages of the PLC:

1. Introduction: The introduction stage is probably the most important stage in the PLC. In fact, most products that fail do so in the introduction stage. This is the stage in which the product is initially promoted; public awareness is very important to the success of a product. If people do not know about the product, they will not go out and buy it. There are two different strategies you can use to introduce your product to consumers. You can use either a penetration strategy or a

skimming strategy. If a penetration strategy is used, then prices are set very high initially and then gradually lowered over time. This is a good strategy to use if there are few competitors for your product: Profits are high with this strategy but there is also a great deal of risk. If people do not want to pay high prices, you may lose out. The second pricing strategy is the skimming strategy. In this case, you set your prices very low at the beginning and then gradually increase them. This is a good strategy to use if there are a lot of competitors who control a large portion of the market. Profits are not a concern under this strategy: The most important thing is to get your product known and worry about making money at a later time.

2. Growth: The growth stage is where your product starts to grow. In this stage, a very large amount of money is spent on advertising. You want to concentrate on telling the consumer how much better your product is than your competitors' products. There are several ways to advertise your product—TV and radio commercials and magazine and newspaper ads—or you could get lucky and customers who have bought your product will give good word of mouth to their family and friends. If you are successful with your advertising strategy, then you will see an increase in sales. Once your sales begin to increase, your share of the market will stabilize. Once you get to this point, you will probably not be able to take anymore of the market from your competitors.

3. Maturity: The third stage in the PLC is the maturity stage. If your product completes the introduction and growth stages, then it will spend a great deal of time in the maturity stage. During this stage, sales grow at a very fast rate and then gradually begin to stabilize. The key to surviving this stage is differentiating your product from the similar products offered by your competitors. Due to the fact that sales are beginning to stabilize, you must make your product stand out among the rest.

4. Decline: This is the stage in which sales of your product begin to fall. Either everyone that wants to has bought your product or new more innovative products have been created that replace yours. Many companies decide to withdraw their products from the market due to the downturn: The only way to increase sales during this period is to cut your costs and reduce your spending.

Very few products follow the same life cycle. Many products may not even make it through all four stages; some products may even bypass stages. For example, one product may go straight from the introduction stage to the maturity stage. This is the problem with the PLC—there is no set way for a product to grow. Therefore, every product requires a great deal of research and close supervision throughout its life; without proper research and supervision, your product will probably never get out of the first stage.

 Apart from the introduction phase, the PLC also needs to add the product development and disposal phases. In the product development phase, product variants are generated to fulfill anticipated market requirements but, at the same time, preventive measures (often on the product architecture level) must be taken to avoid excessive variety generation in later stages of the PLC. During the market phase, further variants are generated (to address perceived market demand) while preventive actions on the architectural level are enforced (to avoid excessive variety). The need for eliminating low-performing variants rises as variety proliferates and efficient handling of the growing portfolio becomes an important success factor.

Product Design Attributes

The presence of particular attributes in the product design can not only increase operational efficiency but also contribute directly to customer satisfaction.

The characteristics of successful products are as follows:

i. Functionality: A product with good functionality works to satisfy customer's needs. Product functionality pertains to the ability of a product to operate as it promises. For instance, a customer who purchases a sports car is interested in the functions of engine performance, sporty styling, and aggressive handling capabilities. Safety-concerned customers would be more interested in buying a car with safety features, such as side air bags, impact absorbing interiors, crash-resistant door pillars, and antilock braking systems. Customers form expectations about the functional benefits they desire from the products they purchase. Customers are satisfied when their functional expectations and usage experience match.

ii. Validity: The validity attribute of a product deals with generating higher values to customers than the cost (and time) spent by them to acquire the product. The function and performance of today's consumer products are entirely adequate for most consumers. But, expending further engineering efforts to increase functionality may not necessarily increase a customer's perception of product usefulness. Product validity can be improved by analyzing and removing unnecessary attributes in products. Only the functional capability (and features) the customer truly seeks in a product should be engineered into the product design. When customers receive the final product, it should have the highest perceived value that the customers desire at the price they are willing to pay. Product validity is essential to the market success of a product.

iii. Manufacturability: Manufacturability is the degree of ease in making products during the production process. This is an important product attribute because a great, innovative product may not be easily producible. This situation occurs when there is a disconnect or communication problem between product design teams and manufacturing personnel. An effective designer should recognize that, while the optimization of product design is essential, it is not always sufficient by itself.

The manufacturability attribute focuses on the efficiency of making the product. A well-designed product can simplify the manufacturing process and reduce the time to market. Decisions made at the product design stage determine to a large extent the product's final cost and quality. Failure to take into consideration the attribute of manufacturability when conducting product design can greatly increase production costs, create poor quality products, and slow down the time to market. Therefore, the ultimate goal of good product design is to optimize both the design and the entire production system, including managing of raw materials, suppliers, manufacturing processes, labor force capabilities, and distribution procedures.

iv. Reliability: The quality of the product often relates to how desirable the product is to the final customer.

Reliability is an aggregate of multiple related attributes like

- Availability
- Usability
- Functionality
- Flexibility
- Efficiency
- Security
- Compatibility

- Manufacturability
- Maintainability
- Portability

A quality product does not necessarily meet all these attributes simultaneously. Therefore, it is important to know the implied needs demanded by consumers and then match these needs with the corresponding quality attributes. The reliability concept is also applicable to the service industry. Customers desire both expedient and courteous service. The quality of the call center experience is one service contact area that often receives low ratings from customers. A frequent complaint is length of the wait-time before they can discuss their problem with the right person. Competing on the basis of time is an important quality consideration in the service industry.

v. Serviceability: The serviceability attribute focuses on the ease of performing maintenance or repairs on the product during its effective life span. Serviceability is the ease in which servicing can be performed on a product during its useful life. The importance of serviceability increases over the life span of products. This is particularly true for industrial products such as automobiles, airplanes, and locomotives. It is necessary that either the original manufacturer or a third-party provider carry replacement parts. Product designs that put cost savings ahead of serviceability have resulted in decreased profitability and increased maintenance costs. In the end, poor serviceability not only increases total cost of ownership (TCO) but also decreases customer satisfaction and product loyalty.

vi. Recyclability: The recyclability attribute considers how the products can be recycled back through the reverse logistics supply chain. Recyclability is the capability within the supply chain to return unusable products, defective items, items to be repaired or recalibrated, and environment-friendly goods back to the original manufacturer or a third-party provider. In order to improve recyclability, a company needs to address various reverse logistics supply-chain activities. The reverse product flow begins with the returning of goods to some contact point, such as the customer service center. After verifying the product warranty and payment records, the customer service representative credits the customer account; the returned product will continue its journey toward its upstream origins by traveling through distribution, product disassembly, repair, calibration, and component separation, until it reaches a point where it is finally recycled or destroyed.

Product Design Approaches

Enterprises can be physically efficient or market responsive. When customer demand is stable and products are commodity or functional goods with low margins, enterprises need to lower operational costs and maximize resource utilization. In contrast, when the customer demand is unpredictable and subject to sudden changes, the challenge is in the ability to accelerate or decelerate product development and production depending on whether the market is favorable or unfavorable toward new products. Operationally efficient enterprises can employ quality function deployment (QFD) and design for manufacturability (DFM) methods to maximize product performance at minimum cost. In contrast, market-responsive enterprises can utilize concurrent engineering (CE) and design for sustainability (DFS) to reduce the time to market and increase responsiveness to market demand for greener products. The following section details some of these product design methods and explains how each method can support the varying needs of enterprises.

Quality Function Deployment

Quality Function Deployment (QFD) is an effective method to understand customer needs. It can be defined as method to transform user demands into design quality, to deploy the functions forming quality, and to deploy methods for achieving the design quality into subsystems and component parts, and ultimately to specific elements of the manufacturing process. Methods used to deploy QFD include the voice of customer (VOC) and prioritization of customer needs. Direct customer interactions can reveal customer needs. This information can be converted into product and service requirements important to customers, after which R&D teams can translate customer requirements into the product design. It is more likely that customers will be satisfied with the developed products and services, because the entire product development process has been constructed to increase customer satisfaction.

The focal point of the QFD process is a matrix called the house of quality (HOQ). The APICS Dictionary (2013) describes the HOQ as a structured process that relates customer-defined attributes to the product's technical features needed to support and generate these attributes.

This technique includes the following steps:

   i. Identify customer requirements. This describes what is to be done.
   ii. Identify supporting technical features to satisfy the requirements. This describes how it can be done.

iii. Correlate the customer requirements with the supporting technical features. This describes how well the hows satisfy the whats.

iv. Identify the relationship among the technical features. This describes how well the hows interact.

v. Assign priorities to the customer requirements and technical features. This describes which of the hows to evaluate first.

vi. Evaluate competitive stances and competitive products. This describes how competing products are satisfying the customer whats.

vii. Determine which technical requirements to deploy in the product design. This describes the hows to be included in the final product.

Design for Manufacturability

Design for Manufacturability (DFM) is a methodology to engineer products for the best manufacturability, which costs less, reduces lead times, and strives for the highest quality in design. Most importantly, effective utilization of DFM can support business strategies, including standardization, mass customization, build to order, and product line rationalization.

In general, product designs should reduce variability, confusion, and complexity in the production process by following rules such as

1. Reducing the number of parts
2. Making assembly foolproof
3. Simplifying the assembly process
4. Making the product easy to test
5. Avoiding excessively tight tolerances

Standardizing design and manufacturing processes can increase flexibility in developing the product line and reduce R&D costs. With decreasing product life cycles, customer demand has been increasingly changing dynamically. Standardization may appear to run counter to being able to satisfy dynamic changes in customer demands; however, a hybrid approach, such as mass customization (see section "Customization and Standardization"), is an effective method to customize customer needs at the mass level. Assemble-to-order or build-to-order strategies help minimize inventory and the need for detailed forecasting. Product line rationalization allows a firm to optimize the productivity of product lines by eliminating or outsourcing unproductive products to a third party. This strategy can free up a strangled production line and optimize its capacity.

Concurrent Engineering

Concurrent Engineering (CE) is another technique to develop new products in response to customer expectations based on the consensus of cross-functional team members. Team members need to collaborate, trust, and share information about customer expectations with each other throughout the product development process. CE expedites the product development process in the parallel rather than the sequential mode. This cycle consists of many stages, including planning, implementation, reviewing, and modifying, in order to continuously improve the product development process. This strategy can shorten the time to market and help to optimize an effective and efficient product development process. A continuous improvement and refinement cycle is a core element of a CE strategy.

Design for Sustainability

Design for Sustainability (DFS) is a technique to meet the increasing customer demand for environmentally friendly goods that can help sustain a business. Offering these goods does more than just meet a growing social trend in society; it also contributes to the well-being of human beings in general. Practising energy conservation, utilizing renewable energy sources, and recycling contaminated by-products are examples of doing good for less and can help a business to stay profitable. Companies must realize that their adverse impact on the environment can also be largely reduced and even eliminated in the long term.

Many business sectors, such as chemical, agricultural, auto manufacturing, and the film developing industry, are embracing the concept of DFS. Another popular term becoming more widely used is the triple bottom line. This is a concept that encourages businesses to aim for profitability, positive social involvement, and improved environmental operation as an integrated approach to their business strategies.

Environmental concern is a key consideration when designing products for sustainability. A good ecodesign approach helps ensure new products do not pollute the environment and retired products can be recycled back to minimize waste. A sustainable product needs to meet these requirements in order to create a sustainable business. Products designed with the welfare of the environment in mind benefit both domestic and international customers. Such green product innovations do not guarantee profit; however, it is important to improve manufacturing efficiency and product quality as well as to exploit the market opportunities that desire these types of products.

Social and environmental problems can easily damage a company's reputation. A number of external stakeholders will exert pressure on the organization to act in a socially responsible manner. Activist organizations and government regulators exert pressure on companies to stop controversial practices. Customers demand safer, healthier, environmentally friendly products produced in a socially responsible manner. Certain legislative requirements require companies to adopt environmental safeguards and disclose their internal business practices concerning the meeting of environmental regulations. Many businesses are beginning to look at these requirements seriously and are seeking to develop profitable and sustainable opportunities out of them. For years, Nike endured accusations of promoting sweatshops when using overseas contractors, despite the fact that they regularly monitor their contractors. More recently, Apple and other companies have incurred negative press reports because of their use of Foxconn, a Chinese company with reported violations in employee working conditions. These types of problems become corporate liabilities, if not prevented and managed properly.

CUSTOMIZATION AND STANDARDIZATION

An enterprise offering customized products caters to a very niche customer base and tailors its every offering to the very needs of one particular customer; the product is differentiated from competitors' by satisfying each and every customer requirement. Consequently, very close ties gets established between the producer and its customers and, often, customers coparticipate in designing the product and express preferences on how it should be manufactured. A customizer's competitive edge is therefore primarily based on product attractiveness.

The more customized a product, the more customers are willing to pay a higher price because the product closely reflects their requirements. As customer benefit increases, the price elasticity of demand decreases, which enables the producer to harvest the consumer surplus. The know-how necessary to maintain such a market position is an invaluable asset, but requires continuous investments. Further costs are incurred by the large product variety, by increasing complexity throughout the value chain, and by highly qualified personnel and so on. This cost disadvantage can only be balanced by a higher price. Some of these negative cost effects can be balanced by the economies of scope that can be realized due to synergies while producing several products simultaneously. If those products have something in common (e.g., fabrication tools, R&D resources, etc.), the shared activities and assets can be "spread" across a group of products resulting in comparatively lower costs of production.

In contrast to customization, an enterprise following a standardization strategy sells homogeneous mass products. Close relationships between customer and producer is no longer possible; products are not made-to-order but are made-to-stock based on market research estimates. As mass-produced, standardized goods cannot consider individual customer preferences, their product attributes are chosen based on an average of preferences taken from a large number of customers. Since individual customers' preferences diverge from this average preference, the benefit provided by the product—and thus the price at which it can be sold—is much lower than in the case of customization. The competitive edge of a mass producer is always based on price.

By producing the same standardized product in large quantities, costs can be saved resulting from the following two effects:

- Economies of scale are achieved due to generally larger facilities (factories, call centers, inventory, etc.), which spreads a considerable fraction of fixed costs to a large number of product units.
- The experience curve effect states that costs drop by 20 to 30 percent every time the cumulative volume doubles. This is mainly on account of increased labor efficiency (resulting from learning), specialization and redesign of labor tasks, product and process improvements, and rationalization, such as introducing more up-to-date technology.

Table 6.2 summarizes the characteristics of Customization versus Standardization strategies for products or market offerings.

TABLE 6.2

Customization versus Standardization Strategies for Products or Offerings

Characteristic	Customization	Standardization
Scope of offering	Specifications of individual customers	Average preference of a large number of customers
Number of customers per offering	One, or very few	Many
Contact to customer	Close; customer integrated in designing and producing product	Not or hardly established (anonymous consumers)
Product fabrication	After order	Before order; in stock
Source of information on customer requirements	Directly from customer	Market research
Similarity of products within line	No product the same; tailored solution; batch size one	All products the same; homogeneous mass product
Product variety	Very large	Only one product variant
Product attractiveness	Inherently high	Inherently low
Customer retention	High	Low
Costs	High	Low
Risk of substitution	Low	High
Competitive effect	Decoupled from competition due to product attractiveness and know-how advantage; opportunity to avoid price-based competition	Risk of price-based competition (especially for firms with low market share); market leader protected by cost advantage
Market entry barrier	Product attractiveness and know-how advantage	Cost advantage of market leader
Price range	Rather high	Rather low

Mass Customization

Mass customization in a way is similar to producing goods and services to meet an individual customer's needs but with near mass production efficiency.
Mass customization production can be achieved with strategies such as

a. Provide quick response throughout the value chain. Reducing the time needed along a firm's entire value chain is known as time-based competition. Speeding up new product development and reducing set-up time in manufacturing significantly decreases variant product-specific costs. Shortening the order-to-delivery cycle in marketing also lowers complexity costs by reducing final goods inventory.

b. Create customizable products and services. This method involves producing goods that customers can easily adapt to individual needs in a "self-service" manner. It changes the focus of development and marketing, while production and delivery remain almost undisturbed. Office furniture that can be adjusted and computer applications that allow users to create their own system environment provide examples of this widely employed method.

c. Provide point-of-delivery customization. As customers know best what they want, this method performs the final customizing step at the point of sale or delivery. For example, men's suits and eyeglasses are individualized to a customer's specific preferences right at the shop. This can be achieved for general products if a firm shifts the entire production process to the point of delivery; however, this would adversely impact the functioning of the whole enterprise. Hence, the method discussed here is more appropriate for products having (say) only one inherently customer-specific attribute on an otherwise relatively standardized commodity. In this way, the standard part can be manufactured centrally, while the customized characteristic can be produced at the point of sale.

d. Customize services around standardized products and services. A standardized product can be tailored by people in marketing and delivery before it reaches customers. For example, car rental companies add customized services such as express service and club memberships for frequent customers to its standard commodity service.

e. Modularize components to customize end products and services. This is considered as the most effective method of mass customizing products: Modularize components that can be configured to a large number of product variants. Economies of scale are achieved through the components, while economies of scope and customization are gained by reusing the components to create a large stream of product variants.

Methodologies for Managing Customization

1. Design for variety (DFV): This method provides a means to estimate the costs incurred by introducing variety into a product line; these costs are commonly indirect and are often not thoroughly understood because they are difficult to quantify.

DFV attempts to capture these indirect variety costs by defining three indices:

i. The commonality index is a measure of the percentage of parts that are reused for other product models and accounts for the utilization of standardized parts.

ii. The differentiation point index considers the points along the value chain where variety is introduced. It is based on the generally agreed premise that later the variety occurs, the better.

iii. The setup cost index relates the estimated setup costs to the overall product costs (material, labor, and overhead).

The method proposes the process sequence graph, which shows the flow of the product through the manufacturing and assembly lines, and visualizes its differentiation points. A quantitative algorithm then shifts those components causing variety as far back in the manufacturing and assembly process as possible. The differentiation points in the process sequence graph are called nodes. The algorithm performs the optimization by minimizing the number of nodes in the process sequence graph of a product. The DFV methodology is primarily concerned with quantifying the costs incurred by product variety and deriving strategies on how to reduce those costs by optimizing the manufacturing and assembly sequence.

2. Design for configuration (DFC): This is a methodology that supports designers in producing and managing information and knowledge needed to configure products. A fixed set of variants can be derived from a configurable product, which can be formed from a fixed set of modules, components, and add-ons with a given variety; the creation of a particular variant is termed as the configuration task. The objective of DFC boils down to offering a relatively broad product portfolio while limiting costs due to the absence of customer-specific designs. Thus, it is able to combine several virtues of mass production and customization, making it a viable tool for implementing mass customization. A configurable product is characterized by the following properties:

i. Each product variant can be clearly specified as a combination of predesigned components and/or modules.

ii. There is a predesigned product architecture which meets a given range of customer requirements.

iii. The sales process does not entail the design of new components. It only requires the systematic configuration of product variants.

iv. As all variants are based on the same common architecture, they are considered a product family.

DFC is an approach mainly concerned with designing a product's architecture to allow for a cost-effective configuring of product variants. The customer requirements that the product family is supposed to cover must be defined before the design process. Therefore, they should be well understood, rendering the consideration of market aspects a fairly important task in the DFC process.

3. Product Modularization: This methodology defines a modular product as consisting of a number of relatively independent units (the modules) sharing decoupled interfaces. As these interfaces are clearly defined and highly standardized, the independently designed modules still function as an integrated whole. Product modularization is supposed to speed up the development process, enhance the ability to adapt to changes in the environment, and reduce the cost of making changes because it increases a company's flexibility by minimizing the interdependencies between the modules of a product. Product modularity enables the customer to choose from a large variety of products while letting the producer profit from economies of scale (shared components) and economies of scope (using modules in different products).

There are several types of modularity:

i. Component-sharing modularity, the same component is used across multiple products to provide economies of scope. It is often associated with the idea of component standardization.

ii. Component-swapping modularity is the complementary case to component-sharing modularity. Here, different components are combined with the same basic product to create a number of product variants belonging to the same product family. Component-swapping modularity is often associated with product variety as perceived by the customer.

iii. Cut-to-fit modularity is the use of standard components with one or more continually variable components. Mostly, the variation is expressed as physical dimensions that can be modified (e.g., length, power).

iv. Mix modularity can use any of the above three types, with the distinction that the resulting product is something different than the constituent components that are mixed together. Therefore, it can only be applied to products consisting of a mixture of various substances, such as colors or fertilizers. For instance, an endless stream of distinct colors can be produced by mixing only a limited number of basic colors.

v. Bus modularity relies on a standard structure with two or more interfaces that can attach any selection of components from a set of component types. While bus modularity allows variation in the number and location of the components, component-swapping, component-sharing, and cut-to-fit modularity only allow variation in the type of component used in an otherwise identical product architecture.

vi. Sectional modularity provides the largest degree of variety and customization. It allows connecting components in any arbitrary way, as long as each component is connected to another through standard interfaces. In this type, the product's scope is not predefined and can be changed to the specific needs of the situation. The classic example is Lego building blocks, from which an infinite number of objects can be built.

When a firm modularizes its products, it is able to respond to the external changes while keeping the internal complexity within reasonable limits. Thanks to widely standardized interfaces, a limited number of standard and customized modules can be combined in many different ways to form a stream of distinct product variants. A broad product portfolio can therefore be maintained that does not cause excessive costs to the enterprise. As the individual modules are highly independent from each other, changes made to one module do not affect other modules, which also saves costs. When a product consists of components that go through life cycles of different lengths, modularization allows for decoupling the life cycles of these modules. For the ensemble as a whole, this results in tremendous gains in flexibility and dramatic reduction in costs.

The primary strength of modularization lies in its ability to provide an agile solution to growing product complexity by rethinking the product architecture.

4. Product Platform: This methodology essentially divides the product architecture into a standardized part (the platform) and customized modules. Combining the two allows the creation of a large number of distinct product variants. The underlying rationale is to optimize the trade-off between cost savings (through scale economies) and

competitive edge (through differentiation). A product platform does not necessarily spread across an entire product, it can also be confined to the level of individual components. A product platform is defined as a set of components or subsystems, and interfaces that form a common structure from which a stream of derivative products that can be developed and produced efficiently.

 Component sharing is mostly performed on an individual product level, but the scope of product platforms is not confined to an individual product level but across entire product families.

SUMMARY

This chapter started with an introduction to the concept of product lifecycle management (PLM). The chapter described the benefits and challenges of PLM before describing the components of a PLM system. The latter half of the chapter detailed the various stages of the Product LifeCycle (PLC) as also the attributes and approaches for the design of products. The last part of the chapter discussed issues regarding the standardization and customization of products in conformance to the Voice of Customer (VOC).

7

Collaborative Enterprise with BPM

Information technology can fulfill its role as a strategic differentiator only if it can provide enterprises with a mechanism to provide sustainable competitive advantage—the ability to change business processes in sync with changes in the business environment and that too at optimum costs. This is achievable on the foundation of Service Oriented Architecture (SOA) that exposes the fundamental business capabilities as flexible, reusable services; SOA along with the constituting services is the foundation of a modern Business Process Management Systems (BPMS). The services support a layer of agile and flexible business processes that can be easily changed to provide new products and services to keep ahead of the competition. The most important value of SOA is that it provides an opportunity for IT and the business to communicate and interact with each other at a highly efficient and equally understood level. That common, equally understood language is the language of business process or enterprise processes in BPMN.

PROCESS-ORIENTED ENTERPRISE

Enterprise systems (ES) enable an organization to truly function as an integrated enterprise, integration across all functions or segments of the traditional value chain—sales order, production, inventory, purchasing, finance and accounting, personnel and administration, and so on. They do this by modeling primarily the business processes as the basic business entities of the enterprise rather than by modeling data handled by the enterprise (as done by the traditional IT systems). However, every ES might not be completely successful in doing this. In a break with the legacy enterprise-wide solutions, modern ES treat business processes as more fundamental than data items.

The significance of a process to the success of the enterprise's business is dependent on the value, with reference to the customer, of the collaboration that it addresses and represents. In other words, the nature and extent of the value addition by a process to a product or services delivered to a customer is the best index of the contribution of that process to the company's overall customer satisfaction or customer collaboration. Customer knowledge by itself is not adequate; it is only when the enterprise has effective processes for sharing this information and integrating the activities of frontline workers and has the ability to coordinate the assignment and tracking of work that enterprises can become effective.

Value-Add-Driven Enterprise

Business processes can be seen as the very basis of the value addition within an enterprise that was traditionally attributed to various functions or divisions in an enterprise. As organizational and environmental conditions become more complex, global, and competitive, processes provide a framework for dealing effectively with the issues of performance improvement, capability development, and adaptation to the changing environment.

Along a value stream (i.e., a business process), analysis of the absence or creation of added value or (worse) destruction of value critically determines the necessity and effectiveness of a process step. The understanding of value-adding and non–value-adding processes (or process steps) is a significant factor in the analysis, design, benchmarking, and optimization of business processes leading to BPM in companies. BPM provides an environment for analyzing and optimizing business processes.

Values are characterized by value determinants such as

- Time (cycle time and so on)
- Flexibility (options, customization, composition, and so on)
- Responsiveness (lead time, number of hand-offs, and so on)
- Quality (rework, rejects, yield, and so on)
- Price (discounts, rebates, coupons, incentives, and so on)

We must hasten to add that we are not disregarding cost (materials, labor, overhead, and so forth) as a value determinant. However, the effect of cost is truly a result of a host of value determinants such as time, flexibility, and responsiveness.

The nature and extent of a value addition to a product or service is the best measure of that addition's contribution to the company's overall goal for competitiveness. Such value expectations are dependent on the following:

- The customer's experience of similar product(s) and/or service(s)
- The value delivered by the competitors
- The capabilities and limitations of locking into the base technological platform

However, value as originally defined by Michael Porter in the context of introducing the concept of the value chain is meant more in the nature of the cost at various stages. Rather than a value chain, it is more of a cost chain! Porter's value chain is also structure oriented and hence a static concept. Here, we mean value as the satisfaction of not only external but also internal customers' requirements, as defined and continuously redefined, as the least total cost of acquisition, ownership, and use.

Consequently, in this formulation, one can understand the company's competitive gap in the market in terms of such process-based, customer-expected levels of value and the value delivered by the company's process for the concerned products or services. Customer responsiveness focuses on costs in terms of the yield. Therefore, we can perform market segmentation for a particular product or service in terms of the most significant customer values and the corresponding value determinants or what we term as critical value determinants (CVDs).

Strategic planning exercises can then be understood readily in terms of devising strategies for improving on these process-based CVDs based on the competitive benchmarking of these collaborative values and processes between the enterprise and customers. These strategies and the tactics resulting from analysis, design, and optimization of the process will in turn focus on the restrategizing of all relevant business process at all levels. This can result in the modification or deletion of the process or creation of a new one.

CONCEPT OF BUSINESS PROCESS MANAGEMENT (BPM)

Business Process Management (BPM) addresses the following two important issues for an enterprise:

1. The strategic long-term positioning of the business with respect to current and envisaged customers, which will ensure that the enterprise would be competitively and financially successful, locally and globally
2. The enterprise's capability/capacity that is the totality of all the internal processes that dynamically realizes this positioning of the business

Traditionally, positioning has been considered as an independent set of functional tasks split within the marketing, finance, and strategic planning functions. Similarly, capability/capacity has usually been considered the preserve of the individual operational departments that may have mutually conflicting priorities and measures of performances (see Chapter 3, section "ERP System Reflects and Mimics the Integrated Nature of an Enterprise").

The problem for many enterprises lies in the fact that there is a fundamental flaw in the organizational structure—organizational structures are hierarchical, while the transactions and workflows that deliver the solutions (i.e., products and services) to the customers are horizontal. Quite simply, the structure determines who the customer really is. The traditional management structures condition managers to put functional needs above those of the multifunctional processes to which their functions contribute. This results in

- Various departments competing for resources
- Collective failure in meeting or exceeding the customers' expectations
- Inability to coordinate and collaborate on multifunctional customer-centric processes that would truly provide the competitive differentiation in future markets

The traditional mass marketing type of organization works well for researching market opportunities, planning the offering, and scheduling all the steps required to produce and distribute the offering to the marketplace (where it is selected or rejected by the customer). It takes a very different kind of organization, namely, the customized marketing type organization to build long-term relationships with customers so that they call such organizations first when they have a need because they trust that such enterprises will be able to respond with an effective solution. This is customer-responsive management, which we will discuss in the section that follows.

BPM is the process that manages and optimizes the inextricable linkages between the positioning and the capability/capacity of an enterprise. A company cannot position the enterprise to meet a customer need that it cannot fulfill without an unprofitable level of resources nor can it allocate enhanced resources to provide a cost-effective service that no customer wants!

Positioning leads to higher levels of revenue through increasing the size of the market, retaining first-time customers, increasing the size of the wallet share, and so on. Positioning has to do with factors such as

- Understanding customer needs
- Understanding competitor initiatives
- Determining the businesses' financial needs
- Conforming with legal and regulatory requirements
- Conforming with environmental constraints

The capability/capacity has to be aligned with the positioning or else it has to be changed to deliver the positioning. Capability/capacity has to do with internal factors such as

- Key business processes
- Procedures and systems
- Competencies, skills, training, and education

The key is to have a perceived differentiation of being better than the competition in whatever terms the customers choose to evaluate or measure and to deliver this at the lowest unit cost.

In practice, BPM has developed a focus on changing capability/capacity in the short term to address current issues. This short-term change in capability/capacity is usually driven by the need to

- Reduce the cycle time to process customer orders
- Improve quotation times
- Lower variable overhead costs
- Increase product range to meet an immediate competitor threat
- Rebalance resources to meet current market needs
- Reduce work-in-progress stocks
- Meet changed legislation requirements
- Introduce short-term measures to increase market share (e.g., increased credit limit from customers hit by recessionary trends)

Business Process

A business process is typically a coordinated and logically sequenced set of work activities and associated resources that produce something of value to a customer. A business process can be simply defined as a collection of activities that create value by transforming inputs into more valuable outputs. These activities consist of a series of steps performed by actors to produce a product or service for the customer. Each process has an identified customer; it is initiated by a process trigger or a business event (usually a request for product or service arriving from the process customer); and it produces a process outcome (the product or a service requested by the customer) as its deliverable to the process customer.

A business process is a set of logically related tasks performed to achieve a well-defined business outcome. A (business) process view implies a horizontal view of a business organization and looks at processes as sets of interdependent activities designed and structured to produce a specific output for a customer or a market. A business process defines the results to be achieved, the context of the activities, the relationships between the activities, and the interactions with other processes and resources. A business process may receive events that alter the state of the process and the sequence of activities. A business process may produce events for input to other applications or processes. It may also invoke applications to perform computational functions, and it may post assignments to human work lists to request actions by human actors. Business processes can be measured, and different performance measures apply, such as cost, quality, time, and customer satisfaction.

 There is a substantial difference between the concept of Business Process Management (BPM) and Business Process Management Systems (BPM Systems). BPM is a concept of much broader scope than the BPM Systems that implement a subset of the tenets of BPM. In this chapter, after introducing the concept of BPM, the chapter focuses on leveraging the BPM-oriented capabilities of the enterprises, while Appendix I includes an overview of the BPM functionality provided by SAP Business Suite (see Appendix I "SAP Business Suite").

BUSINESS PROCESS MANAGEMENT (BPM)

Business Process Management (BPM) refers to activities performed by enterprises to design (capture processes and document their design in terms of process maps), model (define business processes in a computer language), execute (develop software that enables the process), monitor (track individual processes for performance measurement), and optimize (retrieve process performance for improvement) operational business processes by using a combination of models, methods, techniques, and tools. BPM approaches based on IT enable support or automate business processes, in whole or in part, by providing computer-based systems support. These technology-based systems help coordinate and streamline business transactions, reduce operational costs, and promote real-time visibility in business performance.

BPM can be defined as *managing the achievement of an organization's objectives through the improvement, management, and control of essential business processes.* BPM is focused on improving corporate performance by managing a company's business processes.

BPM is a commitment to expressing, understanding, representing, and managing a business (or the portion of business to which it is applied) in terms of a collection of business processes that are responsive to a business environment of internal or external events. The term management of business processes includes process analysis, process definition and redefinition, resource allocation, scheduling, measurement of process quality and efficiency, and process optimization. Process optimization includes collection and analysis of both real-time measures (monitoring) and strategic measures (performance management) and their correlation as the basis for process improvement and innovation. A BPM solution is a graphical productivity tool for modeling, integrating, monitoring, and optimizing process flows of all sizes, crossing any application, company boundary, or human interaction. BPM codifies value-driven processes and institutionalizes their execution within the enterprise. This implies that BPM tools can help analyze, define, and enforce process standardization. BPM provides a modeling tool to visually construct, analyze, and execute cross-functional business processes.

Scenarios suitable for considering application of BPM within various areas are as follows:

a. Management
- Lack of reliable or conflicting management information—process management and performance management and management will assist
- The need to provide managers with more control over their processes
- The need for the introduction of a sustainable performance environment
- The need to create a culture of high performance
- The need to gain the maximum return on investment (RoI) from the existing legacy systems
- Budget cuts

b. Customers/suppliers/partners
- An unexpected increase in number of customers, suppliers, or partners
- Long lead times to meet customer/supplier/partners requests
- Dissatisfaction with service, which could be due to
  - High churn rates of staff
  - Staff unable to answer questions adequately within the required time frames (responsiveness)
- An organizational desire to focus upon customer intimacy
- Customer segmentation or tiered service requirements
- The introduction and strict enforcement of service levels
- Major customers, suppliers, and/or partners requiring a unique (different) process
- The need for a true end-to-end perspective to provide visibility or integration

c. Product and services
- An unacceptably long lead time to market (lack of business agility)
- Product-specific services such as quality, compliance, etc.
- New products or services comprise existing product/service elements
- Products or services are complex

d. Organization
- The need to provide the business with more control of its own processes
- Organization objectives or goals are not being met—Introduction of process management, linked to organizational strategy, performance measurement, and management of people

- Compliance or regulation—For example, organizations currently have to comply with pollution, environment, and forest cover violation norms, hence process projects have been initiated—this process project has provided the platform to launch process improvement or BPM projects
- The need for business agility to enable the enterprise to respond to opportunities as they arise
- High growth—Difficulty coping with high growth or proactively planning for high growth
- Change in strategy—Deciding to change direction or pace of operational excellence, product leadership, or customer intimacy
- Reorganization or restructuring—Changing roles and responsibilities
- Mergers and acquisition scenario—These cause the organization to "acquire" additional complexity or necessitate rationalization of processes. The need to retire acquired legacy systems could also contribute. BPM projects enable a process layer to be "placed" across these legacy systems, providing time to consider appropriate conversion strategies

 Existing functioning processes also are prone to progressive degradation, loss of efficiencies because of altered circumstances, changes in products or services, etc. Business processes may become candidates for BPM because of

- The need for provision of visibility of processes from an end-to-end perspective
- Lack of communications and understanding of the end-to-end process by the parties performing parts of the process
- Unclear roles and responsibilities from a process perspective
- Lack of process standardization
- Quality is poor and the volume of rework is substantial
- Lack of clear process goals or objectives
- Too many hand-offs or gaps in a process, or no clear process at all
- Processes change too often or not at all

ENTERPRISE BPM METHODOLOGY

In this section, we look at the full life cycle of an enterprise's BPM methodology.

 Outsourcing is distancing the company from noncore but critical functions, as against this, reengineering, that is associated with BPM, is exclusively about the core.

We present an overview of the seven steps in a BPM methodology. These steps are as follows:

1. Develop the context for undertaking the BPM and in particular reengineer the enterprise's business processes. Then identify the reason behind redesigning the process to represent the value perceived by the customer
2. Select the business processes for the design effort
3. Map the selected processes
4. Analyze the process maps to discover opportunities for design
5. Design the selected processes for increased performance
6. Implement the designed processes
7. Measure the implementation of the designed processes

The eight steps of the enterprise BPR methodology are shown in Figure 7.1.

The BPR effort within an enterprise is not a one-time exercise but an ongoing one. One could also have multiple BPR projects in operation simultaneously in different areas within the enterprise. The BPR effort involves business visioning, identifying the value gaps and, hence, selection of the corresponding business processes for the BPR effort. The reengineering of the business processes might open newer opportunities and challenges, which in turn triggers another cycle of business visioning followed by BPR of the concerned business processes. Figure 7.2 shows the iteration across the alternating activities without an end.

Strategic Planning for Enterprise BPM

All markets are fluid to some degree, and these dynamic forces and shifting customer values necessitate changes in a company's strategic

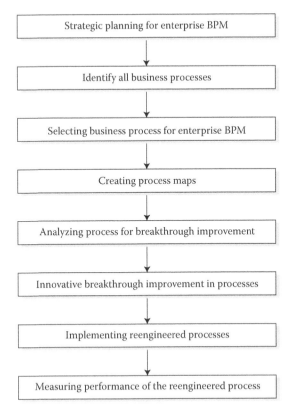

FIGURE 7.1
A cycle of enterprise BPR methodology.

plans. The significance of a process to the success of a company's business is dependent on the nature and extent of the value addition to a product or service. Consequently, as stated earlier, one can understand the competitive value gap in terms of the customer-expected level of value and the value delivered by the enterprise for the concerned product or service.

The competitive gap can be defined as the gap between the customer's minimum acceptance value (MAV) and the customer value delivered by the enterprise. Companies that consistently surpass MAVs are destined to thrive, those that only meet the MAVs will survive, and those that fall short of the MAVs may fail.

CVDs are those business imperatives that must happen if the enterprise wants to close the competitive gap and are similar to the critical success factors (CSF) at the enterprise level. CVDs are in terms of factors like

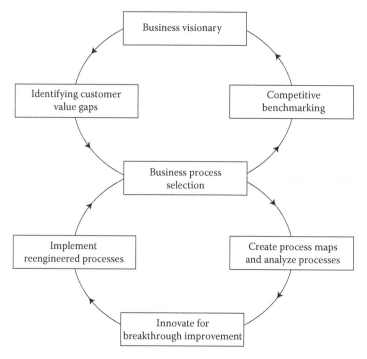

FIGURE 7.2
The alternate activities of business visioning and BPM.

- Time (lead time, cycle time, and so on)
- Flexibility (customization, options, composition, resource network interfaces, and so on)
- Responsiveness (lead time, duration, number of hand-offs, priority, number of queues, and so on)
- Quality of work (rework, rejects, yield, and so on)

Market segmentation is performed based on customer value and the corresponding CVDs. Such market segmentation helps in suggesting corrective strategic and tactical actions that may be required, such as in devising a process-oriented strategic business plan. The strategic plan can in turn help identify the major processes that support these critical value determinants that must be innovatively improved and reengineered.

Identifying the Business Processes in the Company

All business process in an enterprise are identified and recorded. A process can be defined as a set of resources and activities necessary and sufficient to convert some form of input into some form of output. Processes can be internal or external, or a combination of both. They have cross-functional boundaries, they have starting and ending points, and they exist at all levels within the enterprise, including section, department, division, and enterprise levels. In fact, processes exist across enterprise boundaries as well. Processes evolve and degrade in terms of their efficiency and effectiveness.

A process itself can consist of various substeps. The substeps in a process could be

- Value-added steps
- Non–value-added steps
- Legal and regulatory steps (which are treated as value-added steps)

Selecting Business Processes for BPM

Selecting the right processes for an innovative process reengineering effort is critical. The processes should be selected for their high visibility, relative ease of accomplishing goals, and, at the same time, their potential for great impact on the value determinants.

Customers will take their business to the company that can deliver the most value for their money. Hence, the MAVs have to be charted in detail. MAV is dependent upon several factors, such as

- The customer's prior general and particular experience base with an industry, product, and/or service.
- What competition is doing in the concerned industry, product, or service?
- What effect technological limitations have on setting the upper limit?

As mentioned earlier, MAVs can be characterized in terms of the CVDs; only four to six value determinants may be necessary to profile a market segment. CVDs can be defined by obtaining data through

   i. The customer value survey
  ii. Leaders in noncompeting areas
 iii. The best-in-class performance levels
 iv. Internal customers

A detailed Customer Value Analysis analyzes the value gaps and helps in further refining the goals of the process reengineering exercise. The value gaps are as follows:

- Gaps that result from different value perceptions in different customer groups
- Gaps between what the company provides and what the customer has established as the minimum performance level
- Gaps between what the company provides and what the competition provides
- Gaps between what the enterprise perceives as the MAV for the identified customer groups and what the customer says are the corresponding MAVs

It must be noted that analyzing the value gaps is not a one-time exercise; neither is it confined to the duration of a cycle of the breakthrough improvement exercise. Like the BPM exercise itself, it is an activity that must be done on an ongoing basis.

As a goal for the improvement effort, a clear, competitive advantage can be gained if best-in-class performance levels can be achieved in some key customer value areas and at least some MAVs can be achieved in all others.

Creating Process Maps

A process map documents the flow of one unit of work (the unit may be one item, one batch, or a particular service that is the smallest unit possible to follow separately) or what actually happens to the work going through the process. A process map is developed at several process levels, starting at the highest level of the enterprise. It documents both value-added and non–value-added steps. A process map could either be sequential or concurrent in nature.

Process could be mapped in two forms:

- Workflow chart form
- Work breakdown structure form

Process Workflows fall into three categories: Continuous Workflows, Balanced Workflows, and Synchronized Workflows.

Workflow becomes nonsynchronized because of

a. Steps or tasks produced at different rates, that is, an imbalanced workflow
b. Physical separation of operations causing work to move in batches, that is, a noncontinuous workflow
c. Working in batches, causing intermittent flow
d. Long setup or change-over times resulting in batched work along with its problems
e. Variations in process inputs in terms of quality availability on time

All these add time and costs to the process and reduce flexibility and responsiveness.

Using the value-added Workflow analysis of the process map, we can

i. Identify and measure significant reengineering opportunities
ii. Establish a baseline of performance against which to measure improvement
iii. Determine which tools may be most useful in the reengineering effort

Evidently, the major goal in reengineering the process is to eliminate non–value added steps and wait-times within processes. A good rule of thumb is to remove 60 to 80 percent of the non–value added steps, resulting in the total number of remaining steps to be no more than one to three times the number of value-added steps. Even this would be a credible goal for the first iteration of the BPR effort.

Analyzing Processes for Breakthrough Improvements

An enterprise's competitive strength lies in eliminating as many costly non–value added steps and wait-times as possible. The key to eliminating any non–value added steps is to understand what causes them and then eliminate the cause.

For breakthrough improvements, the process maps are analyzed for

- Enterprise complexity: Commonly organizational issues are a major deterrent to efficiency of the processes

- Number of handoffs, especially, other than those associated with resource network interfaces
- Work movement: Workflow charts are utilized to highlight move distances, that is, work movements.
- Process problems: Several factors may have a severe effect on the continuity, balance, or synchronicity of the workflow. Examples are loops of non–value added steps designed to address rework, errors, scraps, and so on. These may be on account of
  i.   Long changeover times
  ii. Process input/ output imbalances
  iii. Process variabilities
  iv. Process yields

These problems need to be identified, measured, analyzed, and resolved through innovative problem-solving methodology.

Innovative Breakthrough Improvement in Processes

The steps involved in innovative problem-solving methods are as follows:

a. Define a problem
b. Find alternate solutions
c. Evaluate the solutions
d. Implement the best solution
e. Measure and monitor the success

The responsive process consists of the following components:

- Diagnosing customer need
- Developing customized solutions specific to organizational interfaces
- Dynamically assigning work to the appropriate delivery unit
- Tracking performance as each task is completed

Business problems fall into three basic categories:

- System problems (methods, procedures, and so on)
- Technical problems (engineering, operational, and so on)

- People problems (skills, training, hiring, and so on): These problems arise because "if you change what a person does, you change what he or she is"

Implementing Designed Processes

This involves the following:

- Reengineered vision and policies
- Reengineered strategies and tactics
- Reengineered systems and procedures
- Reengineered communication environment
- Reengineered organization architecture
- Reengineered training environment

Measuring the Performance of Designed Processes

Measuring the performance of any process is very important, because lack of measurement would make it impossible to distinguish such a breakthrough effort from an incremental improvement effort of a Total Quality Management (TQM) program.

Measurements are essential because they are

- Useful as baselines or benchmarks
- A motivation for further breakthrough improvements, which are important for future competitiveness

The measures for innovative process reengineering should be

- Visible
- Meaningful
- Small in number
- Applied consistently and regularly
- Quantitative
- Involve personnel closest to the process

Table 7.1 enlists tools and techniques for continuous improvement and Table 7.2 lists some of the advanced techniques.

TABLE 7.1

Tools, Techniques, and Benefits for Continuous Improvement

Tools or Technique	Use
External customer survey	To understand the needs of the external customers
Internal customer survey	To understand the perceptions of internal services
Staff survey	To obtain employee feedback on work environment
Brainstorming	To generate ideas for improvements
Cause and effect diagrams	To prompt ideas during brainstorming
Benchmarking	To compare similar processes to find the best practice
Service Performance	To quantify the importance/performance of services
Activity data	To understand the allocation of time in processes
Activity categories	To obtain the level of core/support/diversionary activities
Activity drivers	To relate volumes of activity to causes
High–low diagram	To group objects using two variables
Force-field analysis	To show the forces acting for/against a variable
Histogram	To show frequency of a variable in a range
Scatter diagram	To view the correlation between two variables
Affinity analysis	To measure the strength of functional relationships
Bar chart	To plot the frequency of an event
Run chart	To show how a variable changes over time
Pie chart	To show frequency of a variable in a range

TABLE 7.2

Advanced Techniques for Continuous Improvement

Tools or Technique	Use
Statistical Process Control (SPC)	SPC is a means to understand if a process is producing and is likely to produce an output that meets the specifications within limits
Failure Mode and Effects Analysis (FMEA)	FMEA is a means to understand the nature of potential failure of component and effect this will have on the complete systems
Quality Function Deployment (QFD)	QFD is a structured process to build
Taguchi methods	The design of experiments to create robust processes/products where final quality is subject to many variables

BUSINESS PROCESS REENGINEERING (BPR)

Although, BPR has its roots in information technology (IT) management, it is basically a business initiative that has major impact on the satisfaction of both the internal and external customer. Michael Hammer, who triggered the BPR revolution in 1990, considers BPR as a "radical change" for which IT is the key enabler. BPR can be broadly termed as *the rethinking and change of business processes to achieve dramatic improvements in the measures of performances such as cost, quality, service, and speed.*

Some of the principals advocated by Hammer are as follows:

- Organize around outputs, not tasks.
- Put the decisions and control, and hence all relevant information, into the hands of the performer.
- Have those who use the outputs of a process perform the process, including the creation and processing of the relevant information.
- The location of user, data, and process information should be immaterial; it should function as if all were in a centralized place.

As will become evident when perusing the above points, the implementation of ES especially BPM possesses most of the characteristics mentioned above.

The most important outcome of BPR has been viewing business activities as more than a collection of individual or even functional tasks; it has engendered the process-oriented view of business. However, BPR is different from quality management efforts like TQM, ISO 9000, and so on, that refer to programs and initiatives that emphasize bottom-up incremental improvements in existing work processes and outputs on a continuous basis. In contrast, BPR usually refers to top-down dramatic improvements through redesigned or completely new processes on a discrete basis. In the continuum of methodologies ranging from ISO 9000, TQM, ABM, and so on on one end and BPR on the other, ES especially BPM implementation definitely lies on the BPR side of the spectrum when it comes to corporate change management efforts.

BPR is based on the principle that there is an inextricable link between positioning *and* capability/capacity. A company cannot position the enterprise to meet a customer need that it cannot fulfill without an unprofitable level of resources, nor can it allocate enhanced resources to provide a cost-effective service that no customer wants!

BPR in practice has developed a focus on changing capability/capacity in the short term to address current issues. This short-term change in capability/capacity is usually driven by the need to

- Reduce the cycle time to process customer orders
- Improve quotation times
- Lower variable overhead costs
- Increase product range to meet an immediate competitor threat
- Rebalance resources to meet current market needs
- Reduce work-in-progress stocks
- Meet changed legislation requirements
- Introduce short-term measures to increase market share (e.g., increased credit limit from customers hit by recessionary trends)
- Etc.

 Outsourcing is distancing the company from noncore but critical functions; as against this, reengineering is exclusively about the core.

An overview of a seven-step methodology is as follows:

1. Develop the context for undertaking the BPR and in particular reengineer the enterprise's business processes. Then identify the reason behind redesigning the process to represent the value perceived by the customer.
2. Select the business processes for the reengineering effort.
3. Map the selected processes.
4. Analyze the process maps to discover opportunities for reengineering.
5. Redesign the selected processes for increased performance.
6. Implement the reengineered processes.
7. Measure the implementation of the reengineered processes.

The BPR effort within an enterprise is not a one-time exercise but an ongoing one. One could also have multiple BPR projects in operation simultaneously in different areas within the enterprise. The BPR effort involves business visioning, identifying the value gaps, and hence, selection of the corresponding business processes for the BPR effort. The reengineering of the business processes might open newer opportunities and challenges, which in turn triggers another cycle of business visioning followed by BPR of the concerned business processes.

It must be noted that analyzing the value gaps is not a one-time exercise; neither is it confined to the duration of a cycle of the breakthrough improvement exercise. Like the BPR exercise itself, it is an activity that must be done on an ongoing basis. Above all, selecting the right processes for an innovative process reengineering effort is critical. The processes should be selected for their high visibility, relative ease of accomplishing goals, and at the same time, their potential for great impact on the value determinants.

MANAGEMENT BY COLLABORATION (MBC)

The business environment has been witnessing tremendous and rapid changes in the 1990s. There is an increasing emphasis on being customer focused and on leveraging and strengthening the company's core competencies. This has forced enterprises to learn and develop abilities to change and respond rapidly to the competitive dynamics of the global market.

Companies have learned to effectively reengineer themselves into flatter organizations, with closer integration across the traditional functional boundaries of the enterprise. There is increasing focus on employee empowerment and cross-functional teams. In this book, we are proposing that what we are witnessing is a fundamental transformation in the manner that businesses have been operating for the last century.

This change, which is primarily driven by the information revolution of the past few decades, is characterized by the dominant tendency to integrate across transaction boundaries, both internally and externally. The dominant theme of this new system of management with significant implications on organizational development is *collaboration*. We will refer to this emerging and maturing constellation of concepts and practices as Management by Collaboration (MBC). ES especially BPM is a major instrument for realizing MBC-driven enterprises.

MBC is an approach to management primarily focused on relationships; relationships by their very nature are not static and are constantly in evolution. As organizational and environmental conditions become more complex, globalized, and therefore, competitive, MBC provides a framework for dealing effectively with the issues of performance improvement, capability development, and adaptation to the changing environment. MBC, as embodied by ES packages such as BPM, has had a major impact on the strategy, structure, and culture of the customer-centric enterprise.

The beauty and essence of MBC are that it incorporates in its very fabric the basic urge of humans for a purpose in life; for mutually beneficial relationships; for mutual commitment; and for being helpful to other beings, that is, for collaborating. These relationships could be at the level of individual, division, enterprise, or even between enterprises. Every relationship has a purpose, and manifests itself through various processes as embodied mainly in the form of teams; thus, the relationships are optimally geared toward attainment of these purposes through the concerned processes.

Because of the enhanced role played by the individual members of an enterprise in any relationship or process, MBC promotes not only their motivation and competence, but also develops the competitiveness and capability of the enterprises as a whole. MBC emphasizes the roles of both the top management and the individual member. Thus, the MBC approach covers the whole organization through the means of basic binding concepts such as relationships, processes, and teams. MBC addresses readily all issues of management, including organization development. The issues range from organizational design and structure, role definition and job design, output quality and productivity, interaction and communication channels, and company culture to employee issues such as attitudes, perception, values, and motivation.

The basic idea of collaboration has been gaining tremendous ground with the increasing importance of business processes and dynamically constituted teams in the operations of companies. The traditional bureaucratic structures, which are highly formalized, centralized, and functionally specialized, have proven too slow, too expensive, and too unresponsive to be competitive. These structures are based on the basic assumption that all the individual activities and task elements in a job are independent and separable. Organizations were structured hierarchically in a "command and control" structure, and it was taken as an accepted fact that the output of the enterprise as a whole could be maximized by maximizing the output of each constituent organizational unit.

On the other hand, by their very nature, teams are flexible, adaptable, dynamic, and collaborative. They encourage flexibility, innovation, entrepreneurship, and responsiveness. For the last few decades, even in traditionally bureaucratic-oriented manufacturing companies, teams have manifested themselves and flourished successfully in various forms as super teams, self-directed work teams (SDWT), quality circles, and so on. The dynamic changes in the market and global competition being confronted by companies necessarily lead to flatter and more flexible organizations with a dominance of more dynamic structures like teams.

People in teams, representing different functional units, are motivated to work within constraints of time and resources to achieve a defined goal. The goals might range from incremental improvements in responsiveness, efficiency, quality, and productivity to quantum leaps in new-product development. Even in traditional businesses, the number and variety of teams instituted for various functions, projects, tasks, and activities has been on the increase.

Increasingly, companies are populated with worker-teams that have special skills, operate semi autonomously, and are answerable directly to peers and to the end customers. Members must not only have higher level of skills than before, but must also be more flexible and capable of doing more jobs. The empowered workforce with considerably enhanced managerial responsibilities (pertaining to information, resources, authority, and accountability) has resulted in an increase in worker commitment and flexibility. Whereas workers have witnessed gains in the quality of their work life, corporations have obtained returns in terms of increased interactivity, responsiveness, quality, productivity, and cost improvements.

Consequently, in the past few years, a new type of nonhierarchical network organization with distributed intelligence and decentralized decision-making powers has been evolving. This entails a demand for constant and frequent communication and feedback among the various teams or functional groups. ES packages such as BPM essentially provides such an enabling environment through modules such as BI, PLM, and so on.

Relationship-Based Enterprise (RBE)

A Relationship-Based Enterprise (RBE) builds customer relationships to sustain business growth and to increase the profitability of the business. A relationship is a series of dialogs each consisting of numerous instantaneous interactions with the customer. The Relationship-Based Enterprise has the ability to recognize and interact with different types of customers. The Enterprise uses these dynamic interactions to discover its customers through customer-related and customer's needs-related information, and to create value by organizing itself to serve those customers. Customers and their corresponding needs are changing constantly depending on the market environment and, therefore, it is only because of these dynamic interactions that it can continue to discover the current needs of its customers.

Information-Driven Enterprise

The combined impact on companies of increasing product complexity together with increased variety has been to create a massive problem of information management and coordination. Information-based activities now constitute a major fraction of all activities within an enterprise. Information-based enterprises alone can enable companies to survive in the dynamically changing global competitive market. Only integrated, computer-based information systems such as ES, and especially BPM are (and can be) enablers for this kind of enterprise-level collaboration.

The information-based organization as proposed by management theorist Peter Drucker is a reality today; correspondingly, companies are compelled to install both end user and work–group-oriented enterprise-level integrated computing environments. Only information-based extended enterprises can possibly store, retrieve, analyze, and present colossal amount of information at the enterprise-level that is also up to date, timely, accurate, collated, processed, and packaged dynamically for both external and internal customers. It should be noted that this subsection title uses the phrase "information-driven" rather than "information-based." The primary reason for this is technology in the 1990s permits us to use information as a resource that is a legitimate substitute for conventional resources.

Process-Oriented Enterprise

Collaborations or relationships manifest themselves through the various organizational and inter organizational processes. A *process* may be generally defined as the set of resources and activities necessary and sufficient to convert some form of input into some form of output. Processes are internal, external, or a combination of both; they have cross-functional boundaries; they have starting and ending points; and they exist at all levels within the organization.

Thus, MBC not only recognizes inherently the significance of various process-related techniques and methodologies such as Process Innovation (PI), Business Process Improvement (BPI), Business Process Redesign (BPRD), and Business Process Reengineering (BPR), Business Process Management (BPM) and so on, but also treats them as fundamental, continuous, and integral functions of the management of a company itself. A collaborative enterprise enabled by the implementation of an ES like BPM is inherently amenable to business process improvement, which is also the essence of any Total Quality Management (TQM)-oriented effort undertaken within an enterprise.

Value-Add-Driven Enterprise

Business processes can be seen as the very basis of the value addition within an enterprise that was traditionally attributed to various functions or divisions in an organization. As organizational and environmental conditions become more complex, globalized, and competitive, processes provide a framework for dealing effectively with the issues of performance improvement, capability development, and adaptation to the changing environment.

Along a value stream (that is, a business process), analysis of the absence or creation of added value or (worse) destruction of value critically determines the necessity and effectiveness of a process step. The understanding of value-adding and non–value-adding processes (or process-steps) is a significant factor in the analysis, design, benchmarking, and optimization of business processes in the companies leading to the BPM. ES especially BPM provides an environment for analyzing and optimizing business processes.

Values are characterized by value determinants such as time (cycle time and so on), flexibility (options, customization, composition, and so on), responsiveness (lead time, number of hand-offs, and so on), quality (rework, rejects, yield, and so on), and price (discounts, rebates, coupons, incentives, and so on). We must hasten to add that we are not disregarding cost (materials, labor, overhead, and so forth) as a value determinant. However, the effect of cost is truly a result of a host of value determinants such as time, flexibility, responsiveness, and so on.

Consequently, in this formulation, one can understand completely the company's competitive gap in the market in terms of such process-based, customer-expected value and the value delivered by the enterprise's processes for the concerned product or service. We will refer to such customer-defined characteristics of value as Critical Value Determinants (CVDs). Therefore, we can perform market segmentation for a particular (group of) product or service in terms of the most significant of the customer values and the corresponding CVDs.

Enterprise Change Management

Strategic planning exercises can be understood readily in terms of devising strategies for improving on these process-oriented CVDs based on the competitive benchmarking of these values. The strategies resulting from analysis, design, and optimization of especially the customer-facing processes would in turn result in a focus on the redesign of all relevant business process at all levels. This could result in the modification or deletion of the concerned processes or even the creation of a new process.

Initiating and confronting change are the two most important issues facing the enterprises of today. The ability to change business processes contributes directly to the "innovation" bottom line. The traditional concept of change management is usually understood as a one-time event. But if an enterprise is looking for the capability not only to handle change management, but also management of changes on a continual basis then ES like BPM, is a must!

ES like BPM enables the essential changing of customer-facing processes that are so critical to the success of an enterprise. Business processes that "reside" or are internalized within an organization's employees are difficult to change simply because human beings naturally find it more difficult to change. However, processes that reside within any computerized systems are much easier to change. The consequences of using information technology/information systems (IT/IS) can itself be managed by using more IT! The abstraction and electronic manipulation that have increased the speed of change can itself be used to manage (transparently to end users) these changes. It is reported that in mid-1980s, managers at the Australian bank Westpac concluded that the bank's adaptability to change could be enhanced by first modularizing and then codifying core functions, policies, and knowledge in a computerized system. Linking this separate system to regular operational systems, the bank was able to reduce their time-to-market with new products; thus, the bank was able to enhance its ability to meet changed market conditions in weeks or months instead of months or years.

Learning Enterprise

RBE builds customer relationships based on customer-related information. Evidently, all this information is necessarily finite in nature and also keeps on changing with changes in the customer environment. RBE recognizes that perfect information at any instance and especially on an on-going basis is impossible and, therefore, incorporates them incrementally. Customer Responsive Management enables enterprises to be more adaptable to changing conditions and responsive to smaller markets. It recognizes that forecasting and planning become more difficult as the marketplace and environment become more turbulent. It gives frontline workers more responsibility and authority so that they can innovate. The delivered solution may be expensive, but it is probably less expensive than the traditional deterministic planning and approval process. The solution may not be optimal, but the customer gets served and the first delivered solution occurrence serves as a learning process for a new set of guidelines that will need to be developed. Thus, the detailed planning of work is done at the frontline. Customer responsive management develops numerous best-practice guidelines to guide frontline workers as they interact with customers to plan solutions and also enable them to modify them, if necessary, to improve the customer fit. After the problem has been identified and resolved, it is added dynamically to the best-practice guidelines. It is the dynamic development of best-practice guidelines that keeps the enterprise flexible in responding to new needs and in making continual improvements to the process as new techniques and technologies develop.

MBC also underlies the contemporary notion of the learning organization. To compete in an ever-changing environment, an organization must learn and adapt. Because organizations cannot think and learn by themselves, it is truly the individuals constituting the organization who have to do this learning. The amount of information in an enterprise is colossal. A single individual, however intelligent and motivated, cannot learn and apply all the knowledge required for operating a company. Moreover, even this colossal amount of information does not remain constant, but keeps changing and growing.

The only effective solution is collaborative learning, that is, sharing this learning experience among a team of people. This not only caters to differences in the aptitudes and backgrounds of people, they all can also do this learning simultaneously, thus drastically shortening the turnaround time in the learning process itself. If organizational learning is seen in terms of the creation and management of knowledge, it is very easy for us to see the essential need to share the learning experience among the various member teams at the enterprise level and, within each team, among the members of the teams. Thus, we see another reason for collaboration among and within teams for contributing effectively to the learning process of the organization as a whole.

 What distinguishes learning from mere training is the transformation that results from the former. This, again, can be implemented successfully only by collaborations between various teams as becomes apparent when such collaborations are embodied in the form of ES packages, such as BPM.

Virtual Enterprise

Along with the general economic growth and globalization of markets, personal disposable incomes have increased, so the demand for product variety and customization have increased appreciably. Additionally, technological progress driven by the search for superior performance is already increasing the complexity of both products and especially customer-facing processes. Because volume, complexity, and variety are mutually exclusive, this has invariably led to collaborative endeavors for achieving this with greater flexibility in terms of enhancing of capabilities, minimization of risks, lower costs of investments, shortened product life cycles, and so on.

These collaborative endeavors, which have been known variously as partnering, value-added partnering, partnership sourcing, outsourcing, alliances, virtual corporations, and so on recognize the fact that optimization of the system as a whole is not achievable by maximization of the output at the constituting subsystem levels alone. Only BPMS can provide a backbone for holding together the virtual value chain across all these collaborative relationships.

Outsourcing will become a dominant trend in the millennium enterprise, whereby the enterprise concentrates only on being competitive in its core business activities and outsources the responsibility of competitiveness in noncore products and functions to third parties for mutual benefit. The development and maintenance of its core competencies are critical to the success of its main business; an enterprise cannot outsource these because it is these core functions that give it an identity. On the other hand, competitiveness in noncore functions, which is also essential for overall efficiencies, is outsourced to enterprises that are themselves in business of providing these very products or services; the outsourced products and services offerings are *their* core competencies.

Most of the major manufacturers the world over have become to a large extent "systems integrators," providing only some of the specialized parts and final assembly of subsystems from a network of suppliers (see Chapter 5, section "Networks of Resources"). Their economic role has transformed mainly into the basic planning, coordination, design, marketing, and service, but not complete production per se. For the existence and growth of such virtual enterprises, it is important that the company be able to manage the complexities of managing such relationships on a day-to-day basis. A PRM system provides all the functionality and processes for managing and accounting for such outsourced jobs. But, more significantly, only a PRM system can make it possible for such a collaborative enterprise to exist and grow to scales unimaginable with traditional organizational architectures.

BUSINESS PROCESSES WITH SOA

Every enterprise has unique characteristics that are embedded in its business processes. Most enterprises perform a similar set of repeatable routine activities that may include the development of manufacturing products and services, bringing these products and services to market and satisfying the customers who purchase them. Automated business processes can perform such activities. We may view an automated business process as a precisely choreographed sequence of activities systematically directed toward performing a certain business task and bringing it to completion. Examples of typical processes in manufacturing firms include among other things new product development (which cuts across research and development, marketing, and manufacturing), customer order fulfillment (which combines sales, manufacturing, warehousing, transportation, and billing), and financial asset management. The possibility to design, structure, measure processes, and determine their contribution to customer value makes them an important starting point for business improvement and innovation initiatives.

The largest possible process in an organization is the value chain. The value chain is decomposed into a set of core business processes and support processes necessary to produce a product or product line. These core business processes are subdivided into activities. An activity is an element that performs a specific function within a process. Activities can be as simple as sending or receiving a message or as complex as coordinating the execution of other processes and activities. A business process may encompass complex activities, some of which run on back-end systems, such as a credit check, automated billing, a purchase order, stock updates and shipping, or even such frivolous activities as sending a document, and filling a form. A business process activity may invoke another business process in the same or a different business system domain. Activities will inevitably vary greatly from one company to another and from one business analysis effort to another.

At runtime, a business process definition may have multiple instantiations, each operating independently of the other, and each instantiation may have multiple activities that are concurrently active. A process instance is a defined thread of activity that is being enacted (managed) by a workflow engine. In general, instances of a process, its current state, and the history of its actions will be visible at runtime and expressed in terms of the business process definition so that

- Users can determine the status of business activities and business
- Specialists can monitor the activity and identify potential improvements to the business process definition

Process

A process is an ordering of activities with a beginning and an end; it has inputs (in terms of resources, materials, and information) and a specified output (the results it produces). We may thus define a process as any sequence of steps that is initiated by an event; transforms information, materials, or commitments; and produces an output. A business process is typically associated with operational objectives and business relationships, for example, an insurance claims process or an engineering development process. A process may be wholly contained within a single organizational unit or may span different enterprises, such as in a customer–supplier relationship. Typical examples of processes that cross organizational boundaries are purchasing and sales processes jointly set up by buying and selling organizations, supported by EDI and value-added networks. The Internet is now a trigger for the design of new business processes and the redesign of existing ones.

A business process has the following behavior:

- It may contain defined conditions triggering its initiation in each new instance (e.g., the arrival of a claim) and defined outputs at its completion.
- It may involve formal or relatively informal interactions between participants.
- It has a duration that may vary widely.
- It may contain a series of automated activities and/or manual activities. Activities may be large and complex, involving the flow of materials, information, and business commitments.
- It exhibits a very dynamic nature, so it can respond to demands from customers and to changing market conditions.
- It is widely distributed and customized across boundaries within and between enterprises, often spanning multiple applications with very different technology platforms.
- It is usually long running—a single instance of a process such as order to cash may run for months or even years.

Every business process implies processing: A series of activities (processing steps) leading to some form of transformation of data or products for which the process exists. Transformations may be executed manually or in an automated way. A transformation will encompass multiple processing steps. Finally, every process delivers a product, like a mortgage or an authorized invoice. The extent to which the end product of a process can be specified in advance and can be standardized impacts the way that processes and their workflows can be structured and automated.

Processes have decision points. Decisions have to be made with regard to routing and allocation of processing capacity. In a highly predictable and standardized environment, the trajectory in the process of a customer order will be established in advance in a standard way. Only if the process is complex and if the conditions of the process are not predictable will routing decisions have to be made on the spot. In general, the customer orders will be split into a category that is highly proceduralized (and thus automated) and a category that is complex and uncertain. Here, human experts will be needed, and manual processing is a key element of the process.

Workflow

A workflow system automates a business process, in whole or in part, during which documents, information, or tasks are passed from one participant to another for action, according to a set of procedural rules. Workflows are based on document life cycles and form-based information processing, so generally they support well defined, static, clerical processes. They provide transparency, since business processes are clearly articulated in the software, and they are agile because they produce definitions that are fast to deploy and change.

A workflow can be defined as the sequence of processing steps (execution of business operations, tasks, and transactions), during which information and physical objects are passed from one processing step to another. Workflow is a concept that links together technologies and tools able to automatically route events and tasks with programs or users.

Process-oriented workflows are used to automate processes whose structure is well defined and stable over time, which often coordinate subprocesses executed by machines and which only require minor user involvement (often only in specific cases). An order management process or a loan request is an example of a well-defined process. Certain process-oriented workflows may have transactional properties. The process-oriented workflow is made up of tasks that follow routes, with checkpoints represented by business rules, for example, a pause for a credit approval. Such business process rules govern the overall processing of activities, including the routing of requests, the assignment or distribution of requests to designated roles, the passing of workflow data from activity to activity, and the dependencies and relationships between business process activities.

A workflow involves activities, decision points, rules, routes, and roles. These are briefly described later. Just like a process, a workflow normally comprises a number of logical steps, each of which is known as an activity. An activity is a set of actions that are guided by the workflow. An activity may involve manual interaction with a user or workflow participant or may be executed using diverse resources such as application programs or databases. A work item or data set is created and is processed and changed in stages at a number of processing or decision points to meet specific business goals. Most workflow engines can handle very complex series of processes.

A workflow can depict various aspects of a business process including automated and manual activities, decision points and business rules, parallel and sequential work routes, and how to manage exceptions to the normal business process. A workflow can have logical decision points that determine which branch of the flow a work item may take in the event of alternative paths. Every alternate path within the flow is identified and controlled through a bounded set of logical decision points. An instantiation of a workflow to support a work item includes all possible paths from beginning to end.

Within a workflow, business rules at each decision point determine how workflow-related data are to be processed, routed, tracked, and controlled. Business rules are core business policies that capture the nature of an enterprise's business model and define the conditions that must be met in order to move to the next stage of the workflow. Business rules are represented as compact statements about an aspect of the business that can be expressed within an application, and as such, they determine the route to be followed. For instance, for a health-care application, business rules may include policies on how new claim validation, referral requirements, or special procedure approvals are implemented. Business rules can represent among other things typical business situations such as escalation ("send this document to a supervisor for approval") and managing exceptions ("this loan is more than $50,000; send it to the MD").

Business Process Management (BPM)

BPM is a commitment to expressing, understanding, representing, and managing a business (or the portion of business to which it is applied) in terms of a collection of business processes that are responsive to a business environment of internal or external events. The term management of business processes includes process analysis, process definition and redefinition, resource allocation, scheduling, measurement of process quality and efficiency, and process optimization. Process optimization includes collection and analysis of both real-time measures (monitoring) and strategic measures (performance management) and their correlation as the basis for process improvement and innovation. A BPM solution is a graphical productivity tool for modeling, integrating, monitoring, and optimizing process flows of all sizes, crossing any application, company boundary, or human interaction. BPM codifies value-driven processes and institutionalizes their execution within the enterprise. This implies that BPM tools can help analyze, define, and enforce process standardization. BPM provides a modeling tool to visually construct, analyze, and execute cross-functional business processes.

BPM is more than process automation or traditional workflow. BPM within the context of EAI and e-business integration provides the flexibility necessary to automate cross-functional processes. It adds conceptual innovations and technology from EAI and e-business integration and reimplements it on an e-business infrastructure based on Web and XML standards. Conventional applications provide traditional workflow features that work well only within their local environment. However, integrated process management is then required for processes spanning enterprises. Automating cross-functional activities, such as checking or confirming inventory between an enterprise and its distribution partners, enables corporations to manage processes by exception based on real-time events driven from the integrated environment. Process execution then becomes automated, requiring human intervention only in situations where exceptions occur; for example, inventory level has fallen below a critical threshold or manual tasks and approvals are required.

 The distinction between BPM and workflow is mainly based on the management aspect of BPM systems: BPM tools place considerable emphasis on management and business functions. Although BPM technology covers the same space as workflow, its focus is on the business user and provides more sophisticated management and analysis capabilities. With a BPM tool, the business user is able to manage all the processes of a certain type, for example, claim processes, and should be able to study them from historical or current data and produce costs or other business measurements. In addition, the business user should also be able to analyze and compare the data or business measurements based on the different types of claims. This type of functionality is typically not provided by modern workflow systems.

Business Processes via Web Services

Business processes management and workflow systems today support the definition, execution, and monitoring of long-running processes that coordinate the activities of multiple business applications. However, because these systems are activity oriented and not communication (message) oriented, they do not separate internal implementation from external protocol description. When processes span business boundaries, loose coupling based on precise external protocols is required because the parties involved do not share application and workflow implementation technologies and will not allow external control over the use of their back-end applications. Such business interaction protocols are by necessity message centric; they specify the flow of messages representing business actions among trading partners, without requiring any specific implementation mechanism. With such applications, the loosely coupled, distributed nature of the Web enable exhaustive and full orchestration, choreography, and monitoring of the enterprise applications that expose the Web Services participating in the message exchanges.

Web Services provide a standard and interoperable means of integrating loosely coupled Web-based components that expose well-defined interfaces, while abstracting the implementation- and platform-specific details. Core Web Service standards such as SOAP, WSDL, and UDDI provide a solid foundation to accomplish this. However, these specifications primarily enable the development of simple Web Service applications that can conduct simple interactions. However, the ultimate goal of Web Services is to facilitate and automate business process collaborations both inside and outside enterprise boundaries. Useful business applications of Web Services in EAI and business-to-business environments require the ability to compose complex and distributed Web Service integrations and the ability to describe the relationships between the constituent low-level services. In this way, collaborative business processes can be realized as Web Service integrations.

A business process specifies the potential execution order of operations originating from a logically interrelated collection of Web Services, each of which performs a well-defined activity within the process. A business process also specifies the shared data passed between these services, the external partners' roles with respect to the process, joint exception handling conditions for the collection of Web Services, and other factors that may influence how Web Services or organizations participate in a process.

This would enable long-running transactions between Web Services in order to increase the consistency and reliability of business processes that are composed out of these Web Services.

The orchestration and choreography of Web Services are enabled under three specification standards, namely, the Business Process Execution Language for Web Services (BPEL4WS or BPEL for short), WS-Coordination (WS-C), and WS-Transaction (WS-T). These three specifications work together to form the bedrock for reliably choreographing Web Service-based applications, providing BPM, transactional integrity, and generic coordination facilities. BPEL is a workflow-like definition language that describes sophisticated business processes that can orchestrate Web Services. WS-Coordination and WS-Transaction complement BPEL to provide mechanisms for defining specific standard protocols for use by transaction processing systems, workflow systems, or other applications that wish to coordinate multiple Web Services.

Service Composition

The platform-neutral nature of services creates the opportunity for building composite services by combining existing elementary or complex services (the component services) from different enterprises and in turn offering them as high-level services or processes. Composite services (and, thus, processes) integrate multiple services—and put together new business functions—by combining new and existing application assets in a logical flow.

The definition of composite services requires coordinating the flow of control and data between the constituent services. Business logic can be seen as the ingredient that sequences, coordinates, and manages interactions among Web Services. By programming a complex cross-enterprise workflow task or business transaction, it is possible to logically chain discrete Web Services activities into cross-enterprise business processes. This is enabled through orchestration and choreography (because Web Services technologies support coordination and offer an asynchronous and message-oriented way to communicate and interact with application logic).

Orchestration

Orchestration describes how Web Services can interact with each other at the message level, including the business logic and execution order of the interactions from the perspective and under the control of a single endpoint. This is, for instance, the case of the process flow where the business process flow is seen from the vantage point of a single supplier. Orchestration refers to an executable business process that may result in a long-lived, transactional, multistep process model. With orchestration, business process interactions are always controlled from the (private) perspective of one of the business parties involved in the process.

Choreography

Choreography is typically associated with the public (globally visible) message exchanges, rules of interaction, and agreements that occur between multiple business process endpoints, rather than a specific business process that is executed by a single party. Choreography tracks the sequence of messages that may involve multiple parties and multiple sources, including customers, suppliers, and partners, where each party involved in the process describes the part it plays in the interaction and no party owns the conversation. Choreography is more collaborative in nature than orchestration. It is described from the perspectives of all parties (common view) and, in essence, defines the shared state of the interactions between business entities. This common view can be used to determine specific deployment implementations for each individual entity. Choreography offers a means by which the rules of participation for collaboration can be clearly defined and agreed to, jointly. Each entity may then implement its portion of the choreography as determined by their common view.

SUMMARY

BPMS enable the reconciled, i.e., collaborative working of different cross-company stakeholders of any business process, activity, or decision in compliance with its strategy, policy, and procedures. After introducing the concept of BPM, the chapter described the BPM methodology in detail. The chapter looked at management by collaboration (MBC) as a unifying framework in the context of the customer-centric and customer-responsive enterprise. The chapter also introduced Service Oriented Architecture (SOA) to explain the realization of processes in terms of Web Services.

8

Informed Enterprise with BI

Business Intelligence (BI) enables enterprises to access current, correct, consistent, and complete information on any process or transaction in order to take informed decisions in compliance with its strategy, policy, and procedures.Other than the concept and technologies of BI, the chapter introduces the novel concept of decision patterns that consolidate based on on-going operations and transactions, and then expedite the efficacy of decisions. A BI ecosystem consists of data warehouse management tools, Extract, Transform, and Load (ETL), data integration, and BI tools. The main BI activities include query, reporting, Online Analytical Processing (OLAP), statistical analysis, forecasting, data mining, and decision support.

CONCEPT OF BUSINESS INTELLIGENCE (BI)

A number of enterprises have started to view their data as a corporate asset and to realize that properly collecting, aggregating, and analyzing their data opens an opportunity to discover gems of knowledge that can both automate business decisions in certain well-defined areas of activity, or support business decisions in the context of customary and recurring decision patterns of the past (see section "Decision Patterns as Context"). At the least, they can improve operational processing and provide better insight into customer profiles and behavior. BI is the process of using advanced applications and technologies to gather, store, analyze, and transform the overload of business information into actionable knowledge that provides significant business value. The concept of BI has been introduced into the marketplace in order to enhance the ability to make better and more efficient business decisions.

> There is a substantial difference between the concept of Business Intelligence (BI) and Business Intelligence Systems (BI Systems). BI is a concept of much broader scope than the BI Systems that implement a subset of the tenets of BI. In this chapter, after introducing the concept of BI, the chapter focuses on leveraging the BI-oriented capabilities of the enterprises, while Appendix I includes an overview of the BI functionality provided by SAP Business Suite (see Appendix I "SAP Business Suite").

BUSINESS INTELLIGENCE (BI)

Business Intelligence can be defined as the techniques, technologies, and tools needed to turn data into information, information into actionable knowledge, and actionable knowledge into execution plans that drive profitable business action. Business intelligence encompasses data warehousing, business analytic tools, and content/knowledge management.

BI involves the infrastructure of managing and presenting data including the hardware platforms, relational or other type of database systems, and associated software tools for governance and compliance. It also incorporates query, processing, and reporting tools that provide informed access to the data. Additionally, BI involves analytical components, such as online analytical processing (OLAP), data quality, data profiling, predictive analysis, and other types of data mining. Being able to take action based on the intelligence that has been gleaned from BI is the key point of any BI. It is through these actions that a senior management sponsor can see the true return on investment for investment in BI. A BI program provides insights and/or decision support that increase business efficiency, increase sales, provide better customer targeting, reduce customer service costs, identify fraud, and generally increase profits while reducing corresponding costs. Figure 8.1 presents an overview of the architecture of an Business Intelligence system.

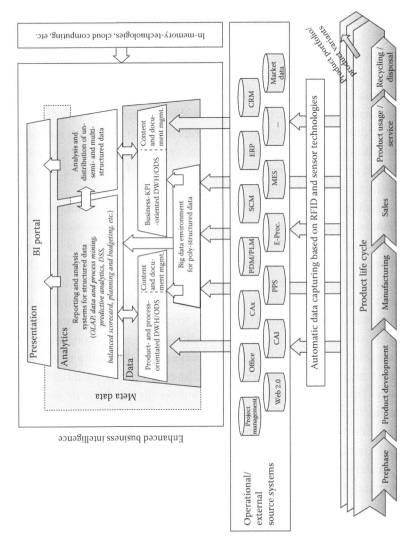

FIGURE 8.1
Business Intelligence Architecture.

BENEFITS OF BI

1. Improve the competitive response and decision-making process

   To realize a long lasting competitive advantage, an organization needs to have rapid and continuous innovation and dynamic coupling of processes so that they cannot be easily duplicated. Moreover, firms also need to leverage on resources such as structural capital, human capital, and relationship capital to achieve sustainable competitive advantage. With BI systems connected to customer relationship management, enterprise resource planning, human resource and finance systems, information can be produced in a more accurate and timely manner. BI systems thus make up a complex solution that allows decision makers to create, aggregate, and share knowledge in an organization easily, along with greatly improved service quality for efficient decision making.

2. Enhancing effectiveness of Customer Relationship Management (CRM)

   Leveraging BI, CRM enhances the relationships between the organization and its customers. With good relationships, customers' loyalty can then be achieved and future sales generated. With timely information available for executives and managers to make better and faster decisions, the organization will be able to provide quality service to its customers and respond effectively to changing business conditions. A BI-enabled CRM provides an organization with the ability to categorize or segment its existing customer base and prospects more accurately. This may be accomplished based on the products or services that a client purchases, demographic information for consumer clients, industry sector, or company size for corporate clients, and so on. BI-enabled

   Customer relationship management allows an organization to better understand the trend or buying pattern of its existing customers and the segmentation of the customer-base would assist sales and marketing to sell products or services (which their customers want) as below:

   i. Revenue generation via customer profiling and targeted marketing: Business intelligence reports and analyses reflecting customer transactions and other interactions enable the development of individual customer profiles incorporating demographic, psychographic, and behavioral data about each individual to support customer community segmentation into a variety of clusters based on different attributes and corresponding values. These categories form the basis of sales and profitability measures by customer category, helping to increase sales efforts and customer satisfaction.

ii. Improved customer satisfaction via profiling, personalization, and customer lifetime value analysis: Employing the results of customer profiling can do more than just enhance that customer's experience by customizing the presentation of material or content. Customer profiles can be directly integrated into all customer interactions, especially at inbound call centers, where customer profiles can improve a customer service representative's ability to deal with the customer, expedite problem resolution, and perhaps even increase product and service sales. Customer lifetime value analysis calculates the measure of a customer's profitability over the lifetime of the relationship, incorporating the costs associated with managing that relationship as well as the revenues expected from that customer.

iii. Risk management via identification of fraud, abuse, and leakage: Fraud detection is a type of analysis that looks for prevalent types of patterns that appear with some degree of frequency within certain identified scenarios. Fraud, which includes intentional acts of deception with knowledge that the action or representation could result in an inappropriate gain, rather than being an exception or a work around, is often perpetrated through the exploitation of systemic scenarios. Reporting of the ways that delivered products and services matched with what had been sold to customers (within the contexts of their contracts/agreements) may highlight areas of revenue leakage. Both of these risks can be analyzed and brought to the attention of the proper internal authorities for remediation.

iv. Improved procurement and acquisition productivity through spend analysis: Spend analysis incorporates the collection, standardization, and categorization of product purchase and supplier data to select the most dependable vendors, streamline the RFP and procurement process, reduce costs, improve the predictability of high-value supply chains, and improve supply-chain predictability and efficiency.

3. Easing corporate governance and regulatory compliance
With increased expectations on traceability of data, the organization must be able to verify the lineage of data, starting at its source

and tracking it through its various manipulations and aggregations, which in turn means having reliable metadata and data auditing that are consistent across the enterprise. In this respect, BI assists in ensuring accuracy of data across the enterprise. It allows reporting and query results to be consistent when they are produced. This is crucial for corporate governance and regulatory compliance when auditing does not find discrepancies in the reports produced.

TECHNOLOGIES OF BI

Data Warehousing and Data Marts

Data warehouses allow sophisticated analysis of large amounts of time-based data, independently of the systems that process the daily transactional data of the enterprise. A data warehouse typically contains time-based summarizations of the underlying detailed transactions; only necessary attributes are extracted from the original source data. Then the data are transformed to conform to the format of the data warehouse and also "cleansed" to ensure quality. In order to create these summary "snapshots," the level of summary detail for the data components must be predefined; and it is fixed for the life of the warehouse, ensuring consistent analysis. This level of summarization is called the granularity of the warehouse. This granularity then determines, for all subsequent data retrieval, the level of transactional detail available for any potential analysis. Aggregating the data reduces the overall number of records necessary to perform specific analyses.

Business Intelligence

Operational enterprise systems are designed to support traditional reporting requirements such as day books, party (customer and supplier) ledgers, balance sheets, income statements, and cash flow statements. Data are captured and maintained at the transaction level and later summarized for specific reporting periods. Enterprise data requirements also tend to be relatively short-term, again to support the most recent statement reporting. Once the data have been processed and the accounting period closed, the data are archived.

On the other hand, business intelligence information is structured to provide real-time data that are essential in current decision-making processes. The transactional data collected by traditional enterprise information systems are useful but are not the only source of data for business intelligence. In today's enterprises, data collection goes beyond the enterprise data, and it is often stored in distributed and heterogeneous environments. Consequently, business intelligence requirements create significant data storage and manipulation problems that are not encountered in standard enterprise reporting. Furthermore, the short-term availability of data for enterprise requirements, because of its archival, is in contrast to the data needs of business intelligence, which tend to require longer time periods (e.g., to support trending and comparative analysis) as well as the need for complex modeling processes. To create useful information, the enterprise data must be aggregated and supplemented by data from other sources that describe the organizational environment.

 The fundamental difference between data warehousing and BI is the data requirements and the need to manipulate it in order to provide alternative views of the data. Typically, enterprise requirements center around repetitive time-based aggregations, whereas business intelligence needs are more dynamic and require sophisticated models.

A major challenge in designing a business intelligence system stems from the relationship between the detailed operational and aggregated data warehouse systems. The data warehouse model creates a design and implementation situation where the supply of data has been predefined (legacy enterprise systems, other internal data collection systems, and external data repositories); but the user requirements have not been defined. User requirements tend to be ambiguous and require significant flexibility to respond to changing competitive requirements (unlike standard enterprise reporting). To address this problem of incongruent levels of granularity among systems, data marts have been employed. A data mart is a more limited data collection, designed to address the needs of specific users, as opposed to the more general audience of the warehouse. The data mart, however, still draws data from the general data warehouse and consequently is still governed by the granularity and scope restrictions dictated for the warehouse. Figure 8.2 shows the general relationship among operational data, data warehouses, and data marts.

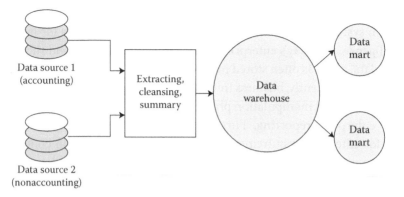

FIGURE 8.2
Relationship among Operational Data, Data Warehouse, and Data Marts.

Data Mining

Data mining is of great interest because it is imperative for enterprises to realize the competitive value of the information residing within their data repositories. The goal of data mining is to provide the capability to convert high-volume data into high-value information. This involves discovering patterns of information within large repositories of enterprise data. Enterprises that are most likely to benefit from data mining

   i. Exist in competitive markets
  ii. Have large volumes of data
 iii. Have communities of information consumers who are not trained as statisticians
 iv. Have enterprise data that are complex in nature

More traditional Business Intelligence (BI) tools enable users to generate ad-hoc reports, business graphics, and test hunches. This is useful for analyzing profitability, product line performance, and so on. Data mining techniques can be applied when users do not already know what they are looking for: Data mining provides an automatic method for discovering patterns in data (see Delmater and Hancock 2001).

Data mining accomplishes two different things:

- It gleans enterprise information from historical data.
- It combines historic enterprise information with current conditions and goals to reduce uncertainty about enterprise outcomes.

Customer-centric data mining techniques can be used to build models of past business experience that can be applied to predict customer behavior and achieve benefits in the future. Data mining provides the following insights:

- Learning patterns that allow rapid, proper routing of customer inquiries
- Learning customer buying habits to suggest likely products of interest
- Categorizing customers for focused attention (e.g., churn prediction, prevention)
- Providing predictive models to reduce cost and allow more competitive pricing (e.g., fraud/waste control)
- Assisting purchasers in the selection of inventory of customer-preferred products

Online Analytical Process (OLAP)

OLAP accommodates queries that would otherwise have been computationally impossible on a relational database management system. OLAP technology is characterized by multidimensionality, and the concept represents one of its key features. Generally, OLAP involves many data items in complex relationships. Its objectives are to analyze these relationships and look for patterns, trends, exceptions, and to answer queries. It is necessary to note that the whole process of OLAP must be carried out online with rapid response time to provide just-in-time information for effective decision making. OLAP operations typically include rollup (increasing the level of aggregation) and drill-down (decreasing the level of aggregation or increasing the details) along with one or more dimension hierarchies, slice and dice (selection and projection), and pivot (reorienting the multidimensional view of data). For instance, it allows users to analyze data such as revenue from any dimension such as region or product line anytime of the year. The ability to present data in different perspectives involves complex calculations between data elements, thus enables users to pursue an analytical process without being thwarted by the system.

APPLICATIONS OF BI

BI is thus applicable to various industries such as communications, education, financial services, government and public sector, consumer product goods, healthcare, pharmaceuticals, retail, technology, manufacturing, etc. for the purposes of improving productivity and enhancing decision making.

1. Banking and Financial Services

   BI has been applied in the banking and financial services industry to perform customer risk analysis and customer valuation on issues such as current profitability, lifetime potential of a customer based on costs, revenues, and future predictive behavior, among others. BI has the ability to do profiling by identifying like-minded customers, thus enabling more accurate segmentation. It also has the ability to create, refine, and target campaigns to win profitable new customers. With these capabilities intertwined with the CRM effort, banking, and financial institutions are able to effectively serve their customers and gain deeper customer insight. In addition, BI automates compliance with reporting standards and regulations which are crucial to these institutions to improve control and productivity.

2. Pharmaceuticals and Life Sciences

   BI has been applied in the pharmaceuticals and life sciences services industry to identify products that yield better results with a clinical trial research process that segments, tracks, analyzes, and shares test results. The systems can also analyze and report on clinical performance data to identify best practices and decide whether to continue, pursue, or terminate a project. BI enables optimizing the supply chain by sharing production information with suppliers, tracking product quality, optimizing stock replenishment, and monitoring vendor performance. Similarly, BI optimizes campaign creation and implementation by analyzing the effectiveness of marketing strategies, and increases sales productivity by understanding sales activities, territory, and representative performances. BI enhances operational, sales, and marketing performance and enables better compliance with regulatory requirements.

3. Retail

   BI has been applied to improve purchasing, forecasting, and distribution management. BI systems help retailers to optimize product profitability and increase the effectiveness of marketing campaigns, identify and segment customers to enable retention strategies, integrate management and financial reporting for improved performance, reduce and control operational costs through optimized store performance and effective customer service. BI is able to help in increasing profit margins by aligning corporate and store operations around critical revenue and profitable targets, providing sales and item movement information to operations, marketing, and merchandising, improving customer satisfaction by identifying trends and responding to customer buying needs and behavior, and optimizing profitability by planning and adjusting resources accordingly. Firms are able to improve store performance by improving visibility and accountability for top controllable expenses like labor and cost of goods sold, by communicating sales and margin information across the chain with enterprise-scale reporting, through identification of high or low performing divisions, stores, channels, products, and staff, by optimizing staffing levels through headcount planning and workforce analytics, and monitoring turnover, customer satisfaction, returns, sales trends, and employee utilization through retail scorecards.

4. Manufacturing

BI has been applied to improve sales performance, increase profitability, improve operational effectiveness, and optimize the supply chain. BI has been applied in the manufacturing industry to analyze cost components and drivers, in order to reduce the cost of goods sold. BI is also able to gain visibility into demand and sales trends in order to optimize investments in inventory. With BI systems, manufacturing companies can identify and analyze excess, obsolete, or slow-moving inventory that can be scrapped or repurposed. Companies can also receive timely notification of events such as late supplier delivery, changes in customer demand, or production stoppages. With the help of BI and integration with CRM, SCM, and PLM efforts, these companies are able to respond quickly to changing markets and company sensitivities.

CONTEXT-AWARE APPLICATIONS

Most mobile applications are location-aware systems. Specifically, tourist guides are based on users' location in order to supply more information on the city attractions closer to them or the museum exhibit they are viewing. Nevertheless, recent years have seen many mobile applications trying to exploit information that characterizes the current situation of users, places, and objects in order to improve the services provided.

The principle of context-aware applications (CAA) can be explained using the metaphor of the Global Positioning System (GPS). In aircraft navigation, for example, a GPS receiver derives the speed and direction of an aircraft by recording over time the coordinates of longitude, latitude, and altitude. This contextual data is then used to derive the distance to the destination, communicate progress to date, and calculate the optimum flight path.

For a GPS-based application to be used successfully, the following activities are a prerequisite:

a. The region in focus must have been GPS-mapped accurately
b. The GPS map must be superimposed with the relevant information regarding existing landmarks, points of civic and official significance, and facilities and service points of interest to people in the past—this is the context in this metaphor
c. There must be a system available to ascertain the latest position per the GPS system
d. The latest reported position must be mapped and transcribed on to the GPS-based map of the region
e. This latest position relative to the context (described in b above) is used as the point of reference for future recommendation(s) and action(s)

It should be noted that the initial baseline of the context (described in b above) is compiled and collated separately and then uploaded into the system to be accessible by the CAA. However, with passage of time, this baseline gets further added to with the details of each subsequent transaction.

We can also imagine an equivalent of the Global Positioning System for calibrating the performance of enterprises. The coordinates of longitude, latitude, and altitude might be replaced by ones of resource used, process performed, and product produced. If we designed a GPS for an enterprise, we could measure its performance (e.g., cost or quality) in the context of the resource used, the process performed, and the product delivered as compared with its own performance in the past (last month or one year back etc.) or in particular cases, that of another target organization. Such an approach could help us specify our targets, communicate our performance, and signal our strategy.

Most of the current context-aware systems have been built in an ad-hoc approach, and are deeply influenced by the underlying technology infrastructure utilized to capture the context. To ease the development of context-aware ubicomp (ubiquitous computing) and mobile applications it is necessary to provide universal models and mechanisms to manage context. Even though significant efforts have been devoted to research methods and models for capturing, representing, interpreting, and exploiting context information, we are still not close to enabling an implicit and intuitive awareness of context, nor efficient adaptation to behavior at the standards of human communication practice.

Context information can be a decisive factor in mobile applications in terms of selecting the appropriate interaction technique. Designing interactions among users and devices, as well as among devices themselves, is critical in mobile applications. Multiplicity of devices and services calls for systems that can provide various interaction techniques and the ability to switch to the most suitable one according to the user's needs and desires. Current mobile systems are not efficiently adaptable to the user's needs. The majority of ubicomp and mobile applications try to incorporate the users' profile and desires into the system's infrastructure either manually or automatically observing their habits and history. According to the perspective being presented here, the key point is to give them the ability to create their own mobile applications instead of just customizing the ones provided.

Thus, mobile applications can be used not only for locating users and providing them with suitable information, but also for

- Providing them with a tool necessary for composing and creating their own mobile applications
- Supporting the system's selection of appropriate interaction techniques
- A selection of recommendation(s) and consequent action(s) conforming with the situational constraints judged via the business logic and other constraints sensed via the context
- Enabling successful closure of the interaction (answer to a query, qualifying an objection, closing an order, etc.)

Decision Patterns as Context

This chapter discusses location-based services applications as a particular example of context-aware applications. But, context-aware applications can significantly enhance the efficiency and effectiveness of even routinely occurring transactions. This is because most end-user application's effectiveness and performance can be enhanced by transforming it from a bare transaction to a transaction clothed by the surround of a context formed as an aggregate of all relevant decision patterns utilized in the past.

The decision patterns contributing to a transaction's context include the following:

- Characteristic and sundry details associated with the transaction under consideration
- Profiles of similar or proximate transactions in the immediately prior week or month or six-months or last year or last season
- Profiles of similar or proximate transactions in same or adjacent or other geographical regions
- Profiles of similar or proximate transactions in same or adjacent or other product groups or customer groups

To generate the context, the relevant decision patterns can either be discerned or discovered by mining the relevant pools or streams of primarily transaction data. Or they could be augmented or substituted by conjecturing or formulating decision patterns that explain the existence of these characteristic pattern(s) (in the pools or streams of primarily transaction data). In the next subsection, we look at function-specific decision patterns with particular focus on financial decision patterns.

 Thus, generation of context itself is critically dependent on employing big data and mobilized applications, which in turn needs cloud computing as a prerequisite.

Concept of Patterns

The concept of patterns used in this book originated from the area of real architecture. Alexander gathered architectural knowledge and best practices regarding building structures in a pattern format. This knowledge was obtained from years of practical experience. A pattern according to Alexander is structured text that follows a well-defined format and captures nuggets of advice on how to deal with recurring problems in a specific domain. It advises the architect on how to create building architectures, defines the important design decisions, and covers limitations to consider. Patterns can be very generic documents, but may also include concrete measurements and plans. Their application to a certain problem is, however, always a manual task that is performed by the architect. Therefore, each application of a pattern will result in a differently looking building, but all applications of the pattern will share a common set of desired properties. For instance, there are patterns describing how eating tables should be sized so that people can move around the table freely, get seated comfortably, find enough room for plates and food, while still being able to communicate and talk during meals without feeling too distant from people seated across the table. While the properties of the table are easy to enforce once concrete distances and sizes are specified, they are extremely hard to determine theoretically or by pure computation using a building's blueprint.

In building architecture, pattern-based descriptions of best practices and design decisions proved especially useful, because many desirable properties of houses, public environments, cities, streets, etc., are not formally measurable. They are perceived by humans and, thus, cannot be computed or predicted in a formal way. Therefore, best practices and well-perceived architectural styles capture a lot of implicit knowledge about how people using and living in buildings perceive their structure, functionality, and general feel. Especially, the indifferent emotion that buildings trigger, such as awe, comfort, coziness, power, cleanness, etc., are hard to measure or explain and are also referred to as the quality without a name or the inner beauty of a building. How certain objectives can be realized in architecture is, thus, found only through practical experience, which is then captured by patterns. For example, there are patterns describing how lighting in a room should be realized so that people feel comfortable and positive. Architects capture their knowledge gathered from existing buildings and feedback they received from users in patterns describing well-perceived building design. In this scope, each pattern describes one architectural solution for an architectural problem. It does so in an abstract format that allows the implementation in various ways. Architectural patterns, thus, capture the essential properties required for the successful design of a certain building area or function while leaving large degrees of freedom to architects.

Multiple patterns are connected and interrelated resulting in a pattern language. This concept of links between patterns is used to point to related patterns. For example, an architect reviewing patterns describing different roof types can be pointed to patterns describing different solutions for windows in these roofs and may be advised that some window solutions, thus, the patterns describing them, cannot be combined with a certain roof pattern. For example, a flat rooftop cannot be combined with windows that have to be mounted vertically. Also, a pattern language uses these links to guide an architect through the design of buildings, streets, cities, etc., by describing the order in which patterns have to be considered. For example, the size of the ground on which a building is created may limit the general architecture patterns that should be selected first. After this, the number of floors can be considered, the above-mentioned roofing style, etc.

Patterns in Information Technology (IT) Solutions

In a similar way, the pattern-based approach has been used in IT to capture best practices how applications and systems of applications should be designed. Examples are patterns for fault-tolerant software, general application architectures, object-oriented programming, enterprise applications, or for message-based application integration. Again, these patterns are abstract and independent of the programming language or runtime infrastructure used to form timeless knowledge that can be applied in various IT environments. In the domain of IT solutions, the desirable properties are portability, manageability, flexibility to make changes, and so on. The properties of IT solutions become apparent over time while an application is productively used, evolves to meet new requirements, has to cope with failures, or has to be updated to newer versions. During this lifecycle of an application, designers can reflect on the IT solution to determine whether it was well designed to meet such challenges.

Patterns in CRM

Traditional marketing theory and practice has always assumed that enhancing revenues and maximizing profits can be achieved by expanding the customer base. While this may be a viable strategy, it may not hold true at all times. For instance, in mature industries and mature markets, customer acquisition may not hold the key to better financial performance: Higher acquisition rates and retention rates do not necessarily result in higher profitability. While key customer metrics such as acquisition, retention, churn, and win-back are essential for establishing a profitable CRM strategy, merely "maximizing" each of these individual metrics is not necessarily a guarantee for success. Implementing specific and tailored strategies for key customer metrics yields a greater impact on customer decisions and can therefore lead to higher profitability. Prevailing patterns in CRM data can help in developing these specific strategies in each of the four steps of the customer—firm relationship life cycle: Acquisition, retention, churn, and win-back.

a. Acquisition: The acquisition strategy involves attaining the highest possible customer acquisition rate by implementing mass-level strategies. Any combination of mass marketing (radio, billboards, etc.) and direct marketing (telemarketing, mail, e-mail, etc.) would be implemented in order to target "eligible" customers rather than "interested" ones. A new approach to CRM pertaining to customer acquisition is gaining ground: There is a conscious move from mass marketing of products to one that is focused on the end consumer. Differentiating and segmenting with regards to demographic, psychographic, or purchasing power-related characteristics became more affordable and possible, and eventually became necessary in order to keep up with competing firms. As firms have become more capable and committed with data analyses, offerings have become more specific, thus increasing the amount of choice for customers. This has in turn spurred customers to expect more choice and customization in their purchases. It is through the continued improvements and innovations in data collection, storage, and analysis that acquisition has moved toward one-to-one acquisition.

b. Retention: Since the early 1960s, companies have changed their focus from short-term acquisition and transactions to long-term relationships and CLTV. In fact, retention studies indicate that for every 1% improvement in the customer retention rate, a firm's value increases by 5%.

c. Churn or attrition: Many firms fail to realize is that the majority of customers who are in the churn stage will not complain or voice their concerns. A study on this found that an estimated 4% of customers in the churn stage will actually voice their opinions, with the other 96% are lost without voicing their discontent. Further, about 91% of the lost customers will never be won back.

d. Win back: Although reacquiring lost customers may be a hard sell, it has been found that firms still have a 20–40% chance of selling to lost customers vs. only 5–20% of selling to new prospects.

DOMAIN-SPECIFIC DECISION PATTERNS

In the following, we discuss as illustrations, decision patterns for two domains or functional areas, namely, finance and customer relationship management (CRM). While the former is a formalized area to a large degree because of statutory and regulatory requirements, the latter is defined and fine-tuned, across an extended period of operational experience, by the specific requirements of the business, offerings, and geographic region(s) in which the company operates.

Financial Decision Patterns

Financial management focuses on both the acquisition of financial resources on as favorable terms as possible and the utilization of the assets that those financial resources have been used to purchase, as well as looking at the interaction between these two activities. Financial planning and control is an essential part of the overall financial management process. Establishment of precisely what the financial constraints are and how the proposed operating plans will impact them are a central part of the finance function. This is generally undertaken by the development of suitable aggregate decision patterns like financial plans that outline the financial outcomes that are necessary for the organization to meet its commitments. Financial control can then be seen as the process by which such plans are monitored and necessary corrective action proposed when significant deviations are detected.

Financial plans are constituted of three decision patterns:

1. Cash flow planning: This is required to ensure that cash is available to meet the payments the organization is obliged to meet. Failure to manage cash flows will result in technical insolvency (the inability to meet payments when they are legally required to be made). Ratios are a set of powerful tools to report these matters. For focusing on cash flows and liquidity, a range of ratios based on working capital are appropriate; each of these ratios addresses a different aspect of the cash collection and payment cycle.

    The five key ratios that are commonly calculated are
    • Current ratio, equal to current assets divided by current liabilities
    • Quick ratio (or acid test), equal to quick assets (current assets less inventories) divided by current liabilities

- Inventory turnover period, equal to inventories divided by cost of sales, with the result being expressed in terms of days or months
- Debtors to sales ratio, with the result again being expressed as an average collection period
- Creditors to purchases ratio, again expressed as the average payment period

There are conventional values for each of these ratios (for example, the current ratio often has a standard value of 2.0 mentioned, although this has fallen substantially in recent years because of improvements in the techniques of working capital management, and the quick ratio a value of 1.0), but in fact these values vary widely across firms and industries. More generally helpful is a comparison with industry norms and an examination of the changes in the values of these ratios over time that will assist in the assessment of whether any financial difficulties may be arising.

2. Profitability: This is the need to acquire resources (usually from revenues acquired by selling goods and services) at a greater rate than using them (usually represented by the costs of making payments to suppliers, employees, and others). Although, over the life of an enterprise, total net cash flow and total profit are essentially equal, in the short term, they can be very different. In fact, one of the major causes of failure for new small business enterprises is not that they are unprofitable but that the growth of profitable activity has outstripped the cash necessary to resource it. The major difference between profit and cash flow is in the acquisition of capital assets (i.e., equipment that are bought and paid for immediately, but that have likely benefits stretching over a considerable future period) and timing differences between payments and receipts (requiring the provision of working capital).

   For focusing on longer-term profitability with short-term cash flows, profit to sales ratios can be calculated (although different ratios can be calculated depending whether profit is measured before or after interest payments and taxation). Value-added (sales revenues less the cost of bought-in supplies) ratios can also be used to give insight into operational efficiencies.

3. Assets: Assets entail the acquisition and, therefore, the provision of finance for their purchase. In accounting terms, the focus of attention is on the balance sheet, rather than the profit and loss (P/L) account or the cash flow statement.

For focusing on the raising of capital as well as its uses, a further set of ratios based on financial structure can be employed. For example, the ratio of debt to equity capital (gearing or leverage) is an indication of the risk associated with a company's equity earnings (because debt interest is deducted from profit before obtaining profit distributable to shareholders). It is often stated that fixed assets should be funded from capital raised on a long-term basis, while working capital should fund only short-term needs.

It is necessary to be aware that some very successful companies flout this rule to a considerable extent. For example, most supermarket chains fund their stores (fixed assets) out of working capital because they sell their inventories for cash several times before they have to pay for them—typical inventory turnover is three weeks, whereas it is not uncommon for credit to be granted for three months by their suppliers.

There is, therefore, no definitive set of financial ratios that can be said to measure the performance of a business entity. Rather, a set of measures can be devised to assess different aspects of financial performance from different perspectives. Although some of these measures can be calculated externally, being derived from annual financial reports, and can be used to assess the same aspect of financial performance across different companies, care needs to be taken to ensure that the same accounting principles have been used to produce the accounting numbers in each case. It is not uncommon for creative accounting to occur so that acceptable results can be reported. This draws attention especially to the interface between management accounting (which is intended to be useful in internal decision making and control) and financial accounting (which is a major mechanism by which external stakeholders, especially shareholders, may hold managers accountable for their oversight).

Financial scandals, such as Enron and WorldCom, have highlighted that a considerable amount of such manipulation is possible palpably within generally acceptable accounting principles (GAAPs). There is clear evidence that financial numbers alone are insufficient to reveal the overall financial condition of an enterprise. Part of the cause has been the rules-based approach of US financial reporting, in contrast to the principles-based approach adopted in United Kingdom. One result of the reforms that have followed these scandals has been a greater emphasis on operating information. In addition, legislation such as the Sarbanes–Oxley Act (SOX) in the United States has required a much greater disclosure of the potential risks surrounding an enterprise, reflected internally by a much greater emphasis on risk management and the maintenance of risk registers.

The finance function serves a boundary role; it is an intermediary between the internal operations of an enterprise and the key external stakeholders who provide the necessary financial resources to keep the organization viable. Decision patterns like financial ratios allow internal financial managers to keep track of a company's financial performance (perhaps in comparison with that of its major competitors), and to adjust the activities of the company, both operating and financial, so as to stay within acceptable bounds. A virtuous circle can be constructed whereby net cash inflows are sufficient to pay adequate returns to financiers and also contribute toward new investment; given sound profitability, the financiers will usually be willing to make additional investment to finance growth and expansion beyond that possible with purely internal finance. Conversely, a vicious cycle can develop when inadequate cash flows preclude adequate new investment, causing a decline in profitability, and so the company becomes unable to sustain itself.

CRM Decision Patterns

This section describes an overview of the statistical models-based decision patterns used in CRM applications as the guiding concept for profitable customer management. The primary objectives of these systems are to acquire profitable customers, retain profitable customers, prevent profitable customers from migrating to competition, and winning back "lost" profitable customers. These four objectives collectively lead to increasing the profitability of an enterprise.

CRM strategies spanning the full customer lifecycle are constituted of four decision patterns or models:

a. Customer acquisition: This involves decisions on identifying the right customers to acquire, forecasting the number of new customers, the response of promotional campaigns, and so on. The objectives of customer acquisition modeling includes identifying the right customers to acquire, predicting whether customers will respond to company promotion campaigns, forecasting the number of new customers, and examining the short- and long-run effects of marketing and other business variables on customer acquisition.

This is a conscious move from mass marketing of products to one that is focused on the end consumer. This is a direct result of increases in data collection and storage capabilities that have uncovered layer upon layer of customer differentiation. Differentiating and segmenting with regard to demographic, psychographic, or purchasing power-related characteristics became more affordable and possible, and eventually became necessary in order to keep up with competing firms. Although segment-level acquisition did not take this theory to the extent that one-to-one customer acquisition has, it reinforced a growing trend of subsets or groups of customers within a larger target market. Being able to collect, store, and analyze customer data in more practical, affordable, and detailed ways has made all of this possible. As firms have become more capable and committed with data analyses, offerings have become more specific, thus increasing the amount of choice for customers. This has in turn spurred customers to expect more choice and customization in their purchases. This continuous firm–customer interaction has consistently shaped segment-level marketing practices in the process to better understand customers.

The decision patterns would incorporate:
- Differences between customers acquired through promotions and those acquired through regular means
- Effect of marketing activities and shipping and transportation costs on acquisition
- Impact of the depth of price promotions
- Differences in the impact of marketing-induced and word-of-mouth customer
- Acquisition on customer equity

b. Customer retention: This involves decisions on who will buy, what the customers will buy, when they will buy, and how much they will buy, and so on. During the customer's tenure with the firm, the firm would be interested in retaining this customer for a longer period of time. This calls for investigating the role of trust and commitment with the firm, metrics for customer satisfaction, and the role of loyalty and reward programs, among others. The objective of customer retention modeling includes examining the factors influencing customer retention, predicting customers' propensity to stay with the company or terminate the relationship, and predicting the duration of the customer–company relationship. Customer retention strategies are used in both contractual (where customers are bound by contracts such as cell [mobile] phone subscription or magazine subscription) and noncontractual settings (where customers are not bound by contracts such as grocery purchases or apparel purchases).

Who to retain can often be a difficult question to answer. This is because the cost of retaining some customers can exceed their future profitability and thus make them unprofitable customers. When to engage in the process of customer retention is also an important component. As a result, firms must monitor their acquired customers appropriately to ensure that their customer loyalty is sustained for a long period of time. Finally, identifying how much to spend on a customer is arguably the most important piece of the customer retention puzzle. It is very easy for firms to over communicate with a customer and spend more on his/her retention than the customer will ultimately give back to the firm in value.

The decision patterns would incorporate:
- Explaining customer retention or defection
- Predicting the continued use of the service relationship through the customer's expected future use and overall satisfaction with the service
- Renewal of contracts using dynamic modeling
- Modeling the probability of a member lapsing at a specific time using survival analysis
- Use of loyalty and reward programs for retention
- Assessing the impact of a reward program and other elements of the marketing mix

c. Customer attrition or churn: This involves decisions on whether the customer will churn or not, and if so what will be the probability of the customer churning, and when. The objective of customer attrition modeling includes churn with time-varying covariates, mediation effects of customer status and partial defection on customer churn, churn using two cost-sensitive classifiers, dynamic churn using time-varying covariates, factors inducing service switching, antecedents of switching behavior, and impact of price reductions on switching behavior.

Engaging in active monitoring of acquired and retained customers is the most crucial step in being able to determine which customers are likely to churn. Determining who is likely to churn is an essential step. This is possible by monitoring customer purchase behavior, attitudinal response, and other metrics that help identify customers who feel underappreciated or underserved. Customers who are likely to churn do demonstrate "symptoms" of their dissatisfaction, such as fewer purchases, lower response to marketing communications, longer time between purchases, and so on. The collection of customer data is therefore crucial in being able to identify and capture such "symptoms" and that would help in analyzing the retention behavior and the choice of communication medium. Understanding who to save among those customers who are identified as being in the churn phase is again a question of cost versus future profitability.

The decision patterns would incorporate:
- When are the customers likely to defect
- Can we predict the time of churn for each customer
- When should we intervene and save the customers from churning
- How much do we spend on churn prevention with respect to a particular customer

d. Customer win-back: This involves decisions on reacquiring the customer after the customer has terminated the relationship with the firm. The objective of customer win-back modeling includes customer lifetime value, optimal pricing strategies for recapture of lost customers, and the perceived value of a win-back offer.

Identifying the right customers to win back depends on factors such as the interests of the customers to reconsider their choice of quitting, the product categories that would interest the customers, and the stage of customer life cycle and so on. If understanding what to offer customers in winning them back is an important step in the win-back process, measuring the cost of win-back is as important as determining who to win back and what to offer them. The cost of win-back, much like the cost of retention or churn, must be juxtaposed with the customer's future profitability and value to the firm.

CRM Decision Patterns through Data Mining

CRM systems like SAP CRM are used to track and efficiently organize inbound and outbound interactions with customers, including the management of marketing campaigns and call centers. These systems, referred to as operational CRM systems, typically support frontline processes in sales, marketing, and customer service, automating communications and interactions with the customers. They record contact history and store valuable customer information. They also ensure that a consistent picture of the customer's relationship with the organization is available at all customer "touch" (interaction) points. These systems are just tools that should be used to support the strategy of effectively managing customers.

However, to succeed with CRM, organizations need to gain insight into customers, their needs, and wants through data analysis. This is where analytical CRM comes in. Analytical CRM is about analyzing customer information to better address CRM objectives and deliver the right message to the right customer. It involves the use of data mining models in order to assess the value of the customers, understand, and predict their behavior. It is about analyzing data patterns to extract knowledge for optimizing the customer relationships. For example,

- Data mining can help in customer retention as it enables the timely identification of valuable customers with increased likelihood to leave, allowing time for targeted retention campaigns.
- Data mining can support customer development by matching products with customers and better targeting of product promotion campaigns.
- Data mining can also help to reveal distinct customer segments, facilitating the development of customized new products and product offerings which better address the specific preferences and priorities of customers.

The results of the analytical CRM procedures should be loaded and integrated into the operational CRM frontline systems so that all customer interactions can be more effectively handled on a more informed and "personalized" base.

Marketers strive to get a greater market share and a greater share of their customers, i.e., they are responsible for getting, developing, and keeping the customers. Data mining aims to extract knowledge and insight through the analysis of large amounts of data using sophisticated modeling techniques; it converts data into knowledge and actionable information. Data mining models consist of a set of rules, equations, or complex functions that can be used to identify useful data patterns, understand, and predict behaviors.

Data mining models are of two kinds:

i. Predictive or Supervised Models: In these models there are input fields or attributes and an output or target field. Input fields are also called predictors because they are used by the model to identify a prediction function for the output or target field. The model generates an "input–output" mapping function which associates predictors with the output so that, given the values of input fields, it predicts the output values. Predictive models themselves are of two types, namely, classification or propensity models and estimation models. Classification models are predictive models with predefined target field or classes or groups, so that the objective is to predict a specific occurrence or event. The model also assigns a propensity score with each of these events that indicates the likelihood of the occurrence of that event. In contrast, estimation models are used to predict a continuum of target values based on the corresponding input values.

ii. Undirected or Unsupervised Models: In these models there are input fields or attributes, but no output or target field. The goal of such models is to uncover data patterns in the set of input fields. Undirected models are also of two types, namely, cluster models, and association and sequence models. Cluster models do not have predefined target field or classes or groups, but the algorithms analyze the input data patterns and identify the natural groupings of cases. In contrast, association or sequence models do not involve or deal with the prediction of a single field. Association models detect associations between discrete events, products, or attributes; sequence models detect associations over time.

Segmentation is much more complex than it may seem; simplified segmentation models when tested in real life, seem to imply that people as customers change behavior radically. If this was really true, there would be no trust, no loyalty and, consequently, no collaboration. The apparent paradox get resolved only when it is recognized that while people as customers do not possess multiple personalities, they have differing customs and, hence, play differing roles based on different contexts or scenarios. The problem arises on persisting with the stance of "one-segment-fits-for-all-contexts-for all-people-on-all-occasions."

Data mining can provide customer insight, which is vital for establishing an effective CRM strategy. It can lead to personalized interactions with customers and hence increased satisfaction and profitable customer relationships through data analysis. It can support an "individualized" and optimized customer management throughout all the phases of the customer lifecycle, from the acquisition and establishment of a strong relationship to the prevention of attrition and the winning back of lost customers.

a. Segmentation: It is the process of dividing the customer base into distinct and internally homogeneous groups in order to develop differentiated marketing strategies according to their characteristics. There are many different segmentation types based on the specific criteria or attributes used for segmentation. In behavioral segmentation, customers are grouped by behavioral and usage characteristics. Data mining can uncover groups with distinct profiles and characteristics and lead to rich segmentation schemes with business meaning and value. Clustering algorithms can analyze behavioral data, identify the natural groupings of customers, and suggest a solution founded on observed data patterns.

Data mining can also be used for the development of segmentation schemes based on the current or expected/estimated value of customers. These segments are necessary in order to prioritize customer handling and marketing interventions according to the importance of each customer.

b. Direct Marketing Campaigns: Marketers use direct marketing campaigns to communicate a message to their customers through mail, the Internet, e-mail, telemarketing (phone), and other direct channels in order to prevent churn (attrition) and to drive customer acquisition and purchase of add-on products. More specifically, acquisition campaigns aim at drawing new and potentially valuable customers away from the competition. Cross-/deep-/up-selling campaigns are implemented to sell additional products, more of the same product, or alternative but more profitable products to existing customers. Finally, retention campaigns aim at preventing valuable customers from terminating their relationship with the organization.

Although potentially effective, direct marketing campaigns can also lead to a huge waste of resources and to bombarding and annoying customers with unsolicited communications. Data mining and classification (propensity) models in particular can support the development of targeted marketing campaigns. They analyze customer characteristics and recognize the profiles or extended-profiles of the target customers.

c. Market Basket Analysis: Data mining and association models in particular can be used to identify related products typically purchased together. These models can be used for market basket analysis and for revealing bundles of products or services that can be sold together.

SUMMARY

This chapter introduced the concept of Business Intelligence (BI), technologies, and applications. It explained how BI enables enterprises to take informed decisions in compliance with its strategy, policy, and procedures.

9

Implementing Enterprise Systems

In this chapter, we consider an overview of the Enterprise Systems (ES) implementation project life cycle. First, we consider the context of launching such a project, which includes the objectives of the project, implementation strategies, and the resource requirements for a company. We also provide an overview of the preimplementation, implementation, and postimplementation phases of the project. The chapter ends by identifying some of the aspects involved with the deployment of ES at remaining sites, as well as the issues of supporting an ES production environment.

It is assumed that after the evaluation and selection of the ES for the company, the company has decided to implement a particular ES as the core solution throughout the company. All other systems, whether they are legacy or that might be implemented in the future, have to interface with the ES backbone that will be implemented within the company. We will also assume that the company has evaluated, selected, and contracted for the hardware and networking infrastructure and the ES implementation partners, as well as any other vendors for training, testing, system and network management support and services, and so forth.

 It must be noted that the approach being presented here is based on the author's experience and perception of ES projects. The situations in particular projects may certainly be different, and the measures presented here may not be applicable; no one is in a position to take a definitive stance on various aspects of such projects. We urge readers to modify the prescriptive message of chapter to suit the particular circumstances of individual companies. This might also be true by reason of the fact that ES implementations for SME enterprises might differ qualitatively from implementations for Fortune 500 enterprises.

MISSION AND OBJECTIVES OF THE ES PROJECT

The mission of the ES project should dovetail into the mission and objectives set forth by the company for the following 3–5 years.

The ES implementation project itself could have a mission similar to the following:

To prepare, implement, and support ES throughout the organization in the planned period of 1 year, with the full participation of all stakeholders of the company and to the satisfaction of all these stakeholders.

Project objectives set for the ES effort are quantifiable items such as

- Reducing by 3% the percentage of customers that deliver 80% of revenues (in total, by product category, by specific product, etc.)
- Reducing by 5% the percentage of customers that deliver more than 100% of profits
- Increasing the marketing spend on existing customers by 15%
- Increasing customer retention by 5%
- Increasing process throughputs by 30%
- Reducing transaction turnaround times by 50%, these could be related to collecting or making payments, responding to internal requisitions or external queries, and so forth

The success of the CRM strategy which is directly related to engaging, acquiring, retaining, and growing customers can be assessed using various CRM metrics like

- Customer Value Metrics
- Customer Behavior Metrics
- Customer Loyalty Metrics

Examples of Cited Reasons for Implementing ES

By now there are more than 500,000 ES installations throughout the world. The reasons cited for undertaking ES vary markedly from company to company. Some of the cited reasons are

- Limitations in expanding on the existing applications
- Application should be able to function on heterogeneous hardware and infrastructure
- Application should provide company-wide uniform user-interface across incompatible front-end hardware
- Application should provide all business events online
- Application should provide access to real-time information
- Application should provide support for cross-functional processes
- Application should enable flexible adjustment of business processes to market demands
- Application should provide integration of customer-facing systems with back-office systems
- Application should ensure that business processes are not hampered by system or national boundaries
- Application must support country-specific functionality
- Application should lead to reduction in lead time

GUIDING PRINCIPLES FOR ES BEST PRACTICES

As an illustration, we will discuss CRM best practices.

CRM is the sum of the people, processes, and technologies working together to

- Attract target customers
- Grow the value of existing customers
- Retain profitable customers for as long as possible

The guiding principles to create CRM best practices are as follows:

a. Define the Customer Relationship strategies required to
  - Acquire new customers by creating awareness of your differentiated product and service offering

- Retain your best customers by better responding to their needs
- Grow the value of the relationship with your customers

b. Design and implement the CRM processes and programs which will allow you to
  - Create a closed-loop relationship with the customer
  - Manage the customer throughout their relationship and lifecycle with the company and its employees
  - Respond and respond in real time to customer needs, inquiries, problems, and opportunities across all channels and touch-points
  - Anticipate customer needs and expectations in order to differentiate the experience you deliver to the customer

c. Select, develop, and integrate the applications, tools, and technology infrastructure needed to
  - Capture all relevant transactions and relationship information about the customer's behavior, requirements, attitudes, and expectations
  - Analyze the information and data in order to create a meaningful relationship experience regardless of the marketing, sales, service, or communication objective
  - Plan the programs, initiatives, and tactics for interacting with the customer based on anticipated customer needs and corporate objectives
  - Execute the process, programs, and initiatives in real time, providing the necessary decision making support for people within the company who are called upon to flawlessly execute specific customer interactions

PROJECT INITIATION AND PLANNING

For business-driven projects such as ES, it is vital that top management should not only be involved, but should also be driving the project at every stage. Therefore, the project initiation would start with the appointment of an executive sponsor for the project. Usually, the executive sponsor should be the CEO of the company. That appointment should be followed by the formation of a project executive committee and a steering committee. These should be followed by the appointment of a Chief Project Officer (CPO) and also the finalization of the scope of the project.

The CPO, under the guidance of the executive and steering committees, should assemble the implementation team, including the identification of module and site managers. The project management policies and guidelines should be finalized. The central project office should be established, including the critical support staff such as the training manager, the resources manager, and the project administrative staff. This team will have to prepare a plan and schedule for the implementation project, including the various activities, the manpower required, the duration, and the schedule for completing each of these activities.

The CPO will have to form another team to look after the procurement, installation, and productive operation of the basic infrastructure, including the hardware servers and clients, networking hardware and software, operating systems, databases, office automation software, and so forth.

CRITICAL SUCCESS FACTORS

Various factors are considered critical for the success of the ES projects. We will look at each of them in this section.

Direct Involvement of Top Management

ES implementation is not an IT project but a business strategy project. As with any other business strategy project for new product development, new marketing strategy, BPM project, and so on, an ES project should get the direct attention and involvement of senior management. If this involvement is confined only to the initial stages of the project, the project is certain to falter later.

One of the issues in which top management is required to demonstrate and encourage full commitment to the ES project is the deputation of key managers from different departments. Particularly in consumer goods industries, participating in IT-oriented projects might be considered a non–value-adding activity in terms of its ability to further managers' career goals. This perception must be corrected because ES implementation is not an IT-driven effort. Furthermore, for employees who would use ES for their routine operations, their full participation in the project is very critical. This can be ensured only by deputing key managers of the company for this effort.

Clear Project Scope

It is very important for a project to have a well-defined scope. Any ambiguities lead only to diffusion of focus and dissipation of effort. There are always adherents especially for increased scope and, a series of such increments in scope would render any project unsuccessful. This is also referred as "scope creep." Hence, the CPO must be vigilant about any creep in the scope of the project.

Covering as Many Functions as Possible within the Scope of the ES Implementation

Companies that are multidivisional and multilocated develop differently at different sites and acquire a character of their own at each site that may not fit into a uniform mold across the enterprise. A CRM package must have the ability to provide a comprehensive functionality to implement such deeply ingrained, differing ways of operations at different locations. It should be able to provide ready-to-use, best-practice processes that incorporate such varying ways of executing any business transaction or process. We have mentioned that the more functions are integrated and performed in real time, the more competitive the organization would be. For this, it is essential that as many functions as possible should go productive together on ES. This "big bang" strategy will have to be adopted in the initial stage of the projects, such as the Discovery and Design stage. Hence, it is critical that at least all the basic components of ES, such as Sales, Services, Marketing, Interaction Center, Partner Channel Management, and E-Business should be implemented at the pilot site.

Standardizing Business Process

Every office or customer service center of a company develops its own character and culture, which are the results of the company's recommended corporate environment blending with the local situation. Such local practices have strong adherents and generate fierce loyalty and pride. These factors often harm the progress of a system implementation across the organization at all its sites and offices, even if it is a computerized system such as ES. As a prerequisite, itis important to streamline and standardize a business process.

Proper Visibility and Communication
in the ES Project at All Stages

It is important to give proper visibility to the ES project. This might entail communicating about the strategic direction of the company, the relevance of ES, the ES implementation project and team, and the implementation plan and schedule. Either there could be a bulletin exclusively focused on the ES project or the company's in-house newsletter must have regular features and articles on ES project-related issues and milestones.

Allocation of Appropriate Budget and Resources

After the company has made the strategic decision to undertake the ES implementation effort, it must also prepare and approve the budget plan and estimates for the complete ES project. Because the project schedules are dependent nonlinearly on the prerequisite at all stages, any changes or deferment of release of funds, and therefore resources, will always have an adverse effect on the successful commencement of the project.

Often the controllers or decision makers will withhold sanction for the resources at a particular stage at a pilot site or for other sites for the optimization of costs. It must be noted that when any business project is launched, and ES implementation is no exception, any deferment of such strategic programs only *increases the opportunity cost* for the period that the project is delayed. Moreover, for an integrated project such as ES, that opportunity cost is not confined only to the local activity or site that contributes to the delay, but extends across the level of the whole company. Thus, for a company with a turnover of $500 million, after the launch of an ES project, that company would effectively be incurring an opportunity cost of $25–$50 million for every delayed month in the schedule.

Full-Time Deputation of Key Managers from All Departments

In traditional IS/IT projects, the personnel normally allocated to such efforts are either members who are young and newly joined or older members who can be spared from their respective departments. In either case, this will not help in a large way to lead the projects to success. ES, being a strategic project, should get allocation of key personnel from different departments because only if the inputs are accurate and functionally correct will the ES truly deliver when it goes into production. SME enterprises, whose staff strength is small unlike large enterprises, must allocate their best people with the conviction that after ES are correctly in production, they will give better returns not only in terms of money, but also in other dimensions such as relationships, satisfaction surveys, improved brands, and so on.

Completing Infrastructural Activities in Time and with High Availability

Consistent with the approach being taken in this book, the infrastructure for an ES project whether it is computer and networking infrastructure or human infrastructure in terms of skills acquisition and training must not be treated as an IS/IT infrastructure. It must be monitored like any other non-IS/IT infrastructure. Any mismatch between the readiness of the infrastructure and the overlaying ES will only lead to delays in the project and, hence, incur opportunity costs.

Instituting a Company-Wide Change Management Plan

Like any other strategy implementation plan, ES implementation is a prime case of organizational change. It should be recognized and planned as such. In parallel with the ES implementation effort, it makes sense to undertake a change management program to address the disorientation and lost sense of direction that might be experienced by a large number of members. If not managed properly, this could jeopardize the success of the whole project.

Top management should note that unlike traditional IS/IT projects, most ES implementations do not have *parallel runs* in which incumbent systems are run along with the older ones for a predetermined time period until the new systems are declared operational and the company switches over to the new regime. This happens because after ES go productive, the transactions and the actual operational tasks are done on the ES itself, and any major error could turn fatal for the company. The situation might seem alarming based on the past experiences of traditional IT systems going productive; however, that is the exact point that we are trying to make in this book. An ES is not like a traditional IT/IS project; it represents a totally different model of computerization (see Chapter 1, section "CRM Represent the Departmental Store Model of Implementing Computerized Systems").

Training of ES Team Members

All training needs for all members of the team should be identified and corporate training programs should be arranged, either on-site or through external training programs. For the SME enterprise, in which project schedules are shorter and the manpower base in the organization is smaller, it is essential that training of the team members is initiated and completed before the scheduled start of the program. Members should be encouraged to take certification tests in their concerned area of activity.

Training of User Members

Awareness, as well as familiarity training for all users who might use the ES productive system, is important. Training plans should not only have training programs, but should also budget refresher courses for all members. Sometimes, when the ES project is reaching critical mass, the user community as a whole might be disadvantaged because of a time lag between the actual training and the commencement of ES going into production. In such cases, refresher courses might have to be undertaken either very close to the actual commencement of implementation or, if all sites and offices go live on ES, on a staggered schedule. Again, top management should allocate a good contingency training budget in light of the fact that when ES go into production, there is no fallback arrangement; once launched, it has to reach "critical mass."

Scheduling and Managing Interface of ES with Other Systems

There are many legacy systems, non-SAP systems, external systems, and even manual functions that might be considered out of the scope of the ES project. ES do not address all the functional requirements of a company. This may involve solutions for security and access, e-mail, CTI, digitizing system, and so on. ES have a complete program of interfacing with, and qualifying, third-party products to leverage on companies with special expertise and products (see Chapter 5, section "Partnering for Growth"). Interfacing these systems should be scheduled in such a way that the interfaces are operational when ES go into production.

In cases in which a peripheral or support system could be replaced by some functionality provided by ES, the steering committee must make the decision as to the schedule of that functionality's implementation in ES.

Considering the onerous agenda of the ES project itself, the committee could decide to continue using the earlier system and transit to the functionality in ES at a more appropriate time.

Transition Plan for Cut Over to ES

The company must have a subsidiary project plan for transitioning from the earlier systems, whether they are computerized or manual, to the ES. This might entail uploading data in a timely fashion into the ES. The timeliness of the data might be dictated by whether it is master unchangeable data or transaction data, or it might be like opening balances for general ledger (GL) accounts and party ledger accounts. It could also be processing jobs that are done on a periodic basis, which might have to be transferred to the ES production system. Because everything cannot just be transferred automatically to ES, a phased approach starting with uploading of data, to transactions, to posting statuses, and subsequent processing steps may have to be designed and executed.

IMPLEMENTATION STRATEGY

In this section, we consider what should be adopted by an SME enterprise for its ES implementation projects.

Big Bang Implementation of ES Components

The enterprise should consider a "big bang" implementation of ES, wherein all the base components of ES (relevant to the enterprise's area of business) are implemented and put in production together. By implementing only certain components of the system, the company should not hope to reap more significant benefits than those accruing from traditional systems. If an ES is not to be used as a past-facing system merely for recording and reporting purposes but more as a future-facing handler of strategic information and relationships, implementation of all the *basic components* corresponding to the businesses of the company is essential. The ES are componentized and, thus, allow component-wise implementations. However, this is one feature that we recommend that should be ignored unless it is unavoidable because of extreme circumstances. A piecemeal approach of progressive implementation should be abandoned because delaying the implementations of all basic components together only delays the benefits of a fully functional ES and, therefore, incurs opportunity costs.

Base Components Implemented First

This strategy clearly dictates that the base components should be implemented with highest priority, though the definition of base component may vary from industry to industry. But, in contrast, other components or interfaces to other systems could be handled more appropriately after the base components as a whole have stabilized.

Implementation of ES Standard Functionality

A standardization of processes usually leads to tremendous gains in terms of maintenance, future upgrades, documentation, training, and even routine operations and the administration of the CRM applications. Custom support is countered to the general emphasis on standardizing the processes and implementing generic ones. It is a business truism that the survival and success of a company depends on how it differentiates itself and its products or services from those of its competitors. To leverage on their competencies or advantages, companies cannot abandon the corresponding differentiating processes and will have to incorporate such fundamental variants in their CRM implementations. But, as far as possible, avoid the bugbear of customization by altering and additional programming in ABAP. Additional programming should be evaluated and adopted only as a last resort. SAP keeps upgrading its suite of products and if custom software is built for a particular version, it will have to be upgraded every time SAP releases new upgrades. Like any other product, SAP goes through oscillating cycles between major functional upgrades followed by technical upgrades and vice versa.

The best solution is to

- Use ES standard functionality
- Accommodate the variation of the business process by using ES flexibility for configuring variant processes
- Adopt a work-around that indirectly takes care of the required functionality, for example, in the absence of the HR module, some

accounts-interfacing HR functions can be managed by treating employees as customers

- Use third-party products that are properly certified and qualified by SAP

Pilot Site Deployment Followed by Rollouts at Other Sites

This strategy entails deploying as comprehensive functionality as possible at the pilot site and preparing the base-reference SAP configuration at the first site. This configuration is merely rolled out rapidly, with minimal changes at other sites. These changes may have to do, for instance, with loading separate master data for a different portfolio of products, or services, or marketing programs, that may be sold or promoted at different sites. Thus, subsequent to the implementation at the pilot site, the project effort at the other sites will mainly involve

    i. Installing ES
   ii. Functional training of super-users and end users
  iii. Training technical personnel in ES administration and management functions
  iv. Uploading corresponding data
   v. Integration testing

Utilize External Consultants to Primarily Train In-House Functional and Technical Consultants

No external consultant can match the know-how of the functional and operational requirements of the company better than its own members, who have the requisite expertise and experience working in various capacities and on different functions in the company. External consultants should be used as facilitators for getting the company's own key members familiarized with the functionality and navigation of the ES.

Considering the tight schedules, external consultants would have to shoulder the main effort and deliverables during the business Design and Configure stages of the ASAP methodology. But the focus of their participation should be in transferring the ES product know-how to the key members of the implementation team. The key members of the implementation team will have the key responsibility of not only rolling out ES to other sites, but also of providing the necessary support for

ES effort in the future. As maybe noted, it is not as simple as it might sound because after gaining expertise on ES product know-how, such key members have a marked tendency to quit their jobs and join the growing number of independent ES consultants or join one of the ES Consultancy firms.

Because of their backgrounds, IS/IT professionals have a critical role in acting as facilitators for non-IS/IT-savvy functional members to clarify, define, and decide on their business requirements, and in assisting the functional members in configuring the system to obtain the desired functionality.

Centralized or Decentralized ES Configuration

ES installations have had centralized database servers. Enterprises with distributed database servers might need to use the decentralized configuration. As we have noted in Chapter 5, "The ES Solution," ES distributed architecture enables the integration of data and processes across the entire system.

User-Driven Functionality

In marked contrast to traditional IS/IT projects, ES projects are user driven. The key members on the implementation team from the functional and business departments play the critical role of documenting and mapping the AS-IS (or existing) processes and deciding on the TO-BE processes. The mapping and configuration of the desired functionality proceeds by an approach closer to the Joint Application Development and prototyping methodology of the 1980s.

ES IMPLEMENTATION PROJECT BILL OF RESOURCES (BOR)

Taking a cue from the Bill of Materials (BOM) employed in Production Planning and Control (PPC) functions, we can define a generalized version of the same for the ES implementation project called the Bill of Resources (BOR). It enables one to define the hierarchy of the inputs, resources, and costs in the same structure. In this section, we provide an overview of what resources are needed for an ES implementation project.

SAP recommends the ASAP methodology as the primary implementation methodology for SME enterprises (see section "Implementation Methodology").

Money

Although it is obviously dangerous to make any kind of generalization, an average ES project cost for SMEs might range from $3 million to $5 million.

In a typical CRM implementation, 28 percent of the total cost goes to buying software, while 38 percent of the cost goes to services such as software customizations, application integration, and training. Hardware makes up 23 percent of the cost, while telecommunications expenses make up the remaining 11 percent.

 Companies may spend about $10,000 per user per year on hardware, software, customization, support, and training.

Materials

The material inputs needed would be

a. Hardware: Servers (database, application, data warehouse, communications, network, email, and so on) and client PCs
b. Networking: Hardware and software
c. Software: ERP, front-end GUI software, data warehouse, DBMS, operating system, office automation systems, and so on
d. Project Office and ES Center infrastructure

Manpower

The manpower resources essential are

a. Executive management
b. Senior officers

    c. Technical personnel

    d. System administrative and support personnel

    e. Office administrative and support personnel

    f. Super-users

    g. End users

Time Period

The duration of an ES project for SMEs might range from 4 to 9 months.

Information

The significant input is the documentation of business process for the whole of the enterprise. This includes documentation on each process, including inputs, outputs, duration, labor, frequency, processing, purpose, interfaces, initiator, supervisor, and so on.

IMPLEMENTATION ENVIRONMENT

The implementation environment consists of several components as listed below:

- ES Applications
- SAP NetWeaver
- SAP Tools and Programming
  - ABAP Custom Development
  - Java Custom Development

IMPLEMENTATION METHODOLOGY

Under ideal conditions, projects can be completed in the most efficient manner in time and on budget. However, what is essential is to have a standardized approach of systems and procedures that could guide a company that is new to ES, to implement ES successfully without any major risk of failure. Such an approach, is called a *methodology*. A methodological approach may not be the *most* efficient one but it ensures success under *optimal conditions*. Companies survive and grow not by planning for the most ideal or adverse conditions, but by planning for optimal conditions. In the case of an ES implementation project, the implementation methodology must ensure success given the usual complexity of businesses, resources, organizational structures, time schedules, and so on.

An enterprise implementation methodology broadly covers the following:

a. Modeling Business Processes: Where the company defines the envisaged or TO BE business processes
b. Mapping Business Processes onto the Processes supported by ES: Where the company discovers the SAP standard processes and functionality that address the requirements of the modeled process
c. Performing the Gap Analysis: Where the company assesses the difference or gap between the ES standard and functionality, and the requirements of the modeled processes
d. Finalizing the scope of the ES implementation project: Where the company decides on the scope of the ES implementation in terms of the processes that would be implemented in the SAP system
e. Configuring the ES: Where the company configures the basic parameters in the ES
f. Validating the customized ES: Where the configured system is tested for delivered functionality with actual data

The identified gaps in functionality can be rectified by any of these measures:

- Devise a work-around for achieving the same functionality and configure it accordingly
- Program the required functionality in ES via user exits
- Suggest third-party ES add-ons or plug-ins that provide the desired functionality and that have been certified for compatibility through ES Complementary Software Program (CSP)
- Defer its implementation to the next wave of implementation or defer it until the ES release update (that will introduce this functionality) becomes available
- Change the business process radically so that it is suitable to the functionality available in ES to achieve the same objectives

- Modify ES software directly, although modified software may lead to incompatibility with future releases of ES

 For the purpose of illustration, we use SAP as reference.

Accelerated SAP (ASAP) Methodology

SAP provides a process-oriented, clear, and concise implementation roadmap for individual implementation projects. This roadmap acts as a project guide that specifies steps, identifies milestones, and generally sets the pace for the entire project to deliver a live system at top speed and quality utilizing the optimal budget and resources. The ASAP roadmap consists of the following phases: Project preparation, business blueprint, realization, final preparation, and go live and support.

Project Preparation

The project preparation phase deals with setting up the project organization, including the teams, roles, and responsibilities. In this phase, the aims and objectives of the implementation are decided. The strategy and draft project plan is prepared. The project infrastructure, including the hardware and networking issues are determined and finalized. Sizing and benchmarking the envisaged installation are performed and the acquisition of the SAP system is initiated. The project starts officially with a kickoff meeting attended by members of the executive and steering committees, project team members, and SAP consultants.

Business Blueprint

The business blueprint phase deals mainly with the documentation and finalization of requirements. The team members and consultants conduct interviews and workshops in different activity areas to ascertain the requirements of various business processes. The functionality provided by SAP is demonstrated using the Information and Design Education

(IDES) and is supported by questionnaires and process diagrams from the Business Engineer. Any gap in addressing functional requirements is identified and appropriate solutions are explored and devised. The final outcome of this phase is the Business Blueprint document, which details the TO BE processes, including written and pictorial representations of the company's structure and business processes. Once this has been approved, the blueprint is the basis for all subsequent phases.

Realization

The goal of realization is to configure the baseline system using the IMG based on the Business Blueprint document. To do so, the business processes are divided into cycles of related business processes. The system is documented using the Business Engineer. The baseline system prepared here is the basis for the production system. The SAP team undergoes advanced training. The system is presented to a team of power users who also undergo requisite training in their respective areas of operations. The baseline system is fine-tuned by the validation done by the power users, who employ an iterative approach. The technical team sets up the system administration and plans interfaces and data transfers. The interfaces, conversion programs, enhancements, reports, end-user documentation, testing scenarios, and user security profiles are defined and tested for effectiveness. The final deliverable is a fully configured and tested SAP system that meets the company's requirements.

Final Preparation

The final preparation phase is aimed at readying the system and company for SAP implementation. It consolidates all the activities of the previous phases. Any exceptions and out-of-turn situations are addressed and resolved. The super-users under the supervision of the SAP team members conduct end-user training. The conversion and interface programs are all checked, volume and stress tests are performed, and user acceptance tests are conducted. This is followed with the migration of data to the new system.

Go Live and Support

The go live and support phase addresses the issues of putting the SAP system in production. The Going Live check is also performed and completed.

This involves solving issues of day-to-day operations including problems and security-related issues reported by end users. SAP is also monitored for possible optimizations. This phase also involves verifying that milestones like day-end processing, first-month end, first-quarter end, and first-year end processes work correctly. It also involves completing any processes or parameters left uncompleted or undefined by oversight. Finally, the business benefits of the new system are measured to monitor the return on investment (ROI) for the project, which may trigger further iterations of the implementation cycle in order to improve business processes. A formal close of the implementation project is also performed.

PROJECT MANAGEMENT

The purpose of project management is to help define the tasks that are necessary to complete a project, control the progress of the activities, and account for the resources expended through the project.

Project Organization

Project organization consists of constitution of the various teams that are assigned to different tasks of the project. It entails nominating the various members of all teams, appointing team leaders, and reporting structures for compiling the progress reports of each team, which are consolidated progressively into higher-level progress reports. Usually, the team will consist of the technical team, the ABAP programming team, and many teams corresponding to major components within Siebel. Each of these later will contain sub teams for performing analysis and design, as well as undertaking documentation and testing of the various components.

Project Control

It is essential that the work of all teams and groups of teams in different areas be controlled for gauging the progress, or lack of it, in the corresponding tasks. For this, the effort and time expended will have to be recorded and monitored on a daily basis. This would be helpful in detecting delays and slippage, reconstituting the teams, and reinforcing any team with additional resources wherever necessary.

Time Recording

Time recording involves recording the time expended under various categories of activities by every member of the team. This is essential not only for external consultants, but also for company members as well. An analysis of the time expended in various activities could be helpful in identifying the effort and cost expended in identifying gaps, resolving gap issues, talking with end users, configuration, documentation, functional and technical testing, debugging functional and technical errors, and so forth.

Meetings

Project meetings could be for all project-related issues, such as

- Scope of the project
- Project strategy
- Constitution of teams
- Project schedule and milestones
- Requirements and business processes
- Gap issues and their resolution
- Issues that have not been resolved
- Decisions on standardizing processes
- Preparation of test plans and data
- Test reports
- Debugging and candidate solutions
- Documentation and updates
- Software upgrades
- Scheduling training programs
- Nominating team members for training
- Resource availability and utilization
- Conflicts and resolutions
- User accounts, access, and authorizations
- Performance and availability
- Hardware and networking vendors
- Providers of implementation services and consultancy
- Bill payments
- Leave and resignations

Project Monitoring

The actual effort and time expended need to be compared to the planned effort and schedule on a frequent basis. Any observed deviations, or pattern of deviations are to be corrected immediately. Any rescheduling of the project plan is addressed only in the project reviews.

Project Reviews

The main objective of project reviews is to ascertain the progress made with reference to the planned schedule. Progress on the action points of the last review is reassessed. Any shortfalls in achieving milestones or delays are diagnosed for the reasons, and corrective measures taken are endorsed or changed. Any suggestions for changing strategies are considered during the reviews. Any unforeseen problems cropping up during the project are analyzed here.

ES IMPLEMENTATION

Unlike a traditional software development project, this involves three main phases: Preimplementation, implementation, and postimplementation.

Preimplementation

Preimplementation involves the formation of the project and steering committees, the constitution of the implementation project team, and the installation of hardware and ES software. The latter involves readying the hardware and infrastructure, installing the operating systems, database software, client software, and ES software. The ES administration function entails systems administration, applications administration, ISS transaction server administration, communications server administration, network administration, database administration, printer administration, client administration, user's authentication and access security administration, and so forth. Another major activity during this phase is training for the implementation team and other users, which is very critical to the success of the project.

Training

Considering the shorter timeframes of the ES implementation projects, training has been identified as an important determinant in the success of any project. ES vendors offer a broad spectrum of training courses covering all stakeholders of an ES project. These courses cover a range of topics from a general overview to in-depth coverage of individual topics.

SAP Partner Academy Technical and Functional courses provide comprehensive training for the entire implementation team. SAP's courses are designed to get a team up to speed quickly and efficiently, some of which are

- Using ES
- SAP NetWeaver
- SAP Tools & Programming
- SAP Enterprise Applications
  - ES Marketing
  - ES Sales
  - SiAP CRM Service
  - ES Interaction Center

ES Installation

This basically involves installing the base licence and designing the system landscape including the SAP NetWeaver Server, the ES Enterprise Applications, and the SAP development environment for ABAP and Java.

Implementation

For the SMEs, ES recommend the Accelerated SAP (ASAP) Methodology (see above). It consists of the following five stages:

i. Project Preparation
ii. Business Blueprint
iii. Realization
iv. Final Preparation
v. GoLive and Support

Postimplementation

The postimplementation phase involves instituting support and services such as the SAP Interaction Center and so on. Following the implementation of the base components, other components such as SAP BI and SAP HANA Workflow, and so on can be implemented.

For effective ES operations, training of the implementation team and user personnel is essential.

ES SUPPORT

Support includes various measures or activities that are undertaken to ensure availability in terms of the application functionality or continued functioning of the system.

It deals with design, organization, and operation of a help desk or a call center for SAP users within the company. Users can register their complaints and queries, and get specific responses that can be implemented by the end users with the help of the super-users in their respective departments.

Hardware availability is ensured by various measures, such as disaster recovery systems and archival of data.

ES DEPLOYMENT

After ES go into production at the pilot site, it is important to have scheduled the focus to immediately shift to the other sites. In fact, at those other sites certain activities, including training of super-users and preparation of data for uploading into the ES, should be undertaken in parallel with the last stages of implementation at the pilot site. It is advised to immediately commence implementation at other sites because doing so enables the company to leverage the momentum generated by the implementation at the pilot site. Moreover, any breaks between the implementations might cause members of the core team to look for other challenging opportunities.

If training super-users and data loading are done in parallel with the finishing stages of the deployment at the pilot site(s), what remains during the actual ES project at the sites is

    i. Deploying the base configuration prepared at the pilot site
   ii. Conducting the integration test

iii. Conducting the training of end users at the concerned site

iv. Going live

WHY SOME ES IMPLEMENTATIONS MAY SOMETIMES BE LESS THAN SUCCESSFUL

There are various reasons why ES projects might be less than successful. Implementing ES is a complex endeavor requiring significant change management expertise, business process experience, and domain knowledge. Failure in ES projects might be because of the following reasons:

- Top management involvement and interest falters or is perceived as faltering
- Lack of clear project scope and strategies; project is too narrowly focused
- Implementation of nonoptimized processes in ES
- Decisions regarding changes in processes and procedures may not be affected; they might be ignored or subverted
- Lack of proper visibility and communication on the ES project at all stages
- Lack of adequate budget and resources such as for training of large group of envisaged end users
- Not deputing key managers on the implementation team
- Support infrastructure and systems delayed inordinately
- Disputes and conflicts in the team not resolved quickly
- Company members of the team may not get along with the external consultants
- External consultants may have differences with end users or user managers
- Core team members may have differences with user departments
- A company-wide change management plan is not implemented
- Too much time between the implementation at the deployment/pilot site and rollout sites
- Members of the company do not participate actively because
  - Members feel the system has been implemented in haste and that it does not address their requirements; they feel they have not been taken in confidence

- Members feel they have not been given adequate training
- Members of the company are apprehensive of their future roles
- Members of the company are afraid that they not be able to learn the new system and perform satisfactorily
- Members of the company feel unsettled by the lack of hierarchy in the system
- Members feel they have been reduced to data entry operators
- Members of the core implementation team might resign and leave the company
- Members of the core team might be averse to moving on projects at rollout sites
- Inexperienced consulting resources
- Slow decision making process
- Scope creep

The solutions for tackling these problems will vary from company to company. The approach to be adopted will depend upon the industry, culture, and history of the company. An approach for handling these type of issues is referred in the earlier section "Critical Success Factors."

SUMMARY

This chapter gave an overview of the complete implementation cycle of a typical ES project. We discussed project planning and implementation strategy, environment, and methodology for undertaking ES projects. We also looked at critical success factors (CSF) for successful projects as well as reasons for unsuccessful ones.

Epilogue: Enterprise Performance Intelligence

An inevitable consequence of organizations using the pyramid-shaped hierarchy is that there was a decision-making bottleneck at the top of the organization. The people at the top are overwhelmed by the sheer volume of decisions they have to make; they are too far away from the scene of the action to really understand what's happening; and by the time decisions are made the actions are usually too little and too late. Consequently, companies suffer by staggering from one bad decision to another. No small group of executives, regardless of their smarts, hard work, or sophisticated computer systems, can make all those decisions in a timely or competent manner. Given the pace of change, companies need something more agile and responsive.

The centralized command and control methods that worked for hierarchies will not work for service delivery networks. Instead of a small group of executives telling everybody else what to do, people need to get the authority to figure out for themselves what to do. The need to be responsive to evolving customer needs and desires creates organizational structures where *business intelligence* (BI) and decision making is pushed out to operating units that are closest to the scene of the action. Closed-loop decision making resulting from combination of on-going performance management with on-going BI can lead to an effective responsive enterprise; hence, the need for *performance intelligence.*

The effect of continuous adjustments and enhancements to business operations can generate a steady stream of savings and new revenues that may sometimes seem insignificant from one day to the next, but as months go by, may become cumulatively substantial. The profits generated in this way can be thought of as the *agility dividend*. Real-time data sharing and close coordination between business processes (sales, procurement, accounting, etc.) can be employed to deliver continuous operating adjustments that result in steady cost savings over time (negative feedback) as well as the delivery of timely new products and services to identified customers that result in significant new revenue (positive feedback).

A company can design and implement instruments ranging from *decision patterns* (DP) to *performance intelligence* (PI) systems that can enable continuous correction of business unit behavior in order for companies to achieve enhanced levels of productivity and profitability.

Appendix I: SAP Business Suite

mySAP Business Suite is a comprehensive family of business applications that allows companies to manage their entire value chain. mySAP applications describe processes and functions from a process point of view. The business applications provide users with consistent results throughout the entire company network and give your company the flexibility needed in today's dynamic market situations. It consists of a number of different products that enable cross-company processes. mySAP Business Suite consists of individual applications. Each application has its own focus area and provides functions to map this area in a flexible and comprehensive way. These applications can be purchased as an entire suite or individually. All the applications are based on the SAP NetWeaver technology platform, an integration and application platform that reduces total cost of ownership across the entire IT landscape and supports the evolution of mySAP Business Suite to a services-based architecture.

Business experience, strategies, and know-how are incorporated in SAP software. The flexibility and comprehensive integration and adaptation options offered by SAP software results in high-performance, industry-specific, and cross-industry e-business applications, namely:

a. mySAP applications describe processes and functions from a process point of view.
b. Applications are SAP's products seen from the point of view of the customer, with an outside-in focus on company processes.
c. Components are not the actual company solutions, simply the technical building blocks; components represent SAP's technical view of software with an inside-out focus.

Figure AI.1 gives an overview of the SAP applications and components.

 SAP installed base is constituted of a spectrum of versions released in the past across a decade or more. For a gargantuan software package like SAP, the nomenclature of its systems and modules frequently undergo changes depending upon the ongoing marketing initiatives and efforts. Keeping this huge spread of versions in mind, we adopt a strategy to adopt a slightly older structure of SAP and its constituting systems (and modules) even though this configuration may have occasionally been superseded in the past whenever there has been a re-positioning or launching of newer products and technologies like SAP NetWeaver.

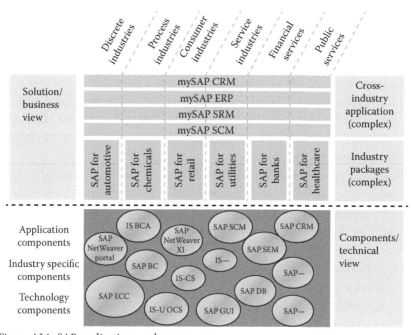

Figure AI.1 SAP applications and components.

SAP CROSS-INDUSTRY APPLICATIONS

SAP ERP provides several solutions that assist firms in achieving operational excellence through process efficiencies, business agility, and streamlined business operations. There is quite a bit of overlap between particular solutions and modules. Although it can be confusing, this flexibility is one of SAP's greatest strengths—the ability to customize a business solution in this way makes it possible to create innovative business processes capable of meeting the needs of almost any organization's finance and executive leadership teams.

SAP provides a breadth of products, each targeted a bit differently at addressing the requirements of customer enterprises. The "best" solution depends on many factors, including cost, required functionality, features, preference for on-site versus hosted solutions, size, and complexity of the business processes to be configured.

mySAP ERP

mySAP ERP Financials

SAP ERP Financials package as enabling financial transformation: New general ledger capabilities streamline the financial reconciliation process, reduce the cost of administration and control, and minimize user error. This in turn frees up an organization to focus strategically—another area SAP ERP Financials enables. By offering more effective collaboration with its customers, vendors, and suppliers, SAP ERP Financials enables governance, helps manage risk and compliance, increases inventory turns, frees up cash and working capital, provides greater financial transparency, and simplifies other complex invoicing and payment processes. The ability to drill down into areas such as profitability analysis and take advantage of built-in analytic solutions empower end users as they make better decisions faster across many different financial domains and, therefore, address financial matters as described below.

Governance, Risk, and Compliance (GRC)

SAP provides a solution for governance, risk, and compliance called SAP Governance, Risk, and Compliance (GRC). With its integrated SAP ERP back end, SAP provides the visibility and transparency organizations demand in response to various regulatory body and internal control requirements. SAP GRC enables a firm to effectively manage risk and increase corporate accountability, thereby improving the firm's ability to make faster, smarter decisions, and protect its assets and people. By giving end users a tool to simply recognize critical risks and analyze risk-reward tradeoffs, the time and expense required to implement SAP GRC is quickly recouped in cost savings. SAP GRC's business benefits include the following:

- Well-balanced portfolios boasting well-vetted risk/reward analyses. Through GRC's transparency, visibility, and company-wide hooks, the solution can enable a firm's decision makers to make smart decisions—decisions based on risk and the probability of return.
- Improved stakeholder value, yielding preserved brand reputation, increased market value, reduced cost of capital, easier personnel recruiting, and higher employee retention.
- Reduced cost of providing governance, risk, and compliance. GRC is no longer an optional service a firm should provide on behalf of its stakeholders but rather a mandatory part of doing business in a global world tainted by less than-ethical business practices. Effective GRC is a differentiator today.
- Enhanced business performance and financial predictability. SAP GRC provides executive leadership teams the confidence they need in their numbers and methods to quickly rectify issues.
- Organizational sustainability despite the risks associated with poorly managed GRC, particularly legal and market ramifications.

All this amounts to increased business agility, competitive differentiation, and other brand-preserving and company-sustaining benefits.

Financial and Managerial Accounting

The Financial and Managerial Accounting module enables end users to enhance company-wide strategic decision-making processes. It allows companies to centrally manage financial accounting data within an international framework of multiple companies, languages, currencies, and charts of accounts. The Financial and Managerial Accounting module complies with international accounting standards, such as Generally Accepted Accounting Principles (GAAP) and International Accounting Standards (IAS), and helps fulfill the local legal requirements of many countries, reflecting fully the legal and accounting changes resulting from the Sarbanes-Oxley legislation, European market and currency unification, and more.

The Financial and Managerial Accounting module contains the following components:

- General ledger accounting—Provides a record of the company's business transactions. It provides a place to record business transactions throughout all facets of the company's business to ensure that the accounting data being processed by SAP is both factual and complete.
- Accounts payable—Records and administers vendor accounting data.
- Accounts receivable—Manages the company's sales activities and records and administers customer accounting data through a number of tools specializing in managing open items.
- Asset accounting—Manages and helps a company supervise its fixed assets and serves as a subsidiary ledger to the general ledger by providing detailed information on transactions specifically involving fixed assets.
- Funds management—Supports creating budgets by way of a toolset that replicates a company's budget structure for the purpose of planning, monitoring, and managing company funds. Three essential tasks include revenues and expenditures budgeting, funds movement monitoring, and insight into potential budget overruns.

Special purpose ledger—Provides summary information from multiple applications at a level of detail specified according to business needs. This function enables companies to collect, combine, summarize, modify, and allocate actual and planned data originating from SAP or other systems. Accounts payable and accounts receivable subledgers are integrated both with the general ledger and with different components in the Sales and Distribution module. Accounts payable and accounts receivable transactions are performed automatically when related processes are performed in other modules.

Cost Controlling

Cost accounting is facilitated by the Controlling module, which provides the functions necessary for effective and accurate internal cost accounting management. Its complete integration allows for value and quantity real-time data flows between SAP Financials and SAP Logistics modules. The Controlling module contains the following:

- Overhead cost controlling—Focuses on the monitoring and allocation of your company's overhead costs and provides all the functions your company requires for planning and allocation. The functionality contained within the Controlling module supports multiple cost-controlling methods, giving you the freedom to decide which functions and methods are best applied to your individual areas.
- Activity-based costing—Enables you to charge organizational overhead to products, customers, sales channels, and other segments and permits a more realistic profitability analysis of different products and customers because you are able to factor in the resources of overhead.
- Product cost controlling—Determines the costs arising from manufacturing a product or providing a service by evoking real-time cost-control mechanisms (capable of managing product, object, and actual costing schemes).
- Profitability analysis—Analyzes the profitability of a particular organization or market segment (which may be organized by products, customers, orders, or a combination thereof).

Enterprise Controlling

SAP's Enterprise Controlling module is divided into a number of components:

- Business planning and budgeting—Comprises high-level enterprise plans that allow for the adaptable representation of customer-specific plans and their interrelationships. This also takes into consideration the connections between profit and loss statements, balance sheet, and cash flow strategies.
- Consolidation—Enables a company to enter reported financial data online using data-entry formats and to create consolidated reports that meet your company's legal and management reporting mandates.
- Profit center accounting—Analyzes the profitability of internal responsibility or profit centers (where a profit center is a management-oriented organizational unit used for internal controlling purposes).

Treasury Management

The Treasury Management module provides functionality needed to control liquidity management, risk management and assessment, and position management. It includes the following components:

- Treasury management—Supports a company's financial transaction management and positions through back-office processing to the Financial Accounting module. It also provides a versatile reporting platform that your company can use to examine its financial positions and transactions.
- Cash management—Identifies the optimum liquidity needed to satisfy payments as they become due and to supervise cash inflows and outflows.
- Market risk management—Quantifies the impact of potential financial market fluctuations against a firm's financial assets. The Cash Management package in combination with the Treasury Management package, helps a firm control for market risks, accounts for interest and currency exposure, conducts portfolio simulations, and performs market-to-market valuations.
- Funds management—Helps create different budget versions, making it possible to work with rolling budget planning. It is tightly integrated with the Employee Self-Services online travel booking function to track estimated and real costs.

Global Trade Services

In reality, the component of SAP GRC known as SAP Global Trade Services (or GTS) is also an SAP ERP Financials solution that further qualifies as an SAP Corporate Services solution and global supply-chain enabler. GTS makes it possible for international companies to connect and communicate with various government systems using a company-wide trade process. In this way, SAP GRC GTS enables the following:

- Meet international regulatory requirements
- Manage global trade by integrating company-wide trade compliance across financial, supply chain, and human capital management business processes
- Facilitate and expedite the import/export process for goods traveling through different country customs organizations
- Facilitate increased supply-chain transparency by sharing cross-border trade-related information with partners (insurers, freight handlers, and so on)

SAP GRC GTS thus enables a firm to mitigate the financial and other risks associated with doing business around the globe. By ensuring compliance with international trade agreements, SAP GRC GTS customers can optimize their supply chain, reduce production downtime, and eliminate errors that otherwise yield expensive penalties. In a nutshell, SAP GRC GTS makes it possible for firms to do business across country borders and to do so more consistently and profitably.

Financial Supply-Chain Management

With all the attention today on driving inefficiencies out of an organization's supply chain, there is little wonder why SAP continues to optimize functionality geared toward financially streamlining supply chains. The Financial Supply-Chain Management (FSCM) module facilitates

- Credit limit management and control
- Credit rules automation and credit decision support
- Collections, cash, and dispute management
- Electronic bill presentment and payment
- Treasury and risk management

mySAP ERP Human Capital Management

SAP HCM also facilitates a human resources (HR) shared services center augmented by reporting and analytics capabilities. In this way, HCM marries what the organization needs to measure internally (related to how well its own HR teams are performing against targets and other metrics such as hiring goals, for example) with the organization's services to its customers—the firm's employees, long-term contractors, and others. This self-service functionality includes or supports a number of roles and company needs, including the following:

- A centralized employee interaction mechanism, which is nothing more than a central point of contact for employees that acts as a single source of company, HR, and other related information. As the primary venue for interacting with the employer, this tool becomes a ubiquitous source of "the answers" company-wide. Meanwhile, the company's HR team uses the tool to access and help manage the information needed behind the scenes.
- Employee Self-Service (ESS), which is perhaps best known as a tool used to maintain personal data, book travel, and conduct other administrative activities that lend themselves to an "online" support environment.

- SAP developed ESS, an effective means of providing real-time access and data upkeep capabilities to employees.
- Workforce Process Management (WPM), or the bundling of common country-specific employee master data. This might include time entry, payroll, employee benefits, legal reporting, and organizational reporting—all of which are brought together and standardized to meet local regulations or country codes. The majority of WPM is not done via self-services but rather by an administrator or through a shared services function.
- Manager Self-Service (MSS), a cockpit of data used by leadership to identify, retain, and reward the firm's top performers; manage budgets, compensation planning, and profit/loss statements; sort and conduct keyword searches of employees' records; conduct the annual employee review process; and address.
- Other administrative matters quickly and from a centralized location.
- Workforce deployment, geared for project teams rather than individuals. Teams are created based on projects, and individual team member competencies and availabilities may then be tracked along with time, tasks, and so on.

Several of these HCM services actually fall into two broad focus areas that SAP still tends to use as labels: Personnel Administration (PA) and Personnel Planning and Development (PD). Each addresses different aspects of a company's HR functions; the integration of the two creates a well-oiled HR machine that, when integrated with a firm's other business processes, creates a competitive advantage for the business.

Personal Administration

The PA module of HCM manages functions such as payroll, employee benefits enrollment and administration, and compensation. Beyond personnel administration, SAP's Talent Management enables recruiters and managers visibility into the various phases of employment, from employment advertising and recruitment through on-boarding, employee development/training, and retention activities. It also provides a company-wide profile of the firm's human capital (people), making it possible to seek out and manage the careers of people holding particular skills, jobs, or roles. Underlying solutions include

- Enterprise compensation management is used to implement a company's pay, promotion, salary adjustments, and bonus plan policies. Functions managed by this solution include salary administration, job evaluations, salary reviews, salary survey results, compensation budget planning and administration, and compensation policy administration. Use it to create pay grades and salary structures and make compensation adjustments—an important piece of functionality to help companies retain their top talent. SAP accomplishes this by marrying performance ratings with compensation standards, industry trends, performance-based pay standards, bonus payouts, and more, which not only helps create bulletproof justifications but reduces the time, the effort, and therefore the risk otherwise germane to such time-sensitive matters.

- E-Recruiting helps companies manage their employee recruiting process. Recruitment initiates from the creation of a position vacancy through the advertisement and applicant tracking of potentials, concluding with the notification of successful and unsuccessful applicants and the hiring of the best candidate. E-Recruiting also ties all the data associated with attracting, acquiring, educating, and developing talent and future leaders into a single system of record.

- Time management provides a flexible way of recording and evaluating employee work time and absence management. Companies can represent their time structures to reflect changing conditions, using the calendar as a basis. Flextime, shift work, and normal work schedules can be used to plan work and break schedules and manage exceptions, absences, and holidays.

- Payroll efficiently and accurately calculates remuneration for work performed by your employees, regardless of their working schedule, working calendar, language, or currency. Payroll also handles fluctuating reporting needs and the regularly changing compliance requirements of federal, state, and local agencies.

Personal Planning and Development

In contrast to these solutions, SAP provides tools to better manage people and traditional HR functions, including organizational management and workforce planning. Some of these include the following:

- Organizational management—Assists in the strategizing and planning of a comprehensive HR structure. Through the development of proposed scenarios using the flexible tools provided, you can manipulate your company's structure in the present, past, and future. Using the basic organization objects in SAP, units, jobs, positions, tasks, and work centers are all structured as the basic building blocks of your organization.

- SAP enterprise learning—Helps a company coordinate and administer company-wide training and similar events and also contains functionality to plan for, execute, confirm, and manage cost allocations and billing for your company's events. By creating an efficient and personalized learning process and environment, SAP enterprise learning takes into account an employee's job, tasks, qualifications, and objectives to create a custom training regimen that aligns with preestablished career development goals.
- SAP learning solution—A component of SAP enterprise learning that also falls under the talent management umbrella (discussed previously), the SAP learning solution links employee learning to a firm's business strategy and objectives. To pull this off, the SAP learning solution brings together SAP ERP HCM with knowledge management and collaboration solutions and provides this in an innovative Learning Portal. Intuitive in form and function, the Learning Portal encompasses not only specialized learning management software, but also tools to author tests and to manage content and collaborate across an enterprise through a customizable taxonomy.

mySAP Operations

Essentially logistics, these solutions encompass all processes related to a firm's purchasing, plant maintenance, sales and distribution, manufacturing, materials management, warehousing, engineering, and construction. SAP Manufacturing and SAP ERP Operations (an aging but still useful term) include the following solutions:

- Procurement and logistics execution, enabling end users to manage their end-to-end procurement and logistics business processes as well as optimizing the physical flow of materials
- Product development and manufacturing, from production planning to manufacturing, shop floor integration, product development, and so on
- Sales and service, which range from actual sales to managing the delivery of services and all the processes necessary to pay out commissions and other sales incentives

Manufacturing

SAP manufacturing connects a firm's manufacturing processes with the rest of its business functions: Logistics, financials, environmental health and safety (EHS) requirements, and more. It also allows a firm to manage its manufacturing operations with embedded Lean Sigma and Six Sigma, both of which help create and improve competitive advantage. SAP manufacturing allows discrete and process manufacturing firms to better plan, schedule, resequence, and monitor manufacturing processes so as to achieve higher yields and greater profitability. This is accomplished through partner and supplier coordination, exception management, embracing Lean and Six Sigma, complying with EHS requirements, and so on—all facilitated by SAP manufacturing. Through continuous improvement, SAP seeks to provide management and shop floor teams alike the ability to view and optimize real-time operations. SAP manufacturing's powerful analytics support the firm's ability to make changes on-the-fly. Thus, SAP manufacturing allows a company to transform itself through enhanced manufacturing capabilities such as the following:

- SAP lean planning and operations—Accelerate and maintain lean operations (through high throughput, high quality, and low overhead)
- SAP manufacturing integration and intelligence—Obtain the data that a manufacturing team needs to take the proper action at the proper time
- SAP supply-chain management—Optimize the supply chain hosted by SAP ERP
- SAP solutions for radiofrequency identification (RFID)—Further optimize the supply chain through more efficient asset tracking and management
- SAP ERP Operations—Enable the manufacturing team to gain greater visibility into its operations and in turn increase control and business insight

Production Planning and Control

Within SAP ERP Operations, the focus of SAP's Production Planning and Control module is to facilitate complete solutions related to production planning, execution, and control. The Production Planning module includes a component called Sales and Operations Planning, which is used for creating realistic and consistent planning figures to forecast future sales. Depending on your method of production, you can use SAP's production order processing, repetitive manufacturing, or KANBAN production control processing. KANBAN is a procedure for controlling production and material flow based on a chain of operations in production and procurement. In the end, Production Planning and Control helps manage the following:

- Basic data
- Sales and operations planning, master planning, and capacity and materials requirements planning
- KANBAN, repetitive manufacturing, assembly orders, and production planning for process industries
- Production orders and product cost planning
- Plant data collection, production planning, and control information system

The implementation of the Production Planning and Control module makes it possible to eliminate routine tasks for the end users responsible for production scheduling. The related reduction in time allows for additional time to be dedicated to more critical activities within the company.

Materials Management

A firm's inventory and materials management business processes are essential to the success of the company. Streamlined day-to-day management of the company's consumption of materials, including company purchasing, managing warehouses and their inventory, tracking and confirming invoices, and so on, are all part of the Materials Management module. Its components include inventory management, warehouse management, purchasing, invoice verification, materials planning, and purchasing information system. In this way, Materials Management saves time and money, conserves resources, and helps optimize the company's supply chain.

Plant Maintenance

The main benefit to SAP's Plant Maintenance module is its flexibility to work with different types of companies to meet differing designs, requirements, and workforces. Different management strategies are supported within the application, including risk-based maintenance and total productive maintenance. Some benefits that your company will derive from the implementation of the Plant Maintenance module involve reduced downtime and outages, the optimization of labor and resources, and a reduction in the costs of inspections and repairs. The Plant Maintenance module includes

- Preventative maintenance
- Service management
- Maintenance order management
- Maintenance projects
- Equipment and technical objects
- Plant maintenance information system

On the whole, the integration of the Plant Maintenance module supports a company in designing and executing its maintenance activities with regard to system resource availability, costs, materials, and personnel deployment.

Sales and Distribution

The Sales and Distribution (SD) module arms a firm with the necessary instruments to sell and to manage the sales process. SD provides a wealth of information related to a company's sales and marketing trends, capabilities, and so on. An SD end user can access data on products, marketing strategies, sales calls, pricing, and sales leads at any time to facilitate sales and marketing activity. The information is online, up-to-the-minute support to be used to service existing customers and to mine for potential customers and new leads. Also included within the SD module is a diverse set of contracts to meet diverse business needs. Agreements concerning pricing, delivery dates, and delivery quantity are all supported within this module.

mySAP ERP Corporate Services

The final SAP ERP business solution, Corporate Services, assists companies with streamlining internal life cycle processes. Modules of Corporate Services include the following:

- Global Trade Services (GTS)—Manages international trade activity complexities, from regulatory compliance to customs and risk management

- Environment, Health, and Safety (EHS)—Assists firms with managing how they comply with matters of product safety, hazardous substance management, waste and emissions management, and so on
- Quality Management—Reflects the controls and gates necessary to proactively manage the product life cycle
- Real Estate Management—Manages the real estate portfolio life cycle, from property acquisition through building operations, reporting, maintenance, and disposal
- Enterprise Asset Management—Addresses design, build, operations, and disposal phases
- Project and Portfolio Management—Manages a firm's project portfolio (including tracking and managing budget, scheduling, and other resource-based key performance indicators)
- Travel Management—Process travel requests to managing planning, reservation changes, expense management, and specialized reporting/analytics

Real Estate Management

SAP's Real Estate module integrates real estate processes into your company's overall organizational structure. The Corporate Real Estate Management model is divided into two components: Rental Administration and Settlement and Controlling, Position Valuation, and Information Management. For a company to successfully use the Real Estate component, special configurations are required in the Materials Management, Plant Maintenance, Project System, and Asset Accounting modules.

Quality Management

The Quality Management module improves product and to some extent process quality. To produce high-quality products, the Quality Management system ensures product integrity, which in turn helps foster good client relations and company reputation. Quality Management services include the following:

- Quality planning, inspections, and quality control
- Quality notifications and quality certificates
- Test equipment management
- Quality management information system

The Quality Management module enables a company to analyze, document, and improve its processes across several dimensions.

Project and Portfolio Management

Once simply called the Project System module, the Project and Portfolio Management module is an important component of SAP ERP corporate services and assists a company in managing its portfolio of projects. Such high-level cross-project insight allows for outstanding planning, execution, and financial oversight, facilitating true project management in the process. As such, it is centered on managing the network of relationships within the system and establishing project management links.

Project and portfolio management is used to manage investments and marketing, software and consulting services, research and development, maintenance tasks, shutdown management, plant engineering and construction, and complex made-to-order production. The components of the Project System module include basic data, operational structures, project planning, approvals, project execution and integration, and project system information system. Like most project management approaches, the system is based on work breakdown structures (WBSs). A WBS is a structured model of work organized in a hierarchical format; work or tasks are managed in a stepwise manner during the course of conducting a project, where large tasks are broken down into key elements that represent the individual tasks and activities in the project.

mySAP CRM

mySAP Customer Relationship Management (mySAP CRM) is a comprehensive solution to the management of your customer relationships. It supports all customer-oriented business divisions, from marketing to sales to service, and even customer interaction channels, such as the Interaction Center, the Internet, and mobile clients. SAP CRM brings together a company's sales, services, and marketing functions. In this way, CRM helps a company focus on three related customer-related areas: Driving topline revenue growth, achieving operational excellence, and increasing customer-facing business agility. Key business scenarios include

Marketing Support

Enhances marketing effectiveness, maximizes resource use, and empowers the sales team to develop and maintain long-term profitable customer relationships. From a user's perspective, this includes marketing resource management, campaign management, trade promotion management, market segment management, lead/prospect management, and marketing analytics.

Sales Support

Helps remove barriers to productivity by enabling teams to work with their customers in a consistent manner. CRM Sales empowers and provides the team with the tools they need to close deals. For example, territory management, account and contact management, lead and opportunity management, and sales planning and forecasting help sales forces identify and manage prospects. Then, by leveraging quotation and order management, product configuration, contract management, incentive and commission management, time and travel management, and sales analytics, the team has the information it needs to keep customers happy while hopefully increasing sales volume and margins and decreasing the costs of doing all this.

Service Support

Assists service management teams in maximizing the value obtained from postsales services. This enables teams to profitably manage a broad range of functions geared toward driving successful customer service and support, including field service, Internet-enabled service offerings, service marketing and sales, and service/contract management. These happier customers benefit from improved warranty and claims management, effective channel service, and depot repair services. And the company's service team benefits from insight gleaned from service analytics, which enable the team to maximize profit per customer.

Web Channel

Increases sales and reduce transaction costs by turning the Internet into a service channel (or sales and marketing channel) geared toward effectively connecting businesses and consumers. This makes it possible to increase profitability of existing accounts while also reaching new markets.

Interaction Center (IC) management support—Complements and arms a company's field sales force. This functionality supports marketing, sales, and service activities such as telemarketing, telesales, customer service, e-service, and interaction center analytics.

Partner Channel Management

Improves processes for partner recruitment, partner management, communications, channel marketing, channel forecasting collaborative selling, partner order management, channel service, and analytics. In this way, a company can attract and retain a more profitable and loyal indirect channel by managing partner relationships and empowering channel partners.

Business Communications Management

Enables inbound and outbound contact management across multiple locations and communications channels. Business communications management integrates multichannel communications with a firm's customer-facing business processes to create a seamless communications experience across several different communications mediums (including voice, text messaging, email, and others).

Real-Time Offer Management

Helps manage the complexities of marketing offers in real time, using SAP's advanced analytical real-time decision engine. This functionality also optimizes the decision-making process across different customer interaction channels, enabling a company to quickly and intelligently enhance its customer relationships.

mySAP SRM

mySAP Supplier Relationship Management (mySAP SRM) is a solution that enables the strategic planning and central control of relationships between a company and its suppliers. It allows very close connections between suppliers and the purchasing process of a firm, with the goal of making the procurement processes simpler and more effective. SAP SRM supports processes such as ordering, source determination, the generation of invoices and credit memos, supplier qualification, and Supplier Self-Services.

SAP SRM helps to optimize and manage the relationship between a company and its suppliers. As another one of SAP's more mature offerings,

SRM integrates seamlessly with PLM, enabling a high degree of collaboration between product buyers and parts suppliers.

mySAP SCM

By transforming a supply chain into a dynamic customer-centric supply-chain network, mySAP SCM enables companies to plan for and streamline the firm's network of logistics and resources that merge to form a supply chain enabling better service, increased productivity, and improved profitability. A supply chain comprises three areas: Procurement, production, and distribution. The supply portion of a supply chain focuses on the raw materials needed by manufacturing, which in turn converts raw materials into finished products; the distribution aspect of a supply chain focuses on moving the finished products through a network of distributors, warehouses, and outlets. mySAP SCM enables increased velocity and improved profitability resulting from cross-company collaboration; enhanced visibility into a company's suppliers, vendors, and customers makes it easier to create a more predictable supply chain capable of capitalizing on circumstances, minimizing costs, and maximizing margins through the following:

- Improving responsiveness via real-time insight into the entire supply chain
- Improving inventory turns by synchronizing balancing supply with demand
- Encouraging collaboration by providing visibility into trends as seen through supply-chain monitoring, analysis, and business analytics

SAP COMPONENTS

SAP ECC

SAP Enterprise Central Component 6.0 (ECC 6.0) consists of the following modules:

i. Sales and Distribution (SD) module records sales orders and scheduled deliveries. Information about the customer (pricing, how and where to ship products, how the customer is to be billed, and so on) is maintained and accessed from this module.

ii. Materials Management (MM) module manages the acquisition of raw materials from suppliers (purchasing) and the subsequent handling of raw materials inventory, from storage to work-in-progress goods to shipping of finished goods to the customer.

iii. Production Planning (PP) module maintains production information. Here production is planned and scheduled, and actual production activities are recorded.

iv. Quality Management (QM) module plans and records quality control activities, such as product inspections and material certifications.

v. Plant Maintenance (PM) module manages maintenance resources and planning for preventive maintenance of plant machinery, to minimize equipment breakdowns.

vi. Asset Management (AM) module helps the company to manage fixed asset purchases (plant and machinery) and related depreciation.

vii. Human Resources (HR) module facilitates employee recruiting, hiring, and training. This module also includes payroll and benefits.

viii. Project System (PS) module allows the planning for and control over new R&D, construction, and marketing projects. This module allows for costs to be collected against a project, and it is frequently used to manage the implementation of the SAP ERP system. PS manages build-to-order items, which are low-volume, highly complex products such as ships and aircrafts.

ix. Financial Accounting (FI) module records transactions in the general ledger accounts. This module generates financial statements for external reporting purposes.

x. Controlling (CO) module serves internal management purposes, assigning manufacturing costs to products and to cost centers, so that the profitability of the company's activities can be analyzed. The CO module supports managerial decision making.

xi. Workflow (WF) module is not a module that automates a specific business function. Rather, it is a set of tools that can be used to automate any of the activities in SAP ERP. It can perform task-flow analysis and prompt employees (by e-mail) if they need to take action. Workflow is ideal for business processes that are not daily activities, but that occur frequently enough to be worth the effort to implement workflow, such as preparing customer invoices.

SAP SCM

SAP Supply-Chain Management (SAP SCM) complements SAP ERP with important components offering planning-based as well as execution-based functions for logistics processes. The components mentioned only briefly here will be examined in more detail in a subsequent chapter:

- SAP Extended Warehouse Management (SAP EWM) is the functionally very extensive successor to the SAP ERP component Warehouse Management (WM). It can be employed as a stand-alone system for complete warehouse management, including all contiguous processes.
- SAP Transportation Management (SAP TM) offers complete transportation processing, from order acceptance, transportation planning and subcontracting, to invoicing customers and service providers. It can be operated as a stand-alone system and was also conceived for use by logistics service providers.
- SAP Event Management is a tool with which processes can be tracked in several ways (such as transport tracking) and critical conditions in a process can be actively determined and reported to users. SAP Event Management can be configured and used for all status management and tracking tasks.
- SAP Auto-ID Infrastructure (SAP AII) integrates RFID technology into business processes. It allows users to establish a bridge between RFID readers and business processes in the application.

Another important component is SAP Advanced Planning & Optimization (SAP APO) consisting of the following:

- Supply-Chain Monitoring serves to monitor the logistics chain.
- Supply-Chain Collaboration enables collaboration with suppliers and customers.
- Demand Planning (DP) allows medium-term planning of requirements based on a prognosis for demand of your company's products on the market.
- Supply Network Planning (SNP) integrates the areas of Procurement, Production, Distribution, and Transport. It thus enables tactical planning decisions and those pertaining to procurement sources based on a global model.

- Global Availability Check (Available-to-Promise) (Global Available-to-Promise, gATP) allows product-availability checks on a global basis. It also supports product substitutions and place-of-delivery substitutions.
- Transportation Planning (Transportation Planning and Vehicle Scheduling) enables optimal intermodal planning for incoming and outgoing deliveries. The actual transportation processing, however, takes place in ERP.

SAP PLM

SAP PLM supports your company in product development, maintenance of assets, and service processing for your products. PLM enables a company to offer the right products at the right time and at the right prices for the customer. Delays increase costs and decrease your competitive ability; costs can often be reduced for service processing through preventative maintenance. And throughout all these activities, the early involvement of customers and subcontractors reduces costs and increases profitability. A company can achieve higher productivity by quickly introducing new products to the market.

SAP PLM has the advantage of being an integrated solution: Product development, quality management, asset management, maintenance, and service management are all integrated and the life cycle is mapped in its entirety. SAP Product Lifecycle Management offers all the functionality needed by any company for integrated product and asset management:

  i. Program and Project Management: Provides advanced capabilities to plan, manage, and control the complete product development process
 ii. Life Cycle Data Management: Provides an environment for managing specifications, bills of materials, routing and resource data, project structures, and related technical documentation throughout the product life cycle
iii. Life Cycle Collaboration: Supports collaborative engineering and project management, employing XML-based Web standards to communicate information such as project plans, documents, and product structures across virtual development teams
 iv. Quality Management: Provides integrated quality management for all industries throughout the entire product life cycle

v. Enterprise Asset Management: Manages physical assets and equipment, covering all components of an enterprise asset management system

vi. Environment, Health, and Safety: Provides a solution for environment, health, and safety issues by enhancing business processes to comply with government regulations

SAP NetWeaver

SAP NetWeaver is the technological platform for all SAP applications, including SAP xApps and the mySAP Business Suite, and forms the basis of solutions of selected partners. Reliability, security, and scalability are the characteristics that ensure that business-critical enterprise processes are processed smoothly using SAP NetWeaver. SAP NetWeaver components are presented in Figure AI.2.

Most organizations have clearly identified the benefits of an integrated enterprise and want to profit from this integration. However, integrating

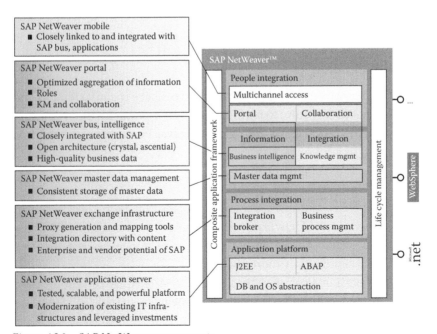

Figure AI.2   SAP NetWeaver components.

heterogeneous systems is always a significant challenge for the IT department. Combining separate systems for individual projects using a point-to-point integration is expensive and means that IT environments of this type become ever more inflexible. To reduce complexity and costs requires a single platform that includes all people, information, and business processes. SAP NetWeaver provides this platform.

SAP NetWeaver is a comprehensive integration and application platform that helps to reduce your total cost of ownership. It combines all users, information, and business processes on a cross-company and cross-technology basis. SAP NetWeaver is also an integrated platform based on Web services. Preconfigured business content reduces the amount of customer-specific integration that needs to be carried out. Unlike other platforms, SAP NetWeaver is compatible and extendible with Microsoft.NET and IBM WebSphere, and supports Java 2 Platform Enterprise Edition (J2EE). In this way, the SAP platform contributes to protecting existing investments in IT systems and employee qualifications. These advantages mean that the total cost of ownership can be considerably reduced not only for SAP solutions, but for the entire IT landscape. SAP NetWeaver helps you to use existing IT investments in a way that adds value while also representing the foundation for future cross-enterprise processes.

People Integration

People Integration ensures that your employees have the information and functions that they require to perform their work as quickly and efficiently as possible. The functions of the SAP NetWeaver Portal play a central role here.

The subareas of People Integration are

i. Portal: Delivers unified, personalized, and role-based user access to heterogeneous IT environments. Business processes in which customers, vendors, partner companies, and employees are involved become significantly more efficient.

ii. Collaboration: Promotes dynamic and cost-effective communication within teams or communities. This includes virtual Collaboration Rooms and tools for collaborating in real time, such as message forums, chat, team calendars, application sharing, and document storage.

iii. Multichannel access: Allows access to enterprise systems through PCs, the Internet, mobile devices, and speech-controlled systems. In this way, you can relocate your business processes to where the business is transacted.

SAP Enterprise Portal (EP)

The SAP NetWeaver Portal gives you access to all relevant data over a service-friendly interface. It also allows you to convert unstructured knowledge into concrete knowledge. SAP NetWeaver Portal brings together information from SAP and non-SAP systems, data warehouses, and desktop documents, as well as Web content and services on a central, unified platform.

The SAP NetWeaver Portal offers a central point of entry to all applications, Business Intelligence functions, documents, and Web services in a company. Users are central players. Users can use information from different sources and collaborate with one another inside and outside the company. Each portal is organized so that an optimal working environment for quickly realizing business opportunities and solving problems is created. This guarantees an extensive provision of pre-defined content, business packages, a fast implementation, and a higher return on investment than for comparable products. This makes the portal into a user-oriented platform for companies and their business partners.

One of the main aims of an enterprise portal is facilitating and accelerating access to information, applications, and services. This happens by allowing users access using a "single sign-on." The target group does not have to be limited to employees of one particular company. You can use external portals to reach partners, customers, or other interested parties.

SAP NetWeaver Portal solution enables

- The integration of all kinds of company data and applications, as well as the opportunity to control heterogeneous IT landscapes
- The optimal use of open standards for securing existing investments
- The conversion of unstructured information into concrete knowledge, and cross-company collaboration
- The provision of enterprise portal content for users, according to their particular role within the company

Information Integration

The Information Integration subarea provides access to all structured and unstructured information in your company. The core component in this subarea is SAP NetWeaver Business Intelligence (SAP NetWeaver BI), which provides data from a large number of different systems for evaluation.

The subareas of Information Integration are

i. Business Intelligence: Enables companies to include, analyze, and distribute business-critical information. This includes an extensive package of tools to develop and publish customized and interactive reports and applications. In this way, decision making is supported at every level.

ii. Knowledge Management: Manages unstructured information such as text files, presentations, or audio files, and allows access to this content. This includes an integrated search, Content Management, distribution of information, classification and workflow functions, and an open architecture for integrating external content.

iii. Master Data Management: Ensures company-wide unification of data and information in heterogeneous IT environments. Master Data Management provides services for consolidation, harmonization, and central management of your master data, including business partner information, product master data and structures, and information about technical systems.

SAP Business Intelligence (BI)

SAP NetWeaver Business Intelligence (SAP NetWeaver BI) allows the evaluation of data from operative SAP applications, from any other business applications, and from external data sources (databases, online services, and the Internet). The Administrator Workbench provides functions for controlling, monitoring, and maintaining all data retrieval processes.

Data from various sources (SAP systems, non-SAP systems, flat files, XML data, databases, and so on) is loaded into the SAP NetWeaver BI using extraction processes and, where necessary, is then transformed. For example, this may take the form of technical modifications or business modifications (such as currency translation). After being processed, the data is saved in InfoProviders. InfoProviders are created with specific business considerations in mind. This simplifies the process of evaluating and analyzing data later for reporting purposes. InfoProviders are objects that make data available for reporting. You can access an InfoProvider and generate reports based on it using the reporting tools provided by the Business Explorer (BEx). This allows you to get a focused readout of your data.

The SAP NetWeaver BI allows Online Analytical Processing (OLAP) for preparing large quantities of operative and historical data. OLAP technology makes multidimensional analysis possible from various business perspectives. The Data Warehouse, preconfigured with Business Content for core areas and processes, guarantees that you can view information in an enterprise-wide context. With Business Content, the information that employees need to fulfill their particular tasks is made available based on roles selected for an enterprise.

With the Business Explorer, SAP NetWeaver BI makes flexible reporting and analysis tools available. This enables strategic analysis and supports decision making within a company. Authorized employees can access and evaluate historic and current data at different levels of detail.

Process Integration

Process Integration ensures that business processes run across system boundaries in a heterogeneous system landscape. This is achieved using XML data packages and workflow scenarios, for instance. The SAP NetWeaver Exchange Infrastructure (SAP NetWeaver XI) plays a central role here.

The subareas of Process Integration are

i. Integration Broker: Realizes XML/SOAP-based communication between application components from various sources. The Integration Broker enables the definition of software components, interfaces, mappings, and content-based routing rules based on open standards.

ii. Business Process Management: Allows the modeling and acceleration of processes in a dynamic IT environment. It allows you to combine existing applications with adaptive integrated processes across the entire value creation chain.

SAP Exchange Infrastructure (XI)

SAP NetWeaver is the integration and application platform for mySAP applications; SAP NetWeaver Exchange Infrastructure (SAP NetWeaver XI) represents the Process Integration layer of the NetWeaver stack, and is a crucial element of the Enterprise Services Architecture (ESA).

Many components in customer system landscapes are directly connected using point-to-point connections, with all integration capabilities hard-wired directly into the application components and individual mapping programs. These systems have been integrated over time using whatever integration technology or middleware was available. The integration knowledge is hidden within the different applications or within the used middleware tools and the interface descriptions. This results in a wildly grown integration landscape with different application systems and multiple individual connections between different interfaces increasing its complexity and renders it very difficult and costly to maintain. The overall key concept of the SAP NetWeaver Exchange infrastructure (XI) is to drive integrated business processes across heterogeneous and highly dynamic IT landscapes in a more manageable and cost-effective way.

The Integration Repository provides integration scenarios, routing objects, mappings, interfaces, and components at design time. It is built in Java and follows Java 2 Enterprise Edition (J2EE) standards. The Integration Directory starts with the same knowledge captured in the Integration Repository, but it adds configuration-specific information that is needed for execution. The collaboration runtime environment enlists all runtime components relevant for exchanging messages among the connected software components and business partners. At the center of execution is the Integration Server, which includes the Integration Engine. The Integration Engine exchanges all messages between the different connected components.

Application Platform

The Application Platform supports J2EE and ABAP in a single environment. It guarantees the independence of databases and operating systems, the complete support of platform-independent Web services and company applications, and an open environment that is based on recognized standards. The central component of the Application Platform is the SAP NetWeaver Application Server (SAP NetWeaver AS).

In addition to the traditional runtime environment for ABAP programs, SAP NetWeaver AS also has a runtime environment for J2EE-based Java programs: The SAP J2EE Engine. Together with functions to control the operating system and database, SAP NetWeaver AS forms the application platform of SAP NetWeaver.

SAP NetWeaver AS offers:

- A reliable and thoroughly tested runtime environment, which has evolved for the past decade
- A framework for executing complex business processes that meets the highest security standards
- A reliable and user-friendly development environment
- Support for open technical standards such as HTTP(S), SMTP, Unicode, HTML, and XML
- High scalability, inherited from SAP Basis
- Support for various operating systems and databases

Benefits of SAP NetWeaver AS are

i. Openness and extendibility: SAP NetWeaver features complete compatibility and extendibility with IBM WebSphere and Microsoft.NET technologies in which companies have made significant investments. SAP will ensure interoperability with IBM and Microsoft solutions, and assist in development strategies, sales activities, and competence and support centers. The integration of SAP NetWeaver with IBM and Microsoft solutions spans all levels and therefore applies to the integration of people, information, and processes. This means that optimal benefit can be gained from existing IT investments in systems and employee qualifications.

ii. Immediate integration: SAP NetWeaver enables complete enterprise integration at all critical levels. SAP NetWeaver also provides valuable preconfigured business content. This ready-to-use content is available at all levels of SAP NetWeaver, drastically reducing implementation time and therefore speeding up return on investment. Among other things, the following business content is provided with SAP NetWeaver:

- Preconfigured portal content and predefined roles for better integration of people
- Reports and analyses for fast integration of information
- Interfaces for linking the business processes in your various back-end systems

iii. Lower total cost of ownership: The technology platform leverages your existing IT investments, since it integrates these and profitably includes systems that are already used in your company. SAP NetWeaver supports the entire software life cycle of business-critical applications with the lowest total cost of ownership. The technology platform is the result of SAP's 30 years of experience with reliable enterprise solutions. This means that you profit from high scalability, continuous uptime, and high security standards.

SAP FINANCIAL PERFORMANCE MANAGEMENT (FPM)

SAP FPM is SAP's solution for defining, executing, and monitoring the corporate strategy of an enterprise. FPM addresses corporate strategy areas such as setting of corporate goals, enabling alignment, communicating priorities, empowering collaboration of stakeholders, corporate scorecard, and management and monitoring of the scorecard.

It consists of following:

a. Business Planning: This entails areas such as budgeting; sales, revenue and capital expenditure planning; staffing and headcount; expense and cash flow planning; forecasting and consensus building.

b. Business Profitability Management: This entails activity-based costing for informed management decisions that optimize customer and product profitability, reduce the cost to serve, and optimize the cost of key processes; shared-services costing and cross charging to align resources and capacities with demand, reduce delivery costs, and gain process transparency; on-demand, what-if scenario analysis; driver-based and activity-based budgeting; and, ongoing dynamic monitoring of the drivers of cost and profitability.

c. Business Consolidation: This entails consolidation including intercompany matching reconciliation, intercompany eliminations, management roll-ups and legal consolidation; financial reporting and analysis including ad-hoc analysis, automated variance analysis and driver analysis (industry, growth, capacity, etc.).

Figure AI.3 presents an schematic of the SAP Financial Performance Management (FPM) suite.

Figure AI.3 SAP Financial Performance Management (FPM) suite.

SAP INDUSTRY-SPECIFIC APPLICATIONS

i. Automotive: SAP for Automotive is designed to streamline and improve disjointed business practices, enabling you to closely manage multitiered networks of customers, suppliers, and partners. This solution set facilitates seamless integration and collaboration across multiple internal and external organizations. It also includes best practices that support critical business processes, providing full visibility into enterprise data and increasing speed and flexibility worldwide.

ii. Banking: Based on a flexible, scalable infrastructure, SAP for Banking provides a robust environment for incorporating new technologies, controlling core banking processes, and extending operations to the Internet. Innovative core banking capabilities seamlessly connect front-office activities with back-office systems, enable low-cost, real-time processing of key financial transactions, and speed the development of multichannel products and services that meet the needs of your demand-oriented market.

iii. Chemicals: SAP for Chemicals delivers capabilities for sales and operations planning, quality management, recipe and batch management, and supply-chain operations. Also included is detailed profit reporting by customer, product, or segment, along with integrated hubs that let you unify process control systems and monitor production execution.

iv. Healthcare: Healthcare is a high-pressure industry facing demands for higher-quality patient care, cost controls, government regulations, and increasing competition. SAP for Healthcare integrates your healthcare processes—from staffing and inventory to financials and patient-centric processes—on an open platform designed for growth. And, when combined with leading, complementary components, SAP for Healthcare provides an end-to-end application for all administrative and clinical processes.

v. Logistics Service Providers: Designed in collaboration with many of the industry's leading companies, our comprehensive set of proven solutions, applications, technology, and services helps you manage your logistics business efficiently and profitably. SAP for Logistics Service Providers handles all order volumes and supports complex business processes in procurement, fulfillment, returns management, warehousing, and value-added logistics.

vi. Mining: Mining consists of multiple processes, each with its own set of challenges, and mining operations must optimize these processes to reduce costs. What is more, mining operations need to ensure regulatory compliance and commit to sustainability, even as commodity prices shift based on global demand and supply. SAP for Mining enables you to meet the specific challenges of the mining industry by helping you manage your assets and operations and leverage global supply-chain networks. As a result, you can increase efficiency and reduce costs.

vii. Oil and Gas: In today's oil and gas industry, companies are caught between rising hydrocarbon prices and ever-growing pressure from customers and regulators. You make every effort to reduce production and distribution costs, but the need for profitability and accountability to your shareholders continues to increase. With SAP for Oil and Gas solutions, you can face the challenges of cost and profitability head on. This set of solutions gives you comprehensive tools that enable you to leverage key data, manage assets effectively, and maximize cash flow.

viii. Public Sector: SAP for Public Sector creates fast, flexible, and responsive e-government by electronically connecting public administrations with citizens, businesses, suppliers, and other organizations via the Internet; enhancing communications; streamlining services;

and cutting costs. With rich functionality tailored to the unique demands of the public sector, this set of solutions helps you meet the challenge of serving the public today.

ix. Retail: Consumers have never been more in control. They have come to expect superb quality, selection, and service, and they are perfectly willing to abandon any retailer that cannot deliver. In today's market, there is no margin for error. SAP for Retail provides a comprehensive solution designed specifically for the new retail environment, where every piece of your retail value chain from forecasting and planning to allocation and replenishment must be focused on meeting and surpassing customer expectations.

SAP COMPOSITE APPLICATIONS

SAP xApps are a new breed of applications that enable you to drive improvements and innovations in your company more easily. With their ability to combine existing, heterogeneous systems to form cross-functional processes, SAP xApps bring people, information, and business processes together to make your company more dynamic and competitive. This flexibility allows you to implement business-wide strategies more easily and efficiently. SAP xApps increase the value of existing investments in the core business area and maximize the return on strategic assets, including employees, knowledge, products, business relationships, and information technology.

SAP xApps realize strategies by using previously unparalleled functions that bring employees, data, and processes in a company together on one interface. SAP xApps provide both continuity and discontinuity. Continuity is ensured by increasing effectiveness and improving productive business transactions; discontinuity is provided in the sense that a company can perform an innovative change in an unusually flexible manner.

By using xApps, a company can optimize a sales process across multiple systems. Functions such as a credit check from the accountancy system, or delivery time and availability (Available to Promise: ATP) from the logistics systems are used to design an integrated sales process. The employee works on just one interface, whereas before they had to perform separate checks in three different systems. The defining characteristics of SAP xApps are

   i. Cross functional: SAP xApps can be implemented with a multitude of applications and information sources. This allows you to run critical integrated processes across heterogeneous systems in compliance with your company's business strategy.

  ii. Composite: SAP xApps execute flexible workflow and business processes independently of the underlying infrastructure. Furthermore, SAP xApps synchronize and improve existing business processes. This makes your company more flexible and, by improving the use of existing investments, it also increases your return on investment (ROI).

  iii. Cross system: SAP xApps support a complex transfer of information (context, relevance), as well as the communication within the business itself, thereby simplifying the collaboration of working groups and sound decision making.

  iv. Information-driven: SAP xApps enable intelligent processes that are driven by decision-relevant business information. This enables a company to make informed, strategic decisions, which you can continually evaluate, and, if applicable, amend.

     Some examples of available xApps:

- SAP xApp Cost and Quotation Management (SAP xCQM): This solution enables the creation of a quotation through the upload of a bill of material (BOM), automatic pricing of existing components, streamlined eRFQ processing for new components, and execution of consolidated costs reports.

- SAP xApp Resource and Portfolio Management (SAP xRPM): SAP xRPM integrates information from existing project management, human resources, and financial systems to provide an overview of the project portfolio with easy drilldown to details for portfolio managers, project managers, resource managers, and project members.

- SAP xApp Product Definition (SAP xPD): SAP xPD is a simple, easy-to-use solution that addresses the hurdles and inefficiencies at the critical front end of product development processes, such as idea management and concept development.

- SAP xApp Emissions Management (SAP xEM): To comply with environmental regulations such as the Kyoto Protocol or the US Clean Air Act, emissions management is a must for all energy-consuming and carbon-dioxide-producing businesses. SAP xEM helps corporations improve their compliance with emerging emissions regulations worldwide and increase revenue through trading of emissions credits.

SAP SMALL AND MIDSIZE BUSINESSES APPLICATIONS

mySAP All-in-One

Each qualified mySAP All-in-One partner solution is a prepackaged, industry-specific version of mySAP Business Suite with built-in content, tools, and methodologies for a cost-effective, turnkey implementation. mySAP All-in-One partner solutions offer out-of-the-box flexibility combined with the power of SAP's world-class business applications.

Qualified mySAP All-in-One partner solutions provide the following advantages:

i. Rapid implementation and transparent costs: mySAP All-in-One is provided by selected, qualified partners who are familiar with the challenges of the respective market segment and industry. The software is implemented using a special implementation method that is based on experience gained from more than 15,000 customer installations in more than 20 industries worldwide. In comparison to traditional implementation projects, customers are able to save costs by 40-percent and reduce implementation time by 30-percent. Due to its scalability, the enterprise solution can be readily extended when the company grows, and can thus keep pace with any company changes.

ii. Increased productivity and cost control: The comprehensive, pre-configured mySAP All-in-One industry solutions integrate financials, human resources, logistics, and customer relationships. As a result, the customer profits from increased transparency and simplified administrative processes. This also means more efficiency not only for the company but also for partners and vendors.

iii. Reliable partners: For several years, SAP's technological know-how has been complemented by the industry knowledge of selected and qualified partners. The mySAP All-in-One partner solutions reflect this valuable experience. SAP partners offer comprehensive solutions consisting of hardware, software, and consulting, all of which are tailored to the needs of small and midsize businesses.

iv. Scalability: The flexible and powerful system technology, which is also used in big enterprises, supports the growth of small and midsize companies. The reason for this is simple: mySAP All-in-One can be easily adapted to changing business requirements.

SAP Business ByDesign

The newest of SAP's SME offerings, SAP Business ByDesign (BBD) includes preconfigured best practices for managing financials, customer relationships, human resources, projects, procurement, and the supply chain. BBD allows customers to focus on their business, leaving SAP to worry about maintaining hardware and software, running database backups, addressing performance and capacity planning, implementing updates and fixes, and so on. SAP takes care of system installation, maintenance, and upgrades so that you can focus on your business rather than on IT. BBD targets to address the market of customers seeking to avoid investing in business software and all the necessary infrastructure and support personnel associated with such an investment.

SAP Business ByDesign solution provides the following advantages:

i. Hosted solution: SAP hosts your Business ByDesign system in an enterprise class datacenter designed to provide high availability and reliability.

ii. Lower efforts and costs: A company deploying BBD does not necessarily require SAP partners or consultants for implementation.

iii. Increased productivity and ease of maintenance: A major advantage of BBD is its ease of configuration for changes and maintenance. Nontechnical users can build business processes using visual modeling tools and web services.

SAP Business One

SAP Business One is an easy-to-use business and operational management application for emerging and dynamic businesses ranging in size from 10 to several hundred employees. The application is simple yet powerful, allowing an immediate and complete view of both business operations and customer activities.

SAP Business One provides the following advantages:

i. Rapid implementation: SAP Business One can be implemented within a few days and can be easily maintained. In addition, its familiar Microsoft Office environment allows occasional users to rapidly learn to use the software. The application is based on open technologies and can be readily extended with special functions, if required.

ii. Lower costs: Because it is cost effective, SAP Business One offers a wide range of functions for an integrated data processing. Thus, decision makers in small and midsize companies benefit from new value potential without exceeding their budgets.

iii. Increased productivity and cost control: As the user interface of SAP Business One is simple and easy to understand, users will quickly learn how to work with the system. This will increase their productivity and help reduce costs. The Drag & Relate technology enables flexible access to business information. For example, by clicking the content of the Customer or Item Number field in the Quotation window and dragging it to another screen, the relevant data will be evaluated. This technology relates different data to each other.

iv. Sound business decisions: SAP Business One allows managers to quickly and effectively access strategic information from all enterprise areas and gives them full control of the relevant information and activities.

v. Scalability: When a company grows, processes usually become more complex and software requirements change. SAP Business One's flexible and efficient system technology can easily keep pace with the company's growth. SAP Business One can be extended by the functions your company requires. It also facilitates the transition to a more comprehensive IT system, such as the mySAP Business Suite.

SUMMARY

This chapter introduced the concept of ERP and the reason for its popularity. It unravels the mystery of ERPs like SAP and their power and potential to transform business enterprises. Customary discussions on ERP systems do not address the key differentiator of ERPs from the earlier mission-critical systems: ERPs, for the first time, are able to treat enterprise-level information not merely as records of information, but as a tangible resource. We then looked at the difference between the functional business model and business process model. Following this we described SAP Business Suite along with its main constituents such as cross-industry applications, components, financial performance management, industry-specific solutions, composite applications, and SAP small and midsize businesses applications.

Bibliography

Albrecht, K. *The Power of Minds at Work: Organizational Intelligence in Action*, Amazon, 2003.

Bell, S. *Lean Enterprise Systems: Using IT for Continuous Improvement*, Wiley, 2006.

Davis, F. W. and K. B. Mandrodt, *Customer-Responsive Management: The Flexible Advantage*, Blackwell, 1996.

Dosi, G., D. J. Teece and J. Chytry, *Technology Organization and Competitiveness: Perspectives on Industrial and Corporate Change*, Oxford University Press, 1998.

Dove, R. *Response Ability: The Language, Structure, and the Culture of the Agile Enterprise*, Wiley, 2001.

Kale, V. *Inverting the Paradox of Excellence: How Companies Use Variations for Business Excellence and How Enterprise Variations Are Enabled by SAP*, CRC Press, 2014.

Kale, V. *Implementing SAP CRM: The Guide for Business and Technology Managers*, CRC Press, 2014.

Koren, Y. *The Global Manufacturing Revolution: Product-Process-Business Integration and Reconfigurable Systems*, Wiley, 2010.

Nightingale, D. J. and D. H. Rhodes, *Architecting the Future Enterprise*, MIT Press, 2015.

Shtub, A. and R. Karni, *ERP: The Dynamics of Supply Chain and Process Management*, Springer, 2010.

Walker, W. T. *Supply Chain Architecture: A Blueprint for Networking the Flow of the Material, Information, and Cash*, CRC Press, 2005.

Waltz, E. *Knowledge Management in the Intelligent Enterprise*, Artech House, 2003.

Weijermars, R. *Building Corporate IQ: Moving the Energy Business from Smart to Genius, Executive Guide to Preventing Costly Crises*, Springer, 2011.

Index

A

ABC, *see* Activity-based costing
ABM, *see* Activity-based management
ABRA, *see* Activity-Based Revenue
        Accounting
Accelerated SAP methodology (ASAP
        methodology), 306, 308, 316;
        see also Enterprise system
        implementation project
    business blueprint, 311–312
    final preparation, 312
    go live and support phase, 312–313
    project preparation, 311
    realization, 312
Activity-based costing (ABC), 188; *see also*
        Activity-based customer
        responsiveness
    advantages, 188
    costs, 190
    customer cost, 189
    drawbacks, 190–191
    product cost, 189
    time-driven ABC vs., 193–194
Activity-based customer responsiveness,
        173, 187; *see also* Activity-
        based costing (ABC);
        Customer responsiveness;
        Time-driven activity-based
        costing (TDABC)
    ABRA, 197–198
    customer-responsive activities, 196
    enterprises objectives, 187
    mass customization, 187
    responsive activity pricing, 196
Activity-based management (ABM), 87
Activity-Based Revenue Accounting
        (ABRA), 190, 197–198
Advanced Planning and Scheduling
        (APS), 41
AF, *see* Application Framework

Agile enterprises, 1; *see also* Agility;
        Construction toys; Enterprise
        agility; Intelligent enterprises
    change proficiency, 9–10
    construction toys, 2–3
    network enterprises, 12–14
    patterns, 8–9
    principles of built-for-change
        systems, 8–9
    strategic adjustments, 6
    strategic reorientations, 6
Agility, 2; *see also* Agile enterprises
    advantages, 7
    aspects of, 6–7
    element of, 14
    stability vs., 4–6
AM module, *see* Asset Management
        module
Application Framework (AF), 42
APS, *see* Advanced Planning and
        Scheduling
ASAP methodology, *see* Accelerated SAP
        methodology
Asset Management module (AM module),
        342
ATP, *see* Available to Promise
Available to Promise (ATP), 355

B

Balance Scorecard (BSC), 68; *see also*
        Enterprise Systems (ES)
    business processes perspective, 72–73
    customer perspective, 72
    financial perspective, 72
    framework, 68, 69
    learning and growth perspective, 73
    strategic management of enterprises
        using, 70
    strategy-focused company creation, 71
    value drivers, 69

BBD, *see* Business ByDesign
BEx, *see* Business Explorer
BI, *see* Business Intelligence
Bill of Materials (BOM), 307
Bill of resources (BOR), 307;
      see also Enterprise system
      implementation project
  information, 309
  manpower, 308–309
  materials, 308
  money, 308
  time period, 309
BOM, *see* Bill of Materials
BOR, *see* Bill of resources
BPEL, *see* Business Process Execution
      Language for Web Services
BPEL4WS, *see* Business Process Execution
      Language for Web Services
BPI, *see* Business Process Improvement
BPM, *see* Business process management
BPMS, *see* Business Process Management
      Systems
BPR, *see* Business process reengineering
BPRD, *see* Business Process Redesign
BSC, *see* Balance Scorecard
B2B, *see* Business-to-business
B2C, *see* Business-to-consumer
B2E, *see* Business-to-employee
Built-for-change systems, 8–9
Business ByDesign (BBD), 358
Business Explorer (BEx), 349
Business Intelligence (BI), 32–33, 45,
      85, 267–268, 294; *see also*
      Context-aware applications
      (CAA); Customer relationship
      management decision patterns;
      Financial decision patterns
  activities, 267
  analytical components, 268
  applications of, 275–277
  architecture, 269
  in banking and financial services, 276
  benefits of, 270–272
  challenge in designing, 273
  CRM effectiveness improvement,
    270–271
  customer satisfaction improvement, 271
  data collection, 273
  data mining, 274–275

  data warehousing and data marts, 272
  domain-specific decision patterns, 284
  governance and regulatory
    compliance, 271–272
  granularity of warehouse, 272
  information, 272
  in manufacturing, 277
  online analytical process, 275
  operational data, data warehouse, and
    data marts, 274
  in pharmaceuticals and life sciences,
    276
  procurement and acquisition
    improvement, 271
  response and decision-making process
    improvement, 270
  in retail, 276–277
  risk management, 271
  technologies of, 272
Business Intelligence Systems, 268
Business models, 113–114
Business process, 107, 234; *see also* Business
    process management (BPM);
    Business processes with SOA
Business processes with SOA, 257; *see also*
    Business process management
    (BPM)
  activity, 259
  business process management, 261–262
  process, 258–260
  process instance, 258
  service composition, 264
  transformation, 260–261
  value chain, 258
  view, 260
  via web services, 263–264
  workflow, 260–261
Business Process Execution Language for
    Web Services (BPEL4WS), 264
Business Process Improvement (BPI), 253
Business process management (BPM),
    32, 42, 107, 235, 253, 261,
    265; *see also* Business process
    reengineering (BPR); Business
    processes with SOA; Enterprise
    BPM methodology; Management
    by collaboration (MBC)
  application areas, 236–237
  approaches, 235

business process, 234, 237
capability/capacity, 233
concept of, 231–233
positioning, 233
process optimization, 235
solution, 235
solution, 261
tools, 262
Business Process Management Systems
(BPMS), 229, 234, 265
Business process model, 94
Business Process Redesign (BPRD), 253
Business process reengineering (BPR), 11,
85, 123, 247, 253; *see also* Business
process management (BPM)
activity-based costing for, 188–190
change in capability, 248
effort, 248–249
seven-step methodology, 248
value gaps, 249
Business rules, 261
Business-to-business (B2B), 42
Business-to-consumer (B2C), 42
Business-to-employee (B2E), 42
Business Web (B-Web), 183
B-Web, *see* Business Web

C

CAA, *see* Context-aware applications
CAD, *see* Computer-aided design
CAE, *see* Computer-aided engineering
CAM, *see* Computer-aided manufacturing
Capacity Requirements Planning
module, 37
CASE, *see* Computer-Aided Software
Engineering
CE, *see* Concurrent engineering
Change proficiency, 9–10
Chief Project Officer (CPO), 298–299
Choreography, 265
CIM, *see* Computer-integrated
manufacturing
CLC, *see* Customer life cycle
CLTV, *see* Customer Life Time Value
COGS, *see* Cost of Goods Sold
Collaborative endeavors, 256; *see also*
Management by collaboration
(MBC)

Collaborative enterprise with BPM,
229; *see also* Business process
management (BPM); Business
process reengineering (BPR);
Business processes with SOA;
Enterprise BPM methodology;
Management by collaboration
(MBC)
Collaborative learning, 255–256; *see also*
Management by collaboration
(MBC)
Commercial off-the-shelf (COTS), 95
packaged systems, 74
CO module, *see* Controlling module
Companies in nonmanufacturing
sectors, 40
Competitive gap, 239
Complementary Software Program
(CSP), 310
Composite services, 264; *see also* Business
processes with SOA; Web
Service (WS)
orchestration, 264–265
Computer-aided design (CAD), 207
Computer-aided engineering
(CAE), 207
Computer-aided manufacturing
(CAM), 207
Computer-Aided Software Engineering
(CASE), 47
-like repository, 78
Computer-integrated manufacturing
(CIM), 39, 85
Concurrent engineering (CE),
218, 220
Construction toys, 2–3; *see also* Agile
enterprises
Erector Set, 3
LEGO, 3, 4
Model Builder, 3, 4
Context-aware applications (CAA),
277, 278; *see also* Business
Intelligence (BI)
concept of patterns, 280–283
context information, 279–280
decision patterns as context, 279
generation of context, 280
GPS-based application, 278
Context-aware ubicomp, 279

Controlling module (CO module), 342
Convergence, 119
Core Web Service standards, 263
Corporate Performance Management
    (CPM), 42
Corporate Performance Monitor
    (CPM), 61
Corporation, 50
Cost of Goods Sold (COGS), 166
COTS, *see* Commercial off-the-shelf
CPM, *see* Corporate Performance
    Management; Corporate
    Performance Monitor
CPO, *see* Chief Project Officer
Critical success factors (CSF),
    239, 319
Critical value determinants (CVDs), 55,
    231, 241
CRM, *see* Customer Relationship
    Management
CSF, *see* Critical success factors
CSP, *see* Complementary Software
    Program
CUG, *see* Customer-differential gap
CUP, *see* Customer-differential period
Current reality tree, 21; *see also* Theory of
    constraints (TOC)
Customer capitalism, 124–126; *see
    also* Customer Relationship
    Management (CRM)
    customer information value
        assessment, 127
    data mining, 128
    increasing returns and, 126
    leveraging, 127–128
    loyalty models, 129
Customer centricity, 115; *see also*
    Customer Relationship
    Management (CRM)
    approach, 138
    communication technologies, 120
    competitive advantage, 122
    convergence, 119
    customer capital, 124–126
    customer database, 124
    customer needs and values, 116, 123
    customer relationship strategy,
        121–122
    customer relationship types, 116–117

customer's attention, 118
    hardware trends, 120
    information, 122–124
    life of customer, 123
    market share, 118
    market spaces, 118
    network effects, 126
    process view, 117
    from products to services to
        experiences, 117–118
    spectrum of offering vs. medium/
        message, 119
    traditional capitalism, 125, 126
    traditional mass marketing vs.
        customized relationship
        marketing, 115
Customer database, 124
Customer-differential gap (CUG), 62
Customer-differential period (CUP), 63
Customer life cycle (CLC), 115, 141; *see
    also* Customer Relationship
    Management (CRM); Lifetime
    value (LTV)
    customer lifetime value, 144–146
    customer types, 141
    customer value, 143–144
    focus of activities during various
        phases, 142–143
    stages of, 142
Customer Life Time Value (CLTV), 62, 146;
    see also Lifetime value (LTV)
    curve, 63
Customer loyalty, 131; *see also* Customer
    Relationship Management
    (CRM)
    characteristics, 132
    cost of winning back, 131
    customer acquiring cost, 131
    Customer Pyramid, 133–134
    customer retention cost, 131
    customer satisfaction orientation, 133
    MVC identification, 132
Customer Pyramid, 133–134
Customer relationship, 134; *see also*
    Customer Relationship
    Management (CRM)
    channel costs and integration, 138
    channel integration, 137–138
    cultivating, 135–136

interaction channels, 136–137
internet, 137
one-to-one marketing, 139–140
permission marketing, 140
responsiveness, 137
understanding customer, 138–139
value of relationship, 134–135
Customer Relationship Management
    (CRM), 31, 41, 42, 59, 85, 96, 109,
    110, 150–151; *see also* Customer
    capitalism; Customer centricity;
    Customer life cycle (CLC);
    Customer loyalty; Customer
    relationship; Customer Value
    Management (CVM)
    business model, 113–114
    compelling customer experiences,
        128–129
    customer loyalty, 131
    customer relationship framework, 111
    customer retention, 111
    effective strategy, 109
    marketing techniques, 112
    mass customization, 114
    metrics, 298
    one-to-one marketing, 112–113
    personalization, 130–131
    principles for best practices, 297–298
    Systems, 110
    TQM movement, 114
    users of, 128
Customer relationship management
        decision patterns, 287; *see also*
        Business Intelligence (BI)
    for customer acquisition, 288
    for customer attrition, 290
    for customer retention, 289
    for customer win-back, 290–291
    data mining, 291, 292
    direct marketing campaigns, 293–294
    market basket analysis, 294
    objectives, 287
    segmentation, 293
Customer-responsive enterprises, 172
Customer-responsive management,
        178, 255; *see also* Customer
        responsiveness
    business webs, 183
    costs, 184

customer-driven change, 179
economics of customer responsiveness,
    183–186
enterprise infrastructure, 181
flexible planning, 179
individual delivery plan, 180
infrastructure development, 182–183
inventory, 184–185
logistics, 179–180
mass production, 178
minimizing wasted capacity, 186
resource network, 181–183
revenues, 184
sense-and-respond enterprise, 179
Customer responsiveness, 170; *see also*
        Activity-based customer
        responsiveness; Customer-
        responsive management;
        Supply-chain management
        (SCM)
    advantages of, 172–173
    aspects of, 174–178
    best-practice guidelines, 174–175
    customer service management,
        177–178
    customized marketing approach,
        171–172
    diagnosis management, 174
    mass marketing, 170–171
    resource interface management,
        176–177
    responsive capacity management,
        175–176
    responsive task management, 175
Customer retention, 111
Customer's attention, 118
Customer value (CV), 143
Customer Value Management (CVM),
        132, 146; *see also* Customer
        Relationship Management
        (CRM)
    benefits, 147
    cocreating systems, 144
    customer as asset, 148–150
    customer capital and brand equity, 147
    marketing mix comparison, 150
    mass customization, 148
    relationship-based enterprises, 148
    value curve, 149

Customization, 221–223; *see also* Product lifecycle management (PLM)
CV, *see* Customer value
CVDs, *see* Critical value determinants
CVM, *see* Customer Value Management

D

Data, 94
Database (DB), 42
Data mining, 128
  models, 292
DB, *see* Database
Decision patterns (DP), 322
Degree of Responsiveness (DOR), 14
Demand Planning (DP), 343
Design for configuration (DFC), 225–226; *see also* Product lifecycle management (PLM)
Design for manufacturability (DFM), 218, 219–220
Design for sustainability (DFS), 218, 220–221
Design for variety (DFV), 224–225; *see also* Product lifecycle management (PLM)
DFC, *see* Design for configuration
DFM, *see* Design for manufacturability
DFS, *see* Design for sustainability
DFV, *see* Design for variety
DMAIC (define, measure, analyze, improve, control), 24, 25–27; *see also* Six Sigma
DOR, *see* Degree of Responsiveness
DP, *see* Decision patterns; Demand Planning
Drum–buffer–rope scheduling methodology, 20; *see also* Theory of constraints (TOC)

E

EAI, *see* Enterprise Application Integration
Earnings, 56
Earnings per Share (E/S), 55
e-Business, 10
ECC, *see* Engineering Change Control
ECC 6.0, *see* SAP Enterprise Central Component 6. 0

ECM, *see* Engineering Change Management
E-Commerce, 43
Economic Value Add (EVA), 59–60
EES, *see* Extended enterprise systems
EHS, *see* Environmental health and safety
Eight-attribute plan, 52
ELM, *see* Employee Life cycle Management
Employee Life cycle Management (ELM), 42
Employee Self-Service (ESS), 330
Engineering Change Control (ECC), 207
Engineering Change Management (ECM), 207
Enterprise, 2, 50
  application architecture, 96
  business model, 113
  change management, 254
  -wide solution, 50
Enterprise agility, 1–2, 10, 30; *see also* Agile enterprises
  business process reengineering, 11
  dynamic business model, 12
  e-Business strategy, 10
  extending business processes with mobility, 12
  extending web to wireless, 12
  mobilizing enterprise processes, 11
Enterprise Application Integration (EAI), 42, 95; *see also* Enterprise Resource Planning (ERP)
  CRM solutions, 97
  enterprise and software applications, 95
  standard template, 96
Enterprise BPM methodology, 238; *see also* Business process management (BPM)
  alternate activities and BPM, 240
  business process identification, 240–241
  business process selection, 241–242
  competitive gap, 239
  for continuous improvement, 246
  CVDs, 241
  cycle of, 239
  MAVs, 241
  process, 240–241
  process analysis, 243–244
  processes improvement, 244–245
  process implementation and performance measurement, 245

process map creation, 242–243
seven steps in, 238
strategic planning, 238
techniques for continuous
improvement, 246
value gaps, 242
Enterprise business processes, 93; *see also*
Enterprise Resource Planning
(ERP)
data, 94
functional model, 94, 95
model, 94
silos, 93
Enterprise intelligence, 30; *see also*
Intelligent enterprises
collaborative enterprise with BPM, 32
customer-centric enterprise with
CRM, 31
customer-responsive enterprise with
SCM, 31–32
informed enterprise with BI, 32–33
integrated enterprise with ERP, 30–31
renewing enterprise with PLM, 32
Enterprise Intelligence Quotient (EQ), 33
Enterprise performance intelligence, *see*
Performance intelligence (PI)
Enterprise portal (EP), 347
Enterprise Resource Planning (ERP),
30–31, 35, 39–40, 42, 76, 77, 80,
85, 96, 107; *see also* Enterprise
Systems (ES); Service-oriented
architecture (SOA)
advantages of, 79, 87–88
approaches, 84
back-office automation vs. relationship
building technology, 86
CASE-like repository, 78
computerized system implementation,
85–86
enterprise application integration, 95–97
enterprise as global enterprise, 81
enterprise business processes, 93–95
enterprise integration level, 40
enterprise into information-driven
enterprise, 80
enterprise knowledge as new capital,
88–89
focus of, 76
information as new resource, 89–91

integrated nature of enterprise, 81–82
IT strategy as part of business
strategy, 84
mass-user-oriented application
environment, 86–87
modeling process-oriented enterprise,
82–83
as new enterprise architecture, 91–93
real-time enterprise, 83–84
sequence, 92–93
shared values, 91
skills, 92
software applications package, 77
staff, 92
strategy, 91–92
structure, 92
success of, 78
timeline of performance improvement
movements, 85
Enterprise Services Architecture (ESA), 350
Enterprise standard time (EST), 83
Enterprise system based enterprise, 50; *see
also* Enterprise system metrics;
Enterprise Systems (ES);
Enterprise value; Value-based
management (VBM)
economic value add, 59–60
eight-attribute plan, 52
enterprise stakeholders, 50–52
enterprise-wide solution, 50
from built-to-last to built-to-perform
enterprises, 52–53
primary stakeholders, 50
Enterprise system implementation, 315;
see also Enterprise system
implementation project
ES installation, 316
implementation, 316
postimplementation, 316–317
preimplementation, 315
training, 316
Enterprise system implementation
project, 295, 319; *see also*
Accelerated SAP methodology
(ASAP methodology); Bill of
resources (BOR); Enterprise
system implementation; Project
management
base component implementation, 305

Enterprise system implementation
        project (*Continued*)
    best practice principles, 297–298
    big bang implementation, 304–305
    budget and resource allocation, 301
    business process standardization, 300
    clear project scope, 300
    company-wide change management
        plan, 302
    critical success factors, 299
    CRM metrics, 296
    ES configuration, 307
    ES deployment, 317–318
    ES support, 317
    failure in ES projects, 318–319
    functions coverage, 300
    implementation strategy, 304, 309–311
    infrastructural activity completion, 302
    key managers, 301–302
    management involvement, 299
    managing interface of, 303–304
    objectives, 296
    pilot site deployment, 306
    project initiation and planning,
        298–299
    reasons for implementation, 297
    standard functionality
        implementation, 305–306
    team members training, 303
    training in-house consultants, 306–307
    transition plan for, 304
    user-driven functionality, 307
    user members training, 303
    visibility and communication, 301
Enterprise system metrics, 63; *see also*
        Enterprise system based
        enterprise
    benefits of, 64
    brand-and customer-level matrices,
        65–66
    categories of, 64
    enterprise performances
        measurement, 67
    sales and distribution measures, 67
Enterprise system packages, 45, 251;
        see also Enterprise Systems (ES)
    CASE, 47
    to confront software crisis, 49
    effort expended during ERP, 48

    reasons for software crisis, 45–46
    software implementation, 47, 48–49
Enterprise Systems (ES), 11, 229, 35, 73–74;
        see also Balance Scorecard
        (BSC); Enterprise Resource
        Planning (ERP); Enterprise
        system based enterprise;
        Enterprise system packages;
        Extended enterprise systems
        (EES); Material Requirement
        Planning (MRP)
    enterprise resource planning, 39–40
    evolution of, 35, 36
    issues for, 232
    manufacturing requirement planning
        II, 39
    materials requirement planning, 37–38
    packages, 45
    traditional, 35
    types of enterprises enabled by, 33
Enterprise value, 53; *see also* Enterprise
        system based enterprise
    cash flow perspective, 56
    earnings, 56
    value to customers, 54–55
    value to employees, 57–58
    value to managers, 56–57
    value to shareholders, 55–56
    value to vendors, 58–59
Environmental health and safety (EHS),
        334, 337
EP, *see* Enterprise portal
EQ, *see* Enterprise Intelligence Quotient
Erector Set, 3
ERP, *see* Enterprise Resource Planning
E/S, *see* Earnings per Share
ES, *see* Enterprise Systems
ESA, *see* Enterprise Services Architecture
ESS, *see* Employee Self-Service
EST, *see* Enterprise standard time
ETL, *see* Extract, Transform, and Load
EVA, *see* Economic Value Add
Evaporating cloud, 22; *see also* Theory of
        constraints (TOC)
Exchange infrastructure (XI), 350
Executable agent, 99–100
Extended enterprise systems (EES), 40;
        see also Enterprise Systems (ES)
    extended functionality, 43–45

framework, 41–43
    layers of, 42
    plug and play environment, 45
Extract, Transform, and Load (ETL), 269

F

Failure Mode and Effects Analysis
    (FMEA), 246
FI module, *see* Financial Accounting
    module
Financial Accounting module (FI
    module), 342
Financial decision patterns, 284; *see also*
    Business Intelligence (BI)
    assets, 285
    cash flow planning, 284–285
    finance function, 287
    financial scandals, 286–287
    performance assessment measures, 286
    profitability, 285
    ratio of debt to equity capital, 286
Financial performance management
    (FPM), 352
Financial scandals, 286–287
Financial Supply-Chain Management
    (FSCM), 330
Flexibility, 2
FMEA, *see* Failure Mode and Effects
    Analysis
Ford Motor Company, 15–16
FPM, *see* Financial performance
    management
Fraud detection, 271
FSCM, *see* Financial Supply-Chain
    Management
Functional business model, 94, 95
Future reality tree, 22; *see also* Theory of
    constraints (TOC)

G

GAAPs, *see* Generally acceptable
    accounting principles
gATP, *see* Global Available-to-Promise
General ledger (GL), 304
Generally acceptable accounting
    principles (GAAPs), 286, 326
GL, *see* General ledger

Global Available-to-Promise (gATP), 344
Global Positioning System (GPS), 278
Global Trade Services (GTS), 329, 336
Goal trees, 27
Governance, Risk, and Compliance
    (GRC), 325
GPS, *see* Global Positioning System
GRC, *see* Governance, Risk, and Compliance
GTS, *see* Global Trade Services

H

Half-life, 12
HCM, *see* Human Capital Management
HOQ, *see* House of quality
House of quality (HOQ), 218
HR, *see* Human Resource
Human Capital Management (HCM), 330
Human Resource (HR), 96, 330
    module, 342

I

IAS, *see* International Accounting Standards
IC, *see* Interaction Center
ID, *see* Identification
Identification (ID), 130
IDES, *see* Information and Design
    Education
IE, *see* Internet Explorer
Individual delivery plan, 180
Information, 89–91
    -driven enterprise, 252
Information and Design Education
    (IDES), 312
Information systems (IS), 79, 254
Information technology (IT), 11, 247
Informed enterprise with BI, 267; *see also*
    Business Intelligence (BI)
Integrated enterprise with ERP, 75;
    see also Enterprise Resource
    Planning (ERP)
Intelligent enterprises, 1, 34; *see also*
    Agile enterprises; Enterprise
    intelligence; Lean; Six Sigma;
    Theory of constraints (TOC)
    improvement programs, 15
    operating strategy, 14
    time-based competition, 28–30

Interaction Center (IC), 339
International Accounting Standards
    (IAS), 326
Internet, 181
Internet Explorer (IE), 178
Inventory turn, 16
IS, *see* Information systems
IT, *see* Information technology

J

J2EE, *see* Java 2 Platform Enterprise
    Edition
Java 2 Platform Enterprise Edition
    (J2EE), 346
JIT, *see* Just-in-Time
Joint venture (JV), 13
Just-in-Time (JIT), 85, 188
JV, *see* Joint venture

K

KANBAN, 335
KMS, *see* Knowledge Management System
Knowledge Management System (KMS), 44

L

Lean, 15, 17; *see also* Intelligent enterprises
    problem solving in, 18
    system improvement cycle, 18
    TPS, 15–16
    value stream mapping, 17
    waste elimination, 17
LEGO, 2, 3, 4
Lifetime value (LTV), 61, 132, 144; *see also*
        Customer life cycle (CLC)
    data essential for calculating, 144–145
    formula for, 145
    prediction, 145, 146
Location-aware systems, 277
LTV, *see* Lifetime value

M

Maintenance, repair, and operations
    (MRO), 159
Management by collaboration (MBC),
        249; *see also* Business process
    management (BPM)

basic idea of, 250
collaborative learning, 255–256
Customer Responsive Management,
    255
enterprise change management, 254
information-driven enterprise, 252
learning enterprise, 255–256
outsourcing, 256–257
PRM system, 257
process-oriented enterprise, 252–253
relationship-based enterprise,
    251–252
systems integrators, 257
value-add-driven enterprise,
    253–254
virtual enterprise, 256–257
Manager Self-Service (MSS), 331
Manufacturing Performance Monitor
    (MPM), 61
Manufacturing Resource Planning
    (MRP II), 39, 75–76, 85
Market share, 118
Market spaces, 118
Mass customization, 114, 148, 187, 223–
        224; *see also* Product lifecycle
    management (PLM)
Mass marketing, 170
    enterprises, 170–171
Master Black Belt, 24
Material Requirement Planning (MRP),
        35, 37–38, 85; *see also* Enterprise
    Systems (ES)
    capacity requirements planning
        module, 37
    closed-loop, 38
    inputs, 37
Materials Management module (MM
    module), 342
MAV, *see* Minimum acceptance value
MBC, *see* Management by collaboration
M-Commerce, 43
Measures of performances (MOPs), 67
MEPs, *see* Message exchange patterns
Message exchange patterns (MEPs), 100
Message queuing system, 101
Methodology, 311
Minimum acceptance value (MAV), 239
MM module, *see* Materials Management
    module

Model Builder, 3, 4
MOPs, *see* Measures of performances
Most valuable customers (MVC), 132
MPM, *see* Manufacturing Performance
    Monitor
MRO, *see* Maintenance, repair, and
    operations
MRP, *see* Material Requirement Planning
MRP II, *see* Manufacturing Resource
    Planning
MSS, *see* Manager Self-Service
MVC, *see* Most valuable customers
mySAP All-in-One partner solution,
    357–358
mySAP Business Suite, 323, 359–360;
        see also SAP components; SAP
        cross-industry applications;
        SAP NetWeaver; SAP small and
        midsize businesses applications
    applications, 323
    components, 324
    financial performance management,
        352–353
    industry-specific applications, 353–355
    SAP composite applications, 355–357
    SAP installed base, 323–324
    SAP xApps, 355–357
mySAP CRM, 338; *see also* SAP cross-
        industry applications
    communications management, 340
    marketing support, 338–339
    partner channel management, 340
    real-time offer management, 340
    sales support, 339
    service support, 339
    web channel, 339–340
mySAP ERP corporate services, 336;
        see also SAP cross-industry
        applications
    project and portfolio management, 338
    quality management, 337–338
    real estate management, 337
mySAP ERP financials, 325–330; *see also*
        SAP cross-industry applications
    cost controlling, 327–328
    enterprise controlling, 328
    financial and managerial accounting,
        326–327
    financial supply-chain management, 330

Global Trade Services, 329–330
    SAP GRC, 325, 326
    treasury management, 328–329
mySAP ERP human capital management,
        330; *see also* SAP cross-industry
        applications
    personal administration, 331–332
    personal planning and development,
        332–333
    self-service functionality, 330
mySAP operations, 333; *see also* SAP
        cross-industry applications
    manufacturing, 334
    materials management, 335
    plant maintenance, 335–336
    production planning and control,
        334–335
    sales and distribution, 336
    sales and operations planning, 334
mySAP SRM, *see* mySAP Supplier
        Relationship Management
mySAP Supplier Relationship
        Management (mySAP SRM),
        340–341

N

Network; *see also* Agile enterprises
    effects, 126
    enterprise, 12–14
Non–value-added processes (NVA
        processes), 81
NVA processes, *see* Non–value-added
        processes

O

Object-oriented system, 101
Offering-based enterprises, 171, 180;
        see also Customer responsiveness
OLAP, *see* Online Analytical Processing
One-to-one marketing, 112–113, 139–140;
        see also Customer relationship;
        Customer Relationship
        Management (CRM)
Online Analytical Processing (OLAP),
        269, 277, 349; *see also* Business
        Intelligence (BI)
OPT, *see* Optimized Production Technology

Optimized Production Technology
(OPT), 85
Orchestration, 264–265
Organizational structure, 232
Outsourcing, 248, 256–257

P

PA, *see* Personnel Administration
Pattern, 8, 280; *see also* Context-aware
applications (CAA)
in CRM, 282–283
in information technology
solutions, 282
links between, 281–282
PD, *see* Personnel Planning and
Development
PDAs, *see* Personal digital assistants
PDM, *see* Product Data Management
PDPs, *see* Product design processes
Performance intelligence (PI), 321–322
Permission marketing, 140; *see also*
Customer relationship
Personal digital assistants (PDAs), 12
Personalization, 130–131; *see also*
Customer Relationship
Management (CRM)
Personnel Administration (PA), 331
Personnel Planning and Development
(PD), 331
PI, *see* Performance intelligence; Process
Innovation
P/L, *see* Profit and loss
Plant Maintenance module (PM module),
342
PLC, *see* Product life cycle
PLM, *see* Product lifecycle management
Plug and play environment, 45
PM module, *see* Plant Maintenance module
Porter's (1980) framework of generic
strategies, 210–212; *see also*
Product lifecycle management
(PLM)
PPC, *see* Production Planning and
Control
PP module, *see* Production Planning
module
Prerequisite tree, 22; *see also* Theory of
constraints (TOC)

PRM system, 257
Procedure oriented language, 101
Process, 240, 252; *see also* Business process
analysis for breakthrough
improvements, 243–244
innovative breakthrough improvement
in, 244–245
instance, 259
-oriented enterprise, 252–253
substeps in, 241
Process Innovation (PI), 253
Process map, 242–243; *see also* Business
process
for improvements, 243–244
Process-oriented enterprise, 229; *see also*
Business process management
(BPM)
process value, 230
value-add-driven enterprise, 230–231
Product Data Management (PDM), 207
Product design processes (PDPs), 32, 202
Production Planning and Control
(PPC), 307
Production Planning module
(PP module), 342
Product life cycle (PLC), 212; *see also*
Product lifecycle management
(PLM)
characteristic product cycle times, 213
concurrent engineering, 220
design for manufacturability, 219–220
design for sustainability, 220–221
product design approaches, 218
product design attributes, 215–217
product development and disposal
phases, 215
quality function deployment, 218–219
S-curve and, 212
stages of, 213–214
Product lifecycle management (PLM), 32,
42, 85, 201, 228; *see also* Product
life cycle (PLC)
advantages of using, 208–210
benefits of, 205–206
challenges of, 204–205
components of, 207–208
customization and standardization,
221–223
design for configuration, 225–226

design for variety, 224–225
generic strategies, 210–212
managing customization, 224
mass customization, 223–224
product modularization, 226–227
product platform, 227–228
specialist networks, 204
Systems, 202
workflow management, 203
Product modularization, 226–227; *see also* Product lifecycle management (PLM)
Product platform, 227–228; *see also* Product lifecycle management (PLM)
Profit and loss (P/L), 285
Project management, 313; *see also* Enterprise system implementation project
meetings, 314
project control, 313
project monitoring, 315
project organization, 313
project reviews, 315
time recording, 314
Project System module (PS module), 342
PS module, *see* Project System module

Q

QFD, *see* Quality Function Deployment
QM module, *see* Quality Management module
Quality Function Deployment (QFD), 207, 218, 246
Quality Management module (QM module), 342

R

Radiofrequency identification (RFID), 334
Range, 2
RBE, *see* Relationship-based enterprises
Recency, Frequency and Monetary (RFM), 141
Relationship, 251
Relationship-based enterprises (RBE), 148, 251–252
Research and development (R&D), 57, 205
Response ability, 2

Responsive enterprise, 170
Return on Assets (ROA), 55
Return-on-Capital-Employed (ROCE), 55
Return on investment (ROI), 51, 59, 147, 313
RFID, *see* Radiofrequency identification
RFM, *see* Recency, Frequency and Monetary
ROA, *see* Return on Assets
ROCE, *see* Return-on-Capital-Employed
ROI, *see* Return on investment

S

Sales and Distribution (SD), 336
module, 341
Sales and operations planning, 334
Sales Force Automation (SFA), 41
SAP, *see* Systems, Applications & Products
SAP Advanced Planning & Optimization (SAP APO), 343
SAP AII, *see* SAP Auto-ID Infrastructure
SAP APO, *see* SAP Advanced Planning & Optimization
SAP Auto-ID Infrastructure (SAP AII), 343
SAP components, 341; *see also* mySAP Business Suite
SAP ECC, 341–342
SAP PLM, 344–345
SAP SCM, 343–344
SAP cross-industry applications, 324; *see also* mySAP Business Suite; mySAP CRM; mySAP ERP corporate services; mySAP ERP financials; mySAP ERP human capital management; mySAP operations
mySAP ERP, 325
mySAP SCM, 341
mySAP SRM, 340–341
SAP Enterprise Central Component 6. 0 (ECC 6.0), 341–342
SAP EWM, *see* SAP Extended Warehouse Management
SAP Extended Warehouse Management (SAP EWM), 343
SAP NetWeaver, 139, 345; *see also* mySAP Business Suite
application platform, 350–352
components, 345
information integration, 348

SAP NetWeaver (*Continued*)
  people integration, 346
  process integration, 349
  SAP business intelligence, 348–349
  SAP enterprise portal, 347
  SAP exchange infrastructure, 350
  SAP NetWeaver AS, 351–352
SAP SCM, *see* SAP Supply-Chain
  Management
SAP small and midsize businesses
  applications, 357; *see also*
  mySAP Business Suite
  mySAP all-in-one, 357–358
  SAP Business ByDesign, 358
  SAP business one, 358–359
SAP Supply-Chain Management
  (SAP SCM), 343
SAP TM, *see* SAP Transportation
  Management
SAP Transportation Management
  (SAP TM), 343
SAP xApp Cost and Quotation
  Management (SAP xCQM), 356
SAP xApp Emissions Management (SAP
  xEM), 356–357
SAP xApp Product Definition (SAP xPD),
  356
SAP xApp Resource and Portfolio
  Management (SAP xRPM), 356
SAP xCQM, *see* SAP xApp Cost and
  Quotation Management
SAP xEM, *see* SAP xApp Emissions
  Management
SAP xPD, *see* SAP xApp Product
  Definition
SAP xRPM, *see* SAP xApp Resource and
  Portfolio Management
Sarbanes–Oxley Act (SOX), 287
SBUs, *see* Strategic business units
SCM, *see* Supply-chain management
Scope creep, 300
SD, *see* Sales and Distribution
SDLC, *see* Software development
  life cycle
SDWT, *see* Self-directed work teams
Self-directed work teams (SDWT), 251
Sense-and-respond enterprise, 179
Service contracts, 103–104
Service-Level Agreements (SLAs), 105

Service-oriented architecture (SOA), 44, 97,
  99, 229, 265; *see also* Enterprise
  Resource Planning (ERP)
  applications, 105
  benefits, 98, 101–103
  business process management, 107
  characteristics of, 103–105
  executable agent, 99–100
  multichannel access, 106
  rapid application integration, 106
  services, 98, 99, 100–101
  with Web Services, 97, 98
SFA, *see* Sales Force Automation
Silos, 93
Six Sigma, 15; *see also* Intelligent
  enterprises
  customer–supplier relationship, 23
  DMAIC, 24, 25–27
  effort, 25
  Goal trees, 27
  investment in infrastructure, 24
  Master Black Belt, 24
  potential projects, 23
  project execution, 25
  solutions, 27
  SPC, 27
  strength of, 27
SLAs, *see* Service-Level Agreements
Small Worlds Networks (SWN), 181
SNP, *see* Supply Network Planning
SOA, *see* Service-oriented architecture
Software development life cycle (SDLC), 79
SOX, *see* Sarbanes–Oxley Act
SPC, *see* Statistical process control
Spend analysis, 273
SRM, *see* Supplier Relationship
  Management
Stakeholders, 50
  types, 51
Standardization, 221–223; *see also* Product
  lifecycle management (PLM)
Statistical process control (SPC), 27, 246
Stockholder capital, 59
Stovepipes, *see* Silos
Strategic business units (SBUs), 71
Strengths, weaknesses, opportunities, and
  threats (SWOT), 5
Supplier Relationship Management
  (SRM), 42, 162

Supply-chain management (SCM),
  31–32, 41, 42, 73, 85, 96, 153,
  198–199; *see also* Customer
  responsiveness
  challenges, 156–158
  characteristics, 159–160
  classic supply-chain operating
    model, 163
  components, 160–163
  concept of, 154–156
  customer relationship management, 161
  demand management, 160
  examples, 164
  framework, 163–165
  funds flow, 159
  globalization, 155
  information flow, 159
  integrated information technologies, 156
  manufacturing flow management, 161
  network structure in, 164
  order fulfillment, 161
  patterns, 165
  performance framework, 165–169
  performance measurement, 169–170
  physical flow, 159
  product development and
    commercialization, 161
  returns management, 162–163
  sourcing management, 162
  supplier relationship management, 162
  Systems, 158
Supply Network Planning (SNP), 343
SWN, *see* Small Worlds Networks
SWOT, *see* Strengths, weaknesses,
  opportunities, and threats
Systems, Applications & Products (SAP)
  Business One, 358–359
  Event Management, 343
Systems integrators, 257; *see also*
  Management by collaboration
  (MBC)

T

Taguchi methods, 246
TBC, *see* Time-Based Competition
TCO, *see* Total cost of ownership
TDABC, *see* Time-driven activity-based
  costing

Theory of constraints (TOC), 19; *see also*
  Intelligent enterprises
  current reality tree, 21
  Drum–Rope–Buffer scheduling, 20–21
  evaporating cloud, 22
  five-step methodology for business
    improvement, 20
  future reality tree, 22
  methodology, 19
  metrics, 21
  prerequisite tree, 22
  thinking process, 22, 23
  tools, 21
  transition tree, 22
Time-Based Competition (TBC), 28–30
Time-driven activity-based costing
    (TDABC), 190; *see also* Activity-
    based customer responsiveness
  activity-based cost, 191
  activity costs, 191
  advantages, 191
  conventional ABC vs., 193–194
  model, 196
  significance of, 194–195
  in strategy and operations of
    enterprise, 195–196
  total costs, 192
TOC, *see* Theory of constraints
Total cost of ownership (TCO), 217
Total Quality Management (TQM), 85,
  114, 245, 253
Toyota, 15
  central organizing concept of, 16
  challenge of synchronization, 16–17
Toyota Production System (TPS), 15
TPS, *see* Toyota Production System
TQM, *see* Total Quality Management
Traditional capitalism, 125, 126; *see also*
  Customer capitalism
Transition tree, 22; *see also* Theory of
  constraints (TOC)

V

Value, 230–231
  chain, 258
  cocreating systems, 144
  gaps, 242, 249
Value-add-driven enterprise, 253–254

Value-based management (VBM), 60; *see also* Enterprise system based enterprise
    financial-oriented, 60
    higher market capitalization, 62
    leveraging, 60
    market capitalization in terms of CLTV, 62
    time value of customers and shareholder value, 61–63
Value Stream Mapping, 17; *see also* Lean
VBM, *see* Value-based management
VOC, *see* Voice of customer
Voice of customer (VOC), 218

W

WAP, *see* Wireless Application Protocol
Warehouse Management (WM), 343
WBSs, *see* Work breakdown structures
WCM, *see* World Class Manufacturing
Web, 137
Webifying, 12
Web Service (WS), 97, 98, 100, 106, 263, 264; *see also* Composite services
Web Service-Coordination (WS-C), 264

Web Service-Transaction (WS-T), 264
WF, *see* Workflow
Wireless Application Protocol (WAP), 12
WM, *see* Warehouse Management
Work breakdown structures (WBSs), 338
Workflow (WF), 260–261
    module, 342
Workforce Process Management (WPM), 331
World Class Manufacturing (WCM), 85
WPM, *see* Workforce Process Management
WS, *see* Web Service
WS-C, *see* Web Service-Coordination
WS-T, *see* Web Service-Transaction

X

XI, *see* Exchange infrastructure

Y

Yield on Investment (YOI), 59
YOI, *see* Yield on Investment
Y-trees, *see* Goal trees